Carnival on Wall Street:

Global Financial Markets in the 1990s

Carnival on Wall Street:

Global Financial Markets in the 1990s

JANE ELIZABETH HUGHES

Brandeis University

SCOTT B. MACDONALD

Senior Managing Director and Partner,
Aladdin Capital Management, LLC

www.wiley.com/college/hughes

Acquisitions Editor   *Leslie Kraham*
Project Editor   *Cindy Rhoads*
Marketing Manager   *David Woodbury*
Editorial Assistant   *Jessica Bartelt*
Managing Editor   *Lari Bishop*
Associate Production Editor   *Kelly Tavares*
Production Editor   *Sarah Wolfman-Robichaud*
Illustration Editors   *Benjamin Reece and Jennifer Wasson*
Cover Design   *Jennifer Wasson*
Cover Image   *© Michael McParlane/PhotoDisc, Inc.*

This book was set in New Caledonia by Leyh Publishing LLC and printed and bound by Courier-Westford. The cover was printed by Phoenix Color Corp.

This book is printed on acid-free paper. ∞

Library of Congress Cataloging-in-Publication Data
Hughes, Jane E. (Jane Elizabeth)
  Carnival on Wall Street : global financial markets in the 1990s / Jane E. Hughes & Scott
  B. MacDonald.
    p. cm.

Includes bibliographical references.
ISBN 0-471-26731-7 (paper)
  1. Capital market--History--20th century. 2. International finance--History--20th century. 3. Stock exchanges--History--20th century. 4. Wall Street--History--20th century. 5. Bull markets--United States--History--20th century. 6. Stock Market Bubble, 1995–2000. 7. Financial crises--East Asia--History--20th century. 8. Globalization--Economic aspects--History--20th century. I. MacDonald, Scott B. II. Title.

HG4523.H84 2004
332'.042'09049--dc22   2003057096

USA ISBN: 0-471-26731-7
WIE ISBN: 0-471-45179-7

Printed in the United States of America

10 9 8 7 6 5 4 3 2 1

Brief Contents

Contents

► **CHAPTER 4** Foreign Exchange Markets: Speculators, Policemen, and Suckers **73**

► **CHAPTER 5** Return of the Neo-Luddites: Globalization and Antiglobalization **107**

Part II   Wall Street: Bubble to Bust   141

▶ CHAPTER 6   The Tech Bubble   143

▶ CHAPTER 7   The Firm and Globalization   162

▶ CHAPTER 8   A Decade of Financial Wrongdoing   186

Preface

The 1990s witnessed one of history's biggest stock market bubbles. For much of the decade, the New York Stock Exchange and NASDAQ captivated people with seemingly endless visions of wealth generation. The combination of technological innovation, the harnessing of that technology in the financial world, and favorable geopolitical events (the most significant of which was the end of the Cold War) set in motion a bull market that centered on Wall Street, but eventually embraced global capital markets. The decade between 1991 and 2001 was one of excessive wealth, greed, and glory, all based on the premise that the free flow of capital was an ennobling force for economic development. This view was molded by a strong faith in globalization, the ability of models to predict markets, and the interrelated belief in the power of technology to surmount any obstacles. Indeed, history will find a track record of strong economic growth rates; the very real physical transformation brought to the home and office (just look to the personal computer and cell phones); and the upward climb of the New York Stock Exchange and NASDAQ (National Association of Securities Dealers Automated Quotation System). The historical ledger indicates that these forces did leave behind a better world or, at the very least, a more technologically advanced and interconnected global civilization.

Yet, the historical ledger also shows that such a leap forward in global civilization was not without its problems, such as worsening imbalances between rich and poor nations, the need for greater transparency and disclosure in corporate affairs, and a serious reappraisal of risk and how it fits into capitalist society. Equally important, the liberalization of capital markets did not always have the intended consequences of its planners—as exemplified by the recurrent emerging markets crises during the 1990s and by the roller coaster rides on the New York Stock Exchange and NASDAQ. While many Argentines and Indonesians had to wonder what they were gaining from the expansion of global capital markets (the two nations ended the 1990s with struggling economies partially due to political problems), many small investors in the United States were left scratching their heads at the antics of a small, but influential, group of corporate chiefs who left a dark scandalous cloud over the stock market and the rest of Corporate America. Sadly, the top leadership of companies such as Enron, WorldCom, and Adelphia were splashed across the headlines and became the public perception of top management in the U.S. business sector.

The bottom line: There were significant advances in the global economy during the decade of 1991–2001 from which there would be no retreat, but there were also lacunas in the overall development process. These lacunas would drive many business leaders, investors, and governments to carefully reexamine the past decade and the business practices of those years, and to ask what type of corporate governance was required to safeguard profits and corporate integrity.

At the core of all of this was the question of what type of capitalism did the post–Cold War order require—a more entrepreneurial system, guided by self-regulation, market discipline, and a referee-like role by the state, or a less flexible and more managed economy, in which the state played a key role in bargaining with big business and big labor. Each side involved trade-offs, but the changes in technology, which percolated through the global economy in the 1980s and 1990s, undermined the managed economy and pushed a more entrepreneurial system. The only problem with this development is that it represented substantial change—change that rocked the socioeconomic system and left the existing order seeking to catch up.

While the 1990s appeared as a new age of finance for many people around the world, students of history would recognize the familiar patterns. Booms often end in a painful period of scandal, as occurred to varying degrees with Dutch Tulipmania in the seventeenth century, the Mississippi and South Pacific bubbles in the early eighteenth century, and the roaring 1920s in the United States. Each case featured new financial techniques coming out of new technology and institutions around the world seeking to catch up. The historical aspect of looking at the 1990s and comparing it to the past for similarities makes considerable sense.

The decades prior to World War I, for example, saw huge technological advances—electrical goods, chemical dyes, internal combustion vehicles, and a shift from sailing ships to steam and then coal power. New sources of cheaply extractable raw materials were discovered. Rising population levels reflected a better-fed and more-healthy global population. There was also a substantial movement of populations from Europe to the Americas, Australia, and New Zealand. Colonial empires drew Africa and Asia into the global market to an unprecedented degree. New rail systems linked the east and west coasts of the United States and Canada, as well as brought Russia closer to Western European economies. In many ways this was a new golden age of international finance, orbiting around London's community of banks, insurance houses, and trading firms. Commerce and capital flowed around the planet, much of it out of Europe and into the then-emerging markets of the United States, Canada, Latin America, and Australia.

In 1910, Norman Angell wrote *The Great Illusion*, which held out that a new age of ongoing progressive development was at hand. Angell's key finding was that the threat of disrupting international credit centered in London—inevitable in a war—would either deter its outbreak or bring it speedily to an end. Angell's view implied two things—one, that the world had become highly interdependent, and two, that it was in everyone's interest to keep the system going. As John Keegan, in his history of World War I, wrote: "It was not only bankers—of whom many of London's foremost were German—that accepted the interdependence of nations as a condition of the world's life in the first years of the twentieth century, a necessary condition and one destined to grow in importance.[1]

The brave new world of interdependent economic and financial relations that was to guarantee ongoing economic development and enrichment, however, fell before the rejection of that system, first by an ethnic Serbian separatist terrorist who shot the heir to the Hapsburg throne, the Archduke Franz Ferdinand, in Sarajevo in 1914; followed shortly thereafter by the European powers that soon became engulfed in one of the world's most deadly conflicts, World War I. The global financial system, which had promised ongoing stability and wealth, proved—at least temporarily—to be a chimera.

In the same sense, the 1990s represented a firm belief in a new system that would continue to evolve, bringing a better life for all of those involved. A compelling and widely read book by Michael Mandelbaum, *The Ideas that Conquered the World*, pointed that the notions of peace, democracy, and free markets "had come to dominate international affairs, not in the sense that each was enthusiastically embraced and faithfully practiced everywhere but rather in the sense that they had no fully anticipated and politically potent rivals."[2]

The act of terrorism that hit the United States in September 2001, however, was a brutal reminder that not everyone concurred with the view that the magic of the marketplace was going to enrich everyone's life, materially as well as spiritually. Indeed, there were elements of the global population strongly opposed to the notion of globalization with an American accent. Some preferred to participate in demonstrations or write books about the evils of globalization, while others preferred to smash the windows at Starbucks or McDonald's. Still others preferred bolder, more deadly forms of protest, combining other traditional political issues with the more mainstream attack on globalization.

Dovetailing with the rise of the anti-globalization movement, faith in the new system was eroding as the dot-com bubble started to deflate in 2000. The events of 9/11, however, accelerated the deflation in the U.S. stock market, helped slow economic activity in the United States, and, by doing so, ensured a cooling of global economic activity. Although faith in the marketplace was to remain, the brutal downturn in the stock market, as well as the threat of new economic crises elsewhere in the world, have eroded confidence in the brave new world stimulated by Silicon Valley's creativity, financed by venture capitalists, and traded on Wall Street. Nonetheless, the great bull market on Wall Street during the 1990s and the related wave of globalization has left the world much more interdependent than ever before—a trend that is likely to continue.

It will take decades to sort through all the implications of the 1991–2001 decade. Although the authors made an effort to capture what we regard as the key points of the decade, we are certain that we missed certain trends and factors. Nonetheless, the following chapters seek to provide a view of the liberalization of the global capital markets and the interrelated boom on Wall Street, which developed into a global carnival, pulling players around the world into the game. The stock market bubble in the United States was only part of the bigger bubble in expectations. Any mistakes made in this book are the responsibility of the authors and no one else.

NOTES

1. John Keegan, *The First World War* (New York: Vintage Books, 1998): 12.
2. Michael Mandlebaum, *The Ideas That Conquered the World* (New York: Public Affairs, 2002).

Acknowledgments

The authors wish to thank our long-suffering families, as well as our editors at John Wiley & Sons who helped us bring this book to life. The students at Brandeis University's Graduate School of International Economics & Finance are a constant source of inspiration. Scott MacDonald would also like to thank the following for their insights into the stock and bond markets: Matt Burnell at Merrill Lynch, Tony Smith at JP MorganChase, and the crew at Aladdin Capital—Amin Aladin, George Marshman, Joe Schlim, Dale Spencer, Darin Feldman, Mark Gros, and Brent Shum. We are also grateful to the reviewers of this book for their helpful comments:

Chetan Ghate, *Colorado College*

Claire Gilmore, *King's College*

Betty Hanson, *University of Connecticut*

Frank Hefner, *College of Charleston*

Austin Jaffe, *Pennsylvania State University*

Lujac T. Orlowski, *Sacred Heart University*

Bryan Ritchie, *Michigan State University*

Tom Sanders, *University of Miami*

While many hands helped stir the pot, the responsibility for the views articulated in the following pages are the authors' and the authors' alone.

CHAPTER 1

INTRODUCTION: GREED, GREATNESS, AND DISASTER

Markets generally work, but occasionally they break down.
—Charles E. Kindleberger

Charles Dickens began *A Tale of Two Cities* with "It was the best of times and the worst of times." Looking at the decade of 1991–2001, we could say the same, especially when considering two images. The first is the July 2000 cover of the now defunct high-tech magazine *Red Herring*. On the cover are two figures, one a housewife (defined by her vacuum cleaner and dishwasher in the background) excitedly waving her arms as U.S. dollars fall from the sky. The other woman has a magic wand in her hand and is wearing a red, white, and blue hat. The title splashed across the cover is "The New and Improved Economy." The message is clear: the new economy is easily delivering a fabulous new lifestyle in which wealth almost falls from the sky. This image epitomizes the widespread perception of the great bull market that began in the early 1990s and ended in 2000.

The other image is that of the World Trade Center towers on fire after terrorists crashed two hijacked airliners into them on September 11, 2001. The attack was clearly a symbolic action aimed at the heart of global financial markets, New York's financial district. With the death of thousands of innocent people, the self-assured swagger of the old era was gone, and Wall Street, in all its multiple reflections around the planet, now faced an uncertain future. Indeed, several years of bear stock markets were to follow, the financial industry underwent a downsizing, and the global economy underwent a marked downturn in 2002.

The decade of 1991–2001 was one of the most dramatic in world financial history and was filled with deeds of greed, disaster, and greatness. Never before had finance been so global, securities trading so actively participated in by so many, and public attention in North America, Europe, and industrialized Asia so rapt with the upward gyrations of the U.S. stock markets. While London, Tokyo, Hong Kong,

Frankfurt, and Paris all played important roles in the globalization of financial markets and helped push along a period of extended economic growth in most countries, New York City remained the key hub, both in terms of hard numbers and symbolically. The city is the headquarters for globe-trotting armies of investment bankers from Merrill Lynch, Goldman Sachs, Morgan Stanley, and Citigroup, as well as a place where other key international players such as Deutsche Bank, Mizuho Financial Group, Barclays, and HSBC are strongly represented. New York City is also the home to the New York Stock Exchange (NYSE), NASDAQ, and the American Stock Exchange. Consequently, we define Wall Street, much along the lines of veteran *New Yorker* staff writer John Brooks, as follows: "It's called Wall Street, a name strictly speaking [that] applies only to a narrow gully in the south of Manhattan but then can be taken as a proxy for Tokyo, London, and other financial markets everywhere."[1] The Wall Street of the 1990s was a massive, multifaceted carnival of financial activity, penetrating every country and touching billions of people well beyond the confines of the small island of Manhattan.

What do we mean by carnival? A common definition of the word *carnival* is a traveling amusement show with sideshows, game booths, and rides; its entertainment value washes away the mundane realities of daily life and replaces it with something pleasing, enjoyable, and, in some sense, a fantasy. With no intention to trivialize the great construct of the marketplace and the massive creativity of human endeavor that undergirds the global economy, what transpired on Wall Street in the 1990s can be considered carnival-like. For many people around the world, the great bull market of the late 1990s was fascinating (and, ultimately, something of a fantasy). It did provide entertainment, creating a new cast of actors in the media, in the so-called New and Old Economy companies, and in the financial world who caught the public's attention. The collapse of the stock market in 2000–2001 and the ensuing scandals also fascinated the public, as many of yesterday's heroes became today's villains. Consequently, we use the word *carnival* in a narrow sense, to capture something of the atmosphere in what were heady days.

By the mid-1990s, the carnival on Wall Street was in full swing. The process of creating a financial bubble was well under way. The once-closed doors of the financial sector, pushed open a crack in the 1980s, were cast wide open to the masses of day traders. The stock market became a daily passion for millions of North Americans and was watched with keen interest in Europe, Asia, and Australia. It appeared that each and every IPO (initial public offering) of stock was a winner; many stocks rocketed to glory on their first day, pleasing investors, as their initial down payment was more than amply returned. China.com, a Chinese Internet company, launched stock on the NASDAQ in July 1999 at around $13 a share. By early 2000, the same stock peaked at a little over $73. This story was frequently repeated as millions of investors sought to follow the seemingly easy path to riches via the stock market. For their part, large institutional investors also were swept along in the herd-like stampede. Not to be engaged meant not to be earning large returns. For seasoned money managers, it was difficult to make the case that the market was wrong as the NYSE and NASDAQ moved relentlessly upward.

Behind the surge of interest in the stock market was the mantra that the revolution in information and communications technology was ushering in a new age of Schumpeter-like creative destruction, much like the era of the railways or the internal combustion engine.[2] This "New Economy" of information technology (IT) and related technologies would deliver a great surge in productivity and profits. Everyone had to have a wireless phone, and companies around the planet rushed to make them smaller, better-designed, and even available in a multitude of colors. Offices needed better computers, and "e-business" became a dire necessity for all sectors, ranging from higher education to pet food sales. *Telephony*—the merger of telecommunication (telecom) and Internet technologies, supplemented with instant access to new entertainment opportunities—was a new word easily slipping off the tongues of Wall Street analysts and small investors, both of whom were active participants in running the Dow Jones Industrial Average over 10,000. The New Economy meant a fast road from rags to riches, especially for racy stocks, such as Lucent, Cisco, Microsoft, Motorola, and Northern Telcom. At the same time, there was a certain degree of contempt, if not scorn, for "Old Economy" companies in such sectors as chemicals, pulp and paper, and manufacturing.

It is important not to understate the real economic significance of the investment binge in the United States. Without millions of individual investors there would have been less capital for corporations, and without that the investment levels in new technology, marketing, and efficiency would have been all the less. Less too would have been the paychecks people brought home, which went a long way to fuel consumer spending, key to the long spurt in expansion of the U.S. gross domestic product (GDP). To this could be added easy access to credit. In a sense, the "democratization of equity" meant that a growing number of Americans bought ownership in corporate America. In the early nineteenth century Napoleon had railed against the English as being a nation of shopkeepers; in the late twentieth century, Americans were on their way to becoming a nation of stockholders. Although there were to be abuses in the system, the penetration of the stock market into the American mainstream (and to other countries) broadened the base of those who firmly believed in the capitalist system and favored the idea of an entrepreneurial-oriented economy.

The entrepreneurial-oriented economy (sometimes referred to as the Anglo-American or Anglo-Saxon model) is defined as an economy that is generally deregulated, with a high level of labor market flexibility, a relatively light tax burden, and a private sector that is promoted as the engine of growth. Central to the private sector's ability to generate growth is the entrepreneur—a key actor in organizing and managing new business ventures, many of which involve risk.[3] The end of the Communist bloc in the late 1980s and the collapse of the Soviet Union in 1992 also played a part in advancing the attractiveness of the entrepreneurial economy. Capitalism, in particular the Anglo-American variety of liberated markets and smaller yet more efficient governments, now appeared dominant. After all, democratic capitalism had won the Cold War.[4] The West's victory over Communism was accompanied by a widespread belief that the Anglo-American model had to be exported to the transitional economies of Central and Eastern Europe and

Central Asia. As *Business Week*'s Robert Kuttner noted: "Get the commissars out of the way, and a free market would simply emerge. By the same token, third-world countries, with shallow markets and often corrupt or dirigiste connections between government and industry, needed much of the same medicine."[5] Indeed, many developing economies in Asia, Latin America, the Middle East, and Africa did require substantial reforms, some of which were affected.

Related to the entrepreneurial-oriented economy as part of the same capitalist economy, the managed economy also came under pressure in the 1990s. That pressure still continues. In brief, a managed economy is one that operates from the premise that the interests of powerful corporations must be balanced by the state and the labor unions to maintain equitable economic development, which, in turn, is supportive of democracy. While the leading capitalist economies were guided in one form or another by managed economies during the 1950s and 1960s, there was a divergence that became most pronounced during the 1990s, with a cleavage between two sides: on one side, the United States, United Kingdom, Canada, and the Netherlands (which witnessed a shift to more entrepreneurial-oriented systems), and on the other side, Germany (which sought to perfect its managed economy) and France (which rethought and tinkered with the system). The problem for the managed economies was that their systems favored a more protracted centralized and formal approach to economic policy that incorporated the state, big business, and labor. The combination of globalization and technological changes hit more fertile soil in those economies that favored flexibility in both management and labor, allowed for rapid decision-making, and provided incentives for small and medium-sized enterprises to flourish. Consequently, economic growth and employment opportunities boomed in the United States, United Kingdom, Canada, and the Netherlands during the 1990s and unemployment fell, while the economies in France and Germany grew at a slower pace and unemployment remained high (close to 10 percent).

To many in North America, it now appeared that their economies were immune from recession, that the jobless rate would remain low forever, and that the stock market would rise inexorably higher. The longer and faster the stock market bubble grew, the more people were sucked in. The lure of easy profits, often based on nothing more than concepts, added millions of small investors to the ranks of the wealthy and powerful institutional investors. One excited commentator emphatically stated in 1998: "We are in the midst of the greatest economic boom and technological revolution in history. ... The Roaring 2000s will come with the aging of the massive baby boom generation into its peak productivity, earning, and spending years and the emergence of their radical information revolution into the mainstream of our economy. Tighten your seatbelts and prepare for the greatest boom in history: from 1998 to 2008."[6]

The investment banking community also played a role in stroking and maintaining the speculative binge. As demonstrated in the aftermath of the tech bubble, in some cases research analysts enthusiastically promoted stocks even though they had misgivings about the company's real value. The clear incentive for promoting a particular stock was the advantage such "research" gave a firm's investment bankers when seeking to obtain a mandate for a lucrative investment banking deal. Although this practice was not widespread, it did achieve considerable notice when companies such as Enron and many of the dot-com enterprises went bankrupt.

During the height of the 1990s carnival, money poured into capital markets at an unprecedented pace. Mutual funds investing in equities expanded rapidly in the 1990s. Between 1990 and the first quarter of 1998, equity mutual funds attracted over a trillion dollars from U.S. investors.[7] In 1996 alone, a total of $221.6 billion was invested in U.S. equity funds, followed by another $231 billion in the next year, leaving the total assets in U.S. mutual funds at $4.2 trillion by year-end 1997. (That sum was greater than the combined GDPs of Canada, Sweden, and France.) The sweeping nature of the Wall Street carnival was best summarized by financial historian Edward Chancellor: "By the middle of the 1990s ... fifty million Americans held shares, and the stock market was being discussed everywhere: in bars, golf courses, clubs, gyms, beauty salons, and on television chat shows."[8] CNBC, the business channel, gained a massive new following, and investment clubs sprang up across the country. The nation enjoyed its wealth. Times were good.

The carnival was not limited to the North Americans but spread to the Europeans and Japanese, Chinese, and Koreans. The tech frenzy became a factor in stock exchanges of Hong Kong, Singapore, and Tokyo, aided by government help in establishing new indexes for high tech, while new rules and regulations were put in place to speed up the process for market entry. Companies all over the world— Israeli and Indian tech and biotech companies, Brazilian and Chilean pulp and paper companies, and Argentine banks—all accessed the U.S. equity markets, tapping into the world's biggest pool of investors.

In Europe, tech, Internet, and telecom stocks gained loyal followings. Eager to gain footholds in the new economy, Europe's once-sleepy state-owned telecom companies, such as Royal KPN N.V. (the Dutch phone company), France Telecom, and Deutsche Telekom, invested billions of dollars in new technology and third-generation (3G) wireless licenses. Companies such as KPN, which emerged from the Dutch postal and telephone monopoly, were partially privatized and made to compete in a new world of globalized telecom. During the 1990s, KPN went out and bought stakes in wireless operators in Belgium, Germany, Indonesia, Czech Republic, and Ukraine. The world was KPN's oyster.

Other European telecom companies also crossed the Atlantic to hunt for assets in the U.S. market. Deutsche Telekom, for example, entered the U.S. mobile market in 2001 by buying VoiceStream Wireless and Powertel. The VoiceStream purchase alone cost $28 billion. Big money was followed by small money as millions placed their bets in the casino-like stock markets networking the global financial system. As the carnival rose to its peak, the bubble in Internet, tech, telecom, and new economy-related stocks took the Dow over 11,000 points.

While the carnival ended symbolically with a bang on September 11, 2001 (9/11), the signs of its demise were evident well before then. The long bull market, beginning in 1991, was over well before 9/11. The long economic growth spurt in the United States had shifted into a sustained slowdown. The stars of the carnival, companies such as Lucent, NorTel, and Motorola, were left struggling with bad accounting in the form of vendor financing, falling demand, and heavy debt burdens. Other companies, such as Xerox and Polaroid, struggled to survive. High-flying dot-com stocks, such as China.com and Korea Thrunet, once trading over $70 a share, plummeted to under $1 a share. The telecom sector, once the highly touted wave of the future, now had to contend with a mountain of debt accumulated by acquisitions and expensive technology, fierce competition, and falling prices for services now priced like a commodity. In 2002, WorldCom and Qwest, two stars of the 1990s, struggled to survive under huge debt burdens, investigations by the Securities and Exchange Commission (SEC), and questions about their basic business models. Indeed, WorldCom would eventually file for bankruptcy—the largest in U.S. history.

In 2001, European growth cooled and Japan slipped into its fourth recession in ten years. As Anthony B. Perkins, editor in chief and chairman of tech magazine *Red Herring*, stated in October 2001, "While our expectations regarding the value of our stock portfolios and the growth prospects of the tech world have been lowered significantly in the last year, we probably need to ratchet these expectations down one or two notches. Another way to put it is that we have yet to escape from the reality-distortion field in which we have been living for the last five years."[9]

Another development was the emergence of an antiglobalization movement, resisting what many thought was the inevitable wave of convergence in branding, marketing, and communications. Angry demonstrations against the summits of G-7 (U.S., Japan, Germany, France, Italy, U.K., and Canada) heads of state, World Trade Organization, and the World Bank and International Monetary Fund, in Seattle, Quebec City, Milan, and Washington, D.C., reflected the uncomfortable fact that not everyone liked the idea of a world without borders. A new generation of protest had emerged as neo-Luddites rose from the political fringes to wave the banner of inward-looking economic models, based on Albanian-like experiments of self-contained existence. While much of the antiglobalization movement was peaceful, there was also a violent element. Moreover, the financial and economic revolution that swept much of the world had left a growing divide between the haves and have-nots. This was brought home by the September 11, 2001 attacks on the United States by terrorists inspired by Saudi Osama bin Ladin, who as a radical Islamist had made it his mission to rid his homeland of American troops. Although religion played a role in the desire to cleanse Islam's holy land (Saudi Arabia is home to the cities of Mecca and Medina), economics also played a role. The destruction of the World Trade Center towers was a symbolic act, aimed at the symbolic heart of the globalized economy, New York City. In many regards, 9/11 marked the abrupt and bloody end of the carnival on Wall Street.

▶ LESSONS OF THE CARNIVAL DECADE

Looking back over the 1991–2001 decade, one can discern eleven major trends that emerged.

1. *The decade of 1991–2001 was one of sweeping technological changes,* increases in productivity, and a substantial move to the integration of

global markets. Along these lines, there was a fundamental shift away from managed economies to more entrepreneurial-oriented economies. This shift was marked by faster rates of economic growth, lower unemployment, and increases in productivity in such countries as the United States, the United Kingdom, and the Netherlands. Even in the aftermath of the boom, the bust has resulted in unemployment levels, which, albeit higher, are still below those of the more managed economies such as those in Germany and France.

2. *There was a downside to the shift to a more entrepreneurial economy,* as the carnival atmosphere blinded many; greed, shortsightedness, and arrogance often overcame analytical rigor in assessing deals, partners, and countries. In a sense, the trajectory of global capital markets, Wall Street in particular, left behind the "efficient market" for one guided more by animal spirits. The overriding investment objective was to make money—as rapidly and as much as possible. The more thought-out investment strategies of diversification, economies of scale, and indexing seemed passé, especially in the face of a rapidly rising NASDAQ.

3. *The era of blind faith was also one in which a crisis of governance emerged.* Corporate governance is the means by which a company is run in regard to rules and regulations to ensure that transparency and disclosure provide investors and regulators with a clear and representative picture of how the company functions. Free markets, technology, and financial models cannot substitute for good governance. In fact, in the absence of strong and credible institutions, free markets, technology, and globalization may enable the proliferation of bad governance in situations as far-ranging as Enron and Argentina. While the vast majority of companies follow good governance procedures, there were enough bad eggs to give the appearance that financial wrongdoing exploded in the 1990s, both in developed countries and in emerging markets.

4. *There was a questioning of the role of research on Wall Street.* Angry investors later claimed that equity analysts had misled them with poor reporting and ongoing buy recommendations, often done at the guidance of investment bankers beholden to the companies issuing equity or debt. In some cases, the institutional pressure from the investment bank side of operations did lead to some absurd recommendations, as in the cases of WorldCom and Enron. Yet, this question must also be asked: Did research on Wall Street have any real value when everything was heading upward anyway? It is easy to forget that equity prices often had little real relationship to company fundamentals, be they good or bad. Many times poor earnings announcements were greeted by a rise in the stock price. Fundamental credit research that stressed cash flow, profits, and debt management often did not factor in, undermining the role of analysts. Consequently, the role of analysts and the perception of what analysts were supposed to do underwent a change during the 1990s—

much of it unfortunate—and the matter has hardly been settled in the early part of the new decade.

5. *Scandals were also a factor.* In any history of bubbles, there is always a tale of shadowy doings, questionable deals, and shocking revelations. Examples include Orange County's $1.6 billion loss in derivatives (1994), bond trader cover-ups at Daiwa Bank and Barings (both in 1995), and trader cover-ups in the copper market at Sumitomo (1997). Nick Leeson's actions in Singapore sank Barings, one of England's oldest and most venerable banking names, while the actions of traders at Daiwa and Sumitomo cost those banks billions of dollars. During the 1990s, which began with the forced closure of BCCI (Bank of Credit and Commerce International, but often known as the "Bank of Crooks and Criminals International") in 1991, world financial leaders displayed increased concern over the role of financial markets and institutions in fostering crime and corruption around the world. However, the decade, which ended with a frantic multilateral attempt to trace the financial assets of the 9/11 terrorists, cannot be credited with a diminution in international financial crime and corruption—quite the contrary. While financial scandals involved a small group of corporate America's leadership, investor and public trust in corporate integrity overall suffered. Public opinion sank as investors learned of the lavish compensation paid to some of the same corporate heads who presided over the collapses of Enron and WorldCom and the massive stock price write-downs of Tyco International, Qwest, and Xerox.[10] It also caused the U.S. Congress to push for new legislation that would improve corporate governance and tighten accounting standards and practices.

6. *The increased emphasis on the Internet and other new technology* led to a blind faith in the ability of technology to deliver a better world. In a sense, the reliance on the Internet as both a source of information and a vehicle for investment was misplaced and misused. Ultimately, the technology was only as good as its users' abilities. As an advertisement in *Forbes* for Sybase aptly stated in October 2001, "… the Internet is only a common set of protocols for the transport of information. It's how well you manage that information that determines the success of your business."

7. *There was an erosion of transparency during the 1990s.* Complicated financial models, the creation of off–balance sheet financial vehicles, and a weakening of accounting standards all conspired to produce scandals like Enron. While the "buyer beware" mentality of credit analysis eroded during the boom years, even sound corporate analysis often had trouble in overcoming opaque accounting terms, especially related to off–balance sheet financial vehicles—many of which proved to hold considerable liabilities.

8. *There was a heavy reliance on financial modeling,* closely linked to both of the previous points, accompanied by a decline in emphasis on

experience and judgment. Long-term capital management (LTCM) was a perfect example of financial practitioners' over-reliance on models and the often-misplaced arrogance that went with it. As financial journalist Roger Lowenstein noted: "Reared on Merton's and Schole's teachings on efficient markets, the professors actually believed that prices would go and go directly where the models said they should. The professors' conceit was to think that models could forecast the limits of behavior. In fact, the models could tell them what was reasonable or what was predictable based on the past. The professors overlooked the fact that people, traders included, are not always reasonable."[11] It was forgotten that models are useful to a point, functioning as rough indicators. As with any analytical tool, too heavy a reliance on one instrument or viewing one set of factors leaves the door open to other potential risks. Financial models are highly important in risk management, especially in dealing with some of the more complicated areas of derivatives and synthetics.

9. *There was a firm belief that the Anglo-American or entrepreneurial model* of small government and an unshackled market, aided by technology and the free movement of capital, was superior to all other models (which it is). Easily glossed over by rosy statistics was the fact that too much marketization and too little regulation have a tendency to fray the social fabric, cheapen values, and raise questions about the potentially competing power of cash versus the public good (which is one of the justifications for a managed economy). Frequently overlooked was the fact that new technology and innovations in finance often outstripped the ability of government institutions to deal with such changes. In a sense, a gap emerged between the demands generated by change and the ability of institutions to deal with these demands.

10. *The Wall Street stock market bubble and the IT (Internet technology) revolution that had pushed globalization eventually created an antiglobalization movement,* which rejects the idea of being interconnected in a world culture dominated by Disney, McDonald's, and Planet Hollywood. While the antiglobalization movement was momentarily silenced by widespread horror at the events of 9/11, it resurfaced shortly thereafter, albeit in a more muted form. However, some of the grievances of the antiglobalization movement are compelling and some are likely to be addressed (as in the case of the transparency of major multilateral lending organizations). At the same time, the very wide range of antiglobalists and their myriad causes—including a more equitable distribution of the earnings of the new Chad–Cameroon pipeline, save-the-Earth environmentalists, and protectionists seeking to save textile jobs in the United States—makes it hard to advance the antiglobalist "cause," which ultimately is to stop globalization. In view of the fact that the genie of globalization in the form of the Internet

and everyday life surrounding the majority of people on the planet is not going back into the bottle (most people appear to like many aspects of globalization), the antiglobalization movement functions best as a form of conscience and as an articulate interest group.

11. *The ripple effects of the Wall Street boom had echoes in Asia,* as the entire region underwent a massive economic and financial reorganization, accompanied first by too much capital and then by too little. Conversely, the 1997–1998 Asian contagion hit the region hard, in particular, Indonesia, Thailand, and Korea. Moreover, Japan remained the odd man out of much of the 1991–2001 Wall Street boom, as it was caught by an inability to emerge from its own set of problems related to its banks, bad debt, and a creaky domestic economy, complicated by a political system based on patronage and protection. By contrast, the inexorable rise of China as a global economic power served as a counterpoint to the decline of Japan, raising important and compelling questions about the future of the region. Throughout the region and during the decade, one of the key themes marching hand in hand with capital market liberalization was the existence of weak institutions, incapable of dealing with a new capital flow environment.

▶ THE APPROACH OF THE BOOK

The approach of this book is to put the great bull market in the U.S. stock market and international capital markets during the 1991–2001 period into its proper perspective—that of a bubble—and to describe how this phenomenon relates back to the kind of economic system that nations choose. There is clearly a risk-reward factor involved, since a more entrepreneurial-oriented economy is going to be more prone to bubbles than a managed economy. However, a managed economy is not likely to experience the great gains in productivity, employment, and wealth generation that occur when there are great innovations in economic life, such as the locomotive, assembly line industrial production, or the Internet. Consequently, we look to the role of innovation in the financial process as part of what helped stimulate the bubble. As Charles R. Morris noted, "The story of finance is therefore one of innovation, crisis, and consolidation. Industrial, commercial, or technological change calls for an innovation—paper trade credits, private-company stocks and bonds, retail stock markets, junk bonds, collateralized mortgage obligations, derivative instruments. In every case, the innovation solves an immediate problem—expanding trade, financing railroads, restructuring companies, stabilizing pension portfolios—and also triggers a period of greatly increased risk and instability, until institutions catch up."[12]

While Morris provides us with an idea of the linkages between industrial, commercial, and technological changes and financial crises, we still need to fully define what is meant by a bubble.[13] After all, a bubble in financial terms remains a somewhat hazy concept, implying something negative. For our purposes, we define a bubble as a condition that arises in a particular market when speculation feeds the market, pushing it sharply upward in terms of prices. As the bubble expands, a greater number of investors are attracted. The expectation on the part of those investors is that the value of the investment will continue to rise. At some point the bubble deflates, but the smart and lucky have already exited with profits. Those last into the bubble, who bought at the highest prices, lose their money as prices plummet. As investors begin to sell, panic sets in, stampeding more investors to dump their investments regardless of price, largely to avoid being the last to exit the market. With the collapse of the market, former wealth creation shifts to wealth destruction.

There are two broad schools of thoughts concerning bubbles: the rationalists and behavioralists (they could be called the irrationalists). The rationalists regard *bubble* as a sloppy term, usually cloaking poor research that fails to find the real reason for financial crashes in underlying, fundamental economic trends. Ultimately, the market is always rational and efficient. Animal spirits or crowd psychology may exist, but the impact of such things is much less than that of financial and economic factors. As Peter Garber, author of *Famous First Bubbles*, observes: "Invoking crowd psychology—which is always ill defined and unmeasured—turns our explanation to tautology in a self-deluding attempt to say something more than a confession of confusion."[14] Along these lines, the rationalists do not have a high regard for such expressions as *mania, bubble, herd behavior, panic, crash, irrational exuberance, Ponzi scheme, contagion,* and the *greater-fool theory*. Rather, there is a quest for any available data and the use of that data to explain market trends in terms of the real economy.

One of the more debated bubbles concerns Dutch Tulipmania during the 1630s. According to Garber, there was no real mania. The high price of tulips could be traced (by various sources) from 1622 to 1637, which clearly demonstrated what he perceived to be a gradual climb in prices. The decline in prices in 1637 was a rational response to the market to changing economic fundamentals. Indeed, as Garber noted, "I conclude that the most famous aspect of the mania, the extremely high prices reported for rare bulbs and their rapid decline, reflects normal pricing behavior in bulb markets and cannot be interpreted as evidence of market irrationality."[15]

The irrationalists believe that in every bubble there is an eventual turn to animal spirits, a point where economic fundamentals go out the door and crowd psychology takes over. One of the earliest advocates of the irrational school was Charles Mackay, the author of the classic *Extraordinary Popular Delusions and the Madness of Crowds*, published in 1841. Although many rationalists regard his research as suspect, Mackay did give a compelling portrayal of some of the frenzied behavior of investors during the Dutch Tulipmania, the Mississippi Land Bubble, and the South Seas Bubble. But Mackay was hardly the last to look upon financial crashes as sparked in part by irrationalities in the stock market. Andrei Schleifer, in Harvard's *Inefficient Markets* (2000), which looks at the big sell-off in the NASDAQ among other things, argues that many investors do poorly in the market because they chase the latest fashion.

Prominent economist Charles E. Kindleberger is clearly in the camp of those who place an emphasis on investor behavior—be it rational or irrational.

Kindleberger regards Dutch Tulipmania as a bubble, driven by a certain degree of irrational market behavior. As to Garber's assertion that there was no mania, Kindleberger replies: "The issue presents a classic test as to whether economic theory 360 years after an event can invalidate its interpretations by the participants and general historians."[16] In addition, Kindleberger points to the fact that there was a depression following the collapse of Tulipmania in Holland and that general historians clearly see the mania as a historical event worth note.[17]

The market bubble that occurred during the 1991–2001 period clearly was a cause of concern for public officials, including Federal Reserve Chairman Alan Greenspan, who commented on what he saw as "irrational exuberance" in the U.S. stock market in December 1996. In the aftermath of the crash, there has been a growing literature denouncing the irrational and immoral conduct of the speculators. This does have a historical ring.

While the debate between the rationalists and irrationalists is likely to continue, we lean toward the latter. However, we would note that there can be a certain rationality to being irrational. In other words, one of the factors worth consideration in the market mania of the 1990s was herding—supported by economic or corporate research. As Garber notes: "If someone enters with a convincing story and structure of thought for organizing otherwise confusing phenomena, he will attract speculative capital. For instance, we know that the Internet stocks are a gamble, but they are backed by a theory of an epochal change in technology that will alter the entire economic structure."[18] For the investor, failure to be engaged can mean failure to put money to work and missing the next big thing. Yet, there is often a leap of faith in making the initial investment that defies the rational market argument. Furthermore, we would also contend that many people are not rational about their relationship with the future and overestimate their ability to beat the market by taking risks. If everything were rational, the market would indeed function without periodic panics and investors would be able to accurately map out the future. Certainly herding occurred throughout the decade.[19]

Along the lines of herding we also see the significance of the "cult of equity" that re-emerged during the 1990s and helped influence the direction of investors. While this may give the idea of dark-hooded priests lurking in the shadows as they pray to sardonic and mawkish gods, the cult of equity was nothing more than a renewed confidence in stocks as a means of personal wealth generation.

Following the market crash of 1929, the American public returned to viewing the stock market as a primitive insiders' game, lacking in transparency and disclosure. As B. Mark Smith noted: "Throughout most of the first half of the twentieth century, the stock market was seen as a vaguely ominous thing to be regarded with skepticism and suspicion."[20] This perception began to change in the 1980s but was briefly interrupted by the October 1987 market crash. However, after the economic slowdown of 1989–1991, the tech revolution and the return to economic growth helped generate a sense of euphoria about prospects for the stock market and individual wealth.

The combination of a period of strong and uninterrupted economic growth, a Democratic presidency inclined to loosen the regulatory environment to help stimulate a greater scale of mergers and acquisitions, and the renewed belief in the stock market led to a massive pouring of national savings into some form of stock market instrument. As Edward Chancellor noted:

> Between 1990 and the first quarter of 1998, equity mutual funds attracted over a trillion dollars from American investors. In 1990, there were 1,100 mutual funds in operation. Seven years later, nearly 6,000 mutual funds became the mainstay of the bull market. ... By the end of 1997, the total assets of U.S. mutual funds had risen
>
> l to the assets in the banking system. Just as in the
> rivate investment in shares by people saving for retire-
> -term support for the stock market.[21]

cult of equity was the view that the biggest risk was to
nk. As British fund manager Ian Rushbrook stated: "It
t of equities, because in the longer term equities always
perceived risk is that your equities fall. The real risk
an investor came into the market, as many Americans
d-1990s, they put their money into a market that was
returns. Consequently, many 1990s investors came to
nts as long-term and essentially rock-solid. They were
ith that also came the false perception that the stock
t continue to climb upward. Hype about the amazing
nomy only fueled expectations further.

an additional dimension, which would come back to haunt the 1990s generation of investors: falling in love with a stock. For many new investors coming into the market for the first time in the 1990s, the only experience they had was a bull market. Even on those occasions, as in 1997, when stocks dipped, recovery came quickly. This was to leave many investors inadequately prepared for the eventual day when stocks did not quickly bounce back but continued to plummet. However, many investors fell in love with a stock and would refuse to abandon it in the hope that it would rise again—perhaps as it had in the past.

This book examines these themes in 1991–2001 by exploring key developments in international financial markets over the decade. The book is divided into ten chapters, including an introduction and conclusion. The first chapter provides a brief history of the development of Wall Street and global capital markets. The two are strongly interrelated, especially in the second half of the twentieth century. It is important to underscore that we have been this way before—the period between 1870 and 1914 was one of substantial technological advances and a globalization of financial markets. The first World War brought that period to an end. Although the United States enjoyed the roaring 1920s, the rest of the world was not as fortunate, and by the end of that decade the Great Depression ended that earlier carnival on Wall Street. The post–World War II period was marked by U.S. economic dominance, and New York clearly became the credit hub of the world. Although Europe and Asia were to recover from the war and there was some dispersion of financial activities to London and Tokyo, New York remained central, so that by 1991 it was primed for a period of rocketing growth.

Chapter 2 provides a brief history of Wall Street and how it evolved alongside global capital markets, commencing with the Dutch settlers to modern Wall Street. Chapter 3 examines developments in emerging markets, while Chapter 4 looks at foreign exchange markets over the decade, focusing on several key issues: the arrival of the euro and consequent decline in trading activity in traditional currencies; the related rise in trading in "exotic" currencies and the change in risk profile that this entails; and the emergence of new players with new muscle and attitude in foreign exchange markets such as George Soros and his compatriots. Chapter 5 discusses the backlash to globalization, with its implications for the conduct of capital markets. Chapter 6 looks at the tech bubble, in particular the close working relationship with the NASDAQ, venture capitalists, and investment bankers. Chapter 7 covers the urge to merger, based on the massive consolidation of major industries such as finance, and the business it generated for Wall Street firms. Chapter 8 discusses the number of scandals and wrongdoings in which a small yet influential number of companies were involved. Chapter 9 examines the decline of Japan and the rise of China and the implications of both to global capital markets—possibly as a future shock.

The final chapter discusses the attack on the World Trade Center towers as a symbolic close to the 1991–2001 decade and considers the significance of 9/11, as well as the key themes highlighted in the book, in pointing the way to future developments in global financial markets. It also deals with the difficult question of how markets and their institutions will regain trust, a critical ingredient to any successful economic and financial experience. At the end of the day, the market-based economy is clearly the superior mode of economic development, and globalization is a major force in providing a sounder business environment and a better path to the improvement of the international standard of living. What is always needed in any system is balance. In the 1990s, that balance was temporarily lost. The first decade of the twenty-first century will be a period of restoring a balance between economic freedom and societal considerations, pertaining to equity, environment, and morals.

This book is meant to be readable and accessible to those interested in banking, finance, politics, economics, and current events. In a sense, it is a history of an amazing decade. We firmly believe that to tell that history, all aspects of the decade must be told. This means that we look at the 1991–2001 era through multicolored lenses of finance, economics, banking, and political science. The absence of one tool would mean the lessening of the sum. We also want to be clear that this is not a book of economic theory or one primarily for the professional economist. Above all else, it is meant for the general reader who has an interest in current events and the forces that shape the world in which we live.

▶ NOTES

1. John Brooks, *Once in Golconda: A True Drama on Wall Street, 1920–1938* (New York: John Wiley & Sons, 1969, 1999), p. v.

2. Joseph Schumpeter (1883–1950) was a widely respected professor of economics at Harvard University who was also associated with the Austrian school of economic thinking. In his *Business Cycles* (1939), he advanced the idea that long-run cycles of economic activity are a

consequence of the cluster of innovations, and downturns come when the spirit of innovation declines. The cluster of innovations is accompanied by a "creative destruction" as new technology and innovation uproot the old system.

3. For a more thorough discussion about the Entrepreneurial Economy, see David B. Audretsch and A. Roy Thurik, *What's New About the New Economy?: Sources of Growth in the Managed and Entrepreneurial Economies* (Bloomington, Ind.: Institute for Development Strategies, Indiana University, July 1998, revised October 2000) and Alfred Chandler, *Scale and Scope: The Dynamics of Industrial Capitalism* (Cambridge, Mass.: Harvard University Press, 1990).

4. As Robert Skidelsky noted: "The collapse of Communism was greeted with a triumphalism appropriate to a crushing military victory. The failure of Communism and all other forms of collectivism seemed to vindicate capitalism and political democracy, and to remove any systematic obstacles to their universal adoption. The optimists looked forward to the reconstruction of post-Communist societies on Western lines and their incorporation into a Western-led international order. A world integrated by trade and democracy would not only soar to unimagined heights of prosperity but would also realize the nineteenth-century liberal dream of universal peace." From his *The Road from Serfdom: The Economic and Political Consequences of the End of Communism* (New York: Penguin Books, 1995), p. vii.

5. Robert Kuttner, *Everything for Sale: The Virtues and Limits of Markets* (Chicago: University of Chicago Press, 1996), p. xiv.

6. Harry S. Dent, Jr., *The Roaring 2000s: Building the Wealth and Lifestyle You Desire in the Greatest Boom in History* (New York: Simon & Schuster, 1998), p. 23.

7. Edward Chancellor, *Devil Take the Hindmost: A History of Financial Speculation* (New York: Farrar, Straus & Giroux, 1999), p. 227. Data cited in the next sentence are from the same source.

8. Ibid, p. 226.

9. Anthony B. Perkins, "The Angler: Getting Real in Silicon Valley," *Red Herring*, October 1, 2001, p. 20.

10. Warren Buffett, one of the investment world's leading figures, was compelled to state to Berkshire Hathaway shareholders in 2002 that he was "disgusted by the situation, so common in the last few years, in which shareholders have suffered billions in losses while the CEOs, promoters, and other higher-ups who fathered those disasters have walked away with extraordinary wealth. To their shame, those business leaders view shareholders as patsies, not partners." Quoted from Arianna Huffington, *Pigs at the Trough: How Corporate Greed and Political Corruption Are Undermining America* (New York: Crown Publishers, 2003), pp. 29–30.

11. Roger Lowenstein, *When Genius Failed: The Rise and Fall of Long-Term Capital Management* (New York: Random House, 2000), p. 235.

12. Charles R. Morris, *Money, Greed, and Risk: Why Financial Crises and Crashes Happen* (New York: A Century Foundation Book, Random House, 1999), p. 7.

13. There is an extensive literature on "bubbles" in history. See Charles E. Kindleberger, *Manias, Panics and Crashes: A History of Financial Crises* (New York: John Wiley & Sons, 1996, Third Edition); John Crasswell, *The South Sea Bubble* (London: Cresset Press, 1960); Edward Chancellor, *Devil Take the Hindmost: A History of Financial Speculation* (New York: Farrar, Straus, Giroux, 1999); John Kenneth Galbraith, *A Short History of Financial Euphoria* (New York: Whittle Books, in Association with Viking, 1993); and D. Hancock, "Domestic Bubbling: Eighteenth Century London Merchants and Individual Investment in Funds," *Economic History Review*, 47, No. 4 (November 1994): 679–702.

14. Peter Garber, *Famous First Bubbles: The Fundamentals of Earlier Manias* (Boston: The MIT Press, 2002), p. 124.

15. Ibid, p. 13.

16. Charles E. Kindleberger, *Manias, Panics, and Crashes: A History of Financial Crashes* (New York: John Wiley & Sons, 1996), p. ix.

17. Two seminal Dutch histories reflect Kindleberger's view: Jonathan I. Israel's *The Dutch Republic* (1995) and Jan de Vries and Ad van der Woude, *The First Modern Economy: Success, Failure, and Perseverance of the Dutch Economy, 1500–1815* (1997). The latter work focused on the issue that contracts made in taverns for tulip trading were unenforceable and that conditions clearly

got out of control. As de Vries and de Woude noted: "Public officials viewed this democratic speculation with both fear and loathing, and once the mania collapsed ... pamphlets appeared
denouncing the irrational and immoral conduct of the speculators." Jan de Vries and Ad van der
Woude, *The First Modern Economy: Success, Failure and Perseverance of the Dutch Economy,
1500–1815* (New York: Cambridge University Press, 1997), pp. 150–151.

18.   Garber, *Famous First Bubbles*, p. 8.
19.   It should be noted that among the behavioral school are the year 2002 winners of the Nobel
Prize for Economics, Princeton University's Daniel Kahneman and Vernon Smith of George
Mason University. Both have conducted research that indicates that people often are irrational
in looking to the future and that they makes mistakes by overestimating their ability to beat the
market by taking risks. Another interesting work is that of Didier Sornette, *Why Stock Markets
Crash: Critical Events in Complex Financial Systems* (Princeton: Princeton University Press,
2002). Sornette proposes that complex-system theory can explain and predict both the emergence of financial bubbles as well as their rupture and path of recovery. He believes that investors
conform to herding behavior much like particles in a magnet and that long periods of "imitative
cooperation" eventually lead first to bubbles and then to short periods of extreme instability, rupture, and catastrophic failure. Although individuals appear to act of their free will when viewed
under a microscope, when viewed macroscopically as a system, he believes, they act in nonran-
dom patterns that (much like molecules in a pressurized container of gas) can be captured with
the precision of a mathematical formula.
20.   Mark Smith, *Toward Rational Exuberance: The Evolution of the Modern Stock Market* (New
York: Farrar, Straus and Giroux, 2001), p. xii.
21.   Chancellor, *Devil Take the Hindmost*, p. 227.
22.   Quoted in Chancellor, p. 228.

PART I

THE GLOBALIZATION OF CAPITAL MARKETS

CHAPTER 2

WALL STREET: FROM FURS TO GLOBAL CAPITAL MARKETS

Wall Street has been and remains a unique market where entrepreneurs and empire builders rub elbows and seek to convert dreams into commercial successes. There is also a colorful history of con men, willing to rob the unsuspecting, greedy, and stupid. Many times the two groups are melded together in the public mind, leaving mixed reviews of the careers of such individuals as J. P. Morgan, Cornelius Vanderbilt, and Ivan Boesky. Transcending all of this is the idea that Wall Street functions as a wellspring for global economic development—both for the betterment of the many and for the enrichment of the few. The two do not necessarily run hand in hand, and history is filled with those who sought and achieved the betterment of themselves over the masses.

Yet the historical record also suggests that the ideas behind Wall Street have helped propel economic development from mankind's early history to the present. In a sense, the pursuit of wealth has led to innovations that have helped push society along, sometimes in a lemming-like rush, other times kicking and screaming, into a new stage of development. Certainly the flow of capital into various channels made the financing of the American Republic's early government possible, as well as the U.S. industrial revolution in the late eighteenth and early nineteenth centuries. It also helped put a man on the moon, facilitated financing for the creation of the world's most powerful military machine, and provided credit for the economic development of a wide range of countries from Argentina and China to Turkey and South Africa. Consequently, Wall Street and the ideas represented by it have a central role to play in the evolution of the global economy, something that is often forgotten in the daily rise and fall of stock prices.

There are six major trends that are significant in the history of global capital markets and Wall Street as part of that process. First, global capital markets evolved in close kinship with the development of capitalism, in particular international trade. As trade created the need for cross-border financial products, it sparked innovation, such as new accounting practices (double-entry accounting) and letters of credit. The second trend is the evolving notion of a stock market, something relatively new in history. Although financial markets did exist in a rudimentary fashion during the Roman Empire, it was not until the late Middle Ages and early modern era that stock markets became important as part of the broader economic picture. In a sense, stock markets provided a geographic location for capital markets.

Closely linked to the idea of stock markets is the growing ability of financial "experts" to manage risk. Without better techniques in risk management, such as insurance as well as the constantly growing expertise in analyzing companies and foreign exchange and interest rate hedging, there would not have been the extension of capital needed to fuel global economic development. Directly related to enhanced risk management is the trend of a long and arduous improvement in transparency and disclosure of financial information. Secrecy long played an important role in how early bankers and financiers ran their operations. Over time, especially in the twentieth century, the culture of opaqueness gave way to public demands for better information about financial transactions. The cloak of transparency has not yet been entirely surrendered. Despite vastly improved supervision and disclosure, the 1990s witnessed their share of scandals and hidden problems.

Related to the issue of transparency and disclosure is the role of the state in providing the rules and structures that capital markets need to perform properly. While self-regulation has evolved, the most important and necessary regulator remains the state, critical in providing infrastructure for the following factors:

1. Information has to flow freely.
2. People have to be able to trust one another.
3. Competition must be ensured.
4. Property rights must be respected.

Without these preconditions, market development remains incomplete and prone to greater volatility.

Finally, as capital markets have progressed through history, the circle of those able to participate, as well as those being affected, has widened. Indeed, this is one of the more intriguing dimensions of the 1990s, which witnessed the "democratization" of equity markets, i.e., substantial penetration of the so-called small investors into the stock market.

▶ FOUNDING FATHERS

The Dutch have the honor of being the founding fathers of Wall Street. They came to the New World at the beginning of the 1600s, led by Henry Hudson, who was searching for the Northwest Passage, a fabled maritime shortcut to the riches of the Far East. Unlike the English, who came to escape religious persecution, and the Spanish, who sought souls and wealth, the Dutch came for profits, starting with the fur trade. By 1626, Manhattan was founded to help support the fur trade, and the outline of what would become New York City and Wall Street was beginning to take shape.

Although the Dutch involvement in settling North America was short-lived, lasting roughly from 1626 to 1676, it left a lasting imprint on the city of New Amsterdam, which is today New York City. The Dutch brought with them a highly entrepreneurial spirit, driven by the pursuit of profits. They were also at the cutting edge of global finance in the seventeenth century, with Amsterdam playing the star role.[1] As Daniel Defoe, the author of *Robinson Crusoe* and a well-traveled man of letters, wrote after a stay in the Netherlands, "The Dutch must be understood as they really are, the Middle Persons in Trade, the Factors and Brokers of Europe. … They *buy* to *sell* again, to *take* in and *send* out, and the greatest Part of their vast Commerce consists in being supply'd from All Parts of the World, that they may supply All the World again."[2]

Because the Dutch were keen traders, they had developed sophisticated finance mechanisms to complement the commodity trade. By the early seventeenth century, Amsterdam had become the dominant market for short- and long-term credit, running hand in hand with markets for stocks, commodity futures, and options. Sound public finances, helped by the creation of the Wisselbank (Exchange Bank of Amsterdam) in 1609, only strengthened what came to be known as "Dutch finance." The bank's role was to facilitate payments in rapidly growing foreign trade as well as to provide a greater degree of stability in the circulation of paper by restricting the circulation of paper credit. Equally important, trade generated wealth in the Netherlands and was a source of excess capital that became available as credit. The Amsterdam bourse made that capital available.

The Amsterdam bourse was used for speculation in grain, herrings, species, and whale oil. Trading in shares first occurred in 1602 and largely involved the Dutch West India Company and a number of other companies. The Dutch also made other contributions to financial techniques. They were to develop short selling (selling stock one does not own in hopes of a fall in prices), bear raids (where insiders conspire to sell a stock short until the outsiders panic and sell out their holdings, allowing the insiders to close these shorts profitably), syndicates (where a person or syndicate secretly acquires the entire floating supply of a commodity, forcing all who need to buy the commodity to do so at their price).[3]

The Dutch were not without their financial mishaps. The Tulipmania was one of the first recorded speculative bubbles. Tulips were first imported into Europe from Turkey in the mid-1500s. Over time tulips gained in popularity, with demand growing for different varieties of the bulbs. The supply (and increasing popularity) of rare varieties of tulip bulbs failed to match demand. Prices rose sharply. By the 1630s soaring prices caught public attention, with ordinary citizens regarding tulip bulb speculation as a certain path to riches. As the mania for tulips reached its height, some people mortgaged their homes and businesses to buy the bulbs. In a sense, the trade in tulips emerged as an alternative to speculation in company shares. The prices for many rare bulb types reached several hundred dollars each. (One bulb of a very rare variety even changed hands for more than $20,000.) By late 1636, people began to see that prices had reached outlandish levels and could only hope that the bulbs could be sold to some "greater fool." Much of the smart money (well-informed investors) had already sold, leaving the door open to a crash in 1637. Government intervention was slow, and by the end of the crash a number of Dutch families lost their homes and businesses they had mortgaged to participate in this "sure thing" investment.

▶ THE RISE OF LONDON

The Dutch were to leave a lasting impression on Wall Street and international capital market development. Dutch ideas concerning finance were to survive in the New World, and Dutch finance was rapidly absorbed in London as well, following the Glorious Revolution of 1688. In 1694, the Bank of England, a central bank, was established. With sound fiscal policies, the establishment of a national debt, relative political stability, strong economic growth stimulated by the gaining momentum of the industrial revolution, and the expansion of trade, Britain was ready to assume the role of the world's banker after the defeat of Napoleon in 1814. In essence, the close working relationship between the Bank of England and other parts of the government and the private sector banks meant that few savings lay idle and the complete financial resources of the economy were fully tapped.

While the British state played an important role in fostering the development of its financial system, the private sector was equally important. The London banks were closely linked to trade; most of the major institutions that held sway in the nineteenth century had their roots in trading activities, including Schroders, Barings Brothers, and the Rothschilds. The Rothschilds, in particular, represented the marriage of banking and political power. As a banking family still active in global markets, the Rothschilds had their beginnings in the Jewish ghetto of Frankfurt, Germany, in the mid-1700s. Mayer Amschel Rothschild, like many Jews of his time, was prohibited from owning land or pursuing other pursuits such as crafts, a prohibition that turned many to financial services and related trades. As his business gradually grew, he sent his five sons to Paris, Vienna, Naples, London, and Frankfurt, where they formed the basis of the Rothschild international network.

The Rothschilds were quick to see that superior information could mean the difference between massive profits and massive losses. Consequently, they constructed their own international intelligence network, with fast packets (packages of letters), agents, carrier pigeons, and couriers. Their emerging importance as the bankers to European governments also provided them with additional access to information. The Napoleonic period was particularly good for them as they became actively involved in smuggling. Napoleon sought to kill England's trade-oriented economy by imposing a continental blockade against English goods. For the Rothschilds this was too good an opportunity to let slip, considering that a strong demand for English goods continued, even if they were now contraband. After 1815 they were in a good position to provide financing for reparations, the initial loans of the Belgian Kingdom, and the boom in railway construction. The business of capital markets was clearly done on a personal basis, with considerable weight given to the banker's ties to high-ranking personnel in a particular government.

The Rothschilds represented a group of growing importance in the financial world—British merchant bankers. Britain was the most powerful country in the nineteenth century, especially after the defeat of the mercantilist French by 1815. Consequently, the British imposed a free trade system on the global economy. A lynchpin to the free trade system was the international acceptance of the gold standard. This meant that the global financial and trade system was founded upon the concept that national currencies were related to the international price of gold, which was set by the British. Consequently, the London bullion market was where most of the newly minted gold came into the international market, and London was where the connection between gold and credit was the strongest.

Within this system, the British merchant banks played a major role, financing foreign trade, bringing new bond offerings to market, and assisting their clients in making sound investments. An additional advantage for the British banks was their ability to issue long-term bonds and loans, which provided them with a competitive advantage over other financial centers. British banks, therefore, were active in financing the industrial and infrastructure development of much of the Americas, continental Europe, and the British colonies in Australia, Africa, and Asia. For most Latin American countries, London was the key financial center if their loans were in pounds (See Table 2.1). The London merchant banks dominated what came to

TABLE 2.1   Foreign Loans to Latin American Governments, 1850–1875

Country	Total No. of Loans	Nominal Value (Br. Pounds, Thousands)	Purpose: Military (%)	Purpose: Public Works (%)	Purpose: Refinance (%)
Argentina	7	13,488	20	68	11
Bolivia	1	1,700	–	100	–
Brazil	8	23,467	30	13	57
Chile	7	8,502	37	51	12
Colombia	2	2,200	–	9	91
Costa Rica	3	3,400	–	100	–
Ecuador	1	1,824	–	–	100
Guatemala	2	650	–	77	23
Haiti	1	1,458	–	–	100
Honduras	4	5,590	–	98	2
Mexico	2	16,960	70	–	30
Paraguay	2	3,000	–	80	20
Peru	7	51,840	10	45	45
Santo Domingo	1	757	–	100	–
Uruguay	1	3,500	–	–	100
Venezuela	2	2,500	–	30	70
Total	51	140,837			

Source: Carlos Marichal, *A Century of Debt Crises in Latin America: From Independence to the Great Depression, 1820–1930* (Princeton: Princeton University Press, 1989), p. 80.

be referred to as *haute finance,* becoming the primary mechanism that facilitated the flow of capital from the areas of surplus to areas of demand.

The British-dominated global capital markets system was not without its periodic defaults and financial panics. The flow of bank loans into Latin America, the United States, and some of the lesser-developed European countries, such as Greece and Turkey (then the Ottoman Empire), carried considerable risk to the country. Other factors weighed heavily on making loans in the developing world for Europe's international bankers during the nineteenth and early twentieth centuries, as amply demonstrated in Table 2.2.

▶ BACK ON WALL STREET

The U.S. stock market developed in the shadow of its more dominant British cousin. Indeed, in the late eighteenth century, the United States was a nation of considerable economic potential but was, nonetheless, a developing nation. Outside of a few major urban centers, such as Boston, New York, and Philadelphia, the country was heavily agricultural. During the British colonial period there was a perennial shortage of coinage, and barter was often used in the frontier areas. Consequently, the American colonial financial system was relatively primitive.

The first steps to the development of a modern capital market in the United States came in the early 1790s with an investment boom caused by the need to finance the American Revolutionary War debt. Despite strong opposition from the Jeffersonian Democrats, the government of President George Washington, under the guidance of Treasury Secretary Alexander Hamilton, issued the first U.S. government bonds—some $80 million. These became the first major issues of publicly traded securities. By 1792, there were a total of five securities traded, including the U.S. government bonds and those of two banks.

Regulation and Organization Commence

At this time, Wall Street was a largely unregulated market, with little transparency and a loose organizational structure. Any regulation was self-induced. While there was strong opposition to any idea of government regulation, there was also a grudging recognition that some basic ground rules were required to guarantee, at the very least, that the major market players were recognizable and had a clear understanding of and agreement on trading practices. The 1792 crash reinforced the importance of reform. Consequently, on May 17, 1792, twenty-four brokers subscribed to what was called the Buttonwood Agreement. This was the first brokers' agreement, signed under a buttonwood tree at what is now 68 Wall Street. The significance of this agreement was that it forced New York's leading brokers to form a private club for securities trading, which was readily identifiable. The Buttonwood Agreement also pledged its signers to fixed commissions of one-quarter percent and to give preference to other club members in their dealings. This was the precedent that started the long history of the New

Transparency?

TABLE 2.2 Selected Crises, 1875–1914

Country of Origin (Date)	Description	Cause
Turkey (1875)	Debt default	Fiscal deficits were funded by foreign borrowing that eventually could not be sustained.
Peru (1876)	Debt default	Falling guano exports and stagnation of other revenues, combined with increasing fiscal deficits, generated a crisis.
Egypt (1876)	Debt default	Increased foreign borrowing to finance consumption led to unsustainable debt growth.
Argentina (1890)	Debt crisis and institutional failure	Argentina's inability to meet debt-service payments led to the bailout of Barings Brothers.
United States (1873)	Financial crisis	Bank runs and failures and fears about U.S. commitment to gold parity were followed by a stock market crash.
Greece (1893)	Debt default	Increased borrowing to finance consumption led to unsustainable debt growth.
United States (1894–1896)	Speculative attack	Speculation against the U.S. gold standard parity followed the Sherman Act (1890) and increasing fiscal deficits.
Brazil (1898)	Debt default	A decline of 64 percent in coffee prices over the preceding five years generated an external crisis.
United States (1907)	Financial crisis	Banking panic and suspension of cash payments followed interest rate hikes and bank failures.
Canada (1907)	Speculative attack/banking crisis	High interest rates in Canada (in response to hikes in the United States) led to excessive credit expansion that generated speculation against the Canadian dollar.
Brazil (1914)	Debt default	A sharp decline in coffee prices in the preceding two years generated a debt crisis.

Source: International Monetary Fund, *International Capital Markets: Developments, Prospects, and Key Policy Issues* (Washington, D.C.: International Monetary Fund, November 1997), p. 238.

WALL STREET'S FIRST SCANDAL:
THE STORY OF WILLIAM DUER AND THE CRASH OF 1792

The first scandal to rock Wall Street occurred in 1792 and was precipitated by William Duer, an Englishman and son of a successful West Indian plantation owner. After a stint in the British Army in India and a period of managing his father's Caribbean estates, Duer settled in New York City in 1773. When the American Revolution broke out, Duer sided with the young Republic and was elected to the Continental Congress, where he was a signer of the Articles of Confederation. He also supplied the Continental Army, making himself a small fortune in the process. Duer's financial situation was not hurt by his marriage to Catherine "Lady Kitty" Alexander, the daughter of a wealthy American general of Scots descent. At their wedding, Lady Kitty was given away by no less a personage than George Washington. Duer quickly became famous for lavish high-society dinners served at his home on Broadway, not far from Wall Street. He also had helped Hamilton establish one of the first banks in the United States, the Bank of New York.

What elevated Duer into a position of financial scoundrel was his access to insider information. As his biographer Robert F. Jones noted: "Interspersed with his public career, and too often depending on it, was his career as a stock speculator, land promoter, army contractor and merchant. For William Duer never tired of combining, or trying to combine, public office with private profit."[1] Since there was no such thing as "insider trading" at the time, Duer was willing to work around moral condemnation to follow through a number of schemes, one of which was to engineer the first market crash on Wall Street. Reflecting Duer's reputation as one of the movers and shakers in the young American Republic with a flair for finance, Treasury Secretary Hamilton asked him to serve as an assistant secretary. Duer served in that capacity from 1789 to 1791. During that time he became involved in the Scotia Land Company scheme, which gave land along the Ohio River to 101 Frenchmen. In fact, there was no land, but Duer led the "speculative" land company that authorized the grants.

Although Duer resigned from the Treasury, he remained in contact with many officials, some of whom were willing to pass on information about the nation's finances. Hamilton was quite proper about not using insider information. Duer was not. After leaving the Treasury, Duer entered into a partnership with Alexander Macomb, scion of one of New York's most affluent families. The pair decided to use Macomb's money and Duer's speculative abilities and Treasury contacts on the stock market.

Their initial target was the Bank of New York. Duer heard that the rival Bank of the United States was going to make an offer to buy the Bank of New York.

(continued)

York Stock Exchange in formulating club rules and regulations designed to promote the interests of its members.

In 1817 New York brokers finally established a formal organization, the New York Stock & Exchange Board, and rented rooms at 40 Wall Street. They also adopted a constitution of rules for the conduct of business. Despite these measures, Wall Street as a capital market remained opaque and poorly regulated. However, business was slowly increasing.

WALL STREET'S FIRST SCANDAL:
THE STORY OF WILLIAM DUER AND THE CRASH OF 1792 *(CONTINUED)*

Consequently, Duer and Macomb bought Bank of New York stock, forming what is called a long position. If the Bank of the United States bought the Bank of New York, they would make substantial gains. Unknown to Macomb, however, Duer had also heard that the merger would not go through and had bet against the stock in his own account (going short). Either way, Duer would win. Hamilton, unaware of Duer's duplicity, abhorred the speculative nature of Wall Street and wrote on March 2, 1792, "Tis time, there must be a line of separation between honest men and knaves, between respectable stockholders and dealers in the funds, and mere unprincipled Gamblers."[2]

Duer's speculative activities did not go unheeded by other investors and the affluent. In particular, the Livingston clan, one of New York State's most powerful families, had financial interests that were threatened by a fall in prices. When the Livingstons moved by gradually pulling out gold and silver from their bank deposits, this in turn caused a contraction in the local money supply and forced the banks to start calling in loans. In the ensuing credit crunch, Duer suddenly found himself indebted well beyond his means of repayment. Compounding matters, Duer had also bought a number of bank stocks for future delivery, speculating that rising prices would allow him to pay for them when the time came. However, with the credit crunch and ensuing panic on Wall Street, the prices for those securities plummeted. Unable to borrow, Duer went into bankruptcy. He was arrested and put into debtors' prison, where he was soon joined by Macomb.

While Duer went from rags to riches and back to rags again—becoming the first American to gain infamy for insider trading—Hamilton became the first Secretary of the Treasury to actively intervene in the stock market and end a panic. Observing that a collapse on Wall Street would be bad for the economy, Hamilton stepped in and ordered the Treasury to buy several hundred dollars' worth of federal securities to support the market. He also urged the bankers not to call in their loans. While Duer was to eventually die in debtors' prison for his acts, he did set in motion an effort by the survivors of the 1792 crash to provide better rules and regulations.

[1] Robert F. Jones, "The King of the Alley": *William Duer—Politician, Entrepreneur and Speculator, 1768–1799* (Philadelphia: American Philosophical Society, 1992), p. vii.
[2] Quoted from Brian Trumbore, "William Duer and the Crash of 1792," www.buyandhold.com/bh/en/education/history/2000/8699.html.

Turnpikes were the first wave of new companies to come to the market. They commenced with the Lancaster Pike, which was completed in 1794. Others soon followed, especially in New York and Pennsylvania. Yet, despite the burst of activity in turnpikes, the real movers and shakers on Wall Street were canal companies. The Erie Canal was particularly popular, because the waterways helped open up the American interior to trade. Instead of having to send grains and other farm staples down the Mississippi to the port of New Orleans, the

Erie Canal facilitated trade to the eastern seaboard via the Hudson River and to New York City and markets beyond. Needless to say, the flow of trade from the west to New York City greatly augmented that city's economic and commercial importance.

Turnpikes and canals were not the only stocks and bonds traded on Wall Street. In the early 1810s, four new bank stocks appeared, New York City provided one of the earliest municipal bonds, and insurance companies were chartered and soon traded. Still, it was a small market. As historian Charles R. Geisst noted, "In 1818 the exchange listed only five U.S. government issues, one New York State issue, ten bank issues and thirteen insurances and several foreign exchange deals."[4]

The New York Stock Market Takes Off

The U.S. capital markets began to take off between 1890 and 1920. This was a period when the American economy underwent a profound structural change from a rural, agrarian, self-sufficient economy to an industrialized, urban, market-oriented one.[5] Advances in industrial technology, in turn, filtered through Wall Street, especially as some of the industries required financing, through either equities or bonds. In step with industrial changes, American finance was also undergoing a transformation, with a new class of entrepreneur coming to the helm.

Chief among these entrepreneurs was John Pierpont Morgan. Born in 1837 in Hartford, Connecticut, Morgan began his career as a finance and investment agent for his father in New York City. In that capacity he developed a familiarity with finance in both the United States and the United Kingdom, then the world's dominant power politically and economically. In 1871, he established the banking house of Drexel, Morgan & Co. Twenty-four years later it was renamed J. P. Morgan & Co., which it was to remain until the firm's purchase by Chase Manhattan in 2000.

Through the offices of J. P. Morgan and other banks, credit was extended to a hungry and growing U.S. corporate sector. Following the financial crash in 1893, Morgan became active in railroads, reorganizing several rail lines in the Eastern United States. He also marketed U.S. government securities on a large scale. In 1889, he entered the field of industrial consolidation, forming the United States Steel Corporation, which became the first billion-dollar corporation in the world. He also had a hand in setting up International Harvester and General Electric. His involvement in the restructuring of the U.S. corporate world was guided by his interest in imposing a measure of order on the turbulent economic development of the United States. He preferred to have large stable systems rather than boom-bust cycles and the wasteful and speculative recklessness of unchecked competition.

Although Morgan was sometimes depicted as one of the "robber barons" of the Gilded Age, he was a firm believer in the development of a more stable U.S. financial system. During the second half of the nineteenth century, the U.S. banking system was plagued by a number of banking panics (1873, 1893, etc.). In 1895, Morgan went to the rescue of the U.S. government, which had run out of gold, by raising $65 million for the Treasury and by making certain that it remained as a reserve. Then, in 1907, a failed effort to corner the copper market on Wall Street spiraled into a major financial crisis. The U.S. government lacked a central bank and was forced to turn once again to Morgan for help. Through his good offices, Morgan spearheaded a major private sector rescue effort, helping to restore confidence in the banking system. His actions also helped sway the argument in favor of a central bank. In 1912–1913, the Federal Reserve System was established to function as a central bank for the United States.

The establishment of the central bank supported the rise of U.S. financial power, and by 1914 Wall Street had emerged as the world's principal money center. London had long been the world's banker, but with the advent of war between Europe's great powers, the British Empire could no longer shoulder the responsibilities associated with such a leadership role. This was painfully evident in August 1914, when the British government suspended gold payments against pounds sterling. Equally significant, London decided to forbid all British investments outside of the Empire. The significance of these developments was noted by the *London Times*, which admitted "the temporary abandonment of our historic claim as an international money center," making it inevitable that "much of the international business we have been accustomed to do should pass to ... the United States," which "is capable of doing it."[6] Although the British were to resume gold payments in 1925, it was too late.

Symbols Matter: The Blast of 1920

Wall Street's newfound prominence in global finance came about from a long chain of historical developments. The Great War accelerated a shift already under way, with financial power gradually making its move to New York City. That trend was reinforced by the circumstances found by the former combatants at the close of hostilities. In Europe and Japan economic activity was down considerably, while even the victors, France and the United Kingdom, were burdened with large debts, part of them to the United States. At the same time, the Allies had insisted on heavy reparations from the Germans to pay for the cost of the war. In the Treaty of Versailles, the Germans were required to pay large sums to the French and British, who then in turn could pay back the United States. The flow of funds was ultimately out of Europe, across the Atlantic and to the United States. Wall Street was decidedly the benefactor of this chain of financing. At the same time, business was picking up on Wall Street in the aftermath of the war, especially with the advent of a new round of technology.

Not everyone was thrilled by Wall Street's rise to the apex of global financial markets. Within the United States there was an active anarchist movement that was strongly opposed to capitalism. Aligned with terrorists in Europe against the "old order" of monarchs, anarchists in the United States were equally open to the use of force. Accordingly, eight Chicago police officers were killed by a bombing in 1886; President William McKinley was assassinated in 1901; a bomb ripped apart the office of the *Los Angeles Times* in 1910, killing twenty people; and in 1919, a series of bombs was mailed to business and government leaders. Adding to concerns about the anarchists was the rise of the forces of international communism, in particular, the successful Bolshevik revolution in Russia in 1917. Both anarchists and communists were vocal enemies of capitalism, which they regarded as exploiting the working class. To both, Wall Street was a blatant symbol of the evils of capitalism: greed, dishonesty, and exploitation.

On September 16, 1920, around noon on a warm Indian summer day, Wall Street was shaken by a massive blast. A driverless, dilapidated wagon pulled by an old horse had pulled up outside the offices of J. P. Morgan in the middle of the financial district. Inside the wagon were an estimated 100 pounds of dynamite with 500 pounds of fragmented steel window sashes. A remote control device triggered the load, driving thousands of jagged metal shards outward into the crowded sidewalks and streets.[7]

The carnage was significant. Survivors described automobiles turned over and burning, plate glass windows shattered for blocks, and wounded people lying on the pavement, like "lifeless lumps of clay." Forty people died and close to three hundred others were wounded. The bombing also left Wall Street badly shaken. In a sense, an act of indiscriminate violence had been conducted against the heart of global capitalism: Wall Street. The attack had absolute shock value.

In the aftermath of September 1920, the Red Scare intensified as anarchists or communists were thought to be the perpetrators. Immigrants were perceived by an apprehensive American public as a dangerous Trojan Horse, being "bearded, crazed bomb-wielding people."[8] Although the expectation was that the government manhunt would catch the evildoers, the perpetrators were never brought to justice, leaving the 1920 Wall Street bombing as one of time's great unsolved mysteries.

Despite the shock of the bombing, Wall Street reopened the next day. One reason for the action was to head off any potential panic in the market. Instead, cheesecloth was placed over the broken windows, the sidewalks were swept clear of most of the debris, and brokers showed up to conduct business as usual. As Columbia University's Beverly Gage noted, "The explosion solidified national support behind Wall Street, transforming the daily routine of finance into an act of defiance and patriotic affirmation."[9] Although the bombings rocked Wall Street, they were unable to derail what was to emerge as one of the century's strongest bull markets.

The 1920s Bull Market and Crash of 1929

In the aftermath of the First World War, the United States economy was the world's largest and had survived the war intact. In fact, U.S. industry was able to rapidly expand overseas because of the weak condition of Europe's major economies, most of them heavily damaged by the war. By 1929, the U.S. economy accounted for over 40 percent of world output.[10] For Wall Street, the expansion of U.S. industry meant expansion in services provided, ranging from trade finance to lending for the development of the manufacturing industry as well as new bond and equity issues.

The 1920s were to be a boom time for Wall Street. U.S. economic activity was pushed along by a new generation of companies and technology. For many the world was now entering a new era: the old economy was fading, and a new economy, based on new technologies, was racing ahead. The years of the Coolidge administration in the mid-1920s were marked by positive economic trends: the extension of free trade, the taming of inflation, the relaxation of antitrust laws, and a more "scientific" style of corporate management (associated with the Harvard School of Business). The relaxation of antitrust laws allowed for a series of mergers among banking, railroad, and utility companies that strongly suggested greater economies of scale and scope.

One of the advocates of the "new era" economy was the eminent Yale University economics professor Irving Fisher. Fisher claimed that modern production "is managed by 'captains of industry'. These men are specially fitted at once to forecast and to mould the future, within the realms in which they operate. The industries of transportation and manufactures, particularly, are under the lead of an educated and trained speculative class."[11] Fisher was hardly alone. Berhard Baruch, a well-known Wall Street financial figure, argued in 1929 that the prospects for peace and free trade, improved statistical information, better comprehension of economics among businessmen, and cooperation among the world's central bankers were producing an "industrial renaissance" in the United States.[12] There was a high sense of confidence that the new order built on science and prosperity would continue forever.

This sense of excitement filtered into Wall Street, fueling the 1923–1929 boom. Adding fuel to the stock market was the emergence of the first mutual funds, Massachusetts Investors Trust and State Street Investment Trust. At the same time as these new sources of capital were available on Wall Street, credit became more widely available to the rest of the population. Consumerism boomed, as banks, credit societies, and companies all opened their doors to provide financing for the growing consumer class in the United States. By 1926, 65 percent of motorcars were purchased on installment credit, while department stores sold over 40 percent of goods on credit.[13] Adding to the credit binge in the 1920s was the ability of investors to take out margin loans, allowing investors to buy stock on credit. By October 1929 brokers' loans and bank loans to investors had climbed to $16 billion, representing roughly 18 percent of the total capitalization of all listed stocks.[14]

As the stock market took off, the sense of public excitement mounted. The mood of the 1920s boom was captured by Harpo Marx, the comedian, who wrote: "This wasn't a boom that was going to go bust. The market was a solid institution and I was being advised by the country's best authorities: Max Gordon (a New York theatrical producer), Groucho Marx, and the elevator operator in the Copley Plaza Hotel. I kept on buying."[15] Marx was hardly alone, as Wall Street also saw the emergence of a number of speculator pools, seeking to ride the wave and make big fortunes for their memberships.

The great Wall Street boom of the 1920s came to a crashing halt in 1929. On October 29, referred to as "Black Tuesday," the party ended. Despite efforts by the banks to brake the bursting of the financial bubble, the stock market collapsed and the slide into the Great Depression was on. A series of banking panics commencing in October 1930 transformed an otherwise serious recession into a depression. The Hoover administration proved unable to adjust to the sharp turn of direction, paving the way for the Roosevelt administration, which came into office in 1933. By then, the United States and the world had become bogged down in a brutal international economic depression, from which there was to be no easy exit. It was estimated that from the peak of U.S. economic activity in 1929 to the trough in 1933, economic output fell by 29.4 percent, a situation mirrored in Europe, Canada, and Australia.[16]

There are many reasons advanced for what caused the Great Depression. While there is considerable finger pointing, they are many actors who helped evoke the crash—greedy investors borrowing from brokers (to trade on what was called the margin), investment bankers who were willing to push stocks and bonds of weak companies, slow-acting central bankers, and well-meaning legislators passing the wrong laws in reaction to rapidly changing economic events. The economic background to all of this was one of false prosperity. A new economic revolution had resulted in an over-dependence on mass production, consumer spending, and marketing. This system had a global element, as the massive improvements in productivity resulted in an overcapacity in autos, farm goods, and textiles. At the same time, real wages did not grow as strongly as did wealth. In many regards, the rich got richer and the poorer got poorer. When the stock market bubble burst, the structural problems in the United States compounded the crisis. Adding to the problem was that the newly formed Federal Reserve tightened money supply, which in turn pushed the banks into a crisis. In 1930 alone, nine thousand banks failed. This panic spread overseas, where many economies were already struggling. Moreover, the U.S. Congress passed the Hawley-Smoot Tariff of 1930, which effectively set off a global round of retaliation and greatly curtailed international trade.

The post-1920 boom period was characterized by a witch-hunt for those who were perceived to have been the most egregious market manipulators, while the government moved to impose tighter regulations. Perhaps most important, the Roosevelt administration soon separated investment and commercial banking with the Glass-Steagall Act of 1933. Many in Congress believed that the stock market bubble had been caused by greedy bankers who lent money to speculators while simultaneously selling stock to these investors. Other key laws were passed. The Securities Act of 1933 required the full and fair disclosure of all material information about the issuance of new securities. The Securities Exchange Act of 1934 established the Securities and Exchange Commission (SEC) to regulate the securities markets and protect investors. The Maloney Act provided for the creation of a self-regulatory organization (the National Association of Securities Dealers) for supervising the over-the-counter securities markets.

The 1929 Wall Street market crash and ensuing Great Depression did considerable damage to international capital markets. While the actual number of those impacted by the market crash was relatively small in comparison with the total U.S. population, the ripple effects of the crash were widespread. Businesses closed, credit became scarce, and there was a dangerous near-collapse of the banking system. More than five thousand banks closed their doors between the 1929 crash and the March 1933 inauguration of Franklin Roosevelt. Following the crash:

- The American public (as well as many Europeans) observed the market as something largely negative.

- This led to a more expansive role of the state in the management of the economy, giving impetus to a round of re-regulation of the financial sector.

■ There was a considerable slowing down in cross-border financial flows. Adding to the last point, the collapse of a pro–free trade international trade order and a search of autarky in a number of major economies, including Germany, did little to reinforce the tendency to avoid international conflict.

Post–World War II Capital Markets: Creation of a New Global Capital Markets Order

Although Wall Street was the dominant force in global capital markets during the 1920s and 1930s, it was after the carnage of World War II that the United States emerged as the leading power. At the same time, even though the United States was the hub of the global capital markets, Wall Street was not humming with activity. Yes, capital flowed from the United States, but part of it came from the Marshall Plan, which sought to put Europe back on its feet. The banks also contributed to the flow of capital. Wall Street as a global stock market, however, was not the hub of capital that it would later become. Rather, Wall Street was largely perceived as a dangerous place for the unwary investor, often run by greedy individuals who had few qualms about taking advantage of the public. Memories of 1929 still lingered.

In the aftermath of the Great Depression and World War II (1939–1945), the leadership of the surviving powers, in particular, the United States and the United Kingdom, pushed for the creation of a new order in the international economy. It was believed that the weakness of international monetary institutions following World War I contributed to the world depression in the late 1920s and 1930s and facilitated the emergence of a regime like Nazi Germany that placed an emphasis on economic self-sufficiency over international trade and cooperation. If such a turn of events was to be avoided in the future, it was essential to establish a new international economic order, founded upon institutions oriented toward providing the necessary coordination of monetary policy between the major economies.

At the Bretton Woods Conference held in 1944, the broad, overarching concepts of the new international monetary order were established. Central to the emerging Bretton Woods system were the International Monetary Fund (IMF), the World Bank, and the General Agreement on Tariffs and Trade (GATT). Influenced by the two major architects of the post-war monetary system, John Maynard Keynes of the United Kingdom and Harry Dexter White of the United States, the IMF was the lynchpin of the new regime. Its primary mission was to promote international monetary cooperation by establishing and maintaining exchange rate stability. The IMF was also to guide and promote the expansion and balanced growth of international trade and bolster confidence in members by making available the Fund's resources (with conditionalities). This was to allow members to correct maladjustments in their balance of payments without resorting to measures detrimental to national or international economic order. The combined mission of the IMF was to help shorten the duration of and lessen the degree of disequilibrium in the international balance of payments. To a world still shaken by the turmoil of the 1930s, this was a welcome force for stability in international capital markets.

The World Bank's role initially was to provide long-term loans for reconstruction following the end of World War II. It was also to provide loans for the economic development of the newly independent nations in Africa, Asia, and the Caribbean, as well as the older and more established republics in Latin America. Over time, the World Bank extended technical expertise to developing economies. As for the GATT, the other element of the Bretton Woods system, its role was to promote a free international trading system through tariff reduction and nondiscrimination. (During the 1990s, the GATT evolved into the World Trade Organization, or WTO.)

The Bretton Woods system worked as long as one nation was willing to bear the burden of providing the world with a reserve currency backed by gold. The United States was willing and able to do this through the late 1940s and into the 1950s. In the 1960s, however, pressures mounted on the U.S. economy and Washington grew increasingly reluctant to shoulder the burden. The United States at the time was running balance-of-payments deficits, was beset by inflationary pressures, and was financing a growing military involvement in Vietnam. In 1971, the Nixon administration took the radical step of pulling the U.S. dollar off the gold standard, effectively ending the Bretton Woods system.

Although the formal Bretton Woods system is regarded as having ended in 1971, many of the institutions created by the system, such as the IMF and World Bank, continue to function. Moreover, the idea of the need for international policy coordination was not discarded, as the Group of Seven (G-7) countries (the United States, Japan, Germany, the United Kingdom, France, Canada, and Italy) continued to meet on a regular basis to discuss international economic policy issues.

▶ THE EUROMARKETS ARRIVE

The postwar years also witnessed the development of the *eurodollar* and *eurobond* markets, sometimes referred to as the *eurocurrency* market. Eurocurrencies are currencies held outside their home country: thus, eurodollars are dollars on deposit outside the United States. Simply stated, the eurodollar market is an international money market focused on short-term credit flows, while the eurobond market is an international capital market dealing with long-term-debt flows (bonds). The development of these two markets was interrelated and mirrored both the structure of Cold War politics and international economics.

The eurodollar market emerged in the late 1940s when large amounts of U.S. dollars ended up outside of the United States, including deposits of dollars in U.S. bank branches located outside the United States. The explosion of U.S. business around the planet meant that U.S. dollars flowed almost everywhere, making the greenback the currency mainstay of international trade. As large American multinational corporations built factories in Germany, France, or Spain, paid their foreign workers, or purchased raw materials, U.S. currency remained outside of the United States. At the same time, efforts to reconstruct Europe's economy (including the Marshall Plan) resulted in public dollar flows into European nations. Although part of the dollar flow was repatriated, the off-shore pool expanded.

The Cold War was another reason to keep U.S. dollars outside of the country. As the great divides of the Cold War became evident, a number of communist countries, such as China and the Soviet Union, decided not to repatriate their dollar earnings to the United States, instead putting them in deposits in carefully selected banks in Europe. In the Cold War environment, communist governments were apprehensive that they would be cut off from U.S. dollar deposits in the United States, which would create problems in their trade with other nations. Consequently, another pool of U.S. dollars developed beyond the borders of the United States. It is important to underscore that although the communist pool of dollars was important, the U.S. dollars that remained in Western Europe for commercial reasons were far more substantial and formed the real foundation for the development of the eurodollar market.

Shortly on the heels of the eurodollar market came the eurobond market, that is, the issuing of bonds outside of the United States in eurodollars. In 1963, Autostrade, an Italian toll road authority, issued the first eurobond for $15 million. This was the first debt issued in dollars outside of the United States. As Europe was regaining its economic strength and the United States was beginning to feel the costs of being a superpower, there was some concern about the large amounts of U.S. currency effectively outside of U.S. monetary control. In 1963, the U.S. government, in an effort to reduce the dollar outflow, imposed an interest equalization tax, which sought to dissuade foreign governments and corporations from borrowing in U.S. bond markets. Moreover, the U.S. Commerce Department ruled that U.S. companies investing abroad had to raise money outside of the United States. The end result was that many U.S. corporations turned to the eurobond market to raise capital. U.S. efforts to contain inflation in the 1966–1969 period provided a further stimulus for the eurobond market. Facing tight money policies at home, U.S. banks turned to the eurodollar market.

Development of the eurodollar market at this time was significant for the following reasons:

- First and foremost, the market served as a source of short-term funds for the trade financing activities of international banks.

- Second, the eurocurrency market facilitated foreign exchange transactions by banks and provided short-term money market trading opportunities.

- Third, international banks used the market as an outlet for placing surplus funds temporarily at attractive yields.

- Fourth, the eurocurrency interbank market became the central mechanism to channel international funds flows among banks. In turn, this gave birth to the London interbank offered rate, or LIBOR (the interest rate for dollars on deposit in London), which became one of the most important international interest rates.[17] The eurocurrency market also provided an outlet for the recycled petro-dollars in the early 1970s.

Back on Wall Street

The expansion of capital market activity from Wall Street to the far reaches of the world economy gathered momentum in the postwar era. While the Bretton Woods system and the emergence of the eurodollar markets were major forces in global capital markets, the way business practices were conducted was heavily influenced by the contributions of two key figures who appeared on Wall Street, setting the stage for the rest of the century. These two men would leave lasting legacies in terms of institutions, the behavior of capital markets, and how they are perceived in an analytical sense. The two are Charles E. Merrill and Benjamin Graham.

Merrill's vision was to "bring Wall Street to Main Street." Although this did not immediately have an impact on global capital markets, it did have a major influence on the way investment banks and investors approached the buying and selling of stocks and bonds. The traditional Wall Street brokerage firm served only a small group of clients, most of whom were wealthy individuals. Some of the larger companies served a slightly wider public, usually through what were called customers' men, whose function was to solicit and handle accounts outside of the relatively closed inner circle of the partners' associates. Those accounts that were the responsibility of the customers' men were usually acquired by word of mouth. The idea of going out and aggressively seeking new customers was unheard of.

Upon his return in the late 1940s, Merrill changed all of this. Unlike many of his contemporaries, he recognized that there was an untapped universe of smaller investors that Wall Street firms were ignoring. Expanding on the old concept of customers' men, he created what were called registered representatives, who underwent training in the fundamentals of the brokerage business. In 1946 the company established the first training school for account executives. The development of registered

CHARLES E. MERRILL

Merrill was born in 1885 in Green Cove Springs, Florida, the son of a doctor and pharmacist. During his long life he was to witness considerable change on Wall Street, some of which he was to shape. Briefly attending Amherst College, Merrill found himself on Wall Street in time for the 1907 panic. By 1914, he established his own firm, Charles E. Merrill, which was soon joined by Edmund Lynch, who was a bond salesman. The new firm became Merrill Lynch and Company. In 1928, Merrill predicted that "the financial skies are not clear" and managed to sell off most of his stocks during the 1929 crash. Although Merrill was to leave Wall Street for a number of years, he returned to his firm in the 1940s. It was during that decade that Merrill and his company began to make significant changes, which would transform the stock industry. Despite the new regulations coming out of the New Deal, Merrill Lynch was to become one of the major Wall Street firms. As for Merrill, he maintained a role in his firm until his death in 1956, leaving a lasting legacy in how Wall Street works.[*]

[*] For more information see Edwin J. Perkins, *Wall Street to Main Street: Charles Merrill and Middle-Class Investors* (New York: Cambridge University Press, 1999).

representatives in turn allowed Merrill Lynch to court the broader market of small investors with the simple message that the U.S. stock market was a safe place to put their money to work. In 1948, Merrill became the first Wall Street firm to take out an advertisement in a newspaper, entitled "What Everyone Ought to Know about the Stock and Bond Business."

Another aspect of Merrill Lynch's success was the use of research. While Merrill recognized the positive aspects of using research, it was another man, Benjamin Graham, who introduced to Wall Street modern financial analysis. Like Merrill, Graham came from a humble background. Born in London in 1894, he moved with his family to New York City when he was one year old. Young Graham did well in school and had a facility with numbers. He graduated from Columbia University and taught from 1928 to 1957 at that university's Graduate School of Business. Despite his academic career, Graham was intrigued by Wall Street. He soon began to formulate means of analysis, based on what was to be called "value investing."

Value investing is based on the idea of investors quietly seeking out bargains in underpriced companies, buying them, and then patiently waiting for their fair value to be realized. How was it that an investor could discover an underpriced company? To Graham the answer was simple: there was a fair amount of data provided by companies from which a valuation could be determined. He popularized the examination of price-to-earnings ratios, dividend records, and noncurrent assets and looked at book values to earnings. He emphasized objective numbers as opposed to more subjective matters, such as management, trends, brand names, and new products.[18] Well after he died in 1976, *Smart Money* (December 1994) was to state that "Graham's ideas formed a framework of thinking about the stock market that has inspired the investment community for nearly a century."

Merrill and Graham represented the changing face of Wall Street. Both men espoused a logical approach to investing, regarded the market as a net positive, and were willing to make their views available to the wider base of potential investors. At the same time, the financial community itself was undergoing some important changes in the 1950s and 1960s. As in the 1920s, a new round of technology was making its way into the economy. In addition, higher federal spending, especially in the area of defense, pushed along a number of new companies.

The Globalization of Wall Street

Financial institutions grew and internationalized in the 1960s and 1970s, with U.S. financial institutions dominating as they were rapidly expanding into foreign markets. The hike in oil prices in the early 1970s meant that petro-dollars—that is, dollars generated by enhanced oil revenues accrued by the largely Middle Eastern hydrocarbon producers—required recycling. U.S. and European banks became active agents in this process, by taking Saudi and Kuwaiti oil profits as deposits and quickly lending them to other countries in Asia, Latin America, and Africa. As already noted, the eurobond market was an important link in the chain. This recycling of petro-dollars reduced potential inflationary pressures in the United States and Europe and met the growing demand for credit from countries such as Argentina, Brazil, Mexico, Turkey, and Poland.

Competition among international banks became increasingly intense as American, German, Japanese, French, and Canadian bankers slugged it out to lead large syndications extending billions of dollars. By the late 1970s there was too much credit being funneled into the developing world as bankers sought to maintain high margins of profit. Despite problems with external debt obligations by Poland, Zaire, and Turkey, international bankers continued to pour money into Latin America. However, in August 1982, the Mexican government informed its international bankers that it was unable to meet its debt repayments, an action that was followed by a series of debt crises throughout the rest of Latin America as well as the Philippines and Nigeria. While Latin America was plunged into a "lost decade," international banks experienced profound problems with debt reschedulings, forced new lendings, and ultimately debt write-offs. The developing world's debt crisis also reduced the number of banks actively engaged in international activities, especially in the United States.

Although U.S. financial institutions sought to reduce their exposure and involvement in the rest of the world, the rest of the world could not be unaware of what was happening in the United States. In the 1970s, Wall Street saw considerable change: in 1972 the Dow Jones Industrial Average first crossed the 1,000 mark; the National Association of Securities Dealers Automated Quotation system (NASDAQ) began operations in February 1971; Congress mandated a true intermarket system in 1975, forcing the NYSE and its rivals (the American, Boston, Cincinnati, Midwest, Philadelphia, and Pacific stock exchanges as well as the Chicago Board Options Exchange and the NASDAQ) to share information on pricing; and new financial techniques were adopted, including the LBO, or leveraged buy-out option. Although the 1970s did not witness a market takeoff, the decade did set the stage for the 1980s.

Global capital markets during the 1980s were dominated by three major trends: extreme volatility in what eventually came to be known as emerging markets; a major round of mergers and acquisitions; and a strong bull market, which ended in the crash of October 1987.

Both the merger mania and the bull market run to October 1987 took place against a background of junk bond takeovers, insider trading scandals, financial excesses, and a new round of "growth" stocks. Those growth stocks were pushed along by technological innovations that were to have a worldwide impact: the desktop computer; computer software that vastly augmented the new, more powerful personal computers (PCs); and biotechnology companies involved in genetic engineering and gene splicing. This was the time when America's once-proud and powerful industrial engine became the rust belt, and discussions were dominated by the decline of U.S. industry, its management, and its work force viewed against the seemingly inexorable rise of Japanese economic power.

As rising international competition impacted the industrial sector, it also impinged on Wall Street, clearly underscoring the ongoing and growing nature of global capital markets, which placed New York as the major hub. Developments in the late 1970s reinforced New York's supremacy. Most important was Rule 415, which allowed companies to preregister their financing needs with the SEC, allowing them to launch new securities issues at any time over the next two years. The impact of the new rule was revolutionary, allowing syndications to be created and new issues to be launched with great speed. Gone were the gentlemen's club days of banking. Increasingly, a bank's ability and expertise in deal launching overshadowed the more traditional banking relationships.

Rule 415 also brought a larger foreign presence into Wall Street, as New York's securities underwriting market expanded by leaps and bounds. Simply stated, New York suddenly became far more attractive for international bankers in Europe and Japan. One of the big moves came when Credit Suisse, the large Swiss bank, bought the old Yankee investment firm of First Boston, the combination of the two becoming Credit Suisse First Boston, or CSFB.

While the movement of European firms into Wall Street was somewhat invisible, the entrance of Japanese companies was a different matter. The yen's appreciation during the 1980s made corporate Japan much more powerful, while facilitating the movement of Japanese firms into new areas of business.[19] In particular, Japanese securities houses became actively involved in the U.S. Treasury bond market. As the U.S. government was active in financing its budget deficit, Japanese investors had a strong demand for U.S. debt. Indeed, the Japanese accounted for almost 30 percent of U.S. government bond purchases from 1985 to 1987.[20] Consequently, Japanese houses such as Nomura were to play a significant role in selling U.S. bonds to Japanese investors.

While the 1980s witnessed a growing globalization of Wall Street via the corporate bond and Treasuries markets, merger mania arose as another critical trend that would have long-term implications. Merger mania was spurred in part by the discovery of the many uses of junk bonds, i.e., bonds of companies that were not rated investment grade by the major rating agencies, Moody's and Standard & Poor's.

Although the "junk" or high-yield bond market grew in the 1970s, it was in the 1980s that it came of age. Two of the key personalities in this were Michael Milken and Ivan Boesky, both working with the firm of Drexel Burnham Lambert. Drexel had become a force in high-yield issuance by finding access to capital for fallen angels, once-strong companies that had skipped below investment grade. Typically, these issuers paid higher interest rates that yielded substantially more to an investor than in the case of an investment-grade bond. In a sense, the investor was being paid more to assume more risk. Rule 415 helped expand the high-yield market by allowing a rapid move to market issuance, which is critical for lower-rated companies.

The junk bond revolution was fueled by deregulation. The Reagan administration sought to liberalize the banking sector through the passage of several acts that eroded the authority of the Glass-Steagall Act, by allowing banks and savings and loans (S&Ls) to buy corporate bonds, and deregulated the S&L sector in other important ways. When interest rates rose rapidly in the late 1970s, the thrifts had to pay a higher rate to depositors than they were charging for their old mortgages.

For the more speculatively oriented new generation of S&L board members and chairmen who came to dominate the industry, these new freedoms proved exceedingly tempting. As financial historian David Colbert noted: "Most deposits were insured by the federal government, thanks to the Banking Act of 1934. So why not bet the farm—and everything else in sight? If the bets pay off, the S&L would profit. If the bets lost, Uncle Sam would make things right with the depositors."[21] The instrument on which to place those bets was junk bonds.

The trends of S&L deregulation and the advance of the junk bond market also had a political component. For a period during the 1980s, the Beverly Hills Hotel in Los Angeles hosted an annual event known as the Predators Ball. Under the master of ceremonies, Ivan Boesky, the function combined bevies of professional models and lavish spreads of food and drink with high-powered politicians and academics brought there to mingle with investors under the overarching theme that market capitalism was great. The bottom line was to help Drexel peddle influence, with an eye to profits in the junk bond market.

The link to merger mania was junk bonds. U.S. industry in the 1980s was ready for consolidation, since after decades of global dominance the rest of the world had caught up with U.S. companies. It was now time to restructure. Changes in tax laws in 1981 helped this along by cutting tax bills and enabling companies to assume more debt. This opened the door to the LBO, which was broadly defined as the acquisition of one company by another through the use of borrowed funds. Usually the acquiring company or individuals use their own assets as security for the funds, with the intention that the loans will be repaid from the cash flow of the acquired company. (At least, that is how it was supposed to be, in theory.)

Milken became the high priest of the LBO and junk bonds. At one point he proclaimed: "People and industries of the future are considered risky. … Junk bond users are the industries of the future."[22] With such an articulated philosophy and backed by Drexel and Boesky, Milken launched the junk bond revolution. With a cast of characters, including T. Boone Pickens, Ron Perelman, and Henry Kravis, LBOs became a mania on Wall Street, generating huge revenues for the consulting firms and investment banks that became involved in providing financing and access to large institutional investors. LBOs also provided a substantial stimulus for Wall Street, stimulating a boom that ran until late 1987. At the same time, the mergers and acquisitions craze was not limited to the United States. In Europe, Sweden's Asea merged with Switzerland's Brown Boveri and France's Cie. Fianciere de Suez took over Societe General de Belgique.

The 1980s bull market began to come to an end with the October 1987 stock market crash. Signs of an impeding slowdown were evident prior to October; confidence in the bull market had already begun to ebb as public attention was brought to bear on the securities industry, showing that there were unprofitable business lines, monstrous overheads, and poor management controls. Scandals loomed over Wall Street, which were soon to hit full force. Although Drexel was not to sink until 1990, the web spun by Milken and Boesky began to unravel as early as 1986. (Both men would serve time in jail.)

An S&L scandal was also looming on the horizon, while the famous investment house E. F. Hutton was heading for oblivion. Hutton was one of the older Wall Street firms and at one time was a close competitor of Merrill Lynch. However, the company was mismanaged. As Brett Duval Fromson, an editor at

Fortune magazine, observed: "The blunders ranged from the ridiculously extravagant (investing $100 million in a glitzy new headquarters when the firm was losing money) to the downright illegal (check kiting)."[23] In addition, Hutton's chairman, Robert Fomon, micromanaged the company, senior management was weak, and internal controls were sadly lacking. The final verdict of Fromson was that "The Hutton saga is a managerial morality tale that has everything but a hero: an actress, a baseball commissioner, several villains, pretty girls, not to mention mismanagement, selfishness, arrogance and greed." Following the October crash, E. F. Hutton disappeared as one of Wall Street's venerable firms, gone in a hasty sale to Shearson American Express.

The nagging doubts about the soundness of the U.S. economy and the finance sector helped undermine confidence in Wall Street. When overseas markets began heading sharply downward, the tide swung against Wall Street. On October 19, 1987, "Black Monday" hit: the Dow Jones Industrial Average plunged 508 points, which was then a one-day record. Nervous concern soon gave way to high anxiety. An entire generation of young traders, who entered into the business enjoying only a bull market, was now confronted with a severe downturn.

Although a depression was avoided following the 1987 market crash, the U.S. economy and others drifted into a recession. Many smaller investors were disillusioned by Wall Street and global capital markets; the business environment was difficult for the companies that survived. Yet, the eclipse of Wall Street was hardly total. Many trends that commenced in the 1980s would resume at a stronger pace in the 1990s, setting the stage for another bull market.

▶ CONCLUSION

In this brief overview of Wall Street and global capital markets, it is important to underscore that the market as such has no moral compass. Money is made; money is lost. However, the individuals and firms involved in the process of making money in the development of international finance faced ongoing moral dilemmas. At the end of the day, the many ebbs and flows of capital resulted in a confluence of global economic development, indeed a globalization of markets. With the fall of communism and the advance of market-oriented economic policies from Central and Eastern Europe into Central Asia, South America, and Africa, the world has drawn closer. Stock markets, foreign direct investment, capital flows, international banks and investment houses, and offshore finance all were tightly bound together by the close of the 1980s. Although the world was far from harmonious and the fall of the Berlin Wall in 1989 represented the advent of a new global disorder, the world and its finances were more tightly bound together than at any time in history. All of this gave birth to the tumultuous 1990s.

▶ NOTES

1.   Amsterdam's arrival at the center of world finance did not occur overnight but was the result of a long chain of events dating back to the northern Italian merchants in the late twelfth century.

The Italian city-states were geostrategically placed to benefit from the Crusades, which helped stimulate trade in the Mediterranean. In this trade, they were well-placed to be middlemen for luxury goods from the Middle East, which were in great demand to the north, beyond the Alps. Trade increased with France, the Lowlands, and southern Germany. In light of the fact that central political authority was often lacking along the trade routes to the north, that bandits were an active risk consideration, and that the sea routes to northern ports carried the risks of adverse weather and pirates, there was a pressing need to create a credit system that precluded the movement of large amounts of coins and bullion. The Italians stepped up to the challenge, contributing greatly to the skills and techniques required for long-distance trade finance. By the thirteenth century, clearance was apparently a standard function of exchange banking throughout the Mediterranean region. It was only in the fourteenth century that northern money-changers adopted the techniques of deposit and transfer banking pioneered and carried across the Alps by the Italians.

What was to carry all of these trading and finance trends to the Netherlands was the change in trade patterns away from the luxury trade (exotic spices and silks) and toward the staple trade (wheat, other grains, and herring) in the North Atlantic. The power of the Italians in Europe's fledgling capital markets declined, and the foci shifted northward, first to Bruges, home of the first stock market (bourse), and then to Antwerp in the 1500s. These cities became cosmopolitan centers attracting traders and bankers from southern Germany (like the Fuggers and Welsers), Italy, England, France, and Portugal. While much of the financial activity was linked to trade, bankers were also active in lending to kings, princes, and dukes, as well as the Roman Catholic Church. Antwerp's dominance as a financial center came to an end during the 1580s, when religious wars resulted in the sack of the city by Spanish troops. The result was a shift of some of the more entrepreneurial and Protestant merchant families to the northern Netherlands, mainly to Amsterdam. This helped stimulate a boom in Amsterdam, which was already doing well as an entrepôt in the transport of grains, precious and common metals, and salt and other bulk goods. For further information see Scott B. MacDonald and Albert L. Gastman, *A History of Credit and Power in the Western World* (Rutgers: Transaction, 2001); Thomas Blomquist, "European Banking," in Joseph R. Stayer, editor, *Dictionary of the Middle Ages* (New York: Charles Scribner's Sons, 1982), p. 82; and Pieter Geyl, *History of the Dutch-Speaking Peoples* (London: Phoenix Press, 2001, reprint of 1932 edition).

2. Michael Kammen, *Colonial New York* (New York: Oxford University Press, 1975), pp. 19–20.
3. John Steele Gordan, *The Great Game: The Emergence of Wall Street as a World Power, 1653–2000* (New York: Charles Scribner's Sons, 1999), p. 23.
4. Charles R. Geisst, *Wall Street: A History* (New York: Oxford University Press, 1997), p. 21.
5. Advances in industrial technology included the evolution from steam to gasoline-run engines, the deeper shift to the use of machines in agriculture (e.g., all-steel threshers, which Case produced in the 1890s), and improvements in refrigeration. The last was particularly significant in that by the 1890s all major breweries used refrigeration, a movement that was picked up by the meat-packing industry over the next decade. Refrigeration meant that meat was able to make it to market without spoilage (in a refrigerated railcar), curing became a year-round activity, and meat quality improved.
6. Quoted in Brooks, *Once in Golanda,* p. 3.
7. Bill Torpy, "Echoes of a Blast," *Atlanta Journal-Constitution*, December 14, 2001.
8. Ibid.
9. Ibid.
10. International Monetary Fund, *World Economic Outlook April 2002* (Washington, D.C.: International Monetary Fund, 2002), p. 110.
11. Irving Fisher, quoted in Edward Chancellor, *Devil Take the Hindmost: A History of Financial Speculation* (New York: Farrar, Straus & Giroux, 1999), 193.
12. Ibid, pp. 193–194.
13. Frederick Lewis Allen, *Only Yesterday* (New York: Mansfield Publishers, 1957), p. 168.

14. Barrie Wigmore, *The Crash and Its Aftermath 1929–1933* (Westport, CT: Greenwood Press, 1985), p. 27.
15. Harpo Marx, "Marxist Economics," quoted from David Colbert, *Eyewitness to Wall Street: 400 Years of Dreamers, Schemers, Busts and Booms* (New York: Broadway Books, 2001), p. 119.
16. International Monetary Fund, *World Economic Outlook*, April 2002, p. 110.
17. Yoon S. Park and Jack Zwick, *International Banking in Theory and Practice* (Reading, Mass.: Addison-Wesley Publishing, 1985), p. 55.
18. Benjamin's publications include his seminal *Security Analysis* (1934), which he wrote with David Dodd, and *The Intelligent Investor*. These two publications made him, in the eyes of many, the father of security analysis.
19. It should be noted that Nomura's first office overseas was in New York and was opened in 1927. It was closed in 1936 after the Japanese military government persuaded the company to ban overseas investment. Nomura reopened its New York office in 1953.
20. Albert J. Alletzhauser, *The House of Nomura: The Inside Story of the Legendary Japanese Financial Dynasty* (New York: Harper Perennial, 1990), p. 244.
21. David Colbert, *Eyewitness to Wall Street: Four Hundred Years of Dreamers, Schemers, Busts and Booms* (New York: Broadway Books, 2001), p. 246.
22. Quoted in Fenton Bailey, *The Junk Bond Revolution* (London, 1992), pp. 39–40.
23. Quoted from Colbert, *Eyewitnesses to Wall Street*, p. 264.

3 *Currency crisis?*
Capital flight

EMERGING MARKETS: GOOD MONEY AFTER BAD?

"Latin America 'vulnerable to shocks'" … "Dervish Lira, Peso Mariachi" … "Specter of contagion returns to haunt markets" … "Brazil's woes threaten recession for region" … "Argentina rattles uneasily and Latin investors shake" … "Navigating dangerous waters" … "Camdessus says crisis 'seems to be over' for emerging economies" … "Investment flow into emerging markets to fall" … "How U.S. wooed Asia to let cash flow in" … "Uncertainty—the one sure thing" … "Taming wild money" … "Poor countries caught in downturn trap" … "Debt rating upgrade gives boost to Mexico" …

After the lost decade of the 1980s, emerging market countries entered the 1990s with a sense of renewed hope and optimism. The Third World debt crisis of the 1980s, which began so dramatically with the infamous "Mexican weekend" of August 1982, was over by the early 1990s, save for a little mopping up. Big-debtor countries, such as Brazil and Mexico, concluded far-reaching debt-restructuring deals with their creditors, and the dark days of the 1980s seemed a distant memory, never to be repeated. Almost unanimously, emerging market countries had embraced the "Washington consensus" set of ideals, driving them to liberalize and reform their economic and financial systems in line with the open-market paradigm preached by the International Monetary Fund (IMF) and World Bank. In turn, liberalization policies were widely credited with laying the foundation for the higher growth and record capital inflows that many emerging market countries enjoyed in the first half of the 1990s.

But something went very wrong along the way. Economist Paul Krugman suggests that future historians may dub the 1990s the Age of Currency Crises. A currency crisis occurs when intense speculative attack against a currency forces the government to defend that currency on foreign exchange markets, usually through some judicious mix of intervention, high interest rates, and jawboning (using the government's moral suasion powers on market participants). Since free-floating currencies are continuously adjusting, currency crises are generally associated with fixed exchange rate regimes. A financial crisis occurs when a country finds itself unable to meet its financial obligations, often because of a currency crisis, capital flight, and/or a shaky domestic banking system. While the two events are closely intertwined and often take place in tandem, they are not synonymous. For example, Britain experienced a currency crisis in 1992 when George Soros and other speculators attacked the pound, but the country's finances were sound and the currency upheaval did not set off a full-fledged financial crisis.

A glance at a time line of the 1991–2001 period explains why Krugman suggested the 1990s be called the Age of Currency Crises.

December 1994: A mismanaged Mexican peso devaluation triggers dramatic capital flight and recession in Mexico; the rest of Latin America suffers a spectacular hangover known as the "tequila effect."

July 1997: Thailand floats its baht, setting off a regional crisis of confidence.

October 1997: The United States contributes $5 billion to an IMF-led bailout of Indonesia, but rioting breaks out and Suharto is forced to resign.

November 1997: Investor panic sends the South Korean won into a tailspin; a new government concludes the biggest IMF bailout in financial history.

June 1998: Investors begin dumping the Russian ruble. A devaluation in August fails to stop the panic, and Russia defaults on its domestic bonds.

January 1999: Brazil devalues its currency, the real, which plunges more than 35 percent as the government raises interest rates to halt capital flight.

December 2001: The IMF withdraws its support from Argentina, which is forced to default on $85 billion in debt. Five presidents in a two-week period are unable to control the panicking financial markets and restore social peace.

By the dawn of 2003, Argentina was still mired in a seemingly intractable crisis, as the world watched nervously. While no one could foresee the long-term consequences of the Argentine default, one lesson was clear: twenty years after the Mexican weekend, emerging markets are still risky and unpredictable.

Financial markets vote with their feet, so an analysis of international capital flows in 1992–2002 tells much of the story (see Figure 3.1). Net private capital flows

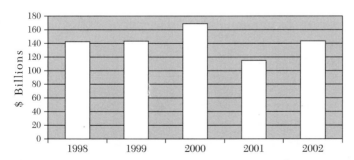

FIGURE 3.1 Net Private Capital Flows to Emerging Market Economies, Total
Source: The Institute of International Finance, Inc.; www.iif.com.

to major emerging market economies rose in the early 1990s to peak at $212 bil-
lion in 1996 and then slipped in 1998–1999 as crises enveloped Asia, Russia, and
Brazil. The level picked up again in 2000 to $169 billion, reflecting recovery in the
Asian markets, but fell sharply in 2001 to just $115 billion, the lowest level in a
decade—clearly reacting to the crises in Argentina and Turkey. Estimates for 2002
range widely, but capital flows to the emerging world probably dipped below $100
billion for the year, well below the peak pre-Asian crisis levels of the mid-1990s.[1]

  Breaking down these data further helps to underline the magnitude and ferocity of shifts in capital flows. Sovereign bond defaults in every year from 1999 to 2001
clearly spooked the financial markets; according to the IMF, net bond flows to developing countries, which fell to zero after 1998, turned sharply negative in mid-2001.
Syndicated bank loans, which are mainly directed to the large private companies of
developing countries, also declined (see Figure 3.3). According to the Institute for
International Finance (IIF), foreign direct investment flows to emerging market
countries in 2002 fell to around $117 billion from $149 billion in 2001 (but the 2001
total was boosted by two very large transactions that accounted for $24 billion).

  Foreign direct investment is relatively stable, though, especially when viewed
in comparison to bank lending and portfolio investment (see Figures 3.2–3.4).
Portfolio investment flows ended 2001 with a net negative figure of $1.7 billion,

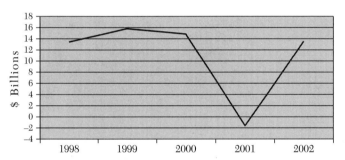

FIGURE 3.2   Net Portfolio Flows to Emerging Market Economies

Source: The Institute of International Finance, Inc.; www.iif.com.

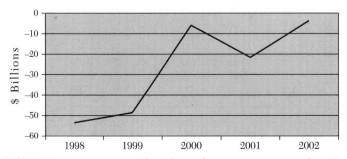

FIGURE 3.3   Net Commercial Bank Lending to Emerging Market Economies

Source: The Institute of International Finance, Inc.; www.iif.com.

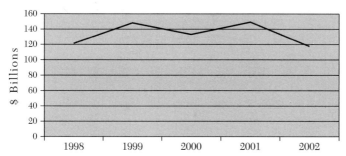

FIGURE 3.4 Net Direct Equity Flows to Emerging Market Economies

Source: The Institute of International Finance, Inc.; www.iif.com.

while bonds saw net repayments of $10 billion in 2001—the first negative total in this area since the revival of the emerging market bond markets in the early 1990s.[2]

The data on capital flows reveal some important shifts in their structure over the past decade. During the 1990s, foreign portfolio investment largely replaced commercial bank loans as the primary channel for international capital flows. Privatization programs and the removal of capital controls facilitated soaring levels of foreign portfolio investment in many emerging market countries. The surge in foreign portfolio inflows began late in the 1980s with Asia; then interest shifted to Latin America (especially Mexico, Brazil, and Argentina) as repatriation of flight capital deepened these markets. Thus foreign portfolio investment ($325 billion) replaced bank lending ($76 billion) as the dominant source of private capital flows into developing countries in 1990–1994. In 1990–1993, for example, capital flows into Mexico totaled $91 billion—of which two-thirds was portfolio investment. Mexico's stock market, not surprisingly, went up by 436 percent during this period.[3] The increasing role of portfolio investment, of course, laid the groundwork for destabilizing speculative flows, as we will see in the next section.

Also, the overall data on capital flows mask the heavy concentration of these flows in just a handful of countries, implying that most emerging market countries were largely excluded from the process. With regard to foreign direct investment in developing countries, just three countries—China, Brazil, and Mexico—accounted for almost one-half of the total in the 1990s. Moreover, even the strength and relative stability of foreign direct investment (FDI) flows into emerging markets during the 1990s may be overrated. These flows largely reflect mergers and acquisitions rather than greenfield investments; mergers and acquisitions (M&A) activity accounted for almost three-quarters of total FDI in developing countries (excluding China) over the decade.

The volatility of capital flows, of course, mirrors the volatility of the emerging market countries themselves. Every one of the currency and financial crises listed here was preceded and accompanied by massive capital flight, facilitated in part by the financial liberalization that governments undertook at the urging of the IMF. During the past decade, economic reform, liberalization, and global integration have been key elements of the development strategy in almost all emerging market countries. Thus, the

CURRENCY CRISES: AN ANALYTICAL FRAMEWORK

While currency crises were a regular feature of international financial markets long before the 1990s, the ferocity of these crises over the 1991–2001 decade was unprecedented. Despite a vast range of academic and empirical work on the origins of these crises, the biggest questions remain unanswered.

Discussion of the analytical framework underlying currency crises always begins with the "canonical" crisis model, which stems from work done in the mid-1970s by economist Stephen Salant. Basically, the canonical currency crisis model, as described by Paul Krugman, "explains such crises as the result of a fundamental inconsistency between domestic policies—typically the persistence of money-financed budget deficits—and the attempt to maintain a fixed exchange rate. This inconsistency can be temporarily papered over if the central bank has sufficiently large reserves, but when these reserves become inadequate speculators force the issue with a wave of selling."

The power of this model, of course, lies in its emphasis on the close link between foreign exchange (FX) market activity and domestic economic policy—a simple but elegant relationship. As Krugman further explains, the canonical model suggests that currency crises are not the result of irrationality or market manipulation but rather "the result of the logic of the situation." Essentially, a currency crisis stems from underlying economic fundamentals—a basic and unsustainable inconsistency between domestic and exchange rate policies.

However, developments on FX markets during the 1980s and 1990s strongly suggested that the canonical crisis model did not represent the reality of many currency crises, which did not appear to be justified by economic fundamentals at the time of the crisis. Thus a "second generation" of currency crisis models gained in importance, as Krugman emphasized: "The main point of second generation models may be stated this way: the real cause of currency crises is not so much what you are actually doing, as what

(Continued)

succession of wrenching crises in spite of this progress—culminating in the still-unresolved catastrophe that is today's Argentina—is unsettling.

▶ 1994–1995: MEXICO AND TEQUILA

The 1994 debt restructuring agreement between Brazil and its creditors marked the final chapter in the painful and prolonged debt crisis that engulfed developing countries in the 1980s. (For the banks, of course, the crisis was easily over by the late 1980s, as they returned to profitability with streamlined and slimmed-down financial statements. The debtor countries, though, took longer to regain their footing.) With the conclusion of the Brazilian deal, about 80 percent of the money that had been lent by commercial banks to developing countries had been restructured,

CURRENCY CRISES: AN ANALYTICAL FRAMEWORK *(CONTINUED)*

the financial markets suspect you might *want* to do." Thus, it is possible for a currency crisis to occur even if not justified by the fundamentals, including self-fulfilling crises in which capital flight forces a policy change that would not otherwise have occurred.

This debate is an important one for FX market analysts and participants. It revolves around a basic question: Are currency crises always justified, or do they reflect irrational but often self-fulfilling expectations on the part of big market players? If the canonical model accurately describes most currency crises, this would suggest that speculators like George Soros play an important and largely benevolent role as global policemen, patrolling financial markets for evidence of inconsistent economic policies and punishing the erring countries. To the extent that the second-generation models are more powerful, this would underline the role of market hysteria, contagion, and market inefficiency in wreaking havoc upon unsuspecting and innocent currency markets.[*]

While the fundamental causes of currency crises are a matter of urgent debate, the immediate early warning signs of a crisis are more obvious. These include the following:

- A large and growing deficit on the country's current account (the net value of its goods and services trade with other countries), especially as a proportion of gross domestic product (GDP)

- A low and declining level of the country's foreign exchange reserves, either as a percentage of GDP or in relation to the months of imports covered

- A sharp increase in the country's real effective exchange rate, meaning that the inflation-adjusted value of the currency has increased rapidly (its inflation rate exceeds the currency's nominal depreciation)

- Volatility in the country's capital account, especially if the country is heavily dependent on inflows of portfolio capital to finance a current account shortfall

[*] Paul Krugman, "Currency Crises," available at web.mit.edu/krugman/www/crises.html.

and the four largest debtors (Brazil, Mexico, Argentina, and Poland) had all revamped their debt. The remaining problem countries, mostly in Africa, were much too small to pose a serious threat to the international financial system.

No sooner were participants done signing the documents and passing out the cigars, though, than Mexico stumbled once again. The crisis was a rude awakening.

In December 1994, the Mexican government found itself unable to service its tesobonos, a series of short-term government bonds, a situation that escalated with remarkable speed into a full-fledged financial crisis for the country. The roots of the Mexican tesobono or tequila crisis, as it came to be called, were well established and not at all difficult to detect. First, the government's policy of maintaining a strong exchange rate via high real interest rates and a budget surplus made the process of economic restructuring more difficult and costly than expected. Highlighted by gaping trade and current account deficits, the data presented a worrisome picture of a country struggling to adjust to free trade with its powerful neighbor. Second, political turmoil (in the form of a rebellion in the impoverished southern state of Chiapas and a number of high-level assassinations, including the ruling party's presidential candidate) erupted at a delicate moment in the economic restructuring process, when the country was heavily dependent on foreign capital inflows to finance its external payments deficit.[4]

The crisis plunged Mexico into a sharp recession, and financial markets throughout Latin America teetered. By the standards of the 1980s debt crisis, though, this one turned out to be relatively short and sweet. Horrified by the specter of its neighbor and free-trade partner facing serious instability, the Clinton administration responded rapidly and generously. The IMF and the U.S. pulled together a massive rescue package to underline U.S. support of its southern neighbor. Also, after its mismanagement of the initial peso devaluation, the Mexican government came through with a credible and well-constructed stabilization program. Taken together, these actions calmed the markets and enabled Mexico to pull out of recession quickly and with relative ease.

Potential contagion for the rest of Latin America, too, was contained. Argentina suffered the most, since its overvalued currency and current account deficit reminded investors of Mexico. The "tequila" effect (referring to the hangover that drinkers get the morning after a tequila binge) brought uncertainty to the entire region, and a broad-based sell-off of Latin American equities and currencies ensued. However, Argentina stood firm against the speculators; a resolute government hiked interest rates and an inflation-phobic public endured steep recession rather than undergo the risks and humiliation of a forced devaluation. In the end, Argentina's victory over the speculators and its determined adherence to austerity won it plaudits from the international financial community (but much more on that later!).

With Argentina remaining stable and Mexico returning to growth, the 1994–1995 Mexican tequila crisis was over quickly. By 1996, Latin America was growing strongly again, and private capital flows to the region were running at record levels. It was time for the attention of world financial markets to shift, once again, to the next firestorm.[5]

▶ 1997–1999: ASIA, RUSSIA, AND BRAZIL

Asian Currency Crisis, 1997–1998

The East Asian financial crisis of 1997–1998 was remarkable in several ways:

- It hit the most rapidly growing economies in the world, resulting in the largest financial bailouts in history.

- It was the sharpest financial crisis in the developing world since the 1982 debt crisis, dwarfing Mexico's 1994–1995 hiccup and the resulting tequila hangover in Latin America.

- It was the least anticipated financial crisis in modern memory. Despite a wealth of research and commentary generated by the 1980s debt crisis and by Mexico's 1994–1995 meltdown, almost nobody saw this one coming.[6]

The crisis began, improbably, with a speculative attack on the Thai baht. The Thai economy had undergone its own bubble of speculative real estate deals, fueled by strong economic growth and easy access to foreign credits. When Thai authorities were forced to devalue the baht in July 1997, markets in the Philippines, South Korea, Indonesia, and Malaysia were rapidly infected by investor panic and capital flight. The quickness and severity of the currency crashes were astonishing. Within a three-month period (July–October 1997), the Thai baht and Indonesian rupiah plunged by around 40 percent each, the Philippine peso and Malaysian ringgit were down by 27 percent, and the South Korean won fell by 35 percent. Even the Hong Kong dollar, linked to the U.S. dollar via its currency board arrangement, came under intense pressure.

What had begun as a speculative attack on currency markets then spread to regional equity markets, resulting in a stock market meltdown and a series of regional banking crises. The turbulence in currency and equity markets across Asia far eclipsed the tequila effect that followed Mexico's December 1994 devaluation—and brought new respect for the power of contagion and herd behavior in financial markets, underlining the relevance of the second-generation currency crisis models.

As noted, the crisis was entirely unforeseen by most market participants and analysts. Risk premiums on bonds and other credits, country risk assessment reports, sovereign credit ratings, and IMF reports on the region all indicated smooth sailing ahead, just weeks before the crisis struck. Even when Thailand devalued the baht on July 2, few understood the consequences.

Nonetheless, the crisis gathered momentum like a snowball rolling downhill. Since many Asian countries were burdened by heavily indebted companies, inflated stock and property markets, overvalued currencies, and bad loans, it was easy to spot similarities to Thailand. Investors began to withdraw their capital, and the dominoes started to fall. In October 1997, Hong Kong's stock market fell by 23 percent over a four-day period, amid widespread panic selling. Indonesia was forced to accept a $23 billion IMF bailout, and pressure on the remaining dominoes—South Korea, Taiwan, Malaysia, Brazil, and Russia—mounted. In November, South Korea too had to accept a $57 billion bailout, the biggest ever. This was the last straw, and embattled investors rushed headlong for the exits.[7]

Much of the post-crisis research and commentary has focused on the causes of the debacle. Were the markets delivering their well-founded judgment on the weak economic fundamentals and mismanagement of the Asian countries, or was it a case of market panic run amok? (These are not mutually exclusive, of course, but there is substantial disagreement over how much weight each factor deserves.) In other words, this represents a classic debate over the power of the canonical crisis model versus the second-generation models.

The one point on which everyone agrees, though, is that the core of the crisis was a huge swing in capital flows. According to IIF estimates, net private capital flows into the five East Asian countries hardest hit by the crisis (Indonesia, Malaysia, South Korea, the Philippines, and Thailand) reversed from a positive $93 billion in 1996 to a *negative* $12 billion in 1997, a swing of $105 billion on a combined pre-shock GDP of $935 billion (see Table 3.1). Of that $105 billion swing, around

TABLE 3.1 External Financing for the Asian Five°

	1994	1996	1997e
Current account balance	−24.5	−55.2	−27.1
External financing, net	45.2	95.2	18.1
Private flows, net	37.9	97.1	−11.9
Equity investment	12.1	18.7	2.1
Direct equity	4.7	6.3	6.4
Portfolio equity	7.4	12.4	−4.3
Private creditors	25.8	78.4	−14.0
Commercial banks	23.4	55.7	−26.9
Non-bank private creditors	2.4	22.7	12.9
Official flows, net	7.3	−1.9	30.0
Resident lending/other, net°°	−15.2	−21.6	−30.5
Reserves excluding gold (− = increase)	−5.4	−18.4	39.5

°Asian Five: South Korea, Indonesia, Malaysia, Thailand, and
the Philippines.
°°Including resident net lending, monetary gold, "errors" omissions.
eEstimate.
Source: The Institute of International Finance, Inc.; www.iif.com.

three-quarters—$77 billion—consisted of commercial bank lending. Foreign direct investment remained more or less constant, and portfolio equity inflows tumbled by $24 billion. So in a sense, this was a "crisis of success," triggered by a boom in international lending followed by a sudden withdrawal of funds.[8]

Still, this begs the real question: *Why* did the capital flows suddenly turn around? No doubt, there is a case for the economic fundamentalists. The East Asian crisis countries featured, among other things:

- corrupt and mismanaged banking systems
- lack of transparency in corporate governance
- sometimes heavy-handed state-managed capitalism, including industrial and exchange rate policies that proved increasingly unsustainable
- related to the first three points, overinvestment in dubious activities in part due to the moral hazard of implicit guarantees, corruption, and anticipated bailouts if necessary
- fixed exchange rates
- heavy reliance on short-term capital to finance large and growing current account shortfalls

These shortcomings were masked by the countries' pursuit of growth and by their investment-driven success in achieving fast-paced expansion, accompanied by relatively moderate inflation.

Eventually, though, the pressures were too much to bear. Ironically, the very financial liberalization policies that had underpinned the Asian countries' success in attracting capital inflows proved a serious liability in times of stress. In the early 1990s, the East Asian countries had liberalized their financial and capital markets, not because they needed to attract more funds (savings rates were already at or above 30 percent of GDP) but because of international pressure. Two prominent economists observed,

> First and foremost, the Asian crisis is a cautionary tale about rapid financial liberalization in emerging markets. The Asian economies had gone far in creating a stable macroeconomic environment and in liberalizing trade and investment regimes, at least for a wide range of tradable manufactured goods. Most of their vulnerabilities in the mid-1990s arose as a result of rapid financial liberalization undertaken in the late 1980s and early 1990s.[9]

This analysis, to some extent, shifts the blame from the Asian governments to the financial markets. No doubt, there is a strong argument here, too. In fact, the Asian Five were in some ways veritable models of good economic management. In this sense the crisis did not really conform to the classic canonical model of speculative currency attacks, which are usually preceded by profligate government spending, large budget deficits, anemic growth, low savings and investment levels, and high inflation. On the contrary, the East Asian countries boasted *surplus* government budgets, *high* savings and investment levels, *low* inflation, and *buoyant* growth. For the most part, the international financial community had applauded their policies, right up to the point where traders and financiers fled for the exits. This suggests that the reversal of capital flows was a case of market hysteria, of "the madness of crowds," rather than a rational response to government ineptitude—a second-generation crisis.

At the very least, the Asian contagion revealed the shortcomings of international capital markets, especially their vulnerability to sudden reversals of market confidence and to herd-based behavior. In the midst of the crisis, much opprobrium was heaped on hedge funds and other speculators (Prime Minister Mahathir of Malaysia was especially virulent in his attacks) for allegedly inciting and profiting from the crisis. Empirical research, though, suggests that for the most part the earliest capital withdrawals were triggered not by hedge funds but by residents of the afflicted countries themselves. Hedge funds, in fact, were generally caught by surprise when the currencies tanked, and even acted against the trend in some cases. (See Chapter 4 for a detailed discussion of hedge funds in FX markets during 1997–1998.)

The wide use of financial derivatives, though, probably did exacerbate the problem, for the following reasons:

■ *Derivatives made it easier for traders to make high-risk bets* on Asian markets, but the amounts were never publicly reported.

■ *The magnitude and high risk* of these positions, in turn, created a mad rush for the exits when the markets headed south, and this scramble fed into huge market swings.

■ *They also magnified linkages* from one country to another. South Korean institutions, for example, had heavy investments in derivatives tied to Indonesia, Russia, Thailand, and even Latin America. When those heavily leveraged investments went sour, the Koreans frantically sold off holdings elsewhere to meet margin calls, triggering plunges on other markets.[10]

So in the end, responsibility for the crisis is shared—in some mysterious formula—by the Asian governments and panicky financial markets. With the benefit of hindsight, it is clear that the myth of frenzied speculators mindlessly attacking countries despite their pure economic fundamentals is just that: a myth. In fact, the East Asian countries had pegged overvalued exchange rates and hefty current account deficits, much like Mexico and the other Latin American countries that suffered similar speculative attacks in previous years. Moreover, the Asian Five financed those shortfalls with capital inflows, increasingly in the form of short-term foreign currency debt, thus heightening their vulnerability to speculative attack and self-fulfilling currency crises. In that sense, there was nothing new about this crisis; it was déjà vu for the old Latin America hands.

The speed and ferocity of the market contagion, though, was new. The troubles first spread within Asia, setting off stormy devaluations and stock market collapses in neighboring countries. Outside the region, the usual suspects—Argentina, Brazil, and Russia—suffered sharp reverses on their equity markets as well, and speculators began to test their currencies.

Russian Default, 1998

An interesting facet of the Asian currency crisis was its ability to rock financial markets halfway around the world, in countries that bore little resemblance to the Asian dominoes. Linkages between markets, it soon became apparent, were much deeper and less obvious than analysts had imagined.

One of those linkages, it turned out, involved Russia. The most obvious transmission point between Asia and Russia was commodity prices, which fell sharply in the wake of the Asian currency crisis. Commodity prices were hit from both sides: excess capacity was already mounting as new supplies of many key commodities came on-stream, while at the same time demand slumped as the Asian economies tumbled into recession. The markets were swimming in Chilean copper, American grain, Colombian coffee, Saudi oil, and Russian steel.

The plunge in commodity prices was especially hard on Russia, whose primary exports are oil and gas. In addition, the Russian economy had been on the skids ever since the breakup of the Soviet Union: tax collection was abysmal, the government budget deficit was out of control, and short-term debt was soaring. Capital flight was massive; Russian citizens converted their money into dollars just as quickly as the IMF and Western donors poured it into the country. Another linkage to the Asian crisis surfaced too, as traders and financial institutions that had lost millions on Asian positions sought to cash out of their positions in other markets, including Russia, to improve their liquidity and reduce their risk profile.

As the ruble struggled and capital flight mounted, it quickly became clear that the Russian government could not contain the panic on its own. Finally, in July 1998 the IMF led a $17 billion bailout to prop up the government's shaky finances. The bailout collapsed just a month later, though; the embattled Russian government stopped propping up the ruble and defaulted on its domestic bonds.[11]

Brazilian Devaluation, 1999

Russia's August 1998 default had a dramatic impact on, of all countries, Brazil. Russia and Brazil had perhaps more in common than Russia and the East Asian countries—both are heavily dependent on commodity exports—but overall the commonalities between the two countries are far from obvious. Nonetheless, Russia's collapse increased the pressure on Brazil.

The most obvious common element, though, was Brazil's overvalued currency and its huge store of short-term debt, by now a well-recognized recipe for financial chaos. Moreover, Brazil's famously difficult political scene and the apparent impossibility of imposing serious fiscal austerity took a toll. Accordingly, the IMF stepped in with a precautionary package of $41.5 billion in November 1998, aimed at calming the markets and averting a crisis.

Even the resources and imprimatur of the IMF, however, were not enough. The crisis exploded anyway when Itamar Franco, a former president and then governor of Minas Gerais state, declared a moratorium on his state's debt to the national government. Franco's apparent defiance of the president spooked investors, who feared that government efforts to push a cost-cutting package through Congress—necessary to comply with the terms of the IMF deal—were doomed. Brazil started hemorrhaging foreign exchange reserves as investor confidence evaporated; reserves plunged from $72 billion to just $26 billion over a three-month period beginning in November.

This was, of course, not sustainable. In January 1999, the Brazilian government bowed to the inevitable and allowed the real to float; it went into free fall, losing almost 50 percent of its value in the next few weeks. The following month, though, Brazil reached agreement with the IMF on a new package to substantially enforce budgetary discipline and keep inflation under control. Recession was inevitable, but the markets began to stabilize and pressure on the real eased.

Having infected virtually every continent, financial contagion seemed to have run its course after Brazil. In part, this may reflect some idiosyncrasies of the Brazilian story. The huge capital outflows from Brazil were largely the work of domestic investors, not foreigners. In contrast to the presence of weighty foreign speculators in Russia and Asia, Western hedge funds and other highly leveraged investors played virtually no role in the Brazilian devaluation. This tended to limit the extent of financial contagion, since hedge funds did not need to sell off positions in unrelated markets to meet margin calls resulting from losses in Brazil (as happened in Russia). Commercial and investment banks, too, had been steadily reducing their exposure to Brazil. The devaluation had long been anticipated—only its timing was unknown—limiting the sense of panic when it finally occurred.

► 2001: TURKEY AND ARGENTINA

Turkey, 2000–2001

So global financial markets enjoyed a relatively peaceful year in 2000. Capital flows to emerging market countries rebounded, sovereign borrowers returned to the market on increasingly favorable terms, and credit ratings improved. Following the lost decade of the 1980s, and the Age of Currency Crises in the 1990s, at long last a period of stability in emerging markets seemed at hand.

The first country to break the relative calm was Turkey. Turkey and the IMF had negotiated a three-year stabilization program back in December 1999, their seventeenth such agreement since 1961. For the most part, Turkey complied with the terms of its IMF pact, implementing measures to reduce the budget deficit, advance privatization, and establish a crawling peg exchange rate to control inflation. Like Argentina, Turkey won praise from the Fund for its fiscal policies and structural reforms.

As it turned out, this was not good enough. The immediate triggers for Turkey's implosion in 2001 were politics and banking. The banking sector had long been troubled by allegations of corruption and mismanagement, including making unsound loans to businesses owned by bank officers and directors and by politically well-connected figures. As struggling banks began to fail in late 2000, the government, under close IMF guidance, implemented a standard-issue austerity program aimed at stabilizing markets. A former vice president of the World Bank, the well-respected Kemal Dervis, was brought in as a sort of "super-minister" to oversee the economy and to spearhead Turkey's negotiations with the multilateral financial institutions.

With interest rates soaring, though, even the relatively sound banks quickly found themselves in serious trouble. Things went from bad to worse when the long-simmering tensions between president and prime minister flared into open warfare in early 2001. Matters were further complicated by the poor health of the prime minister and growing unrest within the ruling coalition. In addition, the fractious nature of Turkish politics and the entrenchment of vested interests continued to slow any substantial progress on privatization of the generally loss-making state-owned enterprises, a major drain on government revenues and an ongoing source of inflation.

Investors, already shaken by the banking crisis, now feared that the new IMF package would be stillborn as the politicians bickered, turning a liquidity crisis into a solvency crisis. A familiar litany of events ensued: stock prices plunged, interest rates soared as high as 5000 percent (putting further pressure on the banks), and inflation seemed set to explode.

Once again, the government negotiated a new program of structural reforms, including bank reforms, as part of a new IMF support package. By mid-2001 the lira had stabilized and markets were calm. However, Turkey left an unpleasant taste in many mouths. The *Wall Street Journal* editorialized:

> If the economic train wreck in Argentina is gruesome, it's worth asking why the United States is cheering one of its most vital allies—Turkey—right down the same track.

Argentina got years of bad advice from the IMF, topped off with a giant bailout that ended in a crisis producing lethal riots, destitute citizens and five presidents in a month. Turkey has also had years of bad advice from the IMF and is now the scene of the Fund's biggest current bailout. Such portents are not good.[12]

The fact is, Turkey *had* been under almost continuous supervision by the IMF for the past several *decades*, so to some extent Turkey's failings are also the IMF's failings. It is also true that the IMF's initial prescriptions in late 2000—fiscal austerity via higher taxes, lira devaluation, higher interest rates—undoubtedly deepened the crisis of early 2001. The sharp spike in interest rates made recession inevitable, while intensifying the pressure on an already struggling banking sector. The economy contracted by more than 9 percent in 2001. By early 2002, Turkey had earned the dubious distinction of being the IMF's largest-ever borrower as its loan program ballooned to over $30 billion. (To some extent, of course, this reflects Turkey's geopolitical importance to the United States, especially following 9/11. Bordering on Syria, Iraq, Iran, and the former Soviet Caucasus, Turkey is a dependable member of NATO, a reasonable democracy, and the only secular state in the Muslim world—all in all, an important ally for the United States in a tough neighborhood.)

Argentina, 2001 to ?

It is hard to know where to begin the Argentina story; certainly, as of mid-2003, there was no end in sight. More than anything else, Argentina is a story of riches to rags—descending from its position as one of the world's most prosperous and promising economic powers in the early twentieth century to one of its worst basket cases at the dawn of the twenty-first century.

As noted, Argentina stood firm against the speculators in the tequila hangover that followed Mexico's 1994 devaluation, and the government was successful in maintaining the peso's peg to the dollar. While growth never really rebounded, markets were stable over the next five years (see Figure 3.5). Like Turkey, Argentina was very much a darling of the multilateral financial institutions during this period, and its policies were widely praised.

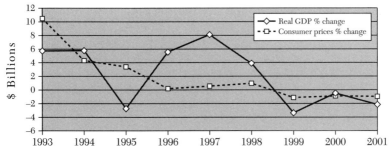

FIGURE 3.5 Argentina: Growth and Inflation

Source: www.bradynet.com.

In fact, also like Turkey, Argentina operated under the auspices of IMF-supported programs and under its close scrutiny virtually throughout the 1990s. The government aggressively opened up financial markets and privatized public companies, while the 1991 Convertibility Law (which established a currency board to tie the peso to the dollar and linked the money supply tightly to the stock of foreign exchange reserves) wiped out inflation. The protection of the IMF's good name, plus the new respect for Argentina that the markets gained from its staunch defense of the peso in 1995, kept speculators at bay.

Nonetheless, the seeds of another crisis were never far from the surface. While the economy and financial markets were stable, they were never robust. Private capital inflows and economic growth never really revived, especially after Brazil's 1999 devaluation. Two fundamental problems were unresolved:

- *Fixed exchange rate*—As the dollar soared in the second half of the 1990s, Argentina's peso—tied to the dollar through the inflexible currency board mechanism—went up with it. Export competitiveness declined, the economy staggered, and unemployment rose. With its relatively closed economy (exports were equivalent to less than 20 percent of GDP), optimists believed that Argentina could survive an overvalued peso indefinitely. However, the domestic economy too was moribund, so the sluggishness of export growth was another blow to an already weak economy.

- *Government spending*—Even worse, both Buenos Aires and the provinces ran up sizable deficits to finance government programs and public employee salaries and pensions. The budget shortfalls (plus expectations of a stable exchange rate) pushed the government to borrow billions of dollars on international capital markets. When recession struck in the late 1990s, government revenues declined and interest rates spiked.

As in Turkey, the country's economic and financial woes were inextricably intertwined with its political travails. With Argentina facing its fifth successive year of economic contraction, by late 2001 the political pressures had become unbearable. Political opposition to austerity had already raised serious doubts about debt and exchange rate sustainability, worrying investors (see Figure 3.6).

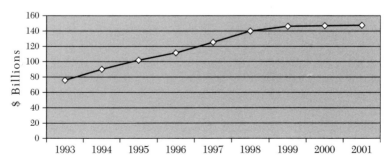

FIGURE 3.6   Argentina: External Debt

Source: www.bradynet.com.

The markets responded to these signs of trouble in their usual fashion. As debt soared and Argentina's political and social problems came to the forefront, lenders became increasingly reluctant to extend new credits. By mid- to late 2001, the country was effectively shut out of private capital markets. The IMF came to the rescue, demanding sharp cuts in the budget deficit via higher taxes and lower spending, designed to win back confidence. Instead, the cuts worsened the economic slump and confidence collapsed. Foreign exchange reserves were enough to back the central bank's $17 billion of monetary liabilities, as required by the Convertibility Law, but nowhere near enough to guarantee the $70 billion of dollar and peso deposits in the banking system, setting the stage for a run on the banks that would eventually topple the currency board. Foreign currency reserves plunged by 40 percent in the first seven months of 2001 and by nearly 25 percent in July alone.

Some investors, perhaps, had expected the IMF to continue supporting Argentina under any circumstances. However, the situation was too much even for the long-suffering Fund, which finally withdrew its support in December 2001. Argentina promptly defaulted on $85 billion in bonds, catapulting the country from a banking/currency crisis into a full-fledged financial and political catastrophe. Overwhelming social tensions exploded into the streets, and multiple governments were formed and just as promptly collapsed. (Argentina had five presidents over a one-month period.) By the close of 2001, the government had scrapped its currency board arrangement, allowing the peso to float; it lost nearly 75 percent of its value in the ensuing crash.

Unlike previous episodes, though, Argentina's crisis did not spread contagion to other financial markets around the world. In large part, this is because it was so well-advertised before the event and thus was thoroughly discounted by the markets—only the timing was unknown. Markets react to surprises, not to well-anticipated events; in this sense, Argentina's crash occurred in slow motion, giving onlookers plenty of time to get out of the way. So this crisis was foreseen by many, including bond investors, who by the late 1990s—viewing Argentina as overindebted and the peso as overvalued—began to cut their lending to the country and hike risk premiums on its paper. Everyone knew Argentina was a time bomb waiting to explode.

▶ WHAT HAVE WE LEARNED?

Argentina and Turkey were poster children for the Washington consensus. As noted, they both operated under more or less continuous IMF guidance throughout the 1990s and earned high praise from the Fund for their dutiful implementation of market-based economic and financial policies.

Thus the implosion of both at the turn of the century is worrisome. Clearly, analysts need to absorb and learn from the lessons of these and other crises over the past decade. As all good historians know, those who do not understand the past are condemned to repeat it. So what are the lessons of the Age of Currency Crises?

- *Fixed exchange rates*—More than ever, it is clear that fixed exchange rate regimes in emerging market countries usually end badly. Pegged rate systems, like Argentina's currency board, are undeniably a powerful weapon against inflation, especially in a country with a history of hyper-inflation (see Chapter 4). However, the lack of an exit strategy for Argentina—as in other countries with fixed rates—eventually is devastating. The 1990s proved, over and over again, the difficulty of exiting from the fixed regime without a wrenching crisis. (Only Israel and Poland have managed to engineer exchange rate–based stability and then move to a more flexible system without a crisis). In almost every country that got into trouble in the 1990s, removal of exchange rate pegs was a contributing factor.

■ *Short-term debt*—Argentina and Turkey shared a reliance on capital flows to finance current account deficits, making them vulnerable to deteriorating external market conditions. Both had, in particular, substantial amounts of short-term debt, heightening the danger that investors would be unwilling to roll over debt at customary interest rates should the markets turn sour. Clearly, high levels of short-term debt are both a leading indicator of trouble ahead and an aggravating factor once the bad times set in.[13]

■ *Domestic banking systems*—Weak domestic banking systems, it turns out, matter a lot, especially with regard to the spreading of currency crises. If foreign capital is generally channeled through domestic commercial banks and the incentives system of these bankers is distorted—often the case in emerging market countries—then foreign funds are likely to be invested inefficiently. Also, if domestic banks have high exposure to foreign currency liabilities, then they will be devastated by a devaluation of the domestic currency.

■ *Contagion*—Analysts have long observed the prevalence of "herd" behavior in emerging markets, leading to episodes of wide overshooting and undershooting relative to economic fundamentals. Crises of the 1990s were invariably accompanied by widespread spillover and contagion effects across countries, even continents. Following Mexico's 1994 devaluation, for instance, Argentina staggered under the weight of speculative attacks. The country ultimately succeeded in defending its currency peg but at a heavy cost.

■ Financial contagion is poorly understood, but it seems to operate in at least three ways:

   ❑ *Economic linkages,* such as trade or bank/other lending. When Brazil stumbled, for example, its close trading ties to Argentina through the Mercosur trading bloc were widely expected to intensify recession in Argentina as well. This heightened investor concern about Argentina, prompting capital flight and pressure on foreign exchange reserves.

   ❑ *Pure contagion,* in which economic actors react because the situation in one crisis-hit country looks similar to the situation in another country. When Russia was hard-hit by sagging commodity prices, investors started to worry about other commodity-heavy countries, such as Brazil. Also, attacks may spread for reasons that cannot be explained by similarities in economic fundamentals; this is usually attributed to "herd behavior" by investors.

❏ *Portfolio readjustment,* by international investors and speculators. Losses in Asia, for example, forced speculators to liquidate investments in Russia in order to meet margin calls, thus roiling Russian markets as well.

■ *Mysteries abound*—Finally, the events of the 1990s force an unbiased observer to conclude that, in fact—despite mountains of learned research and commentary—the international financial community still does not understand crisis prevention and management very well. Some of the most virulent crises were almost entirely unpredicted, and experts still disagree (violently!) on their causes. Moreover, the debate continues to rage on how well these crises were managed and how to prevent further outbreaks.

▶ WHAT *HAVEN'T* WE LEARNED?

So in a sense, the list of questions that were raised—and remain unresolved—by the Age of Currency Crises is much longer than the list of lessons that were learned.

A Cautionary Tale for Globalization?

Among the most difficult and controversial questions at the dawn of the twenty-first century are those relating to the implications of the Age of Currency Crises for globalization and the Washington consensus. As noted, some of the worst crisis-torn countries were considered good and dutiful clients of the IMF—right up until the moment they collapsed. Surely this is the death knell of the Washington consensus?

Economist Robert Kuttner says, "The economic collapse of Argentina is the latest failure of the one-size-fits-all model that the United States tries to impose on developing countries." The model works like this, he explains: developing countries should open up their economies to foreign investment, balance their budgets, restrict the role of government, discipline wages, and limit social outlays. Argentina followed this model (essentially a restatement of the Washington consensus)[14] more faithfully than most, and look where it is today!

Robert Samuelson is just as blunt: "Argentina's default is 'a cautionary tale for globalization.' According to Samuelson, Argentina did a lot of things right in the 1990s: it wiped out hyperinflation and received, as its reward, a solid inflow of foreign investment (almost $80 billion between 1991 and 2000). However, its fundamental weaknesses—government spending, tax evasion, uncompetitive wages, and weak entrepreneurial class—more than offset these gains. "For Argentina," he says, "globalization has been no panacea, because greater trade and international investment don't automatically alter local attitudes and politics. Argentina's predicament applies, in some ways, to much of Latin America and may explain why the gains from rising globalization have been fairly modest. From 1993 to 2001, Latin America's economic growth averaged only 3.3 percent. ..." He concludes: "Perhaps Argentina's crisis will harm only Argentina. But because globalization promised so much more than it has delivered, the crisis may foretell a wider political and psychological fatigue"[15] (see Figure 3.7).

Samuelson's arguments raise a broader question: Does the collapse of such a faithful globalist as Argentina presage a growing disillusionment with globalization throughout Latin America? Richard Lapper of the *Financial Times*, for one, believes that Latin America is in a "time warp," in danger of returning to the policies of populism and authoritarianism that long dominated the region. He views Argentina as just "an extreme version of the broader malaise" affecting Latin Americans, who are increasingly unhappy with the results of liberal market-based reforms.

If so, this would be a major turnaround, with broad-based consequences. During the 1990s, most Latin American countries broke free of dictatorships and accepted the Washington consensus—cutting their public sectors, selling loss-making state companies, and welcoming the market disciplines of low inflation and free trade. This has produced a welcome stability in countries that were previously plagued by hyperinflation. In the first half of the 1990s, it even produced a surge of optimism as capital flowed in, economic growth picked up, and poverty began to decline.

However, these gains proved to be unsustainable. During the second half of the decade, the region was battered by a succession of currency crises and a boom-bust business cycle that has left many bewildered, embittered, and newly impoverished. By mid-2002, for example, about one-fourth of the Argentine workforce was jobless, and thousands of Argentines were falling below the poverty line every day. Paul Krugman writes:

> ... A decade ago, Washington confidently assured Latin American nations that if they opened themselves to foreign goods and capital and privatized their state enterprises they would experience a great sure of economic growth. But it hasn't

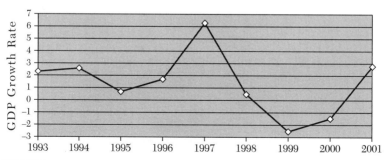

FIGURE 3.7   Latin America: Growth in the 1990s

Source: www.bradynet.com.

happened. Argentina is a catastrophe. Both Mexico and Brazil were, a few months ago, regarded as success stories, but in both countries per capita income today is only slightly higher than it was in 1980. And because inequality has increased sharply, most people are probably worse off than they were twenty years ago. ...[16]

To be sure, Latin American economies were undermined in part by exogenous events: sagging commodity prices and risk aversion among international investors related to fallouts in other parts of the world. But while external shocks certainly played a role, the bottom line is that Latin America by late 2002 was not exactly a poster child for the Washington consensus. As one analyst said recently, "Nowhere in Latin America is thriving."[17] Democracy is holding up (more or less), but polls find a deep dissatisfaction with its failure to improve living standards. (In fact, in late 2002, the Brazilians elected a new president—longtime labor leader and leftist politician Luis Ignacio da Silva, or Lula.)

Even before the latest recession, economic performance was mediocre overall. During the decade of the 1990s, growth in Latin America averaged just 3.3 percent per year (see Figure 3.7), and income per capita rose by just 1.5 percent per year; most inequality indicators ticked upward as well. Latin America's economy expanded by a paltry 0.5 percent in 2001 and probably showed little improvement in 2002. Regional stagnation since the mid-1990s has, in turn, erased whatever progress was made earlier in the decade on fighting poverty. Unemployment remains stubbornly high, and social inequality in the region has risen, frustrating the economists who expected rapid growth to lift all the boats and ease social tensions. According to the United Nations, 15 percent of the region's people live in extreme poverty, unchanged in the past two decades. The Inter-American Development Bank finds that 150 million people in Latin America live on $2/day or less and that the gap between rich and poor widened in the 1990s. As one Caracas-based analyst laments, "In the 1990s there [was] the idea that democracy and the markets were the way to reduce poverty and improve the quality of life. But neither democracy nor markets have solved the problem."[18]

Thus it is not surprising that many in the region are becoming more dubious about the benefits of market-based reforms. While signs of a tentative uptick began to appear in Argentina during 2003, the mood remained sour; the danger of Argentina spreading "ideological contagion" throughout the region appeared quite real. After all, Argentina's collapse in some ways does appear to be a cautionary tale about globalization. While some of Argentina's woes are unique to the country, which at times has seemed bent on self-immolation (remember the Falklands War?), its example still serves as a warning to others. As noted previously, most of Latin America followed similar policies in the 1990s, with very similar results—stability but minimal growth.

Opinion polls across the region, accordingly, show that "while support for reform is declining, populist economic policies, such as more state intervention and much higher social spending, are gaining credit."[19] The prospect of more debt defaults, calls for protection and for state support of national industries, and a return to state largesse seem quite real. On the other hand, so far no country has fully embraced populism either, partly because virtually every government in the region is dependent on overseas markets and investment. International pressure severely limits the degree to which any Latin American country can revert to authoritarianism and populism. Even Lula—whose election as Brazil's president represents the most dramatic shift leftward—has repudiated his earlier radical policies and promises to work closely with multilateral financial institutions on solving Brazil's financial mess.

Also, while it is fashionable to decry market-based reforms, no one has yet presented a viable alternative. In this environment, for example, it might be expected that Venezuela's President Hugo Chavez would benefit from the antiglobalization backlash. Since taking office, he has promoted a radical alternative to what he calls "savage neoliberalism"; his alternative includes a mix of constitutional reforms, state intervention, and radical rhetoric (enthusiastic support of Fidel Castro, for example). Supporters describe him as the "antibody to the twenty-first century disease of globalization."[20]

But Chavez's wildly erratic policies and dismal results have won him few allies. His popularity ratings have plummeted, and he narrowly escaped removal from office in early 2002. In 2002, the Venezuelan economy contracted by 10 percent, and a crippling national oil strike, beginning in December and lasting until February 2003, guaranteed that real GDP would fall by over 25 percent in the first quarter (all of this in a period of high world oil prices). Chavez's economic management has antagonized both big business and labor leaders. If Chavez is the best that the antireformist forces can offer in Latin America, the reformists have little to fear.

A Cautionary Tale for the IMF?

So the implications of the Age of Currency Crises with regard to globalization and market-based reforms remain hazy. By the same token, close analysis of emerging markets in the past decade raises serious doubts about the IMF's approach to these markets, especially its handling of financial crises. If Argentina Redux (2002) is a cautionary tale for globalization, surely it is even more so a cautionary tale for the IMF. Given the fact that the IMF essentially dictated economic policy in Argentina and Turkey over the past ten years and more, it can hardly claim to be responding to crises resulting from those countries' poor policies. To what extent did the IMF's policy failures contribute to the dismal performance of emerging markets over the past ten years, and to what extent will this affect future IMF performance?

Beginning with the IMF's response to the Asian financial crisis, it is indeed difficult to avoid the sense that, to some extent, the Fund was as much a part of the problem as it was a part of the solution. Most analysts, including those at the IMF, were guilty of "catastrophic misdiagnosis" of the Asian illness, leading the Fund to prescribe wildly inappropriate policies. The IMF economists basically began by viewing the Asian crisis as a retread of Latin America's assorted meltdowns and accordingly applied their standard treatment: austerity and aid.[21]

This exacerbated the problems, of course, since the Asian countries were not in fact plagued by profligate government spending. The IMF was castigated, with good reason, for applying the same methods in Asia—where inflation was lower, savings higher, and government budgets in balance or surplus—that it used in Latin America. With the Asian economies teetering on the brink of recession, the Fund's insistence on budget cuts, wage freezes, and interest rate hikes helped push them over the edge. (This is part of the reason why Malaysia's Mahathir opted to impose capital controls rather than submit to an IMF program; his success has always irked the Fund.)

Thus, there is no doubt that the international community's initial response to the Asian flu, led by the IMF, deepened rather than mitigated the growing crisis in its early stages. To their credit, the Fund's economists recognized their misstep fairly quickly and modified their policy recommendations for the Asian situation. But the damage was done, emboldening the IMF's many critics who had always accused it of prescribing an appendectomy, regardless of what symptoms the patient might present.

Joseph Stiglitz, chief economist of the World Bank in 1996–1999, had a bird's eye view of the IMF during the Asian crisis. His observations are particularly damning:

> The last set of financial crises had occurred in Latin America in the 1980s, when bloated public deficits and loose monetary policies led to runaway inflation. There, the IMF had correctly imposed fiscal austerity (balanced budgets) and tighter monetary policies, demanding that governments pursue those policies as a precondition for receiving aid. So, in 1997 the IMF imposed the same demands on Thailand. Austerity, the fund's leaders said, would restore confidence in the Thai economy. As the crisis spread to other East Asian nations—and even as evidence of the policy's failure mounted—the IMF barely blinked, delivering the same medicine to each ailing nation that showed up on its doorstep.
>
> I thought this was a mistake. For one thing, unlike the Latin American nations, the East Asian countries were already running budget surpluses. In Thailand, the government was running such large surpluses that it was actually starving the economy of much-needed investments in education and infrastructure, both essential to economic growth. And the East Asian nations already had tight monetary policies, as well: Inflation was low and falling. (In South Korea, for example, inflation stood at a very respectable 4 percent.) The problem was not imprudent government, as in Latin America; the problem was an imprudent private sector—all those bankers and borrowers, for instance, who'd gambled on the real estate bubble.[22]

Next came Turkey and Argentina. Both countries reflect, in part, the difficulty of engineering a fiscal consolidation—and the IMF's difficulty in cutting off a recalcitrant client. The IMF had long established a pattern of financial assistance in both countries that encouraged market participants to lend without proper regard for the risks. Even more debilitating, despite the urging for fiscal austerity, the IMF's willingness to provide one rescue package after another paradoxically encouraged governments to engage in spendthrift behavior. This was because even when its clients behaved badly, the IMF found it difficult to say no (in part reflecting fears of financial contagion). Barry Eichengreen explains, "Thus, in Argentina and Turkey, as in many prior decisions, the IMF and its shareholders found themselves between a rock and a hard place. Lending threatened to fuel moral hazard, but not lending exposed the world economy to risks too great for the politicians to countenance."

Thus, the role of the IMF deteriorated into that of a multilateral enabler, making it a key source of moral hazard in emerging markets.[23]

Argentina's crisis, in particular, has taken a huge toll on a country that the IMF held up as a shining example of its best work. In December 2001, the democratically elected government collapsed after bloody riots left twenty-seven dead; since then, the peso has lost more than half its value, the economy has gone into free fall, and the once-rich nation is on the brink of economic and political ruin. These developments have prompted the IMF's former chief economist, Michael Mussa, to issue a rare public denunciation of the Fund's policies in Argentina. Mussa begins by pointing to the apparent success of Argentina's Convertibility Law. "Indeed," he notes, "with most of the miracle economies of emerging Asia collapsing into crisis from mid-1997 to early 1998, Argentina became the darling of emerging market finance. ... And, in the official financial community, especially the IMF, many of Argentina's economic policies were widely applauded and suggested as a model that other emerging market countries should take. ..."

Thus, Mussa suggests, it is appropriate to use Argentina to examine the role of the IMF in these countries, both past and future. After all, as noted, Argentina operated under the auspices of IMF-supported programs virtually throughout the 1990s—differentiating it sharply from other countries (Mexico, 1995; Indonesia, South Korea, and Thailand, 1997–1998; Brazil, 1998–1999) where the IMF was called in only after a crisis was under way. In the twelve years leading up to the 2001 default, Argentina was operating under IMF loan agreements for all but five weeks. The government obtained $34 billion in fund loans between July 1991 and August 2001, drawing about $21 billion.

In Argentina, Mussa charges, the IMF made at least two critical mistakes:

- *Failing to push the government* for more responsible fiscal policies, especially after 1995 (the critical flaw of the Argentine economy was its unsustainable, irresponsible fiscal policy)

- *Extending substantial financial support* to Argentina in the summer of 2001, when it was clear that the exchange rate was doomed and that convertibility needed to be scrapped

Mussa concludes: "Argentina's decade-long experiment with hard money and orthodox policies has ended in tragedy—the depths of which are not yet fully known."[24] Indeed, by late 2002 the country had sunk into a steep recession; the economy may have contracted by up to 12 percent for the year. While he does not exempt the country's politicians from their fair share of the blame, in the end he views the IMF's role in the country as a cautionary tale indeed.

The Lessons of China and India?

As noted, opening up domestic capital markets to foreign investment is a key component of the Washington consensus; moreover, it fueled a tremendous surge in growth and development among many emerging market countries in the 1990s. At the same time, most experts also agree that free mobility of private capital set the stage for the series of currency crises that erupted in the 1990s. Clearly, increased capital mobility brings very high costs and limited benefits to countries that lack sound, modern financial institutions.

In this context, it is instructive to look at two big developing countries that escaped relatively unscathed from the gauntlet of the 1990s—China and India. China's transition from a planned economy to a market economy, beginning in 1989, can be described only as a unique process. It has taken place in a piecemeal, bottom-up fashion, often based on cautious experimentation and always incrementally. While China has been troubled by a boom-bust cycle, and observers may quibble with its official data, overall it is difficult to deny that the results have been stupendous. The anti-IMF forces may take heart from China, noting that its reform policies have been entirely home-grown rather than imposed by external institutions.

India, too, managed to avoid the worst of the Asian financial crisis, maintaining its growth rate at close to its average of the past decade. India remains a relatively closed economy; exports account for only 8 percent of GDP, so the adverse effects of the crisis on its balance of payments and domestic economy were modest. Also, India's capital controls limited the country's vulnerability to abrupt swings of short-term capital. Net inflows of private capital in 1992–1996 averaged just 1.5 percent of GDP, compared to 8.8 percent for Thailand, for example.

What, then, are the lessons to be drawn from China and India? Observing these two countries in the context of the crises, a recent UN report notes:

> While the developed world suffered little from the Asian financial crisis that broke out in 1997, and even derived some benefits from it, the impact on the rest of the world has been dramatic. Virtually all developing countries and transition economies were affected. It played havoc in East Asia and Russia throughout 1998, set back the progress achieved in Latin America, and in the most seriously affected countries wiped out the fruits of economic growth and poverty reduction. ...
> The two largest developing countries, China and India, have been striking exceptions in this otherwise bleak landscape. It is notable that both of these countries had resisted the temptation to pursue premature trade liberalization and rapid integration into the global financial system.[25]

Bailing in the Private Sector?

Finally, unanswered questions swirl around the role of the private sector in the succession of financial crises that has engulfed emerging market countries in the past decade. Some of the news on this front is apparently good. Smaller Latin American countries, for example, are finding it easier to borrow on international capital markets at remarkably favorable rates. Issues by El Salvador, Costa Rica, the Dominican Republic, and Guatemala have all successfully raised funds even after the market disruptions of 9/11. Thus there is some evidence that markets are better at differentiating among countries in the same neighborhood, which may reduce the chances of crippling contagion in the future.

At the same time, the decline and fall of the Brady bond market in the late 1990s and early 2000s is generally viewed as an encouraging trend. Brady bonds were devised by U.S. Treasury Secretary Nicholas Brady at the end of the 1980s as part of a solution to the debt crisis that dominated that decade. Brady bonds enabled sovereign borrowers to restructure billions of dollars in defaulted bank loans into bonds, often backed by U.S. treasuries. A vibrant secondary market sprang up. By 2001, though, most countries in Latin America and Eastern Europe had replaced their Brady bonds with new instruments that allow them to reduce their borrowing costs and remove the stigma attached to the bonds.

Brady himself welcomes the trend. He considers the ability of most debtor countries to swap their Brady bonds into global bonds "the end of a transition decade—a decade when many emerging market countries moved from debt restructuring to a fuller participation in the global economy." Market experts predict that the Brady bonds will be replaced completely by new debt by 2006.[26]

At the same time, though, these developments raise the exposure of private capital market participants to emerging markets, and vice versa. If the fuller access of emerging market countries to private capital markets represents the good news, then the bad news part of the story is the open question of what to do when these debts go sour. The problem of how to "bail in" the private sector—how to force these creditors to participate in a bailout (and share the pain) rather than rushing headlong for the exits—is entirely unresolved.

Furthermore, the problem is exacerbated by the changing nature of creditors in today's financial markets. Throughout the Latin American debt crisis of the 1980s and lasting through the Korean crisis of 1997, the bulk of the debt was held by commercial banks yoked together in syndication deals. Thus, when problems arose, the workout was negotiated and implemented by a handful of leading—and well-seasoned—bankers. Now, however, the democratization of credit markets means that the creditor base for emerging markets has shifted toward retail investors. Argentina, for example, defaulted in 2002 on its debt to literally hundreds of thousands of individual bondholders. The difficulty of negotiating a workout under these circumstances, compared to the orderly and well-mapped path of the commercial bankers, is incalculable.

The knottiness of this problem, especially in the wake of Argentina's collapse, has provoked serious discussion of a formal mechanism for private debt workouts for emerging market debtors, relying more on private funding than on IMF bailouts. Clearly, the world needs some alternative to the bailout-or-bust scenario that offers just two dispiriting choices: either an IMF-led rescue of the crippled country (which often, in effect, rescues the private sector creditors as well), or a devastating default with all its attendant risks of financial contagion.

Some sort of international bankruptcy court is one obvious idea. Proponents of this notion observe that over the past twenty years, an average of one country per year has defaulted on its debts. Two methods for dealing with these defaults have been tried:

- *Bailing out countries by plowing money into them,* as the IMF did for Russia in 1998 with its $23 billion package. This was hugely expensive, and a prime example of moral hazard; it enhanced the incentive of both the Russians and their private creditors to behave irresponsibly, knowing that the rich countries would eventually ride to the rescue.

- *Letting the markets sort things out* with voluntary agreements between debtors and creditors, as in Ecuador's default on its public debt in 1998–1999. This was problematic too; the diversity among creditors was a critical obstacle, as some stubborn lenders held things up by insisting on better terms.

Perhaps an international bankruptcy tribunal would address these weaknesses? As proposed by Harvard's Jeffrey Sachs, such a tribunal could be modeled on the procedures available to failing companies in the United States, proceeding through three stages:

- First, the country would receive legal protection from its creditors.

- Next, as restructuring discussions proceeded, creditors would keep the country supplied with cash in return for priority in repayment.

- Third, once the creditors reached agreement, some kind of majority voting would take place to ensure that dissenters do not delay the process.

Critics of such a plan, though, worry that by making it too easy and painless for countries to default, an international bankruptcy tribunal could be swamped by eager takers. Developing countries have about $2.6 *trillion* in external debt outstanding; any procedure that encourages them to default on this debt should be viewed with great caution. Also, what are the chances of a bankrupt country being able to raise fresh capital to finance future growth and development?[27] All of the benefits of access to international capital markets would be lost, at least for some extended period of time.

▶ THE ROAD AHEAD: EMERGING FINANCIAL MARKETS

As the last paragraph underlines, prospects for emerging market countries at the dawn of the twenty-first century are uncertain. The picture is clouded by Argentina's default, the questionable ability of IMF-guided neoliberalism to lay a secure foundation for equitable growth, and an inevitable backlash against globalization and the IMF in many parts of the emerging world.

Latin America, in particular, may be in for a bumpy ride. Increased political instability in Venezuela and a revival of populist politics throughout the continent are worrisome. *The New York Times* notes: "Today the market reforms ushered in by American-trained economists after the global collapse of Communism are facing their greatest challenge in the upheaval sweeping the region." It may be, as one economist warns, "the end of an era."[28] Argentina's political and economic travails are prompting some companies to consider pulling out of the country, potentially imperiling foreign direct investment flows throughout the region. Financial markets reacted with horror to the prospect of a Lula presidency in Brazil (despite his perceptible move toward the center on key economic issues), sending the currency into free-fall and necessitating a $30 billion IMF rescue package in mid-2002. Even Mexico is losing its luster; after two years in office, pro-business President Vicente Fox has accomplished little in the way of serious reform, stymied by a recalcitrant congress and difficult external environment.

On the bright side, the planned creation of a Free Trade Area of the Americas (FTAA), the largest free trade area in the world, by 2006 may spur some investment in the region. An Inter-American Development Bank (IADB) report found that despite a substantial deterioration in the external environment and weakening domestic demand, governments in the region were generally maintaining their austere fiscal policies. The report's authors express little concern that the region will retreat from economic modernization to the old policies of central government control and intervention. (In fact, the IADB is optimistic about prospects for further progress on economic reforms, noting that times of crisis have also generally been times of greatest reform.)

In fact, excluding Argentina and Venezuela, the region *may* be poised for recovery. Brazil's Lula is, in fact, likely to steer a course that hews fairly closely to IMF mandates (disbursement of the rescue package is tied to strict budgetary guidelines). Ecuador's new president also has populist roots but so far has adopted pragmatic policies. Mexico's economy—increasingly tied to the United States and thus largely unaffected by Argentina's troubles—has won its coveted investment grade status from Standard & Poor's. (Latin America grew by a paltry 0.3 percent in 2002, but this partly reflects the sharp contraction in Argentina and the deteriorating outlook in Venezuela.)

On the surface, the outlook in Asia is rosier. Even the most troubled countries of the region have rebounded more dramatically and quickly than expected. By 2001, many of the hard-hit Asian economies had seemingly recovered from the shocks of 1997–1998. In 2000, real GDP rose by around 13 percent in South Korea, 12 percent in Malaysia, and 7 percent in Thailand. The ten member states of ASEAN, plus Japan, Korea, and China, agreed in 2001 on a $1 billion fund for the mutual defense of their currencies against speculators on FX markets. (Bankers, though, deride this effort, pointing out that more than *$1 trillion* passes through FX markets every day.) Investor interest in emerging markets outside of Latin America has perked up, with money flowing back to Russia, Thailand, South Africa, and Indonesia (before the October 2002 bombing in Bali). In part, this reflects a sense that pre-Asian crisis foibles—corporate governance and transparency weaknesses—have been addressed to some extent.

Below the surface, though, the emerging countries of Asia still look vulnerable. Complacent after their relatively quick recovery from the troubles of 1997–1998, many have reverted to their old ways and left vital reforms unfinished. One analyst warns that the region suffers from a "psychological overhang" after the crisis, and that some states "remain deluded, blaming evil external forces." When some of the Asian currencies began to fall again in early 2001, politicians blamed evil speculators and hedge funds in a worrying flashback to the 1997 crisis.

It is clear that in general, the Asian states have not internalized the lessons of the 1997–1998 disaster and have taken few discernible steps to fix the problems that contributed to it. A recent editorial in the *Financial Times* warned, "The Asian financial crisis … was largely the result of the distortions caused by rigid macro-economic policies and the misallocation of capital that flowed from bad corporate governance. Much has changed in Asia since the crisis. But, worryingly, much remains the same."[29] Are those who cannot understand the past condemned to repeat it?

Finally, the continued volatility of world commodity prices is an alarming indicator for many key emerging market countries. Excluding oil, commodity prices plunged by 26 percent between mid-1997 and early 2002. Combined with an inevitable increase in U.S. interest rates, this could spell difficult times ahead for Latin America, Russia, and the Caribbean. As always, countries heavily dependent on commodity exports will be the hardest hit by any global economic slowdown. Coffee prices plummeted by 50 percent in 2000–2002, for example, and cotton prices are down by 66 percent since 1995, with devastating consequences in Latin America and Africa.

Thus, emerging market countries relying on capital inflows and export demand face sharp challenges ahead. With private capital flows weak in recent years, many of these countries have learned to cope without importing huge amounts of capital from abroad. Coping is not the same as thriving, though. Hardest hit will be the poorest countries, which always suffer disproportionately from weak commodity prices. Africa, in particular, has been ignored in much of this chapter because, sadly, most of its markets cannot be said to be "emerging" yet. With the notable exception of South Africa and part of North Africa, the continent has been left out of the worldwide expansion of capital flows over the past few decades. The World Bank and IMF have put twenty-two countries, most of them African, into its Highly Indebted Poor Countries (HIPC) debt relief initiative. But debt relief, even if fully implemented, will not produce growth (see Figure 3.8).

Africa's marginalization from international financial markets differentiates it from the rest of the emerging world. Even for those countries with increasingly favorable access to capital markets, though, huge questions remain. The Age of

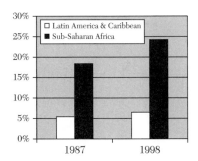

FIGURE 3.8   Latin America and Sub-Saharan Africa: Percentage of Population Living on Less than $1/Day

Source: World Bank.

Currency Crises leaves much uncertainty in its wake: The role of the IMF? Private sector? Backlash against liberalization? Analysis of that decade raises more questions than it answers. The only point on which all can probably agree is that financial convulsions will continue in emerging markets until someone, somehow, can figure out how to answer those questions.

▶ NOTES

1. "Net Private Capital Flows to Emerging Markets," January 2002, available at www.iif.org.
2. Ibid.
3. Jane D'Arista, "Benefits of Capital Flows: New Role for Public Institutions," Financial Markets Center, November 1999, available at www.fmcenter.org.
4. Jane E. Hughes and Scott B. MacDonald, *International Banking: Text and Cases* (Boston, Mass.: Addison Wesley, 2002), p. 384.
5. Ibid., pp. 384-6.
6. Steven Radelet and Jeffrey Sachs, "The Onset of the East Asian Financial Crisis," in *Currency Crises,* Paul Krugman, ed. (Chicago and London: University of Chicago Press, 2000).
7. Nicholas Kristof and Edward Wyatt, "In an Entwined World Market, No Man (Or Nation) Is an Island," *The New York Times,* February 17, 1999.
8. Radelet and Sachs, op. cit.
9. Steven Radelet and Jeffrey Sachs, "Lessons from the Asian Financial Crisis." In: *Global Financial Crises and Reforms,* B. N. Ghosh, ed. (London and New York: Routledge, 2001).
10. Kristof and Wyatt, op. cit.
11. Ibid.
12. Editorial, "Tinkering with Turkey: Don't Let the IMF Create Another Argentina," The *Wall Street Journal,* January 17, 2002.
13. Barry Eichengreen, "Crisis Prevention and Management: Any New Lessons from Argentina and Turkey?" Background Paper for World Bank's Global Development Finance Conference 2002, October 2001, available at www.emlab.berkeley.edu/pub.
14. Robert Kuttner, "U.S. Fueled Argentina's Economic Collapse," *The Boston Globe,* January 7, 2002.
15. Robert Samuelson, "Do Cry for Argentina," *The Washington Post,* January 16, 2002.
16. Paul Krugman, "Who's Being Bailed Out?" *The New York Times,* August 9, 2002.
17. "Losing its Way?" *The Economist,* February 28, 2002.
18. Richard Lapper, "Back to the Revolution," *Financial Times,* February 21, 2002.
19. Richard Lapper, "Region Faces Popular Pressure for Change," *Financial Times,* March 8, 2002.
20. Richard Lapper and Andrew Webb-Vidal, "Chavez's Spent Revolution," *Financial Times,* February 13, 2002.
21. Kristof and Wyatt, op. cit.
22. Joseph Stiglitz, *What I Learned at the World Economic Crisis,* excerpted from *The New Republic,* April 17, 2000, available at www.whirledbank.org.
23. Eichengreen, op. cit.
24. Mussa, op. cit.
25. United Nations Conference on Trade and Development, *Annual Report 1999.*
26. Arkady Ostrovsky and Joshua Chaffin, "Mexico Highlights Demise of the Brady," *Financial Times,* March 27, 2001.
27. Daniel Altman, "A Country in Chapter 11? Yes, but ..." *The New York Times,* January 6, 2002.
28. Juan Foredo, "Still Poor, Many Latin Americans Protest Push to Free Market," *The New York Times,* July 19, 2002.
29. "Asian Values," editorial, *Financial Times,* May 13, 2002.

CHAPTER 4

FOREIGN EXCHANGE MARKETS: SPECULATORS, POLICEMEN, AND SUCKERS

"Currencies in crisis: The wild gyrations are maddening, but the system isn't easily changed" ... "The battered dollar" ... "Now, currencies go wild" ... "Dollar volatility shakes markets" ... "In a key policy switch, U.S. joins Japanese in intervening to prop up the sagging yen" ... "Cheap currency gamblers stung by spurt in the yen" ... "Turnover on foreign exchange markets tumbles" ... "Weak euro lets top car dealers go far in Japan" ... "Chavez may impose controls on forex deals" ... "The false promise of dollarisation" ... "Hong Kong debates link to dollar" ... "G.M. official says dollar is too strong" ...

In the foreign exchange (FX) markets, the decade of 1991–2001 began with a bang, as a handful of well-financed and arrogant traders brought down the mighty Bank of England and humbled the French franc. The decade then progressed through a series of wrenching currency crises in countries as far-flung as Brazil, Thailand, Turkey, and Indonesia. By the close of 2001, the markets were toying with the increasingly hapless Argentine peso, amid widespread wonderment at the seemingly intractable and inexplicable misalignment of major currencies.

So the fundamental mysteries of FX markets remain unsolved. (To paraphrase author William Goldman's observation about the film industry, this is a world where nobody knows anything.) *Plus ca change, plus c'est la meme chose.* (That is, the more things change, the more they stay the same.) And yet, much *did* change over the tumultuous decade that began in 1991. The euro was born, eleven European currencies were retired, the once-proud Southeast Asian currencies were humbled, and the Latin American currencies stumbled through yet another set of crises. Indeed, the FX markets at the dawn of the twenty-first century are fundamentally different from those of the early 1990s.

While FX markets did not become bubbles, as with tech and telecoms, they did reflect a certain frenzied behavior that picked at the vulnerabilities of a world of liberalized capital flows. Like it or not, FX markets functioned in many of the same ways as the stock market: huge volumes of capital flowing in, big profits to be made, a necessary flow of capital into worthwhile development projects, and substantial mistakes, resulting in crises where institutions were inadequate.

▶ STRUCTURAL CHANGE IN THE FX MARKET

The FX markets have undergone substantial structural changes over the past ten years:

- *The euro was born,* replacing eleven European currencies in one fell swoop and transforming the nature of FX trading forever.

- *Breathtaking technological advances* have also transformed the markets, enhancing the role of automated trading and real-time information. The rise of electronic brokering, in particular, led to important changes in the markets; Internet trading is increasingly regarded as the next frontier.

- *Consolidation in the banking industry* erased the names of some key players and joined others together. Consequently, the industry became more competitive, concentrated, and cost-driven.

- *Central banks gave up.* A series of painful and ill-considered interventions, with predictably painful endings, convinced most central bankers that they would not be able to defend or stabilize their currencies through intervention in FX markets. As a result, this once-powerful set of players has largely withdrawn from wide-scale FX activity. (The Bank of Japan is a possible exception, still willing at times to throw big chunks of cash into FX markets to stem the appreciation of the yen.)

- *Huge investment funds,* including hedge funds, replaced the central banks as powerful actors in the FX markets. The role of these giant funds increased sharply over the decade, introducing new levels of volatility and risk for the traditional players (bankers and multinational corporations). To some extent, this may be a case of "nature abhors a vacuum." As central banks left the field, did hedge funds assume their Darwinesque role—picking off the weak in the herd?

- *Fundamental economic factors* were increasingly unable to explain currency behavior. To cite just one example, the Canadian dollar (nicknamed the "loonie") has declined steadily over the past three decades, from U.S. $1.04 in 1974 to just U.S. $0.62 at the close of 2001, in apparent disregard for Canada's stellar economic performance. The gyrations of the dollar, euro, and yen also bear remarkably little resemblance to relative economic trends. As a result, analysts have cast about desperately for new forecasting methods to complement—even replace—the increasingly discredited (but traditional) reliance on inflation, interest rates, balance of payments, and other economic fundamentals to explain exchange rate movements.[1] Economic factors still matter in FX markets, but how and when they matter is increasingly mysterious.

At the same time, much remained the same:

- *The dollar remains dominant.* Despite the advent of the euro and some overheated rhetoric about the newest fad—trading in "exotic" currencies of emerging and transition market countries—the dollar continues to dominate the markets. The vast majority of FX trades still involve the dollar, and most of the world's central bankers still hold the bulk of their FX reserves in dollars.

- *London remains dominant.* The birth of the euro, in which the UK has so far declined to participate, led some observers (mostly French and German) to predict that London would experience a gradual decline in its importance as an international financial center, to be replaced by Frankfurt and Paris. This has not happened. London continues to account for close to one-third of FX trading activity, far more than any of its competitors, and the institutional skills and infrastructure in the City of London command a hefty competitive advantage in the FX business.

- *Citibank remains dominant.* With all of the consolidation and competitive maneuvering in the banking industry, Citibank faced the greatest challenges ever to its historical dominance of the FX industry. In 2000, for the first time since polling began in 1979, Citibank lost the title of best FX bank (to Deutsche Bank) in *Euromoney*'s much-respected annual survey. Citibank regrouped and redoubled its efforts, though, and in 2001 Citibank won back its title. The survey revealed that Citibank captured an impressive 10 percent of the FX market and is widely considered the "best foreign exchange bank" by market participants.[2]

Underlying much of these trends are the key themes of this book: faith in markets, technology, models, and globalization. FX markets reacted sharply and intensely to the gradual liberalization and integration of economies around the world, as surging capital flows were reflected in surging FX market volumes. At the same time, new and changing technologies engineered a virtual earthquake in the nature of FX trading.

▶ THE CONVENTIONAL WISDOM

Perhaps more than any other, the central theme of FX markets in the 1990s was the conventional wisdom being turned inside out. Economists have believed for many years that over the long term, a country's currency should adjust to reflect the relative strength of that currency's underlying economy—a simple concept but a powerful one, and it has dominated thinking about FX markets for generations.

The most basic method for understanding long-term FX market equilibrium is the principle of purchasing power parity, or PPP. Simply, PPP tells us that goods and services should cost the same in every country, regardless of the currency in which they are priced. (If prices deviate, then this creates an opportunity for arbitrage—

risk-free trading—in which a smart entrepreneur buys the goods at country A's cheaper price and sells them in country B at the higher price.) So in a perfect PPP world, currencies adjust for relative price differentials (inflation) in the two countries. Two currencies are at equilibrium when the exchange rate between them equalizes the price of identical goods and services in the two countries.

Economists and FX traders have known for many years, of course, that PPP is a poor predictor of exchange rates in the real world, especially over the short term. Nonetheless, inflation and other economic fundamentals such as a country's balance of payments, fiscal policies, and monetary policy have long been understood to play a vital role in determining FX rates. Like any other asset, the price of a currency is determined by supply and demand for that currency, which in turn should reflect the market's understanding and expectations of the economy that underlies that currency.

While FX market participants have long understood that FX rates can deviate from economic fundamentals for long periods of time, this gap widened dramatically in the 1991–2001 decade. One clear development, the growing importance of capital flows over trade flows, probably sounds the death knell for PPP-based analysis. By the 1990s, FX trading was more than seventy times the level of world trade in goods and services. The new reality—that FX trading is largely driven by capital flows, not trade flows—suggests in turn that new methods for understanding and forecasting FX movements will be necessary. Economic fundamentals will play a more complicated, and probably more subtle, role in these new methods.

Who, What, Where, When, and How

Seismic Shifts in the Markets

The fast pace of globalization over the past decade was reflected in the FX markets. During much of the 1990s, FX market turnover (the total amount of FX traded daily) soared along with global capital flows and economic activity. Daily market turnover shot up by an annual average of 11 percent, from $590 billion in 1989 to a peak of $1.5 trillion in 1998. At the end of the decade, though, an abrupt and surprising contraction occurred. The Bank for International Settlements (BIS) reports:

> ... In 2000 and early 2001 ... turnover in global foreign exchange markets continued to be well below the levels reached before the financial turbulence in autumn 1998. This would be the first reversal of this sort since the first comprehensive survey of foreign exchange market activity was conducted in 1989. ...[3]

In fact, the BIS report indicates that daily turnover on global FX markets tumbled sharply at the end of the 1990s, from an estimated $1.5 trillion in 1998 to just $1.1 trillion at the start of 2001 (Figure 4.1). This is the first reported decline since the BIS began surveying FX markets a decade earlier. While market participants had sensed that the market was less active than in better days, the size of the contraction was still a shock. (To put this in perspective, though, average daily trading volumes on the New York Stock Exchange in early 2002 were around $44.5 *billion* per day.)

What caused the markets to shrink so dramatically? The BIS suggests that three key factors were at work:

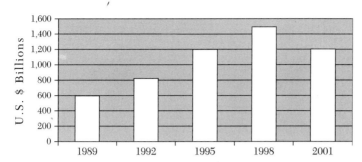

FIGURE 4.1 Total Daily Global FX Turnover

Source: Triennial Central Bank Survey of Foreign Exchange and Derivatives Market Activity 2001—Final Results, Bank of International Settlements at www.bis.org.

1. *The launch of the euro.* As noted, the birth of the euro was one of the landmark events in currency markets during the decade—and stands as a visible, even tactile, symbol of globalization. The BIS explains: "On 1 January 1999, the consolidation of the eleven legacy currencies eliminated at a stroke about 8 percent of global turnover, and this decline was not subsequently reversed by any increase in trading in the euro compared to that in its predecessor currencies."[4] In other words, the decline in trading caused by the disappearance of eleven European currencies was not offset by strong levels of trading in the new euro.

2. *An increased role for electronic brokering in the interbank market, at the expense of voice brokering and direct dealing.* In 2000, around 90 percent of interbank trading in major currencies was conducted by electronic brokers, compared to 50 percent just two years earlier and 25 percent in 1995. This had a dramatic effect on trading volumes. Since electronic brokers automatically provide traders with the best price available to them, FX dealers need to enter fewer transactions in order to optimize their pricing.

3. *Consolidation within the banking industry.* The trend toward consolidation and concentration in this industry has produced a significant decline in the number of active traders and trading rooms. The BIS adds: "The impact of consolidation on trading volumes has been compounded over the last few years by the reported withdrawal of capital from market-making and position-taking and by the reduction in the number and activity of market participants, in particular macro hedge funds."[5]

By the turn of the century the abrupt shift from market growth to market contraction was accompanied by some shifts in the most basic element of FX trading—what's being traded. But perhaps the most interesting story here is the *lack* of change. Through a doubling and then retrenching of market size, through several wrenching currency crises in emerging markets and a yet-unresolved financial crisis in Japan, and through the replacement of eleven European currencies with one infant currency, there was remarkably little change in what traders were actually trading.

What's Being Traded: The Euro

Increasingly, FX markets are operating in a tri-zone world comprising the dollar, the euro, and the yen. However, within this tri-zone world the dollar is still almighty: The dollar figured on one side of a whopping 90 percent of all currency trades in 2001 (Figure 4.2), up from a low of 82 percent in 1992. By contrast, the euro is involved on one side of just 38 percent of all FX transactions, higher than the German mark's share in 1998 (30 percent) but well below the 53 percent share of the eleven component currencies in 1998 (Figure 4.3). In part, this reflects the relatively high cost of doing business in euros. According to a study by one leading think tank, it is 40 percent more expensive to convert euros into dollars than it was to trade German marks for dollars.[6] (The reason for the high costs is not clear. Some market participants charge that European banks have taken advantage of the uncertainty surrounding the launch of the euro to hike transaction costs; others believe that it is an inevitable and temporary byproduct of the new currency's birth.)

The initial failure of the euro to challenge the dollar's dominance both confounded and dismayed europhiles. In fact, altogether the euro's birth pangs were unimpressive. It celebrated its birth by tumbling 14 percent against the dollar in 1999 (Figure 4.4), dampening Europe's political pride and raising fears of a disorderly currency market, which could, in turn, dampen investment and trade. The euro continued to tumble through early 2002, at which point a slow but inexorable dollar decline finally began, bringing the euro back to rough parity with the U.S. currency. (Interestingly, in 2002–2003 the euro's gains against the dollar did not reflect any fundamental shift in the strength of the eurozone economy vis-à-vis the U.S. economy, underlining once again the eternal mystery of FX market behavior— or, more specifically, the declining role of economic fundamentals in determining currency values.)

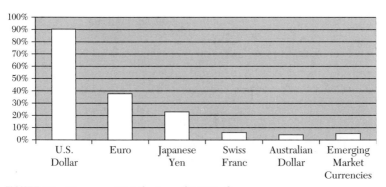

FIGURE 4.2   Currency Distribution of FX Trading

Source: Triennial Central Bank Survey of Foreign Exchange and Derivatives Market Activity 2001—Final Results, Bank of International Settlements at www.bis.org.

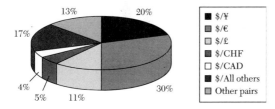

FIGURE 4.3 Currency Pairs
Source: Bank of International Settlements.

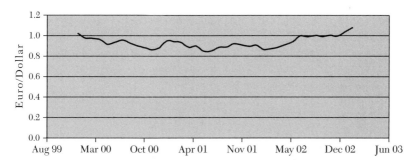

FIGURE 4.4 Euro/Dollar Exchange Rates
Source: Federal Reserve Board; www.federalreserve.gov/releases/h10/Hist/.

After the first flush of enthusiasm had faded, central bankers around the world quietly forgot to convert their FX reserves from dollars into euros. One commentator tartly noted that movements in official reserves are "conspicuous by their absence." In particular, he added, east Asian central banks–which have by far the world's largest holdings of FX reserves—are holding back from increasing the euro portion of their reserves.[7] (In early 2002, China's finance minister commented that the country should switch some of its reserves—the world's largest at over $200 billion—from dollars into euros, in order to reduce its reliance on the dollar. Progress will probably lag well behind the official rhetoric, though.) The estimated $1 trillion of central bank reserves held by the 140 member countries of the International Monetary Fund (IMF) worldwide roughly equals less than one day's average trading volume on FX markets, so this diffidence does not affect markets in any direct way. But the psychological impact of central bankers' demonstrated lack of confidence was a blow to the fledgling currency and raises doubts about its future prospects.

It is important not to overstate the birth pangs of the euro, though. Another market observer noted in 2000: "The euro has been a surprise in two ways. It has dropped nearly 30 percent against the dollar in its first twenty-two months. And it has changed European financial markets, business, and the economy faster than its founders dared to hope."[8] The euro's initial weakness on FX markets was not hard to understand, in fact. In part it reflected the passivity of European economies relative to the aggressively muscular U.S. performance throughout the 1990s. The malady dubbed "eurosclerosis" suggests that European countries remain hobbled by inflexible labor markets, high unemployment, and high levels of regulation compared to the innovative and fast-charging United States. (This should not imply that the U.S. economy did not suffer from structural flaws as well; see Chapter 6 for a critique of that bubble economy, which eventually contributed to a decline in the dollar's value by 2002.) Economic fundamentals, however, seem to play a limited role in currency movements these days, so clearly other factors were present as well. For example, FX traders have been wary of the new currency, still unsure of the ability of European countries in very different stages of the economic cycle to coordinate their policies.

Nonetheless, the potential for internationalization of the euro—its use in transactions not directly involving the eleven component countries—reflects the fact that in some ways it is already well established as a challenger to the dollar.

The euro has made its biggest splash in European stock and bond markets. Despite (or perhaps because of) its lamentably weak showing on FX markets in 1999, the euro ran about equal with the dollar as the debt market's currency of choice. This was the first time that the dollar's supremacy on international debt markets was challenged. During the first half of the year, 45.8 percent of international bonds issued were dollar-denominated, and 43 percent were euro-denominated. For the full year, $602 billion of euro-denominated bonds were issued on international markets, according to Capital Data Ltd., accounting for 45 percent of total issuance. This actually outstripped the $573 billion or 42 percent of all bonds issued that were denominated in dollars.[9] It also stands in sharp contrast to the 22 percent share of international bonds denominated in the eleven eurozone currencies in 1998.

The euro's popularity on debt markets reflected, in part, its weakness on FX markets: non-European borrowers were attracted to the flailing currency in hopes that it would remain soft long enough for them to repay their debt with hardercurrency revenues. To the extent that this factor motivated borrowers, the big role played by the euro on debt markets is less than encouraging. (This also suggests that the euro's recovery on FX markets since early 2002 may stunt further growth in euro-denominated debt.)

However, there are also signs that the euro's position in capital markets reflects more fundamental strengths. The new currency enjoys much greater liquidity than any of the eleven member currencies did individually, encouraging the development of deep and vital capital markets. This is fueling the evolution of bigger and more liquid pan-European stock and bond markets, including a junk bond market that is making international financial markets accessible to companies that were shut out before. In turn, as European capital markets mature, this should reduce the cost of capital for European companies, liberating them from dependence on banks and making acquisitions easier to finance. Fiat, for example, will not be forced to rely on banks as much because it can draw in international investors who once avoided its illiquid Italian lira bonds. Since the euro's arrival, Fiat has issued five billion euros worth of debt; in 1997, the last time it sold Italian lira bonds, the company issued the equivalent of only 200 million euros.[10]

As a general rule, the euro's potential for internationalization may be assessed in three ways: its use as a medium of exchange for Europe's trade with non-European countries; its role as a store of value for stocks and bonds on world capital markets; and its use in official FX reserves held by the world's central banks. By these yardsticks, the picture is mixed.

- *Role in world trade*—The United States accounts for only 14 percent of world trade, but the dollar is used to invoice close to 50 percent of the world's exports. Clearly, there is room for the euro to play a much bigger role in world trade. Countries with close economic and financial links to the "eurozone," like those in central and eastern Europe as well as some former colonies in Africa, may move toward the euro as an anchor currency. This would result in the emergence of a broader eurozone, encompassing countries well beyond the limits of the eleven-plus official members. (More countries are expected to adopt the euro, including even the United Kingdom eventually, although the public remains dubious in many of the potential member countries.)

- *Role on international capital markets*—Once again, the dollar still dominates international stock and bond markets. But the introduction of the euro clearly is playing a big role in broadening the depth, liquidity, and appeal of European capital markets. This could presage the evolution of the euro into a safe-haven currency over time, as investors assess the strength and stability of the euro as well as the credibility of the European Central Bank.

- *Role in official reserves*—The dollar accounts for 57 percent of global FX reserves, and as noted, central banks have been loath to trade in their dollars for euros thus far. Given the initial weakness of the euro and lingering doubts about the long-term viability of European monetary integration, it seems unlikely that the euro will challenge the dollar as a reserve currency in the foreseeable future.[11]

What's Being Traded: The Yen

In many ways, the yen's trajectory over the decade is much more inexplicable than that of the European currencies. Indeed, the yen largely failed to follow its economy downward during the 1990s (Figure 4.5). Despite a largely unbroken stream of dismal news about the Japanese economy and financial system, the yen more or less maintained its value, even making a surge in late 1998 that confounded the analysts and broke the backs of some of the world's biggest hedge funds. Once again, these trends underline the increasing distance between traditional economic analysis and modern currency market developments.

With regard to its share of FX trading, though, the yen stood still. Yen/dollar trading accounted for 20 percent of total turnover in 2001, compared to 18 percent in 1998 and 20 percent to 21 percent in 1995 and 1992. The yen was involved on one side in 23 percent of all trades in 2001, little changed from its historical

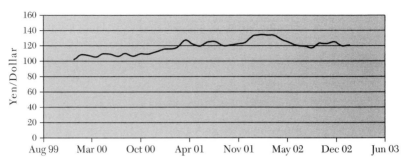

FIGURE 4.5 Yen/Dollar Exchange Rates
Source: Federal Reserve Board; www.federalreserve.gov/releases/h10/Hist/.

performance since 1989 (see Figures 4.2 and 4.3). The yen's lack of momentum in terms of market share probably reflected two offsetting factors: (1) continuing financial liberalization in Japan, which was largely neutralized by (2) the depressed economic and financial condition of the country.

At the same time, the Japanese mounted an intense campaign to promote the yen as an international currency for use in trade, investment, and FX reserves, especially in Asia. Efforts by Japanese officials to heighten the yen's role in Asia were not new, but they were visibly redoubled at the end of the decade, apparently in response to the decision by some Asian countries to end their currency pegs to the dollar following the 1997–1998 financial crisis. Keidanren, Japan's most powerful business organization, appealed to business and government officials in the region to use the yen more, arguing that "it contributes to the reduction of short-term risks, ... the strengthening of international competitiveness of Japanese banks, and the revitalization of Tokyo's financial and capital market."[12]

The campaign to foster internationalization of the yen, though, may prove an uphill battle. Even in Japan itself, only 36 percent of export trade and 22 percent of import trade are conducted in yen.[13] If the currency is the bottom line of the country, then the yen is in for a rough ride on the back of Japan's fundamental economic and financial weaknesses.

What's Being Traded: Exotics

A currency is usually considered "exotic" depending on:

- its liquidity (or lack thereof)
- whether it is quoted on a widely used service such as Reuters
- whether market-makers are needed to create a market (i.e., give a two-way price)

The increasing popularity of so-called Asian exotics markets means that, in fact, fewer and fewer currencies actually fit this description. In the heady days leading up to the 1997 Asian currency crash, it seemed that currencies like the Hong Kong dollar, Thai baht, Singapore dollar, Malaysian ringgit, and Indonesian rupiah were hardly exotic anymore.[14] (As Chapter 3 suggests, that comfortable belief probably played a key role in fomenting the crisis—unfortunately, the Thai baht does *not* behave like the Swiss franc—but much more on that later.)

At any rate, it is clear that liberalization and deregulation, founded on an increasingly unshakable belief in the efficacy of free markets, fostered an upsurge of activity for the lesser-used currencies of East Asia, Latin America, Eastern Europe, and even Africa. This was remarkably well-timed for the trading rooms of international banks, whose profitability was threatened by the decline in trading activity and increased efficiency in markets for the mature currencies of Western Europe and North America. According to one prominent bank economist, during the 1990s the mainstream currencies gradually lost their appeal for big banks in the FX market. He notes, "Big banks ... developed capabilities in exotic currencies to replace or boost revenue from foreign exchange where the increasing competition has made the bigger, more liquid currencies less profitable."[15]

Of course, the flip side of this is increased risk. The impressive efficiency of mainstream currency markets was reflected in tight spreads and disappearing profit opportunities, while the inefficiency of exotics markets became ever more alluring. Traders look for inconsistencies and mismatched prices in the market, signs of inefficiency that can signal a profit opportunity—and, increasingly, are available only in the exotics markets. As the governments of Latin America and Southeast Asia freed up their currency markets, the relative illiquidity of these markets required much higher levels of investment and commitment from the market participants. Spreads were wide, but the higher risk levels underlined by the high spreads demand an excellent support structure. After all, exotics are profitable only for the trader who understands the market better than the others; this requires a labor-intensive infrastructure with up-to-date information on FX controls, among other things.[16]

The fact is, however, that the data on exotics market activity fail to support the overheated rhetoric. Actually, trading in exotic currencies still accounts for a very small portion of total FX turnover. According to the BIS, trading in emerging market currencies comprised just 4.5 percent of total FX market turnover in 2001, compared to 3.1 percent in 1998. This underlines the basic fact that FX markets are still heavily dominated by the major currencies: the dollar/euro is the most traded currency pair, accounting for 30 percent of total turnover, followed by the dollar/yen at 20 percent of turnover and the dollar/pound at 11 percent. In other words, trading in the three main currency pairs accounts for close to two-thirds of total market activity.

Of course, trading in exotics clearly is edging up and is widely expected to play a greater role in FX trading as the mainstream markets get even older and stodgier. However, the Asian currency crisis of 1997–1998 was an unwelcome reminder of the riskiness (Figure 4.6) of emerging market currencies, especially since traders now understand how quickly liquidity can evaporate in these markets under difficult circumstances (but will they remember this lesson?). Remember, an emerging market is one you can't emerge from in an emergency. The events of 1997–1998 have at least slowed the momentum toward increased emphasis on exotics in the FX market.

Still, currency markets can thrive in some unexpected places. Speculation in the afghani, the much-battered currency of Afghanistan, is flourishing in the markets of

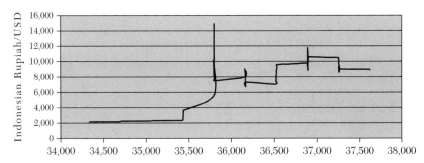

FIGURE 4.6a   Indonesian Rupiah/Dollar Exchange Rates
Source: www.oanda.com.

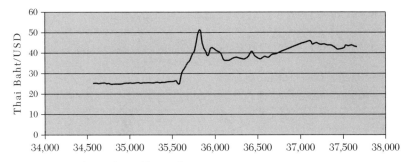

FIGURE 4.6b   Thai Baht/Dollar Exchange Rates
Source: Federal Reserve Board; www.federalreserve.gov/releases/h10/Hist.

central Asia. FX dealers reportedly reaped thousands of dollars in profits on the afghani upon the opposition/United States takeover of Kabul in 2001–2002. Apparently, intrepid currency traders in the region started gambling on an economic revival once the Taliban's end seemed inevitable. This is FX dealing at its most primitive:

> In the concrete courtyard at the center of an ancient four-story walkup [in Peshawar, Pakistan's Faiz Market], scores of Pakistani and Afghan traders throw themselves into a heaving mass of male bodies each morning, shoving their way to the center to call out their bids and positions. An incredible swirling motion sucks the sellers of afghanis into a whirlpool of buyers eager for the best price.[17]

Not a bad description of a London dealing room on a busy day, either!

Where, When They're Trading

Once again, the biggest story here is the lack of change: London, like the dollar, is still almighty. This is especially surprising (and dismaying) to the europhiles who had confidently predicted the decline and fall of London as a financial center due to the British refusal to enter the eurozone in 1999. According to the governor of the Bank of England, the City of London has not been disadvantaged by the United Kingdom's failure to enter the eurozone. He routinely dismisses suggestions that

London's position as Europe's leading financial center is at risk.[18] Surveys of overseas banks generally agree; bankers tend to believe that the euro is irrelevant to the City of London's position as Europe's preeminent financial center.

Lest they be biased, a glance at the BIS data is in order. According to the latest survey, the geographic distribution of FX trading indeed has changed little over the years (Figure 4.7). FX markets are still heavily concentrated in the United Kingdom, which commanded 31 percent of trading business in 2001, compared with 33 percent in 1998 and just under 30 percent in previous studies. The United States remains in second place with a 16 percent market share, also little changed from its historical performance, and Japan comes in third at 9.1 percent. (Japan's market share has declined sharply over the decade, from around 16 percent in 1989, probably reflecting the weakness and resulting consolidation of its financial institutions.) On the basis of the first few years of the euro's life, London has little to fear from other European financial centers in France, Switzerland, and Germany.

The overall decline in FX turnover, though, is bad news for the City of London. With FX volumes down more than 25 percent from their peak in 1998 and further contraction possible, this amounts to serious revenue losses in what has historically been one of the city's most important sources of income. The advent of the euro has cut out trading in "second tier" European currencies such as the Italian lira and Spanish peseta, which were bread-and-butter business for city traders. Overall, the contraction of the FX market is worrisome for the city, which earned huge sums from its FX trading business in the 1990s.[19]

As always, the FX market is nominally a 24/7 market. Trading moves through time zones around the globe, from Asia to Europe to North America and back to Asia again. No matter what the time of day or night, someone is trading the major currencies somewhere in the world—and the top traders sleep uneasily, primed to leap out of bed if their computers detect a sharp shift in markets halfway around the world.

However, the reality is that the most active time in the markets remains the New York morning, when traders in both London and New York are at their desks. With London and New York together accounting for nearly half of all FX turnover,

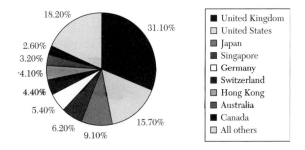

FIGURE 4.7   Where They're Trading
Source: Triennial Central Bank Survey of Foreign Exchange and Derivatives Market Activity 2001—Final Results, Bank of International Settlements at www.bis.org.

those few hours when they are both at work represent by far the deepest and most liquid market for FX.

How They're Trading

Technology has bred a near-revolution in the how of FX trading. As noted previously, electronic brokering has virtually taken over the market in the past ten years. Now the great majority of interbank trades are done via an electronic broker, with a corresponding decline in voice and direct dealing.

The rise of electronic brokering implies, in part, greater efficiency in the markets. The BIS explains:

> While market participants using traditional means of trading typically needed several transactions to obtain information on market prices, electronic brokers automatically provide traders with the best price available to them, depending on their and their counterparties' credit limits. As a result, foreign exchange dealers have tended to enter fewer transactions and turnover has declined. At the same time, the expansion of electronic brok[er]ing, which is more cost-effective than traditional means of brok[er]ing, has led to a substantial reduction in bid-ask spreads in the interbank market.[20]

Internet trading is the next frontier, but progress in this area has been surprisingly slow. In its 2001 report on the FX industry, *Euromoney* magazine notes: "The benefits of moving more business to online and other electronic systems would seem self-evident. By using electronic means to carry out the bulk of trading, operational efficiency should be greatly improved. Fully electronic systems offer a higher level of straight-through processing … reducing the possibility of error, a major headache when manual input is used." (Not to mention fraud.)

But in its next breath, the report acknowledges that "the application of online technology to foreign exchange trading has taken a surprisingly long time to get going."[21] Fear of the unknown is undoubtedly a factor, as is the traditional preference of FX traders for reach-out-and-touch-someone telephone contact with their counterparties. Systems under development will enable traders to hold these conversations—a valuable method of obtaining market information and of developing trusting relationships—over the Internet, perhaps dispelling some concerns. Nonetheless, it is clear that while electronic brokering has made major inroads into the FX markets, Internet trading has not. Recent reports indicate that in spring 2002, volume on two of the biggest Internet platforms for FX trading, FXall and Currenex, amounted to barely $2.5 billion per day, a tiny fraction of the total daily turnover on FX markets.[22]

Who Is Trading

As the march of technology and globalization continues, some dramatic changes in the line-up of FX market participants are well under way. In the 1970s and 1980s, FX market trading was dominated by commercial banks, central banks, and multinational corporations. These participants tend to be highly scrutinized, regulated, and sensitive to public opinion—making them, in general, a fairly stodgy bunch of folks. They remain key participants in FX markets. In the 1990s, however, a host of new players with serious muscle and attitude also invaded the markets. Led by huge investment funds including both pension funds and hedge funds (private investment pools for the wealthy, which borrow massive amounts of money to trade securities and currencies), the impact of these new players is still a topic of intense controversy. Hedge funds, in particular, are often managed very aggressively, and they have the capital and flexibility to take massive positions in expectations of currency swings.

Stung by some heavy losses in 1997–1998, for a time the giant "macro" hedge funds departed from the FX markets at the end of the 1990s. (The impact of the hedge funds on FX markets will be discussed extensively in the next section.) By 2001, though, the funds were back, helping to make the composition of FX market players appear very different in 2001 than it did in 1991.

Another factor, of course, is the trend toward consolidation within the banking industry, which considerably reduced the number of active trading rooms. Between the second quarter of 1997 and the first quarter of 1998 alone, the dollar value of mergers in the U.S. banking industry was an impressive $54 billion (the number of deals was 242). The impact of deregulation and international competitive pressures within the industry no doubt will foster more consolidation and concentration of banking business.[23]

The impact of banking consolidation on FX markets—liquidity, volatility, and profitability—remains uncertain. Some market observers fear that increased consolidation and the resulting smaller number of surviving participants could threaten market liquidity in times of stress. Others believe that the withdrawal of the smaller, weaker players will strengthen the market's ability to respond to stress. Moreover, it is not clear that size is a source of competitive advantage in banking as a whole. (Some studies suggest that the smaller to midsize banks tend to be more efficient and more profitable than the giants of the industry.) In the FX business, though, the biggest players take a disproportionately larger share of the market. Explains one top banker: "This is for the most part a generic high-volume, low-margin business. That it's high volume means it's easier for the big players; that it's low-margin makes it even more challenging for the niche players."[24]

At any rate, it is clear that the business of FX trading is becoming increasingly concentrated among a few key players. The BIS data reveal an overall decline in the number of banks reporting FX trading business, from 3,087 in 1998 to 2,772 in 2001. But these data overstate the level of liquidity and activity in the markets. In fact, the BIS observes that "… together with the expansion of electronic brokering, consolidation has led to a marked shrinkage in the number of banks that quote two-way prices on a wide range of currency pairs. There are currently not more than *twenty global players* [italics added] in foreign exchange markets that can provide such services, a noticeable decrease compared to the mid-1990s."[25]

For all practical purposes, then, FX trading is increasingly concentrated in a handful of huge players, in London and New York. The impact of banking industry consolidation, furthermore, was heightened by the effective withdrawal of macro hedge funds from the FX business at the end of the 1990s. The hedge funds had returned by 2001, though, and studies underline the steadily increasing role of asset managers in FX markets. According to the 2001 BIS survey, FX trading between banks and nonfinancial customers (mostly multinational corporations) has declined markedly since 1998, but the volume of FX trading between banks and financial customers jumped sharply (see Figure 4.8). Thus investment managers are increasingly taking a key role in FX trading, a point that will be considered later in the discussion of how FX markets are evolving.

Why They're Trading

The movements of FX rates remain an unsolved mystery. Why did the dollar appear so weak against the yen in the late 1990s but strong against the euro? Why is the Canadian dollar so anemic? Do economic fundamentals matter anymore? Why did the Thai baht collapse in mid-1997, instead of 1996 or 1998 (or never)? What on earth will happen to the Argentine peso? What makes traders buy the dollar at 11:45 in the morning and then turn around and frantically sell it by 11:50? In other words, what possesses FX markets?

The *Financial Times* commented on this in its 2000 survey of FX:

> The foreign exchange market is a capricious beast at the best of times. But the movements of the world's largest currencies have been particularly mystifying over the past year.
> Seldom has the divergence between economic fundamentals and the performance of currencies been so stark. Traditional currency analysis, based on economic growth, interest rates, and current account balances would, for example, have dictated a rising euro and a falling yen. In fact, the reverse has happened. ...[26]

The yen makes an instructive example. During much of 2001, the best bet for FX traders appeared to be selling the yen, which was clearly overvalued in any fundamental sense of the word at 122 yen/dollar. The Japanese economy was sinking under the weight of huge government debt, banks stuffed with nonperforming loans, and a steady loss of competitiveness in comparison with China and other Asian exporters. Fearful of getting the timing wrong, though, most traders held back.

They were intimidated, in part, by the specter of Julian Robertson and his powerful Tiger Management hedge fund. Robertson, one of the best known bears on

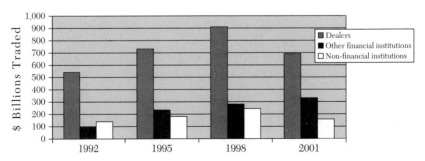

FIGURE 4.8   Who's Trading with Whom
Source: Triennial Central Bank Survey of Foreign Exchange and Derivatives Market Activity 2001—Final Results, Bank of International Settlements at www.bis.org.

Japan, sold the yen short in 1998—getting the fundamentals right but the timing very badly wrong when the yen surged unexpectedly.[27] (In two days of frenzied trading toward the end of October 1998, the dollar plunged against the yen, in open defiance of evidence that the U.S. economy was growing at a 3 percent-plus annual rate, while Japan was sinking back into recession.) Tiger wound up giving its partners their money back and shutting its doors, a frightening example indeed to traders expecting currency fluctuations to have at least a casual relationship to economic fundamentals. And Tiger was not alone: other hedge funds also bet heavily that the yen would reflect the economic downturn in Japan by sinking to 150 yen/dollar. But as the yen rose instead, hedge funds hastily liquidated their short yen positions, selling dollars to buy back the yen and thus driving the yen even higher.

The yen is but one example of how opaque and mysterious the world of currency traders can be. It does illustrate, though, the declining role of economic fundamentals in explaining currency movements, a theme that has run through this entire chapter. One market expert complains,

> Maybe it's our imagination, but it seems like currency analysis is becoming more difficult all the time. The old textbook rules of purchasing power parity (PPP), interest rate differentials, growth differentials and current accounts no longer offer a consistent explanation for currency movements. The dollar, in particular, has often moved contrary to these traditional rules.[28]

Market participants offer several explanations for the increasing tendency of FX trends to depart from economic trends. One is the tendency toward global economic policy convergence, which accelerated sharply during the 1990s. Major countries around the world were in broad agreement on key economic policy goals from the early part of the decade onward (European Monetary Union and the creation of the euro is the most obvious example of this tendency). Over the course of the decade, governments applied largely similar policies aimed at reducing inflation, curbing budget deficits, and aligning interest rates with world levels. This convergence of policies and goals, in turn, narrowed the differentials among countries and thus complicated the role of FX traders immensely.[29]

Perhaps more fundamentally, the "relevant explanatory variables" for FX markets have changed. J. P. Morgan's head of FX strategy explains, "In a world in which capital flows have taken over trade flows, purchasing power parity and current account benchmarks provide little help—input price differentials (relative labor costs, for instance) are a lot more relevant than output price differentials. ... Traditional variables have hence lost their predictive power."[30] The amounts traded in world FX markets are now around seventy times the level of world trade, underlining the dominance of capital flows over trade flows in explaining currency movements. Thus, FX analysis more and more requires analysis of capital flows, especially short-term flows, and the factors that underpin them—which may include traditional economic analysis but a host of other factors as well.

The past decade did serve to clarify at least one point: as FX markets become increasingly sophisticated, there is less and less opportunity for traders to profit from one-way, surefire bets against foolish governments. In the 1980s and early

1990s, traders gleefully rode roughshod over the policies of hapless governments, which were fighting in vain to defend their doomed currencies. French President Jacques Chirac bitterly denounced currency speculators as "the AIDS of the world economy," and he portrayed the international financial system as "an irrational casino, in which twenty-two-year-old traders are able to bankrupt economies."[31] Gregory Millman is even more picturesque:

> ... Like the vandals who conquered decadent Rome, the currency traders sweep away economic empires that have lost their power to resist. Time after time in country after country, when governments can't cope with the new financial realities, traders are the agents of creative destruction.[32]

Casino? Yes, certainly. Irrational? Sometimes, no doubt. But a plague on the world economy? In fact, currency speculators may act as policemen, punishing governments that enact foolish economic policies and rewarding those that act rationally and conservatively. (Seen in this light, currency markets are more efficient and rational than is commonly supposed.) Speculators attack only currencies that are vulnerable, usually because of high inflation, foreign borrowing, and/or balance of payments deficits. This perspective suggests that the newfound refusal of most governments to prop up shaky currencies through market intervention is positive, reflecting the understanding that healthy currencies and healthy economies are not vulnerable to speculative attack; the best way to support a currency is to promote a vibrant and open economy, not to waste billions of dollars in FX reserves to enrich the coffers of currency speculators. (This is related, of course, to the central question of whether currency crises are justified by economic fundamentals or are essentially the result of mindless herds of currency speculators converging on one hapless target. The analytical framework underpinning this is the ongoing debate about canonical theories versus second-generation theories[33] of currency crises, which is discussed in Chapter 3.)

On just one day, for example, July 30, 1993, the Bank of France reportedly spent 300 billion francs of its reserves in an attempt to keep the franc within its European Monetary System (EMS) limits. *Euromoney* further reports: "In the three months of June to September 1992, the Bank of England estimates that it used around $40 billion a month to defend sterling. Neither central bank succeeded. During the same period of 1992, Sweden spent $26 billion in six days trying to defend the krona, even raising interest rates to 500 percent overnight at one point, but to no avail. Finland lost all of its reserves within a few days in an attempt to support its currency; Norway gave up after two days with the loss of 46 percent of its reserves."[34]

Central bankers took note of these escapades and altered their policies accordingly. Thus, when Venezuela's President Hugo Chavez declared war on currency speculators in 2001, it was notable mostly as a vestige of the good old days. Apparently unaware of developments in the FX market over the past decade, Chavez announced that his government would investigate actions on the markets, on the grounds that it had details of a "conspiracy to destabilize the economy through promoting capital flight." His accusations were based on a sharp surge in demand for dollars, which in turn produced a sharp decline in FX reserves as the government sought to defend the currency. Chavez failed to consider, of course, investors' very real concerns about inflation and political risks in Venezuela—not to mention the 35 percent overvaluation of the bolivar.[35] (Venezuela under Chavez would ultimately be forced in late 2002 to impose capital controls aimed at stemming capital flight related to ongoing political turmoil.)

Chavez notwithstanding, for the most part the FX markets have moved way beyond the easy one-way bets against foolish governments that reaped so much in profits for traders in the early 1990s.

Instability and Irrationality

As the earlier comments on the yen reveal, fundamental currency misalignments and sudden, inexplicable shifts in currency values persist despite the sophistication of FX markets and traders. But mature and diversified economies like those of the United States and Japan can cope with the vagaries of currency markets. Emerging and transition economies, on the other hand, are sadly vulnerable. One observer notes,

> Over the past year and a half, vast swaths of the developing world have sunk into recession, dealing a crushing blow to the living standards of millions, as investors dumped the Thai baht, South Korean won, Indonesian rupiah, Russian ruble and Brazilian real. Meanwhile, some major currencies have undergone strange, violent movements—notably the exchange rate between the dollar and the yen, which went from 80 yen per dollar in the spring of 1995 to 147 last June and then back to 108 in January [1999].[36]

Strange and violent, indeed. Fed Chairman Alan Greenspan famously cautioned against "irrational exuberance" in regard to the U.S. stock market bubble of the 1990s, but the well-regulated New York Stock Exchange seems tame by comparison to FX markets. Moreover, economists' comfortable assumption that markets act rationally and efficiently (at least over the long term) is increasingly under attack. A study at the Massachusetts Institute of Technology/Boston University found that professional currency traders react to changing markets not just with their brains but with their entire bodies as well. Researchers monitored the vital signs of traders at work and found that their bodies reacted almost instantaneously to price swings in the market.

These findings add momentum to the notion that financial markets do not always behave rationally; they go through panicky sell-offs and dramatic spikes that cannot be easily explained—at least, not by reference to any rational basis.[37] Lending further credence to this point is the work of 2002's Nobel Prize winners in economics, Daniel Kahnemann of Princeton and Vernon Smith of George Mason University. Kahnemann and Smith found that people often do not behave as classical economic theory would suggest: they make seemingly irrational decisions, especially when faced with uncertainty (as in FX markets). Their research incorporates insights from the world of psychology and the world of economics, with interesting ramifications for understanding the seeming violence and irrationality of FX swings.

At any rate, the tendency of markets to overshoot, a byproduct of irrational exuberance, is well-documented but poorly understood, at least in the FX business. This is reflected in high levels of volatility. Economists might have expected that the success of both Western and emerging market governments in bringing down inflation by the 1990s would, in turn, result in lower volatility on FX markets. In some currency markets and at some times, volatility has indeed declined, reflecting in large part policy convergence among major economic powers. However, periods of calm and low volatility in FX markets alternate at sudden intervals with periods of sharp and inexplicable currency swings. Still-high volatility on FX markets is probably related in part to advances in technology and communications, which make it possible to disseminate new information instantly.[38] The use of computerized trading systems probably also contributes to volatility. The bottom line, though, is that FX markets remain volatile and unpredictable—a combustible mix at best.

► A BETTER MOUSETRAP?

If currency markets are irrational, unstable, unpredictable, and inexplicable, then hapless countries—especially those vulnerable countries in the early throes of creating a market economy—are indeed frighteningly vulnerable. To counter this vulnerability, a rash of new ideas sprang up during the 1990s (and some not-so-new ones were recycled).

Perhaps most important, though, was the demise (except, apparently, in Venezuela) of one old idea: the notion of a fixed currency peg. The debate between fixed and floating exchange rates is a familiar one to students of international economics. Supporters of fixed rates point out that by pegging its exchange rate to a stable peg, either gold or another currency, a country is forced to adopt conservative monetary and fiscal policies in order to maintain the peg. This is especially valuable for countries with a history of profligate spending or hyperinflation, like Argentina in the early 1990s. Also, a fixed rate can lend some credibility to the country's economic policies, reducing uncertainty and therefore encouraging foreign investment.

On the other hand, by pegging its currency a government loses its ability to fine-tune fiscal or monetary policy in line with domestic conditions or business cycles. Since a country cannot gain international market share for its exports via devaluation, the only way to eliminate an external deficit is to deflate the domestic economy, as Argentina learned to its sorrow in the mid-1990s. Export competitiveness can be almost impossible to maintain if the currency is pegged at a high level, thus dampening export growth and domestic employment. Finally, the exit strategy from a fixed exchange rate is often problematic. If a currency is pegged at an artificially high rate, eventually the pressures become so great that a currency crisis ensues—witness Argentina at the end of the decade.

Reflecting this view during the 1990s, the United States urged an end to IMF packages that were used to support pegged exchange rates, arguing that crises in Asia, Russia, Brazil, and, most recently, Argentina all stemmed from pegged exchange rates that proved unsustainable. Former Treasury Secretary Robert Rubin explained, "To paraphrase Winston Churchill's famous statement on democracy, the floating exchange rate system is the worst possible system, except for all others."[39] Most economists concurred, persuaded by the unmistakable evidence that governments are usually foolish to resist a floating exchange rate. Nobody knows precisely *why* markets overshoot, but by the end of the 1990s everyone understood that they *did*, especially when a pegged exchange rate was finally freed.

And so, with the funeral oration for fixed exchange rates etched in stone, the quest was on for a better way. In a burst of candor, former New York Fed president Gerald Corrigan expressed his frustration with the capricious nature of FX markets: "There's got to be a better mousetrap!" he exclaimed.[40]

New proposals for a better mousetrap range from dollarization to a currency stability pact joining the yen, euro, and dollar. All have a common denominator: they reflect "a growing unease about the impact of currency swings on the world's economic health, and they pique oft-asked questions: why doesn't somebody do something about the wild oscillations in foreign exchange markets? Can't we Euroize? Dollarize? Or at least stabilize?"[41]

Dollarization

Dollarization, of course, is the best known of these initiatives. It started as an intellectual but impractical idea and then unexpectedly gained acceptance as a serious policy option over the decade of the 1990s. In 2000, mired in crisis, Ecuador abolished its sucre and adopted the dollar; Guatemala and El Salvador followed its lead, and there has been serious talk of dollarization as a cure for Argentina's latest currency disaster. It is seen as a magic bullet against hyperinflation and currency instability, an instrument to automatically guarantee good macroeconomic management in a shaky economy.[42] (Most recently, Afghanistan has announced that it is considering dollarization, at least for a few years until it can adopt a new currency. Apparently, warlords who refused to recognize the Taliban government printed their own afghanis, so there are several versions of the national currency in circulation and the money supply is hopelessly corrupted.)

The Tobin Tax

Another old-but-new notion is the so-called Tobin tax, whose growing popularity in the 1990s astonished even its namesake, the late economist James Tobin. He first proposed the idea of a tax on currency speculation in a series of academic lectures at Princeton in 1971. It was largely ignored for years but was raised again as the subject of a scholarly symposium at the United Nations Development Program in 1995; since then, it has become a focus of reform and protest movements, especially in Europe among antiglobalization groups such as France's Attac (see Chapter 5). The appeal of the plan lies in its two-pronged approach: first, imposing a tax to discourage destabilizing currency speculation, and second, handing over the proceeds from the tax to an international body working on poverty alleviation. A study by the European Commission found that taxes ranging from 0.01 percent to 0.1 percent of the face value of the transaction would bring in $20 billion to $200 billion per year—vast sums, considering that official development finance totaled just $66 billion in 2000 (Figure 4.9).

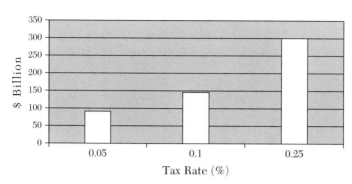

FIGURE 4.9   Tobin Tax Revenues at Different Tax Rates (Expected
Annual International Revenue)
Source: Bank of International Settlements.

Tobin originally viewed the tax as a way to help promote free trade, by assur-
ing countries that they could open their markets without exposing themselves to
disruptive currency speculation. He was dismayed to see his proposal appropriated
by antiglobalization activists, worrying that "the loudest applause is coming from
the wrong side."[43] He wrote, "More than thirty years after I first explored the idea
of a levy on cross-border currency speculation, the 'Tobin tax' is gaining popularity. In Europe, France's Lionel Jospin and Germany's Gerhard Schroder have both
expressed enthusiasm; so, too, have various critics of globalization." Tobin decried,
though, the "mistaken notion that it somehow would be a blow against the alleged
evils of globalization," adding this statement: "I am, like most economists, in favor
of free trade and I welcome developmental capital investment in poor countries,
both private and public. I regard the IMF and World Bank as essential institutions;
while critical of some of their policies and actions, I favor expanding their resources
and functions."[44]

Capital Controls

Tobin's dismay notwithstanding, critics of globalization have embraced his tax as a
potentially powerful weapon against the swath of destruction laid down by currency
traders. Another increasingly popular initiative is an old-fashioned return to capital
controls in order to deter destabilizing inflows and outflows of speculative capital.
Like the fixed exchange rate versus floating exchange rate debate, the controversy
over capital controls is not new. Advocates of capital controls argue that they reduce
a country's vulnerability to destabilizing swings in international capital flows, while
opponents warn that countries with strict capital controls will experience lower levels of incoming foreign investment. Calls for such controls reflect, in large part, public perceptions that global speculators (such as hedge funds) have a huge impact on
FX markets, having spurred massive shifts in the European Monetary System in
1992–1993 and having sowed catastrophe in Asian currency markets in 1997–1998.

It is undeniably true that countries with relatively high levels of capital controls (Malaysia, India, China) fared relatively well in the regional upheavals of 1997–1998. Malaysia's Prime Minister Mahathir has, in fact, led the charge against United States- and IMF-mandated freeing of currency markets. He accused "Soros and an unnamed conspiracy of financiers" of bringing down the Malaysian ringgit in 1997 and moved promptly to institute strict controls on capital flows to prevent further destabilizing speculation.

Virtually all mainstream economists decry the move to capital controls. They argue that liberalization of capital flows led to an unprecedented *inflow* of capital into developing countries during much of the 1990s, sparking an upsurge in growth and development. (And they are absolutely right. The problem, though, is that this argument sidesteps the uncomfortable truth that the bulk of this capital was concentrated in just a handful of countries—mostly those already thought to have good growth prospects, such as China, Brazil, and Mexico.) In any case, the Asian crisis did afford an opportunity to examine the effects of different policy responses, since only Malaysia instituted capital controls, while other Asian countries maintained their commitment to free markets.

On the face of it, Malaysia's policies were not disastrous. Much to the surprise (or dismay) of conventional economists, Malaysia regained its allure for foreign investors in a remarkably short time. The government reopened capital markets in 2001, responding to an upsurge in investor interest and a stable currency market. Thus the Malaysian experience seems to support, to some extent, renewed interest in capital controls to protect emerging market countries. However, the position of mainstream economists remains unequivocal: "Because they deny efficiency and equity, capital controls remain a policy instrument doomed to failure."[45] (Also, it should be noted that Malaysia had some other advantages—a track record of fiscal discipline, relatively prudent economic policies, and adequate FX reserves— that enhanced its chances of success.)

New Analytical Tools

Finally, the evidence of major shifts in the nature of FX market participants has sparked an upsurge of interest in new policy tools to help explain and predict the markets. As noted earlier, asset managers are playing an increasingly important role in FX trading. This suggests, in turn, that currency market analysts should pay more attention to these players. One reporter explains:

> … The refusal of currencies to obey textbook economics has helped bring new analytical tools to the fore—most notably the study of capital flows and market positioning.
>
> Advocates of these new approaches point to profound changes in the forces driving currency valuations. [First], the volume of cross border capital flows has ballooned—increasing the importance of investment decisions on the foreign exchange markets. …
>
> This has led to a change in the mind-set of the foreign exchange market, forcing analysts to contemplate issues which affect longer term investment decisions as well as traditional concerns over monetary policy and inflation. …[46]

As noted, the decreasing relevance of economic fundamentals as an explanatory variable in FX movements is clear. What is less clear, of course, is what should replace the traditional dependence on economic variables in constructing FX forecasting and trading models. For many years, traders have used "chartism" or "technical analysis," especially for predicting short-term market trends. These techniques "plot the historical movement of prices on charts and then attempt to find patterns which indicate changes in market trends or in the direction of price movements." According to one survey, by the beginning of the 1990s, around 90 percent of FX trading institutions used some form of charting or technical analysis in FX trading.

At the same time, many traders are uncomfortable with the lack of explanatory ability inherent in such models, as well as with their "apparent over-simplification of what is clearly a highly complex and dynamic process."[47] A vast literature of empirical work in the 1980s and 1990s examined the performance of technical trading models, with mixed results. Blake LeBaron observed:

> One of the biggest controversies between academic and applied finance is the usefulness of technical trading strategies. These rules, which intend to find patterns in past prices capable of giving some prediction of future price movements, are sold as easy ways to make money, and scoffed at as charlatans. However, evidence in foreign exchange markets has been much more favorable toward the usefulness of technical indicators.[48]

At the end of the decade, though, the performance of technical models was apparently less favorable. In 2000, LeBaron looked at "the performance of these strategies over the decade of the 1990s and [found] earlier claims to their performance to be somewhat exaggerated." Perhaps, he speculated, changes in the FX markets such as lower transactions costs, declining central bank intervention, and the availability of better information were disrupting the performance of the models.[49]

Moreover, since technical models essentially project past trading patterns into the future, the models are obviously unable to deal with major shocks to the market, which are likely to fundamentally alter such trading patterns. Traders often explain their use of these models in terms of the Keynesian beauty contest (the judges don't pick the contestant they think is prettiest; they vote for the one they think the other judges will choose). In this context, the use of technical models is largely defensive, allowing traders to anticipate likely moves by their counterparts. (One trader complained to the authors that technical models are intellectually repugnant. He sighed and then added that maybe that's why they work—FX markets are intellectually repugnant too.)

At any rate, disillusionment with technical models, plus the evident inability of economic fundamental-based models to predict currency movements, leaves traders in a quandary. Market participants are actively casting about for new approaches, mostly based on models that use predictions of capital flows to underpin FX predictions. Some of these approaches are promising, but there is a great deal of work to be done.

► HEDGE FUNDS: POLICEMEN OR THUGS?

The invasion of FX markets by huge hedge funds in the early 1990s and their partial withdrawal at the end of the decade was one of the most controversial stories of the decade. The role of hedge funds in FX markets—policemen or thugs?—is still hotly debated.

Hedge funds began to storm the FX markets in the 1980s but really burst into the public consciousness with the dramatic events on European markets of 1992–1993. Most important were the global macroeconomic hedge funds. These funds took a top-down approach to the markets, betting on big moves in a variety of instruments, including currencies. In mid-1992, financier George Soros became convinced that the British pound was seriously overvalued (despite the government's assurances to the contrary). Soros borrowed heavily to bet around $10 billion against the pound.

Then, in the weeks leading up to September 16 (which became known as Black Wednesday in Britain), Soros led an onslaught of currency speculators in selling the pound. In the end, Prime Minister John Major pulled the pound out of the European Monetary System, and it tumbled by 12 percent. Soros told one reporter, "We must have been the biggest single factor in the market in the days before the ERM [Exchange Rate Mechanism] fell apart." He made a cool $1 billion profit on the pound's collapse and probably even more in the ensuing turmoil that shook the ERM to its very core.[50] He was known within the British Isles as the man who mugged the Bank of England (which reportedly lost 12 *billion* pounds in its futile attempt to prop up the currency).

While Soros led the charge, other big speculators were not far behind. In that tumultuous year of 1992, other hedge funds and leading U.S. banks were big winners too in the "currency turmoil that toppled the pound sterling, the lira and other soft European currencies and humbled the central banks of Europe."[51] These powerful financial institutions, especially Citicorp, J. P. Morgan, Chemical, Bankers Trust, Chase Manhattan, and Bank of America, in the third quarter of 1992 netted around $800 million before tax in excess of their normal quarterly FX trading profits.

In fact, these traders were not rocket scientists. One observer says simply, "They bet on the inevitable."[52] They followed the most simple rule of the market: go short on weak currencies. A close look at Britain's economic fundamentals—and its political will (or lack thereof) to endure higher interest rates in order to defend the currency—made betting against the pound a pretty easy call. (So at least in this one celebrated example early in the decade, economic fundamentals *did* matter in FX markets.)

Unfortunately for the traders, as noted, central bank officials have wised up since then, and economic fundamentals are both less obvious and less important as predictors of FX movements. Most governments have abandoned the effort to defend fixed currency pegs, learning from the unfortunate British experience of 1992, and are leaving their currencies to the mercy of the markets. This has made it much more difficult for big traders—including the hedge funds—to make big profits.

Thus the big macro hedge funds made an ignominious exit from the FX markets at the end of the decade. They were stung, in particular, by big losses on the yen in 1998. One commentator explained in 2000: "Eighteen months ago, George Soros and his hedge funds inspired fear and loathing across much of the developing world. Earlier in the 1990s, he and others like him helped force sterling out of the European exchange rate mechanism and went on to play havoc with the Italian lira." Soros' 1998 experience with the yen—which was overvalued in any economic sense—underscores the pitfalls of relying on economic fundamentals to drive currency rates by the latter part of the decade.

But Soros, who "wielded considerable power in global markets," was on his way out.[53] He announced in spring 2000 his decision to withdraw from large-scale risk-taking, following the lead of Tiger Management's Julian Robertson. These decisions followed a disastrous period for the hedge funds, which had bet heavily on their expectation of a weaker yen. In the end, their actions helped push the yen *up*. In November 1998, the yen soared to its highest level in weeks against the dollar and an eight-month high against the German mark. "Traders said the yen was holstered by hedge funds and other large investment vehicles that scrambled to unwind long-standing carry trades," explained a reporter. Ironically, the main driving force behind the yen's surge was defensive action taken by the hedge funds seeking to close out their exposure to the yen: they purchased huge chunks of yen to offset their short positions.[54]

After being written off as a trading strategy following the disastrous 1998–1999 period, macro investing staged a cautious return to FX markets in 2001. The great macro traders—Caxton, Tudor Investment, Moore Capital, and Soros himself—all did well in 2001, partly because of global interest rate declines and partly because the yen finally staged a decline against the dollar. Caxton and Tudor, for example, racked up 20 percent to 40 percent gains in 2001.[55]

Some hope that the hedge funds will never return to large-scale currency betting. "What in fact Soros was doing was a form of gambling, rather than investing," grumbled James Grant, editor of *Grant's Interest Rate Observer*.[56] Emerging market countries that had been battered by speculation against their currencies were cheered, and pundits noted that the hedge funds' passing would be mourned by few.

Pundits (and Mahathir) notwithstanding, though, there may indeed be reason to hope that these players maintain a strong presence in FX markets. Contrary to conventional wisdom, the macro hedge funds and other huge market players are sometimes an important stabilizing, not destabilizing, factor in currency markets.

Unlike "technical" traders, who buy and sell FX based on advanced computer models and charts that use past patterns to give trading signals, the "macro" hedge funds take large bets based on their analysis of macroeconomic and financial conditions, including balance of payments, inflation, and real interest rates. As Soros himself noted, in their heyday the hedge funds served as policemen, enforcing the use of rational and conservative economic policies by governments around the world. When the hedge funds did help precipitate a devaluation, as in the pound sterling example, it was well deserved and long overdue according to economic fundamentals (an example of the canonical theory of currency crises). Officials knew that Soros and other speculators were watching closely; at the first sign that the government was backtracking on economic reform, the currency would become vulnerable to attack. Thus, in this regard, the macro hedge funds actually may promote good economic management; they are the conscience of financial markets. (This analysis assumes, of course, that over the long term economic fundamentals still matter in FX markets—as indeed they should. Even with the understanding that FX rates are largely driven by capital flows at this point, it still makes sense to assume that capital flows, in turn, are driven to at least some extent by expectations of future economic prospects in a country.)

The empirical evidence on hedge funds' role in currency markets is decidedly mixed but tends to support a more benign view of the funds than Mahathir suggests. A number of researchers have explored the question of hedge funds' ability to destabilize currency markets, first by examining the possibility that they "acquired a distinctive role as lead steers in the herding by investors that sometimes destabilizes these markets." If the hedge funds do play this "lead steer" role, then in fact their bets may become self-fulfilling; enough traders sell a currency to force a devaluation, whether it was originally warranted or not in terms of the fundamentals. This does seem to be a distinct possibility, especially since studies confirm that hedge fund managers are generally regarded as smart and fast. Accordingly, it seems possible that just a hint that the big funds are taking a position can encourage other investors, such as pension funds, insurance companies, and mutual funds, to follow suit—thus prompting the very currency shift that the hedge funds had expected.[57]

In fact, though, the empirical evidence on this ranges from inconclusive to negative. Some studies have found little evidence that other traders are guided by positions previously taken by hedge funds. When big market moves are underway, the data show that hedge funds "often act as contrarians, leaning against the wind, and therefore often serve as stabilizing speculators." Moreover, hedge funds can "be the first to take long positions (buying side) in currencies that have depreciated in the wake of a speculative attack, providing liquidity to illiquid markets and helping the currency establish a bottom." Finally, hedge funds appear to be much more flexible than other market participants and less inclined to buy/sell in the same direction as the market.[58]

On the other hand, some researchers have found that "... the presence of the large investor does make all other investors more aggressive in their selling." One study explored the view that "large traders [such as hedge funds] can exercise a disproportionate influence by fermenting and orchestrating attacks against weakened currency pegs." The famously acrimonious exchange between the financier George Soros and Dr. Mahathir, the prime minister of Malaysia at the height of the Asian crisis, illustrates the widespread belief that Soros led the pack in attacking the Asian currencies.

This study concludes that, indeed, "As a general rule, the presence of a large trader *does* increase the incidence of attack against a peg. The reason is not so much that the large trader's market power manufactures these crises, but rather that the presence of the larger trader makes the small traders more aggressive in their trading strategies."[59]

Translation: the big hedge funds may serve as catalyst and leader, but they do not *create* the crisis, which is generally founded in weak demand underpinning an artificially pegged currency.

Asian Financial Crisis, 1997–1998

What, then, of the 1997–1998 financial crisis? It was widely charged, both in the press and by irate governments, that hedge funds touched off the currency crisis that ravaged Southeast Asia and profited handsomely as a result. (See Chapter 3 for an in-depth discussion of this and other emerging market currency crises of the decade.) This view reflected the fear that hedge funds could act as "big elephants in small ponds," triggering crises that are not justified by economic fundamentals.

A 1998 study by the IMF, though, concluded that hedge funds had in fact not played a significant role in the early Asian market turbulence.[60] Other researchers have looked at the 1997–1998 conflagration, with largely similar findings. With regard to the Thai baht devaluation that started the whole mess, for example, it is impossible to precisely measure total hedge funds' forward sales of Thai baht leading up to the crisis (although they were probably large). But hedge funds were not *early* sellers of baht. The first sellers, in fact, were primarily domestic corporations, domestic banks, and international commercial and investment banks.

In fact, the spread of FX instability through other Asian countries apparently caught the hedge funds off guard. Again, the primary short sellers in the Indonesian, Malaysian, and Philippine currencies were money center commercial and investment banks and domestic investors—not hedge funds. Even more telling, there was a significant buildup of hedge fund positions in the Indonesian rupiah, but most of these were *long* positions taken after the currency's initial decline, reflecting the view of leading hedge fund managers that the rupiah had fallen too far and would soon recover.[61]

One research report concludes: "In sum, we find no empirical evidence to support the hypothesis that George Soros, or any other hedge fund manager, was responsible for the crisis." (Taking it even further, this report looks at other situations since 1993 when hedge funds took huge and correlated positions in currency markets, and it finds that on balance hedge funds did not "move" exchange rates.) The researchers observe that "the global markets can 'absorb' multibillion-dollar positions put on by major currency funds without suffering ill effects." In fact, they concur that to some extent the hedge funds actually played a stabilizing role in 1997–1998: they were big buyers of Malaysian ringgit in the summer and early fall of 1997.[62]

Thus the 1997–1998 story makes it "far from clear that hedge funds, on balance, do more harm in precipitating the fall of asset prices than they do good by helping break the free fall that can affect oversold markets, including markets for currencies."[63] Translation: hedge funds help stabilize currency markets.

▶ SEISMIC MARKET SHIFTS

The withdrawal of the macro hedge funds from large-scale currency speculation around the turn of the century underlined the most fundamental shifts in the nature of the FX market—shifts that are not entirely benign.

A review of the hedge funds' reason for their withdrawal reveals the following:

- First, the sheer size of the funds created some diseconomies of scale. The giant funds simply could not be flexible; they were big enough to make market news with even the most routine of activities. Soros' Quantum Fund, for example, was valued at more than $8 billion at its peak.

- Second, the huge profits that were easily found by making directional bets in markets where central banks chose to defend indefensible currency pegs were no longer available. Politicians in most countries, even among emerging market governments, had learned their lesson and abandoned foolish currency pegs. A reporter explains: "Shifts in policy and declines in trading volume have made it harder for hedge funds to exploit currency markets in the traditional manner. In the past, funds often made money by exploiting efforts by governments to maintain fixed exchange rates. But profits from such bets have fallen as governments have avoided placing themselves in the firing line."[64]

- Also, profits arising from arbitrage in inefficient markets were disappearing as well. The creation of the euro, for example, was all about enhancing market efficiency—bad news for traders who feast on market inefficiency. By the turn of the decade, the only seriously inefficient markets were in highly illiquid emerging market currencies, too risky even for the most aggressive fund managers.

- Finally, the "value-investing approach favored by the Soros and Tiger funds has been an unfashionably long-termist hard slog in a market obsessed by technology." FX trading is increasingly dominated by the technical traders who pay little or no attention to economics, politics, or finance; their bets are governed by the dictates of peculiar and mind-numbingly complex mathematical models based on historical trading patterns. Many of the hedge funds that remain active in FX markets now adopt a technical approach that emphasizes volatility and arbitrage trading, rather than the broad-based macro approach favored by Soros in the early days. Pioneered by hedge fund manager John Meriwether, whose JWM fund has succeeded the ill-fated Long-Term Capital Management, this approach employs sophisticated quantitative methods to develop trading programs that spot market patterns.[65]

The implications of this are mixed. Most obvious, the abandonment of fixed currency pegs and the improvement in market efficiency must be viewed with favor, regardless of the impact on currency traders.

More ominous, though, the takeover of the markets by technical traders suggests that illiberal and ill-managed regimes no longer have to live in fear of Soros and his friends, "so those exits are not all to the good." And perhaps most important, the giant hedge funds added both liquidity and a dollop of stabilizing speculation to the often-disordered currency markets. Their "newfound risk aversion is a bad thing for currency markets that are already short of stabilizing speculation."[66]

The partial return of the hedge funds to currency markets in 2001 thus may be viewed favorably, although the funds seem disinclined to take the huge and dramatic positions of recent years.

Trends to Watch

The peregrinations of the macro hedge funds and the takeover of FX trading by technicians armed with sophisticated computer models are just two pieces in the puzzle that will define the shape of FX markets in the future. Major realignment of currency markets and the players in those markets is well under way. It is not yet clear how these realignments will affect the markets, so many key questions remain open:

- Will volatility in FX markets remain high or decline as the markets become more efficient?

- Will Internet trading take off, or will traders remain glued to their telephones? If Internet trading does expand, what effect will this have on the markets?

- Will trading in "exotic" currencies become an important part of the markets, or will the mainstream currencies remain dominant?

- Will banks be able to profit in the increasingly concentrated and competitive currency markets? Will they have to take unacceptable risks in order to do so?

- Will macro-style trading ever return to currency markets in force, or will the markets be increasingly dominated by technical traders uninterested in the basics of economic fundamentals and capital flows?

In connection with the last question, observers wonder whether the loss of "policemen" like Soros and his cronies—who, for all their sins, understood markets and economics much better than the models ever can—will result in fundamental shifts on FX markets. Old-fashioned macro traders look for currency misalignments, based on fundamental economics, and place huge bets in anticipation of big swings. The new generation of hedge fund managers, by contrast, seeks out arbitrage opportunities in financial markets; the Soros/Robertson traditional approach of placing big directional bets in currency markets is passé for now. In the future, FX trading will be governed by the "state religion of speculators, which is technical analysis, or chart reading."[67] (Technical trading, by the way, is not restricted to the investment funds; commercial and investment bank traders too are increasingly reliant on models for their trading signals.)

The increasing reliance on technical analysis in FX markets has two key implications:

- Models generally cannot anticipate sudden and dramatic shifts in the market. Since the models are based on historical patterns of behavior, anything that generates a sharp deviation from historical patterns will be a shock to technical-based traders. (For proof of this, recall the travails of Long-Term Capital when the markets suddenly acted in a new and different way.) This raises the possibility of huge and unpredictable losses for traders caught unaware by a sudden shift in market patterns.

■ Moreover, the reliance of traders on technical models may also result in even more excessive overshooting than in the past. Recall the evidence that the macro hedge funds sometimes acted as contrarians, helping to buffer or slow currency collapses. Now, with everyone trading on the same models, the tendency for herd behavior is redoubled. Some observers fear, for example, that once the yen finally starts to lose value an orderly decline could fast turn into an avalanche triggered by massive computer-based sell orders.

Increasing reliance on technical models, when coupled with important changes in the line-up of FX market participants, may ultimately bring some unwelcome threats to market stability:

■ First, the possibility of a serious decline in market liquidity, especially in difficult times, is worrisome. FX market participants have complained for the past couple of years that liquidity has become erratic. According to one major dealer, liquidity is "becoming much less reliable. ... Sometimes the market can be remarkably deep and then without warning you can see this liquidity drain away. You can't predict where these areas of illiquidity are until you are in them." The erosion of liquidity reflects several underlying factors: the rise of electronic brokers, who match buyers and sellers but do not serve as market-makers to provide liquidity; banking industry consolidation; and, of course, the higher level of risk aversion among huge hedge funds at the close of the 1990s.

■ Second, the FX markets may prove more herd-like than ever, as trading business is increasingly concentrated among a few large players and the big macro hedge funds play a more cautious role. "With these often contrarian investors on the sidelines, the more herd-like real money investors have come to the fore. But with these herding investors tending to hit risk management limits together, their enhanced influence seems to be damaging liquidity" and threatening more sudden and dramatic currency swings.

■ Next, the markets may prove even more inexplicable than ever. This tendency stems from the growing influence of equities in currency trading, heightened by the growing influence of cross-border mergers and acquisitions: "Increasing M & A [mergers and acquisitions] flows have added to the inscrutability of currency movements, since their effect on currencies depends partly on whether the transaction is financed by cash or shares."[68] Lacking a crystal ball, who can foresee this?

■ At the same time, trading volumes will probably rebound in response to the same factors mentioned here. Once the fallout from the Russian and

Asian crises is fully absorbed and the euro finds its rightful place in the markets, the inexorable march of globalization and resulting rise in cross-border capital flows will almost certainly be reflected in renewed increases in turnover on FX markets. Increased trading volumes could mitigate to some extent the patches of illiquidity that the market will suffer. On the other hand, the larger and more unwieldy the market becomes, the less responsive it will be to government intervention—and the easier it will become for traders to destabilize currencies of smaller and vulnerable emerging market countries.

Interesting times, indeed!

▶ NOTES

1. Harri Ramcharran, "The Profitability from FX Trading Associated With Bank Acquisition: An Empirical Analysis of Large US Banks," *American Business Review*, Vol. 19, No. 2, July 2001.

2. "The World's Best Foreign Exchange Bank," *Euromoney*, July 2001, available at www.euromoney.com.

3. Bank for International Settlements (BIS) 71st Annual Report, 1 April 2000 to 31 March 2001 (Basel, Switzerland: Bank for International Settlements, June 2001). Available at www.bis.org.

4. Ibid.

5. Ibid.

6. Christopher Swann, "Euro Fails to Make Ground as Currency to Rival Dollar," *Financial Times*, October 20, 2001. The reasons for the high cost of trading in the euro are a matter of some debate. Traders' lack of experience and fear of a lack of liquidity in the relatively new currency certainly are a factor. In addition, some market participants charge that European banks have arbitrarily hiked transaction costs in trading the euro, perhaps in order to offset the lost profit opportunities from shrunken intra-European currency trading.

7. "Foreign Exchange 2000," *Financial Times Survey*, available at www.ft.com/surveys.

8. G. Thomas Sims and David Wessel, "The Euro: A Dismal Failure, A Ringing Success," *Wall Street Journal*, November 6, 2000.

9. Edward Luce, "Bonded to a Bright Future," *Financial Times*, June 14, 1999. Also see Michael R. Sesit, "Euro Secures Big Role in International Finance Despite Weakness Against the Dollar and Yen," *Wall Street Journal*, January 4, 2000.

10. G. Thomas Sims and David Wessel, op. cit.

11. Friedrich Wu, "The Arrival of the Euro and its Implications for Asia," *Thunderbird International Business Review*, Vol. 41 (6), November/December 1999.

12. Masayoshi Kanabayashi, "Tokyo Intensifies Push to Promote International Use of the Yen," *Wall Street Journal*, April 20, 2000.

13. Ibid.

14. Jozay Chan, "Exotic Currencies Move Into the Mainstream," *Corporate Finance*, September 1994.

15. Henry Harington, "Exotics Add a Touch of Spice," *The Banker*, Vol. 143, No. 809. 1993

16. Ibid.

17. Indira A. R. Lakshmanan, "Foreign Exchange Dealers Bet on Afghani Values Amid Rise, Fall of Fortunes of War," *The Boston Globe*, November 16, 2001.

18. Christopher Adams, "London 'thriving' outside euro," *Financial Times*, December 8, 1999.

19. Lea Paterson and Caroline Merrell, "Euro Hits Foreign Exchange Volumes," *The Times (London)*, June 12, 2001.

20. BIS 71st Annual Report.

21. Jonathan Brown, "Forex Ventures Beyond the Phone," *Euromoney*, May 2001.

22. Jonathan Fuerbringer, "U.S. Inquiry on E-Trading Shapes Business in 2 Markets," *The New York Times*, May 28, 2002.
23. Harri Ramcharran, op. cit.
24. Jennifer Morris, "Forex transformed by mergers," *Euromoney*, May 2001.
25. BIS 71st Annual Report.
26. Christopher Swann, op. cit.
27. John Dizard, "The Yen Bears Wait for the Moment," *Financial Times*, November 16, 2001.
28. Jeremy Fang, "The Case of the Contrarious Dollar," *The 2001 Guide to Foreign Exchange, Euromoney Research Guides*, September 2001.
29. Ibid.
30. Alfonso Prat-Gay, "Trading Currencies Around Prospective Shifts in Short-Run Capital Flows," *The 2001 Guide to Foreign Exchange*, September 2001.
31. "Finance: Trick or Treat?" *The Economist*, October 23, 1999.
32. Richard O'Brien, "Who Rules the World's Financial Markets?" *Harvard Business Review*, March–April 1995.
33. To economists, the analytical framework for understanding currency crises begins with the canonical model, which postulates that currency crises are founded in weak economic fundamentals—arising when a government's economic policies are inconsistent with supporting the currency at its current level. However, empirical evidence suggesting that currency crises struck even when apparently unjustified by such economic policy divergences led to the development of so-called second-generation models, which focus more on the role of speculators, contagion, and herd mentality in fomenting currency crises. See, for example, Paul Krugman's discussion of the issue at web.mit.edu/krugman/www/crises.html.
34. "Changes in the Foreign Exchange Market," *Euromoney Currency Forecasts*, September 1995.
35. Andy Webb-Vidal, "Chavez May Impose Controls on Forex Deals," *Financial Times*, May 11, 2001.
36. Paul Blustein, "Currencies in Crisis," *Washington Post Weekly*, March 1, 1999.
37. Gareth Cook, "The Biology of 'Irrational Exuberance,'" *The Boston Globe*, October 23, 2001.
38. "Changes in the Foreign Exchange Market."
39. Paul Blustein, op. cit.
40. Ibid.
41. Ibid.
42. Sebastian Edwards, "The False Promise of Dollarization," *Financial Times*, May 11, 2001.
43. Marti Wolf, "Misplaced Hopes in Tobin's Tax," *Financial Times*, March 20, 2002.
44. James Tobin, "An Idea that Gained Currency but Lost Clarity," *Financial Times*, September 11, 2001.
45. Christopher A. Hartwell, "The Case Against Capital Controls: Financial Flows, Crises, and the Flip Side of the Free Trade Argument," *Policy Analysis*, No. 403, June 14, 2001.
46. Christopher Swann, "Mystifying Moves Test Economists," *Financial Times*, FT Survey Foreign Exchange 2000, available at www.ft.com/surveys.
47. "Changes in the Foreign Exchange Market."
48. Blake LeBaron, "Technical Trading Profitability and Foreign Exchange Intervention," *Journal of International Economics,* No. 49, 1999, pp. 125–143.
49. Blake LeBaron, "Technical Trading Profitability in Foreign Exchange Markets in the 1990s," July 2000, Preliminary paper, available at www.brandeis.edu/~blebaron.
50. "Big Winner From Plunge in Pound," *The New York Times*, October 27, 1992.
51. Thomas Jaffe and Dyan Machan, "How the Market Overwhelmed the Central Banks," *Forbes*, October 9, 1992.
52. Ibid.
53. "Hedge Funds and Paper Tigers," editorial, *Financial Times*, May 3, 2000.
54. Sheel Kehli, "Yen Rallies Against Dollar, Mark," *South China Morning Post*, November 3, 1998.
55. Robert Clow, "Glory Days for the World's Largest Hedge Fund Group," *Financial Times*, March 20, 2002.

56. Joshua Chaffin and Gary Silverman, "Sinking Fortunes," *Financial Times*, May 5, 2000.

57. Barry Eichengreen and Donald Mathieson, "Hedge Funds: What Do We Really Know?" *International Monetary Fund, Economic Issues*, No. 19, September 1999, available at www.imf.org.

58. Ibid.

59. Giancarlo Corsetti, Amil Dasgupta, Stephen Morris, and Hyun Song Shin, "Does One Soros Make a Difference? A Theory of Currency Crises With Large and Small Traders," Cowles Foundation Discussion Paper 1273, available at www.econ.yale.edu/~corsetti/soros.

60. Giancarlo Corsetti, Paolo Pesenti, and Nouriel Roubini, "The Role of Large Players in Currency Crises," National Bureau of Economic Research, April 2001.

61. Barry Eichengreen and Donald Mathieson, op. cit.

62. Stephen J. Brown, William N. Goetzmann, and James Park, "Hedge Funds and the Asian Currency Crisis of 1997," National Bureau of Economic Research Working Paper No. 6427, February 1998.

63. Eigengreen and Mathieson, op. cit.

64. Joshua Chaffin and Gary Silverman, op. cit.

65. Ibid.

66. "Hedge Funds and Paper Tigers," editorial, op. cit.

67. John Dizard, op. cit.

68. "Foreign Exchange 2000," *FT Survey*, available at www.ft.com/surveys.

CHAPTER 5

RETURN OF THE NEO-LUDDITES: GLOBALIZATION AND ANTIGLOBALIZATION

"Ireland heads world index of globalization" ... "Simple, if radical agendas lead thousands to protest" ... "Challenging the dogmas of free trade" ... "Davos man takes to the streets of New York" ... "Protesters and police using Internet" ... "Competitiveness and compassion" ... "Anti-globalization warriors shift their ground" ... "Globalization's Chernobyl" ... "Globalization has survived the terrorist attacks" ... "Globalization under fire" ... "In a global tide, beware the undertow" ... "After Genoa" ...

Sporting clown wigs and black masks, they descended on New York for yet another round of antiglobalization protests at the World Economic Forum in February 2002—a motley crew of neo-Luddites squaring off against the Armani-clad businessmen and economists on their way to cocktails at the Waldorf. The Raging Grannies debuted their new anthem, to the tune of "There's No Business Like Show Business":

There's no business like war business,
The worst business we know.
Never mind the homeless and the hungry.
Never mind the people without jobs.
Nowhere can you get that special feeling,
Than when you're piling up the bombs ...

New Yorkers cringed, editorial writers were patronizing, and economists were openly contemptuous. After all, by the last few years of the decade the antiglobalization demonstrations were a standard feature of all major international meetings among the institutions of the globalist mainstream: the International Monetary Fund (IMF), World Bank, World Trade Organization (WTO), and Group of Seven leading industrial countries (G7). The protesters were widely derided as clowns and buffoons (a "traveling circus of anarchists," according to Tony Blair). No doubt the antics of the more radical fringe of Starbucks-smashing rioters reinforced the perception that criticism of globalization was akin to anarchism. Indeed, the newly risen army of malcontents seemed to have their own uniform of blue jeans, disheveled shirts, and torn jackets. Global chic was out; antiglobal grunge was in.

In simultaneous counterpoint to the World Economic Forum, some fifty thousand antiglobalization activists were meeting in Porto Alegre, Brazil, for the World Social Forum—part carnival, part street festival, part economics tutorial. The World Social Forum featured a feminist dance group reinterpreting Harry Belafonte with politically correct lyrics, as well as an elf on stilts handing out wild flower petals and a pop-up drawing of the earth in harmony.

And yet, their central notion—that "another world is possible"—is not funny at all. The goal of the meeting, to develop an alternative agenda to that of the World Economic Forum, is attracting some serious thought and attention. Or at least parts of it are.

Still, the two simultaneous but diametrically different sets of meetings illustrate the crystallization of two points of view in the 1990s: the globalists, represented by the IMF, World Bank, WTO, and pretty much every legitimate government around the globe; and the antiglobalists, represented by an extremely odd set of bedfellows ranging from intellectuals to environmentalists to steelworkers (but also, as we will see, commanding a significant degree of popular support).

▶ A DECADE OF GLOBALIZATION

Globalization is nothing new; countries have been drawing ever closer for hundreds of years, as the world grows ever smaller. (Indeed, the entirety of global economic development can be observed through the lens of growing interconnectedness, evolving from merchants trading between city-states on foot and then by caravans, to roads, sailboats, trains, transoceanic ships, and eventually aircraft.) Considering how much contention has swirled around this term for the past few years, it is surprisingly easy to define. According to the World Bank, globalization is "the growing integration of economies and societies around the world." Essentially, globalization is a multifaceted process by which the world comes closer together. The term is most commonly associated with economic and financial integration— think Citibank or McDonald's—but in fact has social, political, environmental, cultural, and even religious dimensions as well.

Definitions aside, in reality globalization means different things to different people. To economists, it refers to greater economic integration between nations: massive trade flows, investment capital pumping throughout various financial systems, worldwide corporations spanning the globe. (Coca-Cola, for example, is nominally an American company but in fact earns less than 30 percent of its profits from its "home" country. Coke's biggest market is Mexico, where people drink more than one serving per day on average; Figure 5.1.) For people in their everyday lives, it means that they

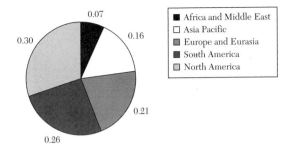

0.07

0.30

0.16

0.21

0.26

- ■ Africa and Middle East
- □ Asia Pacific
- ▣ Europe and Eurasia
- ■ South America
- □ North America

FIGURE 5.1   Coca-Cola's Worldwide Sales
Source: Financial Times, "Coca-Colonisation Covers 200 Countries,"
June 26, 2001.

are more likely to consume products from other countries, invest in other countries, send their children to school in other countries, travel to other countries, know something about other countries, and even talk on the phone to friends in other countries.

Globalization has been a fact of life for hundreds of years. In fact, the fast-paced integration of world economies that marked the 1990s was not unprecedented; similar trends occurred in the late nineteenth and early twentieth centuries. The globalization of the 1990s was distinguished from the past, though, by the sheer speed of advances in communications, market liberalization, and global integration of goods and services. Evidence of globalization is unmistakable; according to Morgan Stanley, global trade soared to a record 26 percent of world gross domestic product (GDP) in 2000, up from 18 percent a decade earlier. Since 1990, the volume of world exports has roughly doubled, and cross-border investments have more than quadrupled.

In fact, the process of globalization has been accelerating since World War II. As the pace of globalization has intensified, the past fifty years have also been a period of spectacular economic growth in many countries around the world. Ireland, for example, is considered the world's most globalized economy according to a new index published in 2002; it boasts the most open economy in the world. Not coincidentally, Ireland is also considered Europe's "tiger" economy, the fastest growing country in the region during the 1990s. The confluence of fast-paced globalization and fast-paced growth obviously suggests a strong correlation between the two. Another report, the Heritage/*Wall Street Journal* Index of Economic Freedom, is even more suggestive (Table 5.1). Even the most cursory glance at this index reveals the high correlation between economic freedom and prosperity. The countries with the highest degree of economic freedom (as measured by trade, fiscal burden, government intervention, monetary policy, foreign investment, banking/finance, wages/prices, and property rights) tend to rank among the world's wealthiest. By contrast, with the exception of oil producers, the countries with the least economic freedom also tend to be the poorest.

At the same time, many of the world's poorest countries, especially in Africa (where a majority of the world's remaining dictatorships still thrive), have seen little

TABLE 5.1 2002 Index of Economic Freedom

Overall Rank (the Top)	Country	Overall Rank (the Bottom)	Country
1	Hong Kong	140	Bosnia/Herzegovina,
2	Singapore		Equatorial Guinea
3	New Zealand	142	Suriname, Yugoslavia
4	Estonia, Ireland,		(Federal Republic)
	Luxembourg,	145	Burma, Syria
	The Netherlands,	147	Zimbabwe
	United States	148	Belarus, Uzbekistan
9	Australia	150	Turkmenistan
12	Denmark,	151	Iran, Laos
	Switzerland	153	Cuba, Libya
14	Finland	155	Iraq, North Korea
15	Bahrain, Canada		

Source: The Heritage Foundation/*Wall Street Journal* Index of Economic Freedom, available at www.heritage.org/index/indexoffreedom.

to no benefit at all. In essence, this defines the debate over globalization. Is it a force for good or evil? Does it promote economic progress for all, or an ever-sharper division between the haves and have-nots? As *Financial Times* commentator Martin Wolf notes, "This globalizing process is not a new one. Over the past five centuries, technological change has progressively reduced the barriers to international integration. … The question that remains, however, is whether today's form of globalization is likely to have a different impact from that of the past."[1]

Thus, the acceleration of globalization in the 1990s was accompanied by an extraordinary division of views on the topic, expressed both in scholarly reviews and on the streets of Genoa, Seattle, and Washington, D.C.

▶ THE GLOBALISTS

Globalization has become the mantra of major power players around the world. It is espoused by every major financial institution on the planet: the World Bank, IMF, WTO, central banks of industrial countries, and commercial and investment banks worldwide. It must also enjoy a substantial level of popular support, considering that most democratically elected governments are enthusiastic globalists; certainly the U.S. consumer is a great fan of globalization. The euro, a new currency replacing the centuries-old currencies of eleven European countries, serves as a dramatic physical representation of the process. As Harvard's Dani Rodrik observes, there is now "a remarkable consensus on the imperative of global economic integration." Openness to trade and investment, he adds, is now viewed as "the most potent catalyst for economic growth known to humanity."[2]

IRELAND: FROM TIGER TO PUSSYCAT?

Today it is all but forgotten that Ireland used to be one of the economic backwaters of Western Europe, characterized by high levels of unemployment, low per capita income in comparison with other Western and Northern European countries, and poor performance in terms of trade. For a long time, Ireland actually exported highly educated workers, as there were no job opportunities at home.

During the 1990s, though, globalization and clever policies targeted to capitalize on the changing world sparked strong and broad-based growth in the once-sleepy economy. The country enjoyed a steady decline in unemployment, coupled with remarkable inflows of foreign investment. Ireland's most severe and deeply embedded problems—high unemployment and emigration—were eradicated in the 1990s, to the point that the outward flow of workers actually reversed and immigration levels soared. As Dublin-based economist Paul Sweeney noted, "For the first time ... there has been a substantial growth in the number of new jobs, averaging more than 1,100 a week, each year between 1994 and 2000. This compares to a decline in total employment in the 1980s. Between 1986 and 2000, 513,000 new jobs were created—an increase of 47 percent—a remarkable achievement."* Even the Organization for Economic Cooperation and Development (OECD) joined in the praise: "It is astonishing that a nation could have moved all the way from the back of the pack to a leading nation within such a short period, not much more than a decade in fact."

To what did Ireland owe its success? In large part the answer is globalization: Ireland enjoyed two competitive advantages that allowed it to ride the latest wave of globalization: a highly educated, English-speaking workforce and a government with some degree of institutional flexibility, which enabled it to pioneer tax-free zones, duty-free shopping, and zero tax on export profits.

* Paul Sweeney, *The Celtic Tiger: Ireland's Continuing Economic Miracle* (Dublin, Ireland: Ode Tree Press, 1999), p. 3.

(Continued)

The doctrine of globalization is largely enshrined in the so-called "Washington consensus," a phrase coined by economist John Williamson in 1989 to describe a widely accepted set of policies urging:

- measures to improve trade and investment flows
- a new economic orthodoxy, including:
  - fiscal discipline
  - removal of subsidies
  - tax reform
  - liberalized financial systems
  - competitive exchange rates
  - privatization of state industries
  - deregulation
  - measures to secure property rights

IRELAND: FROM TIGER TO PUSSYCAT? *(CONTINUED)*

However, by the dawn of the twenty-first century, Ireland was something of a poster child for the darker side of globalization, much as it had highlighted the glories of globalization for much of the previous decade. Ireland's high level of integration into the world economy and its heavy dependence on foreign investment left it vulnerable to:

- the worldwide high-tech meltdown, which "helped cut growth to a fraction of its peak in the 1990s and stripped away thousands of jobs"

- the growing competition for foreign investment inflows from lower-cost, fast-globalizing countries in eastern Europe

These developments left many questioning Ireland's fundamental strategy. Said one local official, "Eastern Europe at the moment is the cheapest option, and all those countries will come into the European Union. The multinationals will get ten or twelve years there and make their profit and then move on, just like they did here. There's no loyalty in all this."[2]

Despite that sentiment, Ireland is a far richer society now than it was before it adopted a strategy of globalization. Even though unemployment has gone up from its historical low of 3.9 percent in 2001, it is well below historical averages. Unemployment of 4 percent to 5 percent (expected in the 2003–2005 period) is far better than the average of 14.3 percent unemployment during the 1986–1997 period. In addition, real GDP growth in 2002 was down to 3.6 percent, but it was still by far one of the fastest rates of growth in the European Union and the OECD.

[2] Alan Cowell, "Ireland, Once a Celtic Tiger, Slackens Its Stride," *The New York Times*, February 19, 2003.

(Williamson's phrase, in fact, referred largely to the policy advice being given by Washington-based institutions to Latin American countries struggling with a massive debt overhang. In later years, Williamson himself became concerned that the phrase could be misinterpreted as implying that the liberalizing economic measures undertaken by developing countries in the past two decades were imported from Washington-based institutions. Rather, he meant to underline the process of intellectual convergence that had emerged to support these policies.)

The central question for economists is the impact of economic integration on developing countries and the poor: Does globalization accentuate or reduce poverty? In a much-quoted article in *Foreign Affairs*, Jay Mazur asserted: "Globalization has dramatically increased inequality between and within nations." There is no doubt that the world economy has become much more globally integrated—and much more unequal—over the past two centuries. "If correlation meant causation, these facts would imply that globalization has raised inequality between nations," explains another commentator. In fact, though, mainstream economists argue that globalization has probably *mitigated* rising inequality among nations.[3] The World Bank sums up its view with three key findings:

- *Successful integration* into the world economy generally supports poverty reduction. Poor countries containing about three billion people, such as China, India, Bangladesh, and Vietnam, have broken into world markets for goods and services over the past twenty years. These new globalizers have experienced a substantial decline in poverty during the same time period; during the 1990s, the number of poor people in these countries declined by 120 million.

- *Inclusion,* though, is an issue. Within countries that have broken into global markets, integration has *not* generally produced a higher level of income inequality. However, a less welcome trend is the plight of countries containing two billion people that are in grave danger of becoming hopelessly marginalized from the world economy. Income in these countries has declined, poverty has risen, and participation in world trade is lower than it was twenty years ago. Some failed nations, mostly in Africa, or countries stymied by geography or disease are thoroughly sidelined from the globalization process. Clearly, there are winners and losers in this process. Even within the globalized countries, owners of firms and workers in formerly protected sectors lose from liberalization.

- *Standardization or homogenization* is also a serious concern. Opinion polls in many countries reveal high levels of anxiety that economic integration will lead to cultural homogeneity. Reality tends to belie these fears; highly globalized countries such as Japan, the United States, and France retain highly individual cultures and identities. (The World Bank comments: "Diversity may be more robust than is popularly imagined.") Nonetheless, fears of cultural domination—especially by the United States—are underlined by the proliferation of Starbucks, McDonald's, and Citibanks on High Streets around the world.

The World Bank concludes that globalization generally reduces poverty. Globalized economies tend to grow faster, and this growth is usually widely diffused, with a salutary effect on income distribution as well. Many countries have experienced rapid declines in poverty as they integrated into the world economy (Figure 5.2). While economists are cautious about leaping from correlation to causality, the potential for global integration to alleviate poverty is well illustrated by the examples of China, India, and Vietnam.[4]

Thus, globalists urge developing countries to implement policies of economic and financial integration because they offer the best chance of success. Mainstream economists believe that the best evidence demonstrates that the current wave of globalization, beginning around 1980, has promoted economic equality and reduced poverty around the world. Much empirical work supports the contention that there is a strong correlation between higher rates of participation in international trade and investment and higher rates of growth.

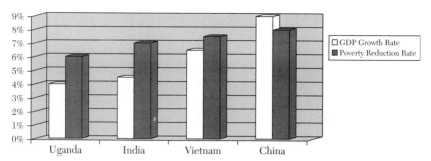

FIGURE 5.2 Poverty Reduction and GDP Growth (Annual Percentages, 1992–1998)
Source: World Bank; www.econ.worldbank.org/files.

The most widely circulated and widely respected study in this area, by David Dollar and Aart Kraay, divides the developing world into a "globalizing" group of countries that embraced rapid growth in trade and investment and a "nonglobalizing" group of countries that did not. Dollar and Kraay's results are impressive: annual per capita GDP growth for the globalizing group accelerated steadily from 1.4 percent in the 1960s to 5.0 percent in the 1990s, while growth rates for the nonglobalizers actually declined to only 1.4 percent per annum by the 1990s (Figure 5.3). The study further suggests that globalization has not increased income inequality within countries either. Inequality has risen in some countries, such as China, but this is due to other factors (education, taxes, domestic social policy) rather than globalization. In general, the study finds, higher growth rates in globalizing countries produce higher incomes, even for the poor.

Dollar and Kraay conclude:

> The integration of the world economy over the past twenty years has been dramatic. The experiences of the post-1980 globalizers show that the process can have great benefits, contributing to rising incomes and falling poverty and enabling some of the poorest countries in the world to catch up with richer countries. The real losers from globalization are those developing countries that have not been able to seize the opportunities to participate in this process.[5]

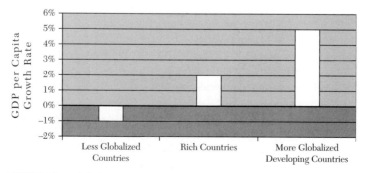

FIGURE 5.3 Globalizers versus Nonglobalizers in the 1990s
Source: World Bank.

Other empirical work also supports the notion that global capitalism benefits all participants. World Bank studies indicate that openness to free trade benefits the poor as well as the rich in emerging market countries. In fact, the very poorest countries and people are suffering from too little globalization, not too much. Economist Pierre-Richard Agenur, for example, set out to examine empirically the extent to which globalization affects the poor in low- and middle-income countries. He found that at very low levels, globalization may hurt the poor, but beyond a certain threshold it seems to reduce poverty, possibly because it brings renewed impetus for reform. Thus, he concludes that globalization may hurt the poor—not because it goes too far, but because it has not gone far enough.[6]

Other studies concur, finding no particular correlation between openness to trade and inequality. While these averages do gloss over some serious problems, such as pockets of deep and intractable unemployment,[7] overall the results are impressive. Perhaps most dramatic is the work of economist Surjit Bhalla, who finds even the World Bank too negative on globalization. According to his calculations, the percentage of persons living in poverty in 1985–2000 declined at a much faster pace than at any time in world history, from 37.4 percent of the world population to just 13.1 percent (this is well below the World Bank's estimate of 23 percent in 1999). Bhalla also takes issue with the World Bank's finding that during the golden age of globalization, 1980–2000, there was a large increase in income inequality; he finds that inequality actually fell to its lowest level in fifty years. Bhalla reports: "We are also told by the World Bank that ... poor countries have grown at a slower pace than rich countries. I reach the opposite conclusion. As a group, poor countries have grown more quickly. ... The globalization period has been the golden age of development."[8]

For countries with the right skill sets, the necessary degree of social organization, and flexible political institutions, then, globalization is the opportunity of a lifetime. An IMF spokesman sums up: "There are no doubt winners and losers in globalization. But we still think that global economic integration offers the best route to lift the poor out of poverty."[9]

Take China, for instance. A huge beneficiary of globalization, China enjoyed annual growth rates of 8 percent to 10 percent in the 1990s precisely because it can make products that are used globally.

▶ THE ANTIGLOBALIZERS

But the example of China illustrates the other side of the coin as well. China is a clear winner for a number of rather idiosyncratic reasons, including geography, politics, and history. (Also, its policies are not exactly in line with those suggested by the Washington consensus; moreover, the same could be said of the Asian tigers in general, especially when compared to much of Africa and Latin America.) For millions and millions of people without the skills to compete in an open world economy, like those living in the chaotic social environments of central Africa, for example, the globalization process may actually accelerate declines that were already under way. The widening gap between winners and losers underscores the

THE ANTIGLOBALIZATION ARGUMENT

Labor leader Jay Mazur published an influential (and surprisingly compelling) article in *Foreign Affairs* in early 2000 that essentially laid out the best arguments that
the antiglobalists can marshal. His central point:

> Globalization has reached a turning point. The future is a contested tension
> of very public choices that will shape the world economy of the twenty-first
> century. The forces behind global economic change—which exalt deregula-
> tion, cater to corporations, undermine social structures, and ignore popular
> concerns—cannot be sustained. Globalization is leaving perilous instability
> and rising inequality in its wake. It is hurting too many, and helping too few.

Mazur supports his arguments by reference, in part, to research done by the
United Nations (UN) and World Bank. He cites, for example, a UN report showing
that globalization has been associated with a sharp increase in inequality, both within
and among nations. Incredibly, the assets of the richest two hundred people in the
world now exceed the combined income of the two billion-plus people at the bottom
of the economic food chain. He further notes that the benefits of the global economy
are reaped disproportionately by the handful of countries and companies that "set the
rules and shape the markets." Some 80 percent of foreign direct investment into developing and transition economies in the 1990s, for instance, went to just twenty countries, and much of it went to China. Most damning, the most recent wave of global
trade and investment has not produced uniform growth. In fact, eighty countries have
lower per capita incomes now than they did a decade ago.

Also, Mazur points out the ancillary damage done even when globalization seems
to work. As the former chief economist of the World Bank, Joseph Stiglitz, notes, the
deregulated global economy has fostered a "boom in busts"—financial crises of
increasing depth and regularity that have a devastating effect on poor and working
families. (Stiglitz further notes that the Washington consensus on globalization does
not take into account the damage done by globalization's byproducts, such as environmental damage, child labor abuses, and the hazardous workplace.)

At the very least, Mazur's arguments cannot be dismissed as those of a fool or
anarchist. It is clear that the data are less conclusive than the globalists would suggest and that an intelligent and serious argument can be made by the other side.

Source: Jay Mazur, "Labor's New Internationalism," *Foreign Affairs*, January/February 2000.

basic argument of the antiglobalists: globalization enriches a few and worsens the
misery of many, many more.

Who Are They?

The public face of the antiglobalization movement is unfortunate. When most people think of the antiglobalists, they think of Starbucks-smashing, black-masked rioters—stoned, drunk, or just bent on mischief—disrupting traffic, destroying
property, and defying authority. Appearing foolish at its best and dangerous and

destructive at its worst, the antiglobalization movement has acquired a reputation that makes it easy for critics to decry and deride it. Truly, the movement is its own worst enemy.

In fact, it is not even a movement. It is an uneasy confederation of some of the oddest bedfellows the world has ever seen: trade unions, environmentalists, anarchists, church groups, human rights advocates, and many, many more. One organizer explains: "We are a fragmented movement, maybe a disunited movement, and here we are trying to build a dialogue between ourselves and our networks. We are a big bunch of different groups with different tactics, different pressures, different passions. We are trying to understand our goals." This loose coalition of organizations and individuals shares concerns about the impact of economic liberalization and globalization, if not much else. They offer an overlapping set of arguments about free trade, poverty, privatization, and environmental protection, generally opposing the growing power of multinational corporations at the expense of consumers and governments. They express deep concern about the spread of market forces and open markets around the world. However, beyond these broad-brush themes, their areas of commonality with respect to goals, tactics, and issues are limited.

The *Financial Times* conducted an exhaustive study of the antiglobalists in 2001 and concluded: "It is a movement of movements, an unruly, unregulated, and unaccountable check on corporations, politicians, and the institutions of democracy." The movement has no leadership and no cogent philosophy; until the shock of 9/11, its momentum alone helped to disguise its fundamental diversity of interests. The only common element: "Antiglobalization has essentially been a movement of self-doubt in the globalizing, capitalist west."[10]

So the antiglobalists are fragmented, diverse, and leaderless and share only a common enemy: global capitalism. But, ironically, they are drawn from the most globalized generation the world has ever known. (Perhaps this is best illustrated by a sign held by one protestor in New York: "World Coalition Against Globalization.") Militants of the movement carry cell phones and multistamped passports and think nothing of hopping a plane for Milan, Rio, or wherever the action will be.

Their technological proficiency is also remarkable. One group, the Ruckus Society, offers a sophisticated Web site that highlights its workshops for "technical activists" to discuss how they are using the Internet and other technologies to work for change. The workshops, aimed at "activists seeking to harness technology for their own causes," include:

- *electronic organizing*, which involves using the Internet to organize and advance activist causes
- *independent media*, including "digital witnessing," to harness video, the Internet, satellite phones, and other technologies to guard against environmental destruction by recording and broadcasting these activities to the general public
- *secure collaboration*, which includes the use of encryption, computer viruses, and firewalls and covering digital footprints left when activists surf the Web[11]

In fact, as their worldliness and technological acuity may suggest, many of these activists are "children of affluence" rather than children of poverty. The vast majority are products of globalization, the movement itself welded together by the Internet and enabled by products that represent the very core of globalization itself: cell phones, cheap air fares, and the laptop. Moreover, the movement is, to some extent, a result of the boom years of the 1990s; as one commentator notes, "affluence brings people the confidence to protest."[12]

A Movement Is Born

The antiglobalization movement emerged in the mid-1990s, catalyzed in the United States by the fight against NAFTA, the North American Free Trade Agreement. Protestors first took center stage in late 1999 with a set of violent and disruptive demonstrations at the WTO meeting in Seattle. (The Seattle protestors featured youths dressed as endangered sea turtles, Korean sweatshop workers, French farmers, U.S. labor union organizers, and environmentalists.) They followed up this first act with subsequent and increasingly violent demonstrations at summits of global leaders in Washington, D.C., Quebec City, and Genoa. Public safety authorities and global leaders alike floundered in their response. Tough security clearly was not the answer; the riots in Genoa were met by massive police resistance that left 231 injured, 1 dead, and 280 in jail.

While the movement is fragmented and leaderless, a few core organizations should be mentioned:

- *Fifty Years Is Enough*, a coalition of more than two hundred "U.S. grass-roots, women's solidarity, faith-based, policy, social-and-economic-justice, youth, labor, and development organizations, dedicated to the profound transformation of the World Bank and the IMF." According to its Web site, it works with more than 185 partner organizations in more than sixty-five countries. It was founded in 1994, on the fiftieth anniversary of the founding of its targets, the IMF and World Bank.[13]

- *The Ruckus Society*, which "provides training in the skills of nonviolent civil disobedience to help environmental and human rights organizations achieve their goals." Founded in 1995, Ruckus runs training camps across the United States to provide classroom-style instruction, advice on media communications, and courses on nonviolent philosophy and practices. (For those who may be interested, its Web site includes detailed information on "hanging yourself from a billboard."[14])

- *Jubilee*, which focuses on the issue of emerging market debt and urges widespread debt forgiveness to give poor countries a chance to grow and prosper. Jubilee bills itself as the world's first Internet-driven grassroots movement, founded in 1996, and it has gained support from Christians across the political spectrum (amazingly, it has the support of both Jesse Helms and U2's Bono—strange bedfellows indeed!).

- *Jobs With Justice*, founded in 1987, which aims to protect workers rights as part of a larger campaign for economic and social justice.

- *Attac*, a European organization founded in 1998, which focuses on promoting the "Tobin tax." This is a modest tax on transactions in foreign exchange markets aimed at stabilizing the markets and raising funds for international poverty alleviation. (See Chapter 4 for a fuller discussion of the Tobin tax.)

- *Global Exchange*, founded in 1988, which promotes environmental, political, and social justice around the world. It is especially concerned with battling the proposed Free Trade Area of the Americas, calling it a "dangerous elevation of corporate rights above human rights."[15]

Despite its fragmentation, the movement is surprisingly well-organized and well-financed. European groups are financed in part by the European Union (EU) and by grants from charitable trusts; U.S. groups are financed by wealthy individuals and groups, including the Ford and Rockefeller foundations, and church-related foundations.

Still, the public face of the movement has been unfortunate, making it easy to dismiss the protestors as fools or thugs. Because they are such a motley crew, they are easy to write off and hard to negotiate with. The challenge that the movement has yet to overcome is this: to develop a manifesto and methodology that differentiates the serious thinkers from the mischief-makers, anarchists, and bomb-throwing malcontents. But as one observer admits, "… in among all their weak arguments, dangerous good intentions, and downright loony notions, the skeptics are hiding some important points."[16]

What Do They Want?

What are those important points? The movement is so fragmented and, indeed, so loony at times that its true goals are not always easy to discern. In essence, though, the movement revolves around five key themes:

- *Poverty*—As the rich get richer, the number of very poor people in the world has risen in absolute terms.

- *Inequality*, which has risen both within and among nations since the Industrial Revolution.

- *WTO rules*—Activists charge that these are grossly unfair, forcing poor countries to accept goods that destroy local jobs while barring their most competitive exports (usually agricultural) from rich country markets. Everyone agrees that trade integration does create losers, especially in the short term. Moreover, rich countries have not always opened their markets to free competition, even while they urge/force these policies on poor countries. Vested interests in rich countries ensure many exceptions to free trade, often in areas where the poor could compete most effectively, such as textiles and agriculture. Mike Moore, director general of the WTO, admits, "The playing field is no more level than the earth is flat."[17] A recent Oxfam report further notes: "The problem is not that international trade is inherently opposed to the needs and interests of the poor, but that the rules that govern it are rigged in favor of the rich." Oxfam explains that barriers to imports in developed countries are biased against the exports of developing countries. Moreover, at the same time that rich countries keep their markets closed, poor countries are being forced to open theirs, "often with damaging consequences to the poor communities."[18]

■ *IMF/World Bank policies,* which are likened to economic imperialism over poor and highly indebted countries. Critics charge that debt relief schemes, when they have occurred, are too little, too late, and too conditional on back-breaking austerity policies. Volatile international capital flows, which are facilitated by the financial liberalization insisted upon by the IMF, have proven immensely disruptive to emerging market countries.

■ *Global capitalism,* which the activists say is distorted in favor of profit-seeking multinational corporations at the expense of poor people, poor countries, and the environment.[19]

Poverty, Inequality, and Imperialism

The twin issues of poverty and inequality are central to the arguments of many antiglobalists, who reject the key IMF/World Bank assertion that globalization reduces both. A succession of crises in the 1990s—in Mexico, Thailand, Indonesia, Korea, Russia, Brazil, and Argentina—suggests that financial crises and serious stresses in emerging market countries are an unwelcome byproduct of globalization, challenging its ability to raise living standards in poor countries. Mexico, where "government statistics show that economic liberalization has done little to close the huge divide between the privileged few and the poor, and left the middle class worse off than before," is a potent example. In 2000, around one-half of all Mexicans lived on $4/day, 10 percent of the people controlled close to 40 percent of the country's wealth, and the middle/working classes made up just 35 percent of the population, compared to 60 percent in the early 1970s. An observer notes: "… it seems a sorry outcome for a nation that adopted the economic tenets of globalization as gospel."[20] (On the other hand, Mexico has avoided a major economic/financial crisis even in the stormy years since 1994. It has benefited from a huge inflow of foreign investment, much more than most countries in Latin America and Africa; it enjoys far greater transparency in its financial markets than most emerging market countries; it has made the shift from a boom-bust cycle to a more healthy business cycle; and it will probably be well-positioned for the next uptick in the North American economy.)

To support their arguments, antiglobalists point to two billion people in countries where poverty is rising, economic growth is stagnant, and trade is declining as a proportion of GDP. A large chunk of the world, holding about one-third of its people and including much of Africa and the Muslim world, has been marginalized. Nearly one-half of the people in the world live on less than $2 per day; one-fifth survive on $1 or less. Most people in Latin America, the Middle East, and

BIG MAC ATTACKS

A victim of its own success, McDonald's has become the favored target of antiglobalization protesters worldwide. With more than twenty-five thousand restaurants in 119 countries, McDonald's earns most of its revenues from outside the United States; during the late 1990s, it opened a new restaurant somewhere in the world every seventeen hours. McDonald's prides itself on its localization policies, going out of its way to use local suppliers and managers and adjusting its menus to appeal to local tastes. It may be viewed as the quintessential globalization success story: Thomas Friedman even points out that two countries that have a McDonald's within their borders have never gone to war against each other.

Somewhere along the way, though, McDonald's became the poster child for U.S. cultural imperialism. The first round was the now-infamous McLibel Trial in 1996. Two British environmental activists passed out leaflets attacking McDonald's, and the company promptly took them to court for libel. McDonald's won the court battle, though it may have lost more than it gained in the process. In the end, the McLibel incident was a public relations disaster for McDonald's, which was widely viewed as Goliath triumphing over its Davidian challengers. During 1996–2001, McDonald's outlets were the targets of hundreds of violent and nonviolent protests, including bombings and arson attacks, in more than fifty countries.

In August 1999, for example, French farmers dumped tons of manure and rotting apricots in front of a local McDonald's to protest U.S. trade policies. The seventeenth annual Worldwide Anti-McDonald's Day was observed on October 16, 2001, but an anti-McDonald's Web site reminded its visitors, "Remember, however, that any day is a good day to protest against the promotion of junk food, the unethical targeting of children, exploitation of workers, animal cruelty, damage to the environment, and the global domination of corporations over our lives."[*]

Why McDonald's? There is no doubt that activists target McDonald's in part because it guarantees them media coverage. But in addition, as James Watson explains, "McDonald's is more than a purveyor of food; it is a saturated symbol for everything that environmentalists, protectionists, and anticapitalist activists find objectionable about American culture." Ronald Steel expanded on this in a 1996 editorial:

"It was never the Soviet Union, but the U.S. itself that is the true revolutionary power. ... We purvey a culture based on mass entertainment and mass gratification. ... The cultural message we transmit through Hollywood and McDonald's goes out across the world to capture, and also to undermine, other societies. ... Unlike traditional conquerors, we are not content merely to subdue others: We insist that they be like us."[†]

[*] www.mcspotight.org.
[†] James L. Watson, "China's Big Mac Attack," *Foreign Affairs*, May/June 2000.

Central Asia are no better off than they were at the end of the Cold War, despite the economic integration of the 1990s; Africans live no longer and have no higher incomes than they did forty years ago.

In fact, the empirical evidence on the benefits of globalization is not as clear as mainstream economists would suggest. If the world's income distribution had become more equal in the past few decades, this would be powerful evidence that globalization is working to the benefit of all, quelling the worst fears of the antiglobalists. Unfortunately, the "evidence" is a matter of growing controversy. The Dollar-Kraay study, for example, has spawned thousands of Web pages and a number of serious studies to support and dispute its results. World Bank economist Branko Milanovic and Columbia University's Xavier Sala-I-Martin have studied trends in global inequality, with sharply conflicting findings. According to Sala-I-Martin, inequality is declining; Milanovic says it has either remained steady or risen slightly. As the *Boston Globe* laments in trying to make sense of the problem, the devil is in the data.[21]

Everyone agrees that world income distribution became much more unequal after the Industrial Revolution (the IMF itself acknowledges that the gap between rich and poor countries has been widening for many decades). But what of the past two decades, when globalization accelerated rapidly? Huge statistical difficulties complicate the analysis enormously (Should economists weight countries by population? Measure economic growth in terms of purchasing power parity or actual exchange rates?). However, at least two reputable studies at the end of the 1990s using household income/expenditure data showed a rapid rise in global income inequality since the late 1980s.[22] By the turn of the century, 10 percent of the world's population received 70 percent of total income; 50 percent of the world's population—three billion people—produced only 6 percent of world output and lived on less than $2 per day.[23]

No doubt the rich did get richer during this period. In the United States between 1979 and 1997, the average income of the richest 20 percent of the population rose from nine times that of the poorest 20 percent to fifteen times. In the United Kingdom, income inequality reached its highest level in forty years during 1999.[24] It was a good time to be rich: in 2001, the world had 7.2 million people with investable assets of at least $1 million, up from 5.2 million in 1997. These people controlled about one-third of the world's wealth. Overall, in 1900 the average income per capita in the richest country in the world was fifteen times that of the poorest; by 1990 this figure had jumped to fifty times that of the poorest.[25]

Research by Attac looks at major economic and social indicators around the world to produce a virtual scorecard on globalization. Researchers compared the last twenty years of accelerated globalization (1980–2000) to the previous twenty years, examining changes in GDP per capita, life expectancy, infant mortality, literacy, and education. Their conclusion: for economic growth and almost all other indicators, the last twenty years have shown a marked decline in progress in comparison with the previous two decades. At the same time, the 1980–2000 period saw many changes, most under the rubric of globalization or the Washington consensus: the removal of trade and capital barriers, and fiscal and monetary contraction as the IMF/World Bank economists prescribed. While the Attac study does not claim to prove causality—that these changes produced the broad decline in progress—it certainly shows no evidence that the policies associated with globalization have *improved* outcomes for most low- to middle-income countries.[26] President Truman said more than fifty years ago that it was intolerable that "more than half the people of the world are living in conditions approaching misery," but Attac's supporters point out that that fact remains relatively unchanged today.[27]

For critics, this is powerful evidence of a correlation between globalization, poverty, and inequality. It buttresses the main point of the antiglobalization movement: that globalization has widened the gap between haves and have-nots, benefiting the rich while doing little for or even harming the poor. The apparent failure of globalization to alleviate poverty is alarming to many. With global poverty on the rise, James Gustave Spaeth wrote in *Foreign Affairs,* "The risk of a huge global underclass undermining international stability is quite real."[28] (It should be noted, though, that the terrorists who planned and executed the attacks of 9/11 were hardly representative of any underclass; they were generally well-educated, well-traveled, and solidly middle class.)

The antiglobalists thus decry the impact of globalization on poverty and inequality. Some take the argument further, suggesting that globalization and the Washington consensus are *deliberately* designed to meet the needs of the rich rather than the poor. The liberalization of financial markets, for example, delivers windfall profits to domestic and foreign speculators while delivering punishing financial crises to the poor. In essence, they say, economic imperialism by rich countries has replaced military imperialism, with much the same effect.

One commentator explains: "To the protestors, large nations led by the U.S. have turned globalization into a form of economic colonialism through the lending policies of the IMF and World Bank." These financial institutions lend money to poor countries. Then, in order to service the debts, the poor countries must lure multinational corporations by offering low wages and lax environmental standards. So instead of maturing into self-sustaining, modern economies, the poor countries remain economic colonies of the rich, exporting cheap products and importing basic goods and services from the United States and Western Europe. In support of this argument, the critics note that the huge debt overhang burdening many countries—$220 billion for the forty poorest countries in the world—forces many nations to spend more on debt service than on education and health, effectively undermining any prospects for growth and progress.[29]

Economists Reexamine Globalization

Among their most powerful evidence, the antiglobalists assert, is the string of financial crises and boom-bust cyclicality that emerging markets suffered through the 1990s (see Chapter 3). By the end of the decade, even respectable economists were expressing doubts about some aspects of globalization, in particular citing the ferocity of emerging market collapses as a worrisome outcome of the globalist manifesto. Most would not go as far as former World Bank chief economist Joseph Stiglitz, who charges that "globalization became a neo-imperialist force that left hundreds of millions of people worse off in 2000 than they were in 1990."[30] But many thoughtful economists, by the end of the decade, were increasingly convinced that hardcore globalization, as practiced in the 1990s, needed some retooling. A new centrist consensus was beginning to emerge.

James K. Galbraith, for example, writes:

The doctrine known as the Washington Consensus was, after its fashion, the Apostle's Creed of globalization. It was an expression of faith that markets are efficient, that states are unnecessary, that the poor and the rich have no competing interests, that things turn out for the best when left alone. It held that privatization and deregulation and open capital markets promote economic development, that governments should balance budgets and fight inflation and do almost nothing else. ... But none of this is actually true.[31]

Galbraith charges that the policies urged on developing countries in the name of globalization have actually darkened their economic prospects in most cases. Where, he asks, are the success stories, the "emerging markets that have emerged?"

More specifically, economists at the Center for Economic and Policy Research looked at the assumption that globalization generally helped to spur growth in 1980–2000 throughout most of the world. They find this assumption invalid; more important, they find that the exceptions to their findings tell the most interesting story of all. While growth lagged in much of the developing world, China and India forged ahead, but their accomplishments are hardly a success story for Washington consensus–based globalization. The economists explain,

In short, there is no region of the world that the Bank or Fund can point to as having succeeded through adopting the policies that they promote—or in many cases, impose—upon borrowing countries. They are understandably reluctant to claim credit for China, which maintains a non-convertible currency, state control over its banking system, and other major violations of IMF/Bank prescriptions. ...[32]

Harvard's Dani Rodrik concurs, noting that the fastest growing countries in the developing world, China and India, have implemented trade and investment liberalization in a decidedly unorthodox fashion: gradually, sequentially, and as part of a policy package with many unconventional features.[33] (At the same time, it can be argued that much of China and India's success, especially with regard to high-tech goods and services in India, is dependent upon open markets and thus globalization.)

Many economists save their most vituperative analysis for the disastrous events in Asia of 1997–1998. In its 1999 report, the United Nations Conference on Trade and Development (UNCTAD) observed,

The humbling of the Asian tigers since 1997 has revealed the vulnerability of even the strongest developing economies to the powerful forces unleashed by globalization. Indeed, the twentieth century is closing on a note of crisis and a growing sense of unease about the policy advice that was proffered in the past decade.

Even more damning, the report finds that "the empirical record has been at odds with the promises." After more than ten years of globalization and liberal market reforms in developing countries, their underlying problems are every bit as acute as ever.[34]

What They Want: Key Policies

With some justice, the antiglobalists have been criticized for being *against* many things (the Washington consensus, IMF, World Bank, WTO, etc.) but *for* very little. In fact it has been easier for the antiglobalization movement to attack its common enemy than for it to set forth coherent and positive recipes for change. Nonetheless, there are some cogent proposals that deserve serious consideration:

- *Debt Relief*—A central theme of the movement, debt relief is seen as a necessary precondition for the rebirth of poor countries. The activists attribute the accumulation of foreign debt to:
  - predatory lending practices by commercial banks
  - lending for huge infrastructure projects that were either poorly conceived or poorly executed (did Kuala Lumpur really need the world's tallest building?)
  - the oil crisis of the mid-1970s, a catastrophe for poor oil-importing countries
  - dramatic hikes in U.S. interest rates at the end of the 1970s
  - the disappearance of massive amounts of borrowed money into the pockets of dictators and corrupt government officials, often facilitated by see-no-evil Western bankers

    The Jubilee organization cites World Bank data to illustrate the impossibility of the debt burden for poor countries. In 1999, $128 million was transferred *daily* from the sixty-two most impoverished countries to the wealthy countries; for each $1 that a country received in grant aid, it repaid $13 on old debts. The impact of the debt is felt in two ways:
  - diversion of natural resources to debt service
  - negative social and economic consequences of Structural Adjustment Programs (SAPs) that debtor countries are forced to adopt
- On its Web site, the organization Fifty Years Is Enough explains,

  Debt is necessarily the starting point in explaining the state of siege that grips the economies of most developing countries today. That's because the efforts by governments to pay this external debt, or at least calm the pressures exerted on them to make interest payments, are what have allowed officials of the IMF and World Bank to take those countries' economic policies hostage. The remedies prescribed by these experts have only exacerbated the twin problems of debt and poverty.

  The most important step needed to accomplish the goals of Fifty Years: eliminate the enormous debts of the poorest, southern hemisphere economies.[35] Jubilee concurs, calling for 100 percent cancellation of developing country debt as its primary goal.

■ *Reform of the IMF and World Bank*—Antiglobalists decry the prescriptions of the IMF and World Bank, which they believe have served rich companies and countries at the expense of the poor. SAPs imposed by the IMF, for example, ensure that the government will save and earn enough hard currency to service its debts to foreign bankers—and impose painful austerity policies on its citizens. (One banker told the authors: "When I started traveling to South America in the early 1980s, my Spanish wasn't good. The first phrase I learned was 'Death to the IMF,' because it was scrawled on every building between the airport and my hotel.")

The SAPs imposed by the IMF on heavily indebted countries are a particular target for critics. Jubilee asserts, "… SAPs have almost invariably caused increased poverty, unemployment, and environmental destruction, while also leading to an increase in the overall size of a country's multilateral debt. The universal failure of the standard SAP recipe has meant that debt and structural adjustment simply end up fueling each other" (Table 5.2). For proof, the critics point to Argentina, a loyal client of the IMF that descended into financial chaos in 2002 despite years of religious adherence to SAPs. The IMF's "monumental failure in Argentina," says Fifty Years, will lead to more calls for a transformation of global policies than 9/11 or the war in Afghanistan. Argentina has become the poster child for what's wrong with the Washington consensus model.

Thus, critics of the IMF and World Bank charge that these institutions represent a veritable "globalization of policymaking," in which rich countries wield all the power and poor countries have no influence. Accordingly, as Martin Khor explains in his book on globalization, the domestic economic policies of developing countries worldwide are being formulated in Washington.[36] Another author, Diane Coyle, writes in *Paradoxes of Prosperity* about the annual IMF/World Bank meetings in Prague in September 2000. She describes the conference attendees standing out against the backdrop of Prague's beautiful and historic city center: "They always walked in pairs, all wore expensive navy or gray suits and sober ties, all carried briefcases even while sightseeing."[37]

Joseph Stiglitz, former chief economist at the World Bank, makes a similar point. The IMF and World Bank economists, he notes, often know more about a client country's five-star hotels than about the intricacies of its economic and political life. "It's not fair to say that IMF economists don't care about the citizens of developing nations," he comments. "But the older men who staff the fund—and they are overwhelmingly older men—act as if they are shouldering Rudyard Kipling's white man's burden."[38] (When asked during a news conference in Argentina in 2002 why Latin Americans are increasingly rejecting the policy prescriptions of globalization, then-U.S. Treasury Secretary Paul O'Neill replied, "I have no idea." Even for an official whose tenure was marked by gaffes and a tone-deaf approach to financial markets, this was damning evidence of willful blindness at its worst.)

TABLE 5.2   Structural Adjustment: An Antiglobalist Perspective

IMF/World Bank Condition	Impact on Elite (Corporations, Investors, Wealthy)	Impact on Poor
Cut Social Spending: Reduce expenditures on health, education, etc.	More debts repaid including to World Bank and IMF	Increased school fees force parents to pull children—usually girls—from school Poorly educated generation not equipped for skilled jobs Higher fees for medical service mean less treatment, more suffering, needless deaths
Shrink Government: Reduce budget expense by trimming payroll and programs	Fewer government employees means less capacity to monitor businesses's adherence to labor, environmental, and financial regulations Frees up cash for debt service	Massive layoffs in countries where government is often the largest employer Makes people desperate to work at any wage
Increase Interest Rates: To combat inflation, increase interest charged for credit and awarded to savings	Investors find country a profitable place to park cash, though they may pull it out at any moment	Small farmers and businesses can't get capital to stay afloat Small farmers sell land, work as tenants or move to worse lands Businesses shut down, leaving workers unemployed
Eliminate Regulations on Foreign Ownership of Resources and Businesses:	Multinational corporations can purchase or start enterprises easily Countries compete for foreign investment by offering tax breaks, low wages, free trade zones Once in the country, corporations can turn to WTO for enforcement of rights	Control of entire sectors of economy can shift to foreign hands Governments offer implicit pledges not to enforce labor and environmental laws
Eliminate Tariffs: Stop collecting taxes on imports; these taxes are often applied to goods which would compete with domestically produced goods	Allows foreign goods easy access to domestic markets Makes luxury items cheaper for those in the country Allows country to comply with WTO agreements	Makes it harder for domestic producers to compete against better-equipped and richer foreign suppliers Leads to closure of businesses and layoffs
Cut Subsidies for Basic Goods: Reduce government expenditures supporting reduced cost of bread, petroleum, etc.	Frees up more money for debt payments	Raises cost of items needed to survive Most frequent flashpoint for civil unrest
Reorient Economies from Subsistence to Exports: Give incentives for farmers to produce cash crops for foreign markets rather than food for domestic ones; encourage manufacturing to focus on simple assembly for export rather than manufacturing for own country; encourage extraction of valuable mineral resources	Produces hard currency to pay off more debts Law of supply and demand pushes down price of commodities as more countries produce more, meaning guaranteed supply of low-cost products to export markets Local competition eliminated for multinational corporations Increased availability of low-cost labor	Law of supply and demand pushes down price of commodities as more countries produce more, meaning local producers often lose money Best lands devoted to cash crops; poorer land used for food crops, leading to soil erosion Food security threatened Women often relegated to gathering all food for family while men work for cash Makes country more dependent on imported food and manufactured goods Forest and mineral resources over-exploited, leading to environmental destruction and displacement

Source: www.globalexchange.org.

Time for change, say the critics. The Mobilization for Global Justice circulated the following proposals in 2001, endorsed by hundreds of organizations around the world:

- Open all World Bank and IMF meetings to media and the public.

- End all World Bank and IMF policies that hinder people's access to food, clean water, shelter, health care, education, and the right to organized labor. (SAPs generally include user fees for public services, privatization, and economic austerity programs.)

- Stop all World Bank/IMF support for socially and environmentally destructive projects, such as oil, gas, and mining projects.

- Cancel all impoverished-country debt to the IMF and World Bank.

- *Tobin Tax*—This is the primary cause of the European organization Attac, founded in 1998 to advance the Tobin tax idea. First proposed several decades ago by economist James Tobin, the tax is a modest

THE IMF, WORLD BANK, AND STRUCTURAL ADJUSTMENT

The missions of the IMF and World Bank are so commendable, at least on paper, that it is astonishing to see how much rage the institutions have produced. The World Bank makes loans to poor countries, usually for specific infrastructure-type projects, at interest rates that reflect their fiscal conditions. The IMF sends teams of economists and makes billions of dollars in loans to rescue countries facing financial crises.

Noble goals notwithstanding, the two institutions have become a target for critics of globalization worldwide. In particular, the SAPs prescribed and overseen by the IMF for countries in crisis are widely despised. (According to the critics, it is as if every patient who visits a doctor is given an appendectomy, no matter what his symptoms.) In return for IMF/World Bank assistance, the SAPs usually require debtor countries to impose strict budgetary discipline, lift all subsidies for food and other basic products, raise the cost of public services such as health care, and eliminate trade barriers. The antiglobalist organization Global Exchange, in fact, charges that these SAPs are used to maintain the interests of the wealthy at the expense of the poor (see Table 5.2).

Unfortunately, as former World Bank economist Joseph Stiglitz observes, IMF/World Bank policies have never brought a country to prosperity. In Haiti, for example, the World Bank supported forty-one projects over the past fifty years with more than $1 billion in loans, and the IMF lent $150 million in the past twenty years. Even so, more than 80 percent of Haiti's population still lives in poverty, up from 65 percent in 1987. And Argentina's recent collapse, despite its slavish devotion to the policy prescriptions of the IMF, threw millions of middle class families into poverty. *The New York Times* acknowledges, "The two institutions have often failed to turn deep political backing, world-class brainpower, and billions in funds into good results."[*]

[*] Daniel Altman, "As Global Lenders Refocus, a Needy World Waits," *The New York Times*, March 17, 2002.

charge on all transactions in foreign exchange markets, aimed at discouraging destabilizing speculation and at raising money for the international community. At a rate of 0.1 percent, the Tobin tax would raise $166 billion/year according to its proponents—sufficient to eradicate poverty in a matter of years. The Tobin tax has gained wide support in Europe, including that of some leading politicians, but it runs directly counter to the IMF's mantra of financial market liberalization.

Results: Constructive Engagement

Despite the antics of their fringe elements, the serious antiglobalists are being heard—and were even before the shocks of 9/11. The Tobin tax, in particular, has engaged the mainstream and is widely discussed by center-left politicians in Europe. Recent meetings of the establishment institutions, including the World Bank, IMF, and World Economic Forum, have featured dialogues between antiglobalist activists and representatives of the globalist establishment. Both the IMF and World Bank, in fact, have responded to the criticism by expanding and accelerating their programs in debt relief and poverty alleviation (Figure 5.4).

Whether the proglobalist economists and businessmen are truly listening remains an open question, but by the dawn of the new century they were at least paying lip service to the notion of constructive engagement. In some ways, even before 9/11 the "system" was clearly under pressure, and the antiglobalist forces had scored some victories. Local activists in India, Nigeria, and Turkey slowed or halted large projects by multinationals; Napster and its progeny were challenging the multimillion-dollar music distribution industry. As Diane Coyle observed, "this system ... is drawing to a close."[39]

▶ GLOBALIZATION, ANTIGLOBALIZATION, AND 9/11

The world changed on September 11, 2001. The impact of the terrorist attacks on the globalization movement, as well as the antiglobalization movement, is a topic of intense speculation and controversy. The only point on which all agree is that 9/11 will have a profound effect on the globalization debate. But how?

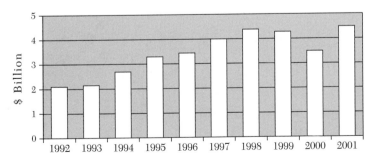

FIGURE 5.4 Poverty Alleviation Program Spending
Source: World Bank, International Monetary Fund.

Did Globalization Contribute to 9/11?

In classrooms, coffee shops, and Internet chat rooms around the world on September 12, people wondered aloud: Did globalization—and the stresses, resentments, and inequities that it has caused—contribute to the terrorist attack? Did globalization play a role in laying the groundwork for 9/11?

A possible link between globalization and the seeds of terrorism has been much debated since 9/11. Indeed, the choice of the World Trade Center—a proud and prominent symbol of global capitalism—as a target is suggestive. As Martin Wolf wrote in the *Financial Times:*

> The terrorists who attacked the U.S. on September 11 were mortal enemies of the U.S. But the U.S. is not just a country, it is also a set of ideas. Among the ideas it has stood for over more than half a century is a liberal world economy. ...[40]

On the one hand, some point out that the terrorists hate the United States because it is an imperialistic power, gradually imposing its values on the rest of the world. Conquest is achieved through economic weapons (such as WTO rules, Big Macs, and SAPs), rather than military/diplomatic means. Nonetheless, it is conquest just the same. One observer explains: "The generals who matter in this war are mostly to be found in the upper echelons of capitalist corporations, which is why the attack on the gleaming towers of the World Trade Center had such symbolic importance for the Muslim extremists."[41]

Western economists, though, reject this argument as utter nonsense. In their view, the spread of a global market economy is purely technical and has nothing to do with any particular set of values, ethics, or political views. Indeed, the market economy is consistent with any value system, including Islam. As proof that market institutions are culturally neutral, they point to the United States itself—a society where many strong and diverse religious faiths coexist in one economic system.

This may be disingenuous, though. Michael Prowse comments: "A theocratic Muslim state has every reason to fear U.S.-led globalization, because market institutions are most unlikely to prove compatible with the kind of communal life that it favors. Whatever else markets may be, they are not value-free. They promote one value above others: personal freedom. ..." Also, he adds, ideas flow in along with goods and services. (For proof of this, consider the Chinese government's hard lesson in how difficult it is to open its economy to global forces while maintaining repressive control over the political and social system—an effort that is doomed, above all, by the facsimile [fax] and Internet.) So the individualism and materialism that are associated with global capitalism are inherently inimical to autocratic Muslim states, which may explain *some* (not all!) of the terrorists' hatred of the United States.[42]

9/11: The Death Knell to Antiglobalization?

Just as important in the wake of 9/11 was the question of how it would impact the antiglobalization movement, which had just succeeded in engaging the attention of the mainstream and putting some of its causes, like the Tobin tax, on the mainstream agenda. Antiglobalization protests were decidedly muted at the first large post-9/11 meetings, the WTO meeting in Doha, Qatar, and the IMF/World Bank meetings in Ottawa, Canada. Enthusiasm for large and noisy demonstrations against economic liberalization and the institutions of the West plummeted, and the taste for violence virtually evaporated.

In fact, after 9/11 pundits were quick to predict the imminent demise of the antiglobalization movement. Shocked by the attacks and fearing that their demonstrations could suggest some tacit support for, at the very least, the goals of the terrorists, the leaders of the antiglobalization movement were quiescent. Furthermore, to the extent that the antiglobalization movement is, in some sense, anti–United States (after all, the key institutions and corporations targeted by the movement are all U.S.-based), in the immediate aftermath of 9/11 any action that hinted at anti-Americanism was taboo.

In addition, proponents of globalization were quick to seize on 9/11 as proof that globalization had not gone far *enough*. U.S. administration officials commented that the best means of combating terrorism was by promoting probusiness global policies, to bring the angry and disenfranchised into the fold. President Bush told a group of business executives in October 2001 that more free trade and greater unrestricted commerce were crucial to fighting terrorism. Along the same lines, economists argued that a contributing factor to 9/11 was too little globalization, not too much. Restrictions on the migration of people around the world, for example, contributed to marginalization and anger. The central theme: "… Globalization, far from being the greatest cause of poverty, is its only feasible cure."[43]

Kofi Annan, secretary general of the United Nations, supported this argument as well. Noting that people were asking why he was attending the World Economic Forum, viewed as a bastion of world capitalism, he responded, "Some even seem to think that by doing so I align myself with the glitterati and the global elite, turning my back on the downtrodden masses who—in these people's eyes—are the victims of globalization." In fact, he continued, the poor are far from victims of globalization: their problem is that they are *excluded* from global markets.[44]

The antiglobalization movement faced a more practical problem after 9/11 as well. As noted, the appetite of even the most fervent activists for loud and noisy demonstrations aimed at Western institutions had waned enough to rob the movement of much of its momentum. Unlike a political party or trade union, the antiglobalization movement has no formal, hard-core membership to fall back on in lean times. This is potentially a serious problem for a movement that lacks coherent leadership and ideology, since it is sustained largely by its momentum—by activism itself. Since the 1999 demonstrations in Seattle, the movement had largely been defined and invigorated by a series of mass street protests. With each mobilization, the activists' sense of their own power increased. Now, nobody wanted to participate in mass street protests, robbing the movement of its momentum and even its core identity. "Activists need to be active," one observer fretted.[45]

Finally, by mid-2002 the antiglobalization movement faced another threat—paradoxically, from its newest set of adherents. While the movement had always been an amalgamation of strange and uneasy bedfellows, it gained some of its most uncomfortable allies yet in the wake of 9/11. In spring 2002, traditional antiglobalist protesters in Washington were marching cheek by jowl with antiwar and anti-Israeli protestors, wearing T-shirts emblazoned with "We are all Palestinians" and "Up With Saddam," and carrying signs demanding a U.S. withdrawal from Afghanistan.

At a time when most U.S. polls indicated solid support for the antiterror effort, these demonstrations were not likely to win much favor with the general public. (Even in Europe, where sympathy for the Palestinian cause is much greater, there are few fervent supporters of Saddam Hussein.) The appearance of these new and largely unwelcome allies in the antiglobalization movement underlines the leaderless and uncontrolled nature of the movement and its vulnerability to hijacking by radical and potentially unwelcome adherents.

Or a Vindication of the Movement?

But while the public face of the movement has been defined and energized by mass street protests, its core still revolves around a set of serious issues and themes that were invigorated—indeed, vindicated—by the attacks of 9/11. While nobody was celebrating, some antiglobalists felt that 9/11 helped to prove the urgency and essential rightness of their arguments. One commentator explains: "The terrorist attacks on America were the Chernobyl of globalization. Just as the Russian disaster undermined our faith in nuclear energy, so September 11 exposed the false promise of neoliberalism."[46] In this viewpoint, the promise of neoliberalism to remedy the world's ills through a judicious mixture of deregulation and free market forces has irrevocably failed. At the very least, chimes in another writer, "The confidence of 'Davos man' [participants in the World Economic Forum, usually held in Davos, Switzerland] in the irresistible march of globalization—and his belief in his own righteousness and cultural condition—has been shaken."[47]

The sense that 9/11 had exposed the flaws of blind faith in globalization was compounded by the global economic slowdown that quickly followed, the implosion of Enron, and Argentina's slide into financial ruin. Taken together, these events seemed to suggest that the antiglobalization movement had been vindicated, rather than decimated, by recent developments. At the very least, 9/11 confirmed some doubts about the promise of globalization. John Gray, a British political scientist and well-known critic of globalization, claimed that "the era of globalization is over … the entire view of the world that supported market faith in globalization has melted down." And Stephen Roach, chief economist at Morgan Stanley, suggested that the terrorist attacks and their aftermath would deal a serious blow to globalization, especially when added to Argentina's economic meltdown, which "cast doubt on the free market economic philosophy underpinning the drive to globalization."[48]

Also, distaste for mass street action in the aftermath of 9/11 seemed likely to rein in the radical fringe of the antiglobalization movement, always its Achilles' heel.

A diminished appetite for physical confrontations with the authorities and police can only be good for the movement's public image. In addition, leaders of the movement acted quickly to reject the rabid anti-Americanism at the core of the terrorist attacks, defining their own positions more clearly in the process and helping to pave the way for more well-considered and reasoned arguments. At the very least, 9/11 gave rise to a sense that civilized countries and peoples needed to stick together, not reject each other, which could only strengthen the serious thinkers of the movement while weakening its violent fringe.

The Reality: "Sand in the Gears"

So the forecasts of an imminent demise for both globalization and antiglobalization in the wake of 9/11 turn out to be vastly exaggerated. There are a few realities, though:

- *Slowing Economic Integration*—A slowing in the expansion of trade and capital flows that has underpinned globalization seems inevitable, at least in the short term. There are two problems, one structural and one cyclical.

  - *Cyclical*—The world economy turned sluggish in 2001–2002; while recovery was inevitable, prospects for a return to the fast-paced growth of the 1990s were dim. In the boom-bust cycle that seems to characterize world trading and investment patterns, the immediate future was uncertain. According to the IMF, world trade soared by a record 12.4 percent in 2000 but then crept up by just 1.4 percent in 2001. International capital flows were also disrupted by the 9/11 shock, as well as by crises in Argentina and Turkey. Net private capital flows to major emerging market countries fell from $169 billion in 2000 to $115 billion in 2001, the lowest level in a decade. Economists believe that these flows picked up in 2002 but remain well below their peak level of 1995–1997.[49]

  - *Structural*—Even more important, the post-9/11 world will inevitably be burdened by higher barriers and costs to economic integration. Cross-border activities will be more expensive and more difficult—think of lines at airport check-in counters and delays at border crossings. Factors such as higher transportation costs, insurance premiums, border congestion, immigration troubles, even fear of flying, will restrict the mobility of people and goods for the foreseeable future. In effect, this introduces a new and hefty tax on cross-border activities, which is likely to slow growth.

    Essentially, the problem is that pre-9/11 globalization was founded on the free flow of goods, services, and people, facilitated by the erosion of trade and investment barriers. Now, these flows will be slower and costlier. Businesses will have to spend heavily on nonproductive activities such as insurance and security; tougher border inspections will slow cargo movements; labor mobility will decline; and companies will be forced to stock more inventory to guard against lags in cargo shipments. Stephen Roach warns, "What drove the rapid expansion in trade and capital flows was the notion that the world was becoming a seamless, frictionless place. Now, there's sand in the gears of cross-border connectivity."[50]

■ *Government Is In Again*—The other reality about 9/11 is the enhanced role for governments that seems inevitable in its aftermath. Globalization and neoliberalism embrace the market above all; their mantra is deregulation, privatization, and de-bureaucratization. Get the government out of the markets, and everything will work better.

Suddenly, in the post-9/11 world, governments are in vogue again. Flags are waving all over the United States; all at once, the role of government and of cooperation with the government is enhanced. This is perhaps best symbolized by the U.S. decision to federalize airport security workers—a decision that seemed to fly in the face of the Washington consensus position on privatization but was hailed by most Americans. All of a sudden the government, rather than a private security firm, was seen as the best guarantor of Americans' safety. One writer comments, "The 1990s produced a paradigm through which to view the world: globalization. It held that capitalism, trade, and technological revolutions were transforming the world and breaking down old obstacles and mandates. Global capitalism was the only game in town, and countries had to play by its rules or be left behind—far behind." Since 9/11, he continues, a new paradigm is emerging. "Politics is back, culture is back, ideology is back, and above all, government is back."[51]

■ *The Antis Are Vindicated*—Finally, it is difficult for even the most enthusiastic cheerleader of globalization to deny that 9/11 has refocused attention on the failings of the global "system." While the terrorists were hardly victims of poverty or U.S. imperialism, they do share a fundamental distaste for U.S. economic and cultural domination with the antiglobalists. At the very least, 9/11 suggested that after two fast-paced decades of global integration, the world harbors pockets of deep hatred and marginalization that need to be addressed. (This line of thinking requires great care, however; it is important to underscore that the serious antiglobalists in no way support or sympathize with the actions, goals, or tactics of the 9/11 attackers.) "Serious protestors who are concerned about the marginalization of the poorest countries," writes the *Financial Times*, "about ways of alleviating their intolerable debt burden, and how to give them greater access to rich country markets, have been reinforced in their convictions."[52]

By the same token, the path of the world economy since 9/11 has underscored some of the antiglobalists' concerns about blind faith in the power of globalization to deliver economic progress. In 2001, world growth slipped below the 2.5 percent annual rate that the IMF defines as the breaking point between progress and slippage. The United States, Japan, and Europe probably saw their first collective contraction since the oil price shock of the mid-1970s, "revealing a dark side to the increasing economic integration of the last decade." Stephen Roach again: "One by one, each major country is tipping into a rare and possibly lethal recession. It is far-reaching and deep, and much of that has to do with the fact that we've become much more interconnected."[53]

The worldwide economic slippage, of course, gives powerful ammunition to the opponents of economic integration. To make matters worse, countries that enthusiastically courted foreign investment, following the Washington consensus advice to keep their markets open and their currencies freely convertible, have suffered the most. Loyal Washington consensus adherents such as Singapore, Taiwan, Mexico, and Argentina have been hardest hit; China, Russia, and India moved much more slowly toward global economic integration and are suffering much less in the current economic slowdown.

▶ A TURNING POINT, BUT TOWARD WHAT?

The one point that everyone agrees on is that 9/11 probably marked a turning point for both the globalization and antiglobalization movements. The question is, toward what? After all, the economic history of the twentieth century reminds us that globalization is not inevitable. War in 1914 abruptly ended a period of economic openness and integration; the 1930s, too, were marked by beggar-thy-neighbor policies adopted after the Depression. This raises the possibility that governments will turn their backs on open trade and capital flows in the next decade, reacting to the shocking events of 9/11 and beyond. In this sense, the attack may prove a turning point similar to the assassination of Archduke Ferdinand in Sarajevo in 1914, which brought an end to the first great age of globalization. This time, though, the danger is a gradual reversal of market integration policies rather than a cataclysmic world war. (In fact, globalization is evolutionary in its nature and probably inevitable. It moves forward in a series of stops and starts—great leaps forward due to technological breakthroughs, followed by periods of adjustment and sometimes steps backward, like the World War I and II periods.)

Or did 9/11 give new impetus, even urgency, to the globalization movement? The *Financial Times* further notes, "Globalization is an economic reality, even if the growth of world trade may have slowed, and investment flows are down." In this viewpoint, 9/11 and the subsequent blows to capitalism (Argentina, Enron, and the world economic slowdown) will eventually underscore the sturdiness—indeed, the inevitability—of globalization. Even after a series of wrenching shocks, the system is recovering and reforming. Trade and capital flows picked up smartly in 2002, underscoring the fundamental reality that globalization is here to stay (Figure 5.5).

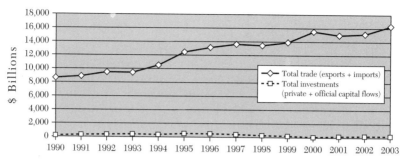

FIGURE 5.5 World Growth in Trade and Investment
Source: IMF.

World Economic Forum versus World Social Forum

The distance between the two paradigms can, above all, be represented by the distance between the World Economic Forum in New York and its evil twin, the World Social Forum (WSF) in Porto Alegre, Brazil, in early 2002. Part carnival, part teach-in, the WSF demonstrated that the antiglobalization movement had regained some of its lost momentum. The gathering was largely peaceful, and most participants took great care to distance themselves from the violence and vandalism of Seattle and Genoa. Attendees included high-ranking public officials, such as the UN High Commissioner for Human Rights, the director-general of the International Labor Organization, and influential parliamentarians, judges, and mayors from Europe. In fact, the WSF featured, above all, a serious exchange of ideas and proposals, including:

- debt forgiveness for the poorest countries
- tariff exemptions for exports from the poorest countries
- an increase in development aid to 0.7 percent of rich countries' GDP
- "flexibilization" of the WTO's intellectual property laws
- access to basic drugs, especially those used to control AIDS and malaria, at the lowest possible prices
- a larger cut in carbon emissions by industrial countries
- implementation of International Labor Organization rights, including the right to unionize and prohibitions on child and forced labor worldwide
- creation of taxes on global financial transactions (the Tobin tax) and abolition of tax havens[54]

If the WSF showed that the antiglobalization movement had regained its momentum, it also revealed a decided drift toward the center. The ideas and proposals listed may not win the approval of conservative voters and politicians, but they cannot be dismissed as anarchism or foolishness either. In fact, this is quite a respectable set of themes that can be seriously discussed by economists and politicians worldwide.

And the mainstream is paying attention. The antiglobalists may be repudiating their radical fringe and drifting toward the center, but the globalists too have been shaken enough by 9/11 and subsequent events to question their blind faith in the universal rightness of global economic integration. The WSF certainly proved beyond any doubt that the antiglobalists are not going to fade away. They are too well-financed, too well-organized, and perhaps too right. Many of their concerns about global inequities between rich and poor are more relevant than ever today, and these issues are commanding increased attention in the wake of 9/11.

Public opinion, of course, plays a role in this. The popularity of Malaysia's Prime Minister Mohamed Mahathir, who has often delighted in bashing the Washington consensus, is instructive. By 2002, Mahathir was the sixth longest-ruling head of state in the world, preaching unabashedly against the spread of market capitalism and globalization (notwithstanding, of course, the fact that Kuala Lumpur is home to a Planet Hollywood and Tower Records and that Malaysia is developing a multimedia investment corridor near the modern airport). In France, antiglobalization activist Jose Bove, who was convicted for destroying a McDonald's to protest U.S. trade policies, is viewed more as a folk hero than a criminal. There is no doubt that popular support for at least some elements of globalization, such as trade liberalization, is lagging—even in developed countries. (Witness the U.S. imposition of hefty steel import tariffs in 2002.) The institutions that represent global economic integration—the World Bank, IMF, and WTO—are "reviled more widely than they are admired."[55]

While distaste for those institutions is widespread, public support for nongovernmental organizations (NGOs)—including some of those at the core of the antiglobalization movement—has never been stronger. Polls in the U.S. reveal that NGOs enjoy a level of public trust almost equal to that of the largest companies. The popularity of both is exceeded only by that of the government, which rose sharply after 9/11. In Europe, NGOs are *more* trusted than the government, companies, and the media. Some NGOs, like Amnesty International, Greenpeace, and the World Wildlife Fund, are now viewed as "superbrands" topping the public trust rankings in Europe. They come in well above the trust ratings for Microsoft, Ford, and Bayer, which are the three most trusted corporate brands.

The fact is, though, that unlike the 1930s there is no plausible alternative to globalization on the table today. And herein lies the key lesson: *most serious critics of globalization are not antiglobalists;* their goal is to reform and tweak the process so that it plays a much more positive role in alleviating poverty, inequality, and injustice worldwide, not to derail it altogether. At the same time, in the wake of 9/11 many globalists are also softening their positions; globalization is still good for all, but the process clearly could use some refining. Some new ideas are emerging. Harvard's Dani Rodrik, for example, has proposed including labor mobility on the WTO's agenda, to allow people from poor countries to work for a set period of time in rich countries.

Underlining the more reflective stance that had begun to emerge even before 9/11, the managing director of the IMF commented at the 2000 annual meeting in Prague:

It is the task of international economic policy to tap the opportunities of globalization, while limiting its risks. The opportunities it affords are higher productivity, increased trade, stronger growth dynamics, and more jobs and higher income. ... The risks lie in overstretching the abilities of societies and political infrastructures to adapt, and in financial crises caused as a consequence of excessive volatility in capital flows. The central problem is, however, the fact that too many people have so far had no share of the gains in the prosperity that was brought about by globalization. The successful fight against poverty is, in my view, the key to peace in the twenty-first century.[56]

With both sides moving toward a more accommodating stance, future dialogue should be more promising than in the past. Globalization is here to stay, but many power players are beginning to concede that parts of the process are flawed and even that the antiglobalists may serve an important role as a "check on the excesses and inadequacies of global capitalism."[57] Increasingly, post-9/11 dialogue is being marked by a repudiation of the antiglobalization movement's violent and radical fringe and by a new willingness on the part of globalizers to question their blind faith in the merits of global economic integration.

▶ NOTES

1. Martin Wolf, "Will the Nation-State Survive Globalization?" *Foreign Affairs*, January/February 2001.

2. Dani Rodrik, "Trading in Illusions," *Foreign Policy*, March 2001.

3. Peter H. Lindert, Jeffrey G. Williamson, "Does Globalization Make the World More Unequal?" NBER Working Paper No. w8228, April 2001.

4. "Globalization, Growth and Poverty: Building an Inclusive World Economy," (Washington, D.C: World Bank, 2002), available at www.econ.worldbank.org.

5. David Dollar and Aart Kraay, "Spreading the Wealth," *Foreign Affairs*, January/February 2002; David Dollar and Aart Kraay, "Growth Is Good for the Poor," World Bank Policy Research Department Working Paper No. 2587 (Washington, D.C.: 2001), available at www.worldbank.org /research/growth.

6. Pierre-Richard Agenur, "Does Globalization Hurt the Poor?" World Bank Policy Research Working Paper, October 31, 2002, available at www.worldbank.org.

7. Editorial comment, "An Answer for the Protestors," *Financial Times*, January 31, 2002.

8. Surjit Bhalla, "Imagine There's No Country: Poverty, Inequality and Growth in the Era of Globalization," (Washington, DC: Institute for International Economics, September 2002), available at www.iie.com.

9. Leslie Wayne, "For Trade Protesters, 'Slower, Sadder Songs,'" *The New York Times*, October 28, 2001.

10. James Harding, "Clamor against Globalization Stilled," *Financial Times*, October 10, 2001.

11. www.ruckus.org.

12. Diane Coyle, *Paradoxes of Prosperity* (New York, Texere, 2001).

13. www.50years.org.

14. www.ruckus.org.
15. www.globalexchange.org.
16. Clive Crook, "Globalization and its Critics," *The Economist*, (Survey: Globalization), September 27, 2001.
17. Coyle, op. cit.
18. Martin Wolf, "Doing More Harm than Good," *Financial Times*, May 8, 2002.
19. Editorial comment, "An Answer for the Protestors."
20. Ginger Thompson, "Free Market Upheaval Grinds Mexico's Middle Class," *The New York Times*, September 4, 2002.
21. Laura Secor, "Mind the Gap," *The Boston Globe*, January 5, 2003.
22. Robert Wade, "Winners and Losers," *The Economist*, April 26, 2001.
23. Martin Wolf, "Growth Makes the Poor Richer," *Financial Times*, January 23, 2001.
24. "Does Inequality Matter?" *The Economist*, June 14, 2001.
25. Coyle, op. cit.
26. "1980-2000: 20 Years of Diminished Progress," available at www.attac.org.
27. Joseph Kahn and Tim Weiner, " World Leaders Rethinking Strategy on Aid to the Poor," *The New York Times*, March 18, 2002.
28. Dollar and Kraay, op. cit.
29. Leslie Wayne, "For Trade Protestors, 'Slower, Sadder Songs'."
30. Joseph Kahn, "Review of Globalization and its Discontents," by Joseph Stiglitz, *The New York Times Review of Books*, June 23, 2002.
31. James K. Galbraith, "The Crisis of Globalization," *Dissent*, Summer 1999, Vol. 46 No. 3.
32. Mark Weisbrot, Robert Naiman, and Joyce Kim, "The Emperor Has No Growth: Declining Economic Growth Rates in the Era of Globalization," Center for Economic and Policy Research, May 2001.
33. Dani Rodrik, "Trading in Illusions," *Foreign Policy*, March 2001.
34. *United National Conference on Trade and Development (UNCTAD) Report*, 1999.
35. www.50years.org.
36. www.jubilee2000uk.org.
37. Coyle, op. cit.
38. Joseph Stiglitz, *What I Learned at the World Economic Crisis*, excerpted at www.whirledbank.org.
39. Ibid.
40. Martin Wolf, "A Free World," *Financial Times*, September 4, 2002.
41. Michael Prowse, "Why a Peace-Loving Nation is Seen as a Threat," *Financial Times*, October 20–21, 2001.
42. Ibid.
43. Clive Crook, op. cit.
44. Kofi Annan, "The Bottom Line is Hope," *Financial Times*, February 4, 2002.
45. James Harding, op. cit.
46. Ulrich Beck, "Globalization's Chernobyl," *Financial Times*, November 6, 2001.
47. Virginia Postrel, "Economic Scene," *The New York Times*, January 31, 2002.
48. "Going Global," *The Economist*, February 1, 2002.
49. "Net Private Capital Flows to Emerging Markets," Institute of International Finance, January 30, 2002.
50. "What's at Stake: How Terrorism Threatens the Global Economy," *Business Week*, October 22, 2001.
51. Fareed Zakaria, "A Plan for Globalization," *Newsweek*, December 17, 2001.
52. Editorial comment, "Global Warnings," *Financial Times*, January 31, 2002.
53. Joseph Kahn, "The World's Economies Slide Together Into Recession," *The New York Times*, November 22, 2001.
54. Raymond Colitt, "Serious Ideas Behind the Theatrics," *Financial Times*, February 5, 2002.

55.   Clive Crook, op. cit.

56.   "The Challenge of Globalization and the Role of the IMF," remarks by IMF Managing Director Horst Kohler, April 2, 2001, available at www. imf.org. It is worth noting, however, that he went on to say that the IMF would therefore redouble its efforts to help poor countries gain macroeconomic stability, adopt conservative fiscal and monetary policies, and address capital markets issues. Insofar as this reflects the conventional wisdom followed by the IMF for the past two decades, it is unclear how much the IMF has really absorbed from the antiglobalization movement.

57.   James Harding, op. cit.

PART II

WALL STREET: BUBBLE TO BUST

CHAPTER 6

THE TECH BUBBLE

"Net gains" ... "Earnings Push Dow Over 11,000: Can They Last?" ... "Tech Stocks That Rule" ... "Next Stage in the Internet Revolution" ... "Next Stage in the Cellular Tour" ... "Internet Selloff Brings NASDAQ a Correction" ... "From Boom to Bust" ...

The tech or Internet bubble clearly left its imprint on the 1990s. As the personal computer (PC), the Internet, and cellular telephones first penetrated and then completely restructured everyday life, both at home and at the office, the excitement of the new order percolated from the realm of techno-nerds and into the universe of first venture capitalists and finally the larger world of the investor. In an even broader sense, the reordering of daily life included entertainment and media. Movie tickets, books, and even food could be picked up via the Internet. Airplane tickets became paperless. Shopping for groceries and clothes via the Internet was yet another option. Consumerism entered into a new decade of fingertip shopping.

The tech sector—in all its manifestations—experienced all of the excitement and adrenaline rush of inflated expectations and prices. By the late 1990s, the tech bubble (some have called it the Internet or dot-com bubble) reached amazing heights as investors fought to get into IPOs (initial public offerings), and the NASDAQ (National Association of Securities Dealers Automated Quotation System) moved ever higher. The Dow Jones Industrial Average climbed from a low of 2,365 in 1990 to hit 10,000 in March 1999, a dizzying increase of more than 300 percent. (Eventually it peaked at 11,000, before tumbling in 2001.) The excitement from Wall Street flowed outward, helping to create similar upward swings in stock markets in Europe and Asia. It can be argued that the tech bubble was a key factor in defining the shape and tone of international capital markets during the 1990s and early 2000s.

As the bubble inflated, common sense tended to evaporate. Analysis of company financial statements meant little as a tidal wave of new firms, some backed by savvy venture capitalists, rushed to the market to issue stock. In some cases, all that was being sold behind the company name and the reputation of management was an idea. And ideas sold. For those who clung stubbornly to the analysis of corporate fundamentals, it was difficult to understand how a company could be marketed to investors with no cash flow or profits, only the projection that at some point in the future the money would pour in. As one observer of the Wall Street tech bubble stated: "During the boom, you could throw a dart at a list of technology names and most likely come up with a winner. Analysis really didn't seem to matter." Market momentum swept aside the naysayers.

However, by early 2000 the tech bubble was beginning to burst as the lack of profits, questionable cash flows, and growing debt burdens reflected the sad reality that even the high-flying tech sector was bound by the inescapable law of gravity. The air slipped out of the tech bubble throughout 2000–2001, eventually rippling into the broader stock market. From October 2001 to December 2002, seventeen tech companies with a market capitalization of $90 billion filed for bankruptcy protection. With the deflation of the bubble came a massive loss of wealth, on Wall Street as well as around the world.

The tech bubble was a reflection of the bubble phenomenon that gripped Wall Street in the 1990s. The bubble phenomenon, which has a lengthy history, came in six stages.[1]

1. The first stage was the advent of a new technology that offered to change the world in which we live.

2. Once the new technology began to make an impact there was interest in it by the financial world. In the meantime, the average person was becoming increasingly aware of the Internet and other aspects of the new economy.

3. The third stage witnessed the shift of new technology from being incubated by a select number of investors (during the late twentieth century, venture capitalists) to going to the broader stock market for funding. The use of the Internet spread, and more people came on board with the revolutionary aspects of the innovation.

4. The fourth stage was where the new technology caught the imagination of the investing public. This stage begins as prudent investment but ends up being dominated by hype and the emergence of more questionable (or, as some would argue, dodgy) investment schemes involving new technology. Excitement about the new technology sector spreads outward to the rest of the market, pushing up stock values. The boom is on.

5. The next to last stage is the peak, where the smart and lucky money exits, leaving the field to the less well informed and less lucky. Delusion becomes a factor for many investors.

6. The last stage is the crash, in which some catalyst erodes confidence in the market and many of the financial instruments of new technology companies. Investors flee the market and the crash ripples through the entire market. Delusion becomes disillusion.

▶ THE "NEW ECONOMY" STORY

The first stage of the bubble phenomenon came with the development of new technology. PCs came along in the late 1970s. In 1981, Microsoft founder Bill Gates launched MS-DOS to run on IBM's new PC. Between these two developments, the tech revolution began to help reshape the way we live. As Robert Cringley, author of *Accidental Empires*, aptly noted:

> Personal computers came along in the late 1970s and by the mid-1980s had invaded every office and infected many homes. In addition to being the ultimate item of conspicuous consumption for those of us who don't collect fine art, PCs killed the office typewriter, made most secretaries obsolete, and made it possible for a 27-year-old M.B.A. with a PC, a spreadsheet program and three pieces of questionable data to talk his bosses into looting the company pension plan and doing a leveraged buy-out.[2]

The American public became familiar with the PC and the tech world's new cast of stars: Bill Gates, John Doerr, Jim Clark, and Steve Jobs. They were the vanguard of the tech revolution, turning California's Silicon Valley into a new Mecca for the entrepreneur and venture capitalist, as well as a source of new companies soon to hit first the United States and eventually the global investor.[3]

Silicon Valley's rise accelerated other developments, and companies began experimenting with cell phones (making them more compact and flashier), broadband was sold cheaply by the U.S. government to a new set of entrepreneurs who began making en masse pagers, and computers were just beginning to be introduced to the workspace.[4] By the 1990s, the new technological revolution was in full swing, leading to considerable upheaval in the U.S. corporate world, akin to the industrial revolution, which shook the United States and international economy during the late nineteenth and early twentieth centuries. The focus on information technology, or IT, was based on computers and various networks; it was creating what was called the New Economy. Presumably, the New Economy would uproot the old economy of brick and mortar and replace it with a seamless, information-driven, universally connected world. The Internet was a core element in this vision, of course, as it created a new cosmos for marketing and interconnectedness that had otherwise not existed.

Key to the New Economy was the belief that IT was able to magnify labor productivity. According to a study conducted by the International Monetary Fund (IMF), there are three stages that occur with technological revolutions.

1. First, technological change raises growth in the innovating sector.
2. As the innovations become widespread, they cause prices for capital spending in the economy at large to drop.
3. There is a significant reorganization of production around the capital goods that embody the new technology.[5]

Thus, in plain English, IT and related technology increase productivity, as their impact ripples outward from the starting sector into the broader economy. This explanation also implies that the process of enhancing productivity could take time, i.e., not occur on a fast track to overnight conversion. If we look back to our six stages, clearly what the IMF was talking about was how the new technology made the shift from being the arena of a few players (the tech innovators and their initial financiers) to the bigger markets. The fourth stage, "take off," came with a lot of hype.

The tone of the tech bubble was best epitomized by Harry S. Dent, Jr., in his book *The Roaring 2000s: Building Wealth and the Lifestyle You Desire in the Greatest Boom in History*. Educated at Harvard University and a corporate advisor to several Fortune 500 companies, Dent clearly put his finger on the excitement behind the tech bubble, proclaiming: "In fact, we are on the brink of the most exciting boom period since the Roaring Twenties. I call it the Roaring 2000s, because it will usher in the kind of sweeping economic and social changes that turned post–World War I America upside down."[6] He argues: "Now, new technologies, industries, products and services are again about to burst forth." Significantly, the baby boomers are expected to be big spenders of what the New Economy will provide. Following demographic trends, Dent asserts, "the economy is highly predictable." Moreover: "The simple but powerful truth is that we can easily project long-term economic trends. Our economy is fundamentally driven by predictable family spending cycles of each generation and the predictable movement of new technologies and industries into the mainstream of our society."[7] The key words for many investors listening to Dent and other boosters of the New Economy were *easily predictable*. This suggested that anyone with any common sense could make a killing in the stock market by just buying stock in the right companies. This was indeed a truth during a bull market, but over the long term it was obviously a bit misleading. (His historical emphasis on the Roaring Twenties did not immediately bring one's attention to the Great Depression of the 1930s.)

Beyond the hype, a more balanced approach of the New Economy was given by Bob Davis and David Wessel, two veteran journalists. In a far less sensationalistic way than Dent, they argued that the 1990s witnessed a confluence of trends in technology, education, and globalization, which were to "see the flowering of an era of broadly shared prosperity for the American middle class."[8] Accordingly, the massive $2 trillion investment in computer and communications technology would lead to increased productivity and rising living standards. This trend is reinforced by the rise of community colleges and other educational institutions that will help reverse the forces that have widened the chasm between the educated classes and working poor. Finally, globalization is expected to create new and better jobs, both from U.S. companies exporting to developing countries and from foreign companies building in the United States. In addition, many of the Old Economy companies moved to adopt the new technology.

It is important not to understate the power of the idea. The Internet and all related technology represented a powerful new idea that tied together economics and politics—business and lifestyle—into one package. As Mark Ingebretsen explained:

> A kind of hip youth culture, flowing out from tech firms in California, in many ways pressured Americans to accept the new-economy credo. A generation before, baby boomers had rallied against the political establishment. This new generation's goals were far more defined and pragmatic: Dismantle the old capitalism system and replace it with a faster, cheaper, better version run via the Internet. If you were not

on board, you did not get it. And if you hung on to the dreary old ways of doing business, you were a Luddite and deserved to be squashed.[9]

Although there was a considerable amount of hype about the creation of the new economy, in reality there was a degree of creative destruction. Certainly, one strength of the new economy was its dual ability to enhance productivity and absorb new and displaced workers. As Thomas L. Friedman wrote in August 1999: "… U.S. companies are quick to absorb new, more productive technologies because they can easily absorb the cost of the new investment by laying off the workers who used to perform that task. And as the overall economy becomes more productive, these workers get rehired elsewhere."[10]

It is also important to emphasize that the New Economy was not limited to the United States but was global in its impact. In fact, the wireless revolution in telecommunications in Asia and Europe was more advanced than in the United States, while the application of PCs and the Internet expanded users massively. (Table 6.1 reflects a substantial penetration of the Internet from very small numbers in the early 1990s.) This obviously had an impact on the major global economies as well as on the lesser-developed regions, such as in Africa, Central Asia, and parts of Latin America. The tech revolution funneled into many Latin American and Eastern European nations as the privatization of local telecommunications monopolies brought foreign capital into such a diverse set of countries as Argentina, Brazil, Peru, the Czech Republic, Poland, and Hungary. With upgrades in communications came greater Internet penetration, and with that came "B to B" (business to business) communications, Internet shopping, and new forms of entertainment. The New Economy, symbolized by Silicon Valley and Silicon Glen (in Scotland), was a harbinger of globalization, making Sao Paulo and Shanghai all part of the same grid, sharing many of the same expectations of what this meant to enhancing productivity and augmenting commerce. (It should be added that the great leap forward in technology and communications increased the gap between the wired, most of whom were in the more developed world, and the unwired, the majority being in the lesser-developed parts of Africa, the Middle East, Asia, and Latin America.)

TABLE 6.1 Headway of the Internet: Worldwide Internet Users in 2000

Country	Millions of Users
United States	135.7
Japan	26.9
Germany	19.1
UK	17.9
China	15.8
Korea	14.8
Italy	11.6
Brazil	10.6
France	9.0

Source: Red Herring, December 18, 2000, p. 55.

▶ THE GREAT TECH GOLD RUSH

The forces behind the great tech rush were numerous, including the savvy investment strategies of venture capitalists, a rush of new technology, and a public ready to absorb the new line of tech products. A steady period of economic growth since the beginning in 1991 and low inflation also put many Americans in a position where they were ready and able to invest in the stock market, largely attracted to the stocks of the new econ-omy. This was certainly the case of cellular phones.

The cellular phone story has its roots as far back as 1896, when the young Italian inventor, Enrico Marconi, patented the world's first wireless telegraph. In 1901, he made history when he tapped away the Morse Code from Newfoundland, Canada, to a transmitter in Cornwall, England. Marconi proved what had been speculated about: radio waves travel around the curve of the earth. But still, the cellular rev-olution was slow in coming. Size was an issue; many of the early models of the cel-lular phone were too heavy and bulky, while there were major issues with spectrum. Simply stated, spectrum is the airwaves through which sound travels, with numer-ous frequencies that can be used. As James B. Murray, Jr., noted, spectrum "is the commodity on which every kind of wireless communications runs, from garage door openers to pagers to satellite dishes and beyond ... like real estate in the sky."[11] In the 1980s, though, a growing number of individuals began to see the promise of cellular communications, especially as other technological innovations, such as pagers, were showing promise. This combined with the U.S. government's move to dismantle AT&T, the telephone monopoly, in 1984 and a shift in the policy of the Federal Communications Commission (FCC) to begin selling spectrum licenses in the early 1980s.

While the 1980s saw the fundamentals align for the formation of cellular phone companies, the mid-1990s saw the sector take off. The economic slowdown in 1990–1991 briefly interrupted the process, but by 1993–1994 the telecommunica-tions sector was gearing up. Venture capitalists found the tech revolution fertile soil for sowing large profits. At the same time that the FCC moved to sell spectrum, it set the wheels in motion for expansion of the telecommunications industry, already being reshaped by wireless technology advances. Part of the impetus behind such products as cell phones and personal computers was everyone's fear of being left behind. As one observer noted of the cell phone: "Technically speaking, no one really needed one. But once people started using them, no one wanted to be with-out one. ..."[12] The corporate world moved to keep abreast of the changes in telecommunications as well as with the Internet. Although the Internet was not used in a commercial sense until 1995, it quickly spread. In addition, the U.S. Congress passed the Telecommunications Act of 1996, which was the first over-haul of the telecommunications industry in sixty-two years and was a major step to deregulation of the sector. This new law let anyone enter into the communications business and let any company compete in any market against any other company. Suddenly, the wide world of telecommunications was open to all who could raise the money to enter. Consequently, in the 1997–1999 period there was a massive surge in technology budgets on the part of corporate America.

Telecommunications was hardly the only element of the convergence of tech-nology and finance. The birth of the Internet also opened the door to a wide realm of entrepreneurs, tech experts, and new companies, ready and willing to seek ven-ture capital. Companies like Critical Path embodied the new order of the Internet boom. Founded by David Hayden, Critical Path was one of the first to move into e-mail. Hayden was able to raise $40 million in venture funding to fill a former chocolate factory in San Francisco with engineers. The new company had no profit and less than $1 million in revenues. However, it was able to raise almost $600 million in a year from investors, while its shares started at $24 and climbed to $150 in a month, fueling a $1.8 billion acquisition binge.[13] For investors looking for "hot" companies, Critical Path was a definite prospect. (The company would later file for bankruptcy protection and re-emerge in 2003.)

An additional element of the tech bubble was the rise of the NASDAQ. Although the NASDAQ had its beginnings in the 1940s, it became a real force in stock trading only in the 1970s, when trading was automated for the first time. The NASDAQ was traditionally for institutional investors trading large quantities of common stock on the over the counter (OTC) market. "OTC" referred to stocks not listed on one of the national exchanges or one of the regional exchanges. Instead, the stocks were traded "over the counter" by licensed brokers.

It is important to underscore that the NASDAQ was revolutionized by technology. As computer trading and telecommunications improved, so did the stock exchange's ability to handle larger volumes of trade. This opened the door to a new sea of investors, beyond the traditional large institutional investors. By the mid-1990s trading was executed through a sophisticated computer and telecommunications network that eventually came to transmit real-time quote and trade data to more than one million users in over eighty countries. Consequently, the NASDAQ, a market based on the juncture of technological and financial innovations, attracted many of the new companies, such as Apple, Oracle, and Microsoft. The close association between the new wave of tech companies and the NASDAQ helped open a new world of investment as the small investor discovered technology. All of this helped pump up the NASDAQ as a key element in the 1990s bull market. Although the New York Stock Exchange (NYSE) would regain its prominence, the NASDAQ was more closely associated with the gold rush.

By 2000, the tech bubble was at its height. For those involved in telecommunications, the Internet, media, and anything remotely related to tech, the world was an exceedingly busy place, marked by an amazing upward march of the NASDAQ and Dow and fueled by an ongoing flow of IPOs and mergers and acquisitions. The media were ready to capture the hurly-burly of the tech bubble. In an article in *The Boston Globe*, the dash of one venture capitalist, Sheryl Marshall, is captured:

> Sheryl Marshall is living the transition. In August, she quit her longtime gig as a high-profile stockbroker for Donaldson, Lufkin & Jenrette Inc. She pushed her Christian Dior suits to the back of her closet and cut off her mane of curly hair. "I've got the venture capital haircut," she says. No time for bad hair while she's jetting around the country, raising $50 million from investors. Marshall's Axxon Capital Inc. aims to invest in hot young companies, especially those run by women.[14]

The article also discussed how venture capital was much more rewarding for those individuals who made the switch from traditional investment banking. In a sense, the article represented venture capitalists as rugged individualists (or at least people seeking their independence from large, stodgy corporations), dedicated to "building longer-term relationships with entrepreneurs and helping to build companies." This obviously appealed to the image many Americans have traditionally had of themselves, reminding people of those hardy pioneers who went forth to tame the Wild West in the second half of the nineteenth century.

The appeal of venture capital and the tech sector percolated into Wall Street even beyond the rush for stocks. As the dot-com craze gained momentum in the late 1990s, a brain drain from investment banking began. At many business schools, MBAs were more interested in joining dot-com companies or venture capital firms than Wall Street investment banks, a significant shift from the 1980s and mid-1990s.[15] In 1999, at the Harvard Business School, 12 percent of the graduating MBA class went into venture capital, up 50 percent from 1997. At the same time, 10 percent went into investment banking, down from 16 percent in 1997 and much higher levels in the 1980s. In this environment, an MBA with only two to three years' experience could command a considerable pay package at almost any job.

The lure of the tech rush (in its broadest sense) to the investor was enormous. Consider the following observation by one newspaper in January 1999:

> Just eight days ago, shares in Internet-site developer CMGI Inc. sold for $57.25 apiece; yesterday they traded for more than twice that, $130.75. Yahoo, Inc., the search-engine company, has seen its stock nearly double over the same period, to $402. And Broadcast.com, an Internet radio and television provider, ended the session at $233 a share, nearly three times what the stock fetched at the beginning of the year.[16]

The rush into tech stocks was contagious. As Ken Pasternak, president of the brokerage firm Knight Securities in Jersey City, which handled orders for Internet trading companies, stated: "Everybody's buying them. Everybody, down to taxicab drivers and housewives and anyone else who has felt the empowerment of the Internet."[17] Delusion had clearly become a factor in the market by 1999. The cult of equity was now deeply rooted in the market's psychology.

Many of the companies that were the most attractive to investors still had not made a profit. The large online bookseller Amazon.com, in business since 1995, did not make a profit through the rest of the decade. Nonetheless, the idea of selling books online attracted enough investors to pump up the company's market capitalization to a massive $26 billion in 1999, six times the combined value of its two major rivals, Borders Group and Barnes & Noble, both of which would eventually be forced to launch their own online sales.

Adding to the contagious nature of the stock market rush was the emergence of the day traders—individuals who worked from a computer hooked into the Internet and traded on momentum during the day. Day traders did not have to be licensed broker-dealers, did not have to work with a major brokerage firm, and did not have to deal with the pressures of a 9-to-5 job. Instead, the day trader could roll out of bed, sit in his pajamas, and trade stocks. She could be a student or someone operating from the living room. In a sense, the day trader embodied many of the substantial technological changes in how finance was conducted in the 1990s. The Internet democratized trading and brought empowerment—outside of the control of the Wall Street insiders. This loss of control by Wall Street firms and major institutional players added another force to the gold rush mentality.

One profile of a day trader in 1999 featured a twenty-year-old computer science major at the Massachusetts Institute of Technology who made $10,000 trading in Internet stocks and other issues over a month.[18] Each morning he booted up a personal computer loaded with software that tracks the NASDAQ stock exchange. While admitting that he had not mastered the art of valuing stocks over the long term, he also indicated that he had no intention of doing so. Rather: "This is about seeing a pattern and stepping in front of it." (This is what many refer to as momentum trading. When a trend in trading becomes apparent, other traders jump up, giving the buying wave further momentum.)

While a number of industry actors were growing wary of the Internet bubble in 1999, the market boom was hardly over. There were still large groups of investors who strongly believed that the Internet was going to continue to reap further riches. Bob Adler, president of CCBN.com in Boston, an online financial data provider, stated in January 1999: "The supply of [Internet stocks] is grossly limited compared to their place in the world. The fact is that everybody thinks that the Internet is going to open up a lot of new electronic channels of commerce, and they want to have a piece of that in their portfolios."[19] Added to this were industry pundits' statements that revenues would top $1.2 trillion by 2002 and might someday reach $33 trillion worldwide.[20]

By early 1999, it was estimated that the combined market value of publicly traded Internet stocks was around $250 billion. In a sense, the NASDAQ ran off the reality track in 1999, as tech stocks pulled it far ahead of every other index. It was not just the Internet stocks that were climbing amazing highs, but virtually anything related to tech, including telecommunications (Qwest, WorldCom, and Sprint), telecommunications equipment makers (Lucent, Nortel, and Motorola), and fiber optics producers (Corning). Even small foreign Internet companies that ventured on to the NASDAQ, such as China.com and Korea Thrunet, did exceedingly well, despite showing exceedingly little prospect for profits.

A major factor in the Internet bubble was the strong view that the new economy was for real and that technology spending would continue at an impressive pace. For many investors considering further investing in tech stocks in 2000, the feeling was that technology investment boosted American productivity, kept inflation in check, and prolonged the expansion into the longest in recorded history. Many of the same ideas were evident elsewhere in the world. In Europe and industrialized Asia, investors expected that major new investments in technology would continue indefinitely. Moreover, American business increasingly purchased tech-related services from Asian countries, including Singapore, Korea, Taiwan, the Philippines, and Malaysia. India became an important offshore computer center, providing a well-educated and computer-literate workforce. Israel emerged as an important part of the global grid as local companies tapped into the highly educated labor pool and developed expertise in everything from biotechnology to electronics.

Another offshoot of the Internet revolution was the transformation of the gaming industry, i.e., video games. Long perceived as the realm of the nerd, the Internet radically changed the gaming world, pumping it into the mainstream of the entertainment business. In fact, big business could not ignore the gaming industry. By 1999, game-related revenue topped movie box office figures, and some 145 million Americans—more than half of the population—admitted to playing video games.[21] What made all of this more attractive was that 43 percent of the players were women, a large and somewhat untapped market. Like so much else in the tech bubble, the expectation was that gaming would continue to rapidly expand: online consoles and computers were soon expected to allow players to come together in cyberspace.

Despite some fears to the contrary, 2000 was another record year for the stock market. Indeed, in 2000 tech and telecom stocks together made up more than a third of the overall market capitalization of U.S. equity markets. Twelve of the top twenty best-performing stocks over 1995–2000 were tech companies. The high fliers were Nortel Networks, Nokia, Broadcom, Yahoo, and Applied Materials. Yet, the words of Robert Brusca, chief economist in the New York office of Nikko Securities, rang true: "The image you get is of Wile E. Coyote having stepped off a mesa but still smiling because he hasn't looked down yet."[22] Although the comment was made in 1999, it was really more appropriate for 2000, when the carnival on Wall Street entered its last round.

▶ THE END OF THE PARTY

The great bull market in the NASDAQ and related tech stocks on the Dow had a very strong allure for the smaller investor. Yet, not everyone was sold on the running of the bulls on Wall Street. As early as December 1996, Federal Reserve Chairman Alan Greenspan warned investors about their "irrational exuberance" and suggested they should let prices slide to lower, more realistic levels. At the time of his warning, the Dow was at 6,382. It would continue its dizzying ascent up to a little over 11,000 in 2001. Greenspan was not alone in foreseeing the dangers of the stock market bubble. In January 1999, financial commentator Martin Mayer stated: "The NASDAQ market is an obvious bubble. Bubbles that pop make a lot of money disappear, with unpredictable consequences—especially in our time, when math Ph.D.s burnish analyses that link different markets together and carry economic disease around the world as the Norway rat carried the bubonic plague."[23]

Red Herring, a tech-oriented magazine, was also filled with concerns about the Internet bubble. Indeed, in the fall of 1999, the top executives of the magazine published a book called *The Internet Bubble*, in which they concluded: "Our advice to Internet investors is simple; if you hold any of these stocks, it's time to sell." The first deflation in the tech bubble came in April 2000, when dot-com shares started to fall. During the week of April 10, the NASDAQ fell 25 percent, a trend that would gather momentum in the months to come. In December 2000, *Red Herring*'s Arnold Berman followed through with the same theme in an article on the "next big thing," in which he wrote: "Technology investment will likely be less about hype, the open-ended potential of the addressable market, and press releases. Instead, it will be about stock picking, earnings growth, and hard work."[24]

What finally caused the bubble to burst? The bottom line was a loss of confidence by the investor in the ability of the Internet to be an ongoing creator of wealth. There was a shift from blind faith in the stock market and tech to climb forever higher to a growing concern that perhaps the boom would not go on forever. In time, growing concern was replaced by nagging doubts that were increasingly tied to financial realities that companies eventually needed to earn profits and that larger and larger amounts of debt could not forever be accumulated. At some point, companies had to make profits and debt had to be repaid. As this process of awareness accelerated, the economic backdrop changed for the negative. After a long growth spurt, the U.S. economy slowed abruptly in the second half of 2000. A convergence of forces was responsible: a severe winter, a fall in consumer demand, power shortages in parts of the country, and companies cutting spending. This fed into the computer sector, which saw sales plunge. This in turn eroded confidence in the tech sector's profitability. Suddenly, the high debt levels and lack of free cash flow in many tech companies looked really bad. While these companies struggled for profits in a healthy economy, this thought now gained momentum: How would these same companies fare in a poor economic environment?

Although the number of Internet users worldwide continued to climb in 2000 and 2001 to more than five hundred million people around the planet, there was a massive fall-out and consolidation in the tech industry. Many dot-coms, having been unable to generate profits, finally lost the confidence of the investors. As fast as investor money had been poured into the dot-com world, it now flowed out. And this fear was to ripple into the rest of the tech world. More attention was given to the balance sheet and such matters as financial flexibility, embodied in access to credit and leverage. The idea no longer sold by itself; the ability to make profits, backed by a good idea, did. What this meant was that as investors put companies under the microscope, many in the tech sector were found wanting. In addition, a number of companies, some of them very large, increasingly appeared to be houses of cards, constructed on weak foundations, with substantial debt burdens. Eventually, as the bubble deflated, there were a number of major corporate crashes.

While the tech bubble deflated through 2000–2001, what accelerated the process was the Enron scandal in late 2001. Enron was an energy company that during the 1990s morphed into an energy-trading company, making extensive use of derivatives and off-balance-sheet financial entities. Although Enron is discussed at greater length elsewhere in this book, the scandal that rocked the company revealed that parts of the management intentionally deceived the public by overstating profits and hiding losses. What was particularly disturbing was the involvement of the company's accounting firm, Arthur Andersen, in destroying records and obscuring financial transactions. Following the company's bankruptcy in December 2001, the term "Enronitis" was used to describe companies that employed questionable accounting techniques intentionally misleading the public in terms of profits. The search for companies with Enronitis took investors to the telecom sector—in particular, WorldCom.

Under Bernie Ebbers in the 1990s, WorldCom rose to become the second largest long-distance and data services company in the United States and carrier of about half of all Internet traffic. Originally from Edmonton, Canada, Ebbers founded WorldCom in Mississippi in 1983. Tall, bearded, and often pictured wearing cowboy boots with expensive suits, Ebbers had a distinctive persona. Usually at his side was Scott Sullivan, the chief financial officer (CFO), well dressed, articulate, and persuasive. The company followed an aggressive strategy involving sixty acquisitions, the high point of which was the audacious $37 billion purchase of MCI in 1996. By 1999, WorldCom generated close to $40 billion a year in revenues, and its stock peaked at $61.99, tripling in value from January 1, 1998. Ebbers and Sullivan had taken a small company based in Clinton, Mississippi, and converted it into a major global player in the international telecommunications industry.

WorldCom's push to become a major powerhouse, however, came at a cost. To wheel and deal in the telecom market, a considerable sum of capital was borrowed from banks and raised by Wall Street firms. Impressed by Ebbers' rag-to-riches tale and his ability to sell the company, investors lined up. By year-end 2001, WorldCom group's debt was a massive $30 billion. The stock was widely held by both large institutional investors, including state retirement funds, and small investors, many of whom held it in retirement funds. In the late 1990s, the money poured in. However, the telecom industry began to undergo a dramatic change. WorldCom's once highly specialized product of long-distance communications became a lower-priced commodity. Fierce price competition ultimately generated less revenue, just in time for the tech bubble to burst in 2000–2001, taking WorldCom's stock with it.

Complicating matters for WorldCom, Ebbers had gone on a personal buying spree and accumulated a number of acquisitions, ranging from a massive timber farm in British Columbia to a boat called the *Aquasition* and a mansion in Mississippi. Ebbers used WorldCom stock to secure bank loans to make these purchases. When stock prices began to fall, the bank called the loans. Ebbers then turned to his board at WorldCom, which first guaranteed the loan and then assumed the debt itself. Consequently, Ebbers came to borrow money, some $408.2 million, from his own firm, an action that is regarded as poor corporate governance and raises serious moral questions. If nothing else, the loans were a factor in the decision of the Securities and Exchange Commission (SEC) to investigate WorldCom. Under pressure from disgruntled shareholders, Ebbers stepped down as CEO in April 2002. *The Globe and Mail*'s Mathew Ingram best captured the change in Ebber's fortune: "It's been quite a ride for Bernie Ebbers, the Edmonton-born former basketball coach with the cowboy boots and the sprawling B.C. ranch, the poster boy for the New Economy, fiber-optic data revolution that was sweeping through the telecom industry. Now, having resigned as CEO of the company he started in 1983, he represents the opposite—the collapse of most of the industry's multibillion dollar dreams."[25]

The accumulation of falling profitability, questionable corporate governance, and an SEC investigation all made WorldCom a focal point for frustrated investors looking for someone to blame. WorldCom stock was severely punished, falling to under $1 a share. However, the real blow came in June 2002, when it was revealed that the company had intentionally hid $3.88 billion in current expenses by counting them as capital investments that could be written off over twenty-five years. The SEC charged the company with fraud. This was followed by the firing of seventeen thousand employees (20 percent of the staff), while the company's employees' 401K retirement plan lost more than $1 billion. In July 2002, WorldCom filed for bankruptcy—the largest in U.S. history. In early August, the company announced that it had discovered another $3.3 billion in overstated earnings, dating back to 1999. Shortly following that revelation, the public was given the memorable picture of WorldCom's CFO Scott Sullivan being led off in handcuffs by the FBI.

What made the demise of WorldCom sit so badly with many Americans was that Bernie Ebbers, who presided over the demise of his company and the destruction of his employees' jobs and retirement savings, was paid exceedingly well. The company paid him $46.5 million in salary and bonuses from 1997 to 2001, while the value in WorldCom shares hovered at about $1.5 billion in 1999. As one former WorldCom Internet engineer who lost his job stated: "It looks like Bernie Ebbers pulled out of this very well. I have a whole list of people who have been devastated by this. People with families and bills to pay, mortgages, and not on ranches, on their homes."[26]

By late 2002, the list of criminal charges against some of the former high fliers of corporate America's leadership had grown. Those implicated included members of WorldCom's top management and senior executives at Arthur Andersen, Adelphia Communications, and biotech firm Imclone Systems (as well as Martha Stewart, as a stockholder of the latter). In addition, a number of companies were under criminal investigation, including media giant AOL (over questions pertaining to how America Online recorded revenue before its 2001 merger with Time Warner), Computer Associates (questions over inflating sales and profit by booking revenue on contracts many years before it was paid), Global Crossing (suspected of inflating sales and profit by making sham transactions with other telecommunications companies), and Qwest (ditto). In the case of Qwest, the company's decline also marked the departure of its former CEO, the pugnacious and highly ambitious Ralph Nacchio.

The bursting of the tech bubble quickly rippled into the world of investment banking. After enjoying a long bull market, marked by lax regulatory supervision, huge fees from IPOs, merger and acquisitions, and sky-high investor confidence, the world shifted. Confidence—so critical to making markets work—was badly eroded by the scandals that followed the market slump in 2001 and into 2002. The Enron scandal and the implications for Arthur Andersen did considerable damage in eroding investor confidence in corporate America, including not only the tech sector but the entire range of companies from accounting to energy. Eventually, this erosion of investor confidence was to focus on Wall Street itself.

In March 2001, a lawsuit was brought against Merrill Lynch by Debases Kanjilal, who claimed he lost $500,000 investing in Infospace, Inc., an Internet stock he said his Merrill Lynch broker urged him not to sell when it was trading at $60 a share. By the time Kanjilal sold the stock it had fallen to $11. In the suit against Merrill Lynch, it was alleged that the investment bank's star Internet analyst, Henry Blodget, had misled investors by fraudulently promoting the stocks of companies with which the firm had investment banking relationships. While there was nothing new about angry investor suits against Wall Street firms, in this case it helped stimulate an investigation by New York State Attorney Eliot Spitzer. Spitzer was to undertake a hard-hitting investigation of Merrill Lynch and a number of other firms, including Solomon Smith Barney, Morgan Stanley Dean Witter, and others.

In the course of the investigation, the public was shocked when Spitzer released some e-mail exchanges between Merrill Lynch's analysts and bankers. In particular, the e-mails gave the appearance that there was a degree of collusion between the investment bankers and research analysts to boost prices for companies that were really not worthy of such recommendations. In the private e-mails, analysts disparaged stocks as "crap" and "junk," even as they publicly maintained buy recommendations. Theoretically, Chinese walls—the corporate policy of strict separation of the different lines of business conducted under the same roof—existed to prevent any such abuses. As *BusinessWeek* noted, Chinese walls "were supposed to keep the bankers honest and free from corruption."[27] Although some bankers surely turned a blind eye to this before the 1990s, a lot of people had lost money investing in stocks. Billions of dollars of wealth disappeared with each downward twist in the stock market. The earlier Enron scandal had already raised these issues, as many of the major Wall Street analysts maintained buy recommendations on the stock even as it plummeted toward a dollar and under. The investigation of Merrill Lynch now added fuel to the flames of public anger. It also badly eroded the confidence of investors, who already were deeply worried about a hard economic landing.

Adding to the popping of the tech bubble was the loss of jobs. The number of companies filing for bankruptcy rose sharply in the aftermath of the bubble. In early 2003, the American Electronics Association released a report noting that more than a half million U.S. citizens lost their high-tech jobs from January 2001 to December 2002. In particular, 560,000 workers employed at high-tech firms such as Hewlett-Packard, IBM, and Lucent were laid off in the two-year period that saw the dot-com bubble burst.

The demise of a number of major U.S. telecommunications companies demonstrated—in case anyone still doubted it—that at least part of the stock market rise during the 1990s was not constructed on firm foundations. Rather, there was a degree of intentional obscuring of transparency, which led to one scandal after another. It also led to some of the largest bankruptcies in U.S. corporate history (Table 6.2). These bankruptcies resulted in the loss of thousands of jobs, wiped billions of dollars from shareholders' accounts, and hurt companies conducting business with the crippled giants. Significantly, some of the most dramatic bankruptcies came in the once high-flying telecommunications and tech sector, as mirrored by WorldCom, Global Crossing, Adelphia Communications, and NTL.

While U.S. telecommunications high fliers WorldCom and Qwest crashed, non-U.S. companies did not escape the agony of the tech bubble. Europe has also found itself caught up in the tech-telecom-media investment binge. France Telecom, Deutsche Telekom, British Telecom, and KPN, the Netherlands phone company, suffered from the accumulation of too much expansion, too much debt, and an inability of top management to come to terms with the changes in the

TABLE 6.2   The Largest Bankruptcies: 1980 to Present

Company	Bankruptcy Date	Total Assets Pre-Bankruptcy	Filing Court District
Worldcom, Inc.°	7/21/2002	$103,914,000,000	NY-S
Enron Corp. †	12/2/2001	63,392,000,000	NY-S
Texaco, Inc.	4/12/1987	35,892,000,000	NY-S
Financial Corp. of America	9/9/1988	33,864,000,000	CA-C
Global Crossing Ltd.	1/28/2002	25,511,000,000	NY-S
Adelphia Communications	6/25/2002	24,409,662,000	NY-S
Pacific Gas and Electric Co.	4/6/2001	21,470,000,000	CA-N
MCorp	3/31/1989	20,228,000,000	TX-S
Kmart Corp.	1/22/2002	17,007,000,000	IL-N
NTL, Inc.	5/8/2002	16,834,200,000	NY-S
First Executive Corp.	5/13/1991	15,193,000,000	CA-C
Gibraltar Financial Corp.	2/8/1990	15,011,000,000	CA-C
FINOVA Group, Inc., (The)	3/7/2001	14,050,000,000	DE
HomeFed Corp.	10/22/1992	13,885,000,000	CA-S
Southeast Banking Corporation	9/20/1991	13,390,000,000	FL-S
Reliance Group Holdings, Inc.	6/12/2001	12,598,000,000	NY-S
Imperial Corp. of America	2/28/1990	12,263,000,000	CA-S
Federal-Mogul Corp.	10/1/2001	10,150,000,000	DE
First City Bancorp of Texas	10/31/1992	9,943,000,000	TX-N
First Capital Holdings	5/30/1991	9,675,000,000	CA-C
Baldwin-United	9/26/1983	9,383,000,000	OH-S

°WorldCom, Inc., assets were taken from the audited annual report dated 12/31/2001.

†Enron assets were taken from the 10-Q filed on 11/19/2001. The company has announced that the financials were under review at the time of filing for Chapter 11.

Source: BankruptcyData.com.

business environment from boom to bust. Billions of euros were spent on Germany's third-generation wireless licenses, while Central and Eastern Europe saw Western European telecom giants buying up cheap new assets. However, all of this was to come at a price. As stock prices fell in 2001, pressure grew for tough restructuring measures and for changes at the top. Within a few months in 2001 and 2002, the heads of British Telecom, KPN, and Vivendi were ousted by angry shareholders. Still other companies, such as the United Kingdom's telecommunications equipment maker Marconi, struggled to survive heavy debt burdens and falling revenues.

Vivendi Universal is a good example of a company whose aspirations to become a major media/entertainment/telecommunications powerhouse exceeded its capabilities. Starting from its humble beginnings in the mid-nineteenth century as a water company in Lyons, France, Vivendi underwent sweeping changes in the 1990s, eventually accumulating Canada's Seagram (owner of Universal Music Group and Universal Studios), the entertainment assets of USA Networks, and various publishing companies (including Boston's august Houghton-Mifflin). Vivendi also owned European pay-TV provider CANAL+ Group (which reaches sixteen million subscribers), 44 percent of telecom provider Cegetel, and about 40 percent of Vivendi Environnement, the world's leading water distributor. By 2001, Vivendi was the world's number three media company, behind only AOL TimeWarner and Disney.

Vivendi's great acquisition binge was led by Jean-Marie Messier, who vowed to bring an Anglo-American management culture to the former water utility turned into media-entertainment-telecom empire. Indeed, the well-connected Messier was one of the movers and shakers of the French business world. Prior to running Vivendi, he had held a number of senior roles in the French economy ministry during the 1980s and then worked as an investment banker. He was a friend of the Socialist Prime Minister Lionel Jospin. In 1994, he became CEO of the staid Compagnie Generale des Eaux. Messier's vision was to convert the 150-year-old company, whose core activities were refuse collection and running sewage plants, into a global media and telecommunications conglomerate. Riding a string of acquisitions, partially financed by bank loans and bonds, Messier managed to remake his company, renaming it Vivendi.

Good-looking, well-dressed, and articulate, Vivendi's CEO was popular in French business circles, especially as he demonstrated that French companies could compete globally and head to head with U.S. and British companies. As one reporter noted, "The colorful chief executive, still in his early 40s, became known as J6M, short for Jean Marie Messier, Moi Meme Maitre de Monde (master of the world)."[28]

Messier's empire building came at a huge cost. While the dashing Vivendi CEO built up a trans-Atlantic business, he also amassed a huge mountain of debt. During the 1990s, when times were good, the well-connected Messier enjoyed easy access to credit from international banks and capital markets. Vivendi's bond issues were well-received, and the stock was bought on both sides of the Atlantic. However, when the stock market bubble burst and the impact rippled into Europe, helped along by the events of September 11, 2001, Messier's empire began to unravel. As revenues fell, the company's Euro 19 billion ($18.6 billion) debt began to weigh heavily. Vivendi's unprecedented expansion had been based on acquisitions, and as economic growth faltered, concerns mounted that the company had paid too much for its many purchases.[29] The former hero was now accused of hubris, his position at the helm not helped by a Euro 13.6 billion loss for 2001, falling stock prices, and his comment that "the French cultural exception is dead" (widely interpreted as a condemnation of government subsidies for French art and culture).[30] The fact that Messier moved to New York City, with a very chic and expensive Park Avenue address, did not go down well with his former circle of contacts in France. By early July 2002, Messier was ousted in a nasty and protracted board fight.

Messier's legacy, like that of his Canadian counterpart Bernie Ebbers or Qwest's Ralph Nacchio, was to leave his company in freefall, its future highly uncertain. By August 2002, there were serious doubts that Vivendi would survive. If nothing else, it would be forced to sell off a substantial amount of assets, perhaps leaving it not much more than where it started—a water company. Vivendi was destined to become yet another example of too rapid expansion, not enough integration, and too much hype paid to the wonders of the New Economy.

By 2002, the bull market of the 1990s was a distant memory. From the beginning of June through July 17, 2002, investors sold about $46 billion more of stock mutual funds than they bought. The $46 billion represented almost 1.5 percent of all stock mutual funds held in the United States, marking this as the largest redemption over a two-year period since 1990.[31] The money was fleeing the stock market and went into bonds, cash, and real estate. As journalists David Leonhardt and Jennifer Bayot noted in July 2002: "The fall of the broad market by almost half since early 2000 has left many people questioning stocks, at least over the short term, for the first time in their lives." The questioning of stocks reflected the end of the cult of equity. The new reality was a swing to the opposite—lack of confidence in the stock market, suspicion of accountants, CEOs, and CFOs, and little tolerance of any potential problems.

In all fairness, it is important to indicate that not all tech and tech-related companies failed in the aftermath of the bubble. In fact, a large number of companies survived the boom and bust. Companies such as Nokia, Qualcomm, Vodafone, and Microsoft have not only survived but also demonstrated that they are able to adjust to a new, more difficult post-bubble business environment defined by lower debt burdens, lower production costs, and greater financial flexibility. And, for all the dismal loss of jobs in the tech sector, the industry has become part of the economy, demonstrating that it is not a passing fad. Instead, the tech sector is finding a new equilibrium that places an emphasis on growth and profitability and a more measured reliance on financing from the stock market.

▶ CONCLUSION

The 1990s stock bubble was driven by the converging trends of technology and finance. With improvements in automated trading led by the NASDAQ, better communications via the Internet and telecommunications, and greater prosperity on the part of the average American, the great bull market of the 1990s was able to take off, reaching more investors than ever before. The cult of equity and hype from Wall Street all helped blow air into the bubble. There was also a willingness on the part of the investing public to have confidence (or, as some would argue, blind faith) in the ever-rising charts that marked the upward valuations of the NASDAQ and NYSE stocks. The future looked rosy. Conversely, the end of the tech bubble lead to considerable gloom about the future. In a sense, the draining of the once vast pool of investor funds that so readily functioned as credit for innovation—and waste—brought the tech sector into a state of disequilibrium in the early 2000s. With so many companies having filed for bankruptcy and so many billions of dollars lost, many were left to ponder whether the tech sector had a future.

Yet, tech is not dead, nor is its relationship with finance. Despite the wreckage that the tech bubble left behind, innovation has not left the stage. The savage reduction in money available for developing new technologies and perfecting old ones has meant that investors are much more scarce as well as prudent. A large number of tech, telecommunications, and semiconductor companies are still in existence, and many of them are in the process of reducing debt, cutting costs, and squeezing out profits. The world has moved on the post-bubble stage. This now means that the standards for companies have changed in everything from disclosure and transparency to corporate goals concerning profitability, debt management, and accounting. Hubris is out and humility is in. At the end of the day, the tech/telecommunications/dot-com bubble reflected the meddling of three major forces: a huge step forward in technology, the harnessing of that technology into financial economics, and a belief in the equity market as a means of wealth generation for many people. All three of these forces were interrelated and supplemented each other. The tech bubble sucked in a large number of people, including many of those who lacked any degree of financial sophistication but were driven by the herd instinct and attracted by prospects of making easy money. In this case, it was very much like previous bubbles. In the end, the 1990s proved to be a time when a carnival-like investing atmosphere lured both those armed with cutting-edge financial software and those with little idea about investment, and in many cases the results, ironically, were the same.

▶ NOTES

1.   Market analyst Martin Pring argues that market bubbles typically play out over twelve steps. During the first stages of the bubble a new idea emerges. It is an idea that captivates the public's imagination and appears capable of creating unlimited wealth. Stage by stage reinforces this until it is widely accepted by the public. Eventually the peak comes and the market crashes. While we like Pring's idea, we simplified the number of stages to six. See his *Investment Psychology Explained* (New York: John Wiley & Sons, 1993).
2.   Robert X. Cringley, *Accidental Empires* (New York: Penguin Books, 1996), p. 4.
3.   Journalist David Kaplan was to comment of Silicon Valley: "If the Valley were a nation, it would rank among the world's twelve largest economies. Back during the Cold War, the area ranked near the top of the Soviet's list of nuclear targets. But far more than the mother lode of economic miracles, fount of overnight millionaires, and international symbol of high-tech know-how, the Valley competes with Hollywood as a place in the culture of money and celebrity, success and excess. Washington and Wall Street have been left gasping for air in the rearview mirror." From his book, *The Silicon Boys and Their Valley of Dreams* (New York: Perennial, 2000), p. 13.
4.   In 1983, after many years of development, Motorola's first DynaTAC cellular system began commercial operation. Motorola devoted fifteen years and $100 million to the development of its cellular program.
5.   See Markus Haacker and James Morsink, "You Say You Want a Revolution: Information Technology and Growth," *IMF Working Paper*, April 2002.
6.   Harry S. Dent, Jr., *The Roaring 2000s: Building Wealth and Lifestyle You Desire in the Greatest Boom in History* (New York: Touchstone Books, 2000), p. 30.
7.   Ibid.
8.   Bob Davis and David Wessel, *Prosperity: The Coming 20-Year Boom and What It Means to You* (New York: Times Books, 1999), p. 3.
9.   Mark Ingebretsen, *NASDAQ: A History of the Market That Changed the World* (Roseville, California: Forum, 2002), p. 226.
10. Thomas L. Friedman, "An American in Paris," *The New York Times*, August 20, 1999, p. A21.

11. James B. Murray, Jr., *Wireless Nation: The Frenzied Launch of the Cellular Revolution in America* (Cambridge, Mass.: Perseus Publishing, 2001), pp 20–21.

12. Murray, *Wireless Nation*, p. 51.

13. Victoria Murphy, "Critical Juncture," *Red Herring*, January 20, 2003, p. 62.

14. Beth Healy, "It's Not Just a Job, It's a Venture: Money Hotshots Bail Out of Traditional Firms to Finance High-Tech Start-Ups," *The Boston Globe*, March 27, 2000, p. C1.

15. Healy, "It's Not Just a Job," *The Boston Globe*, March 27, 2000.

16. Kimberly Blanton and Ross Kerber, "Internet Stocks Defying Wall Street's Gravity," *The Boston Globe*, January 13, 1999, p. A1.

17. Ibid.

18. Ibid.

19. Ibid.

20. Ingebretsen, *NASDAQ*, pp. 217–218.

21. "Leader: The Nature of the Game," *Red Herring*, December 18, 2000, p. 33.

22. Kimberly Blanton, "Nightmare on Wall Street as Market Soars Closer to Once-Unthinkable Height of 10,000: Analysts Detail Their Worst Fears," *The Boston Globe*, January 10, 1999, p. J1.

23. Martin Mayer, "Higher and Higher: It's Been Boom Times in the US for 7 Years, With No Bust in Sight," *The Boston Globe*, January 3, 1999, p. E1.

24. Arnold Berman, "Tactics: Now's Not the Time for the Next Big Thing," *Red Herring*, December 18, 2000, p. 238.

25. Mathew Ingram, "WorldCom Founder's Rocket Ride Comes to an End," *The Globe and Mail*, April 30, 2002, p. 1.

26. Rob Urban, "Ebbers May Lose the Ranch to WorldCom Shareholders, Creditors," *Bloomberg*, August 12, 2002.

27. Marcia Vickers et al., "Wall Street: How Corrupt Is It?" *BusinessWeek*, May 13, 2002, p. 38.

28. Myles Neligan, "Profile: Jean-Marie Messier," *Financial Times*, July 2, 2002, p. 24.

29. Ibid.

30. Ibid.

31. David Leonhardt and Jennifer Bayot, "Out of Stocks and Into What?" *The New York Times*, July 24, 2002, p. C1.

CHAPTER 7

THE FIRM AND GLOBALIZATION

"The Making of Global Citizenship" ... "Striving for First-Rate Markets in Third-World Economies" ... "Mexico Attracts Japanese Investors" ... "Unions of Giants" ... "Consolidation of the Global Energy Industry" ... "Megamergers a Go-Go" ... "Megamergers Are a Clear and Present Danger" ... "Bigger and Better: Mergers Continue to Grow in Size" ... "How to Merge: After the Deal" ... "Credit Suisse Ousts Chief after a Series of Blunders" ...

The 1990s witnessed a massive number of changes in how firms interacted with the world around them. New technology turned the workplace on its head, and globalization opened up new universes of opportunities as well as risks. There are three major dimensions of how globalization forced the firm to reconfigure, all of which have a relationship to capital markets during the 1990s.

1. Most companies were forced to reassess the way business was conducted. Part of this was learning how to deal with mature home markets and how to access new growth markets. Many of those who did not learn these lessons either failed or were bought by more aggressive and innovative rivals. While Kmart floundered, Wal-Mart excelled.

2. Globalization also gave new impetus to multinational corporations (MNCs) and the role of foreign direct investment (FDI). MNCs are briefly defined as companies actively engaged in business in two or more countries, usually via FDI.

3. Related to the above trends, the 1990s were to see a substantial surge in mergers and acquisitions, many of them across national borders. The urge to merge was not solely left to the high-flying tech sector but was a phenomenon that swept through both the new and old economies as well mature and emerging markets. The second part of the decade witnessed some of the largest combinations in history: Citibank and Travelers, WorldCom and MCI, Daimler and Chrysler, and British Petroleum and Amoco. Although the United States was at the core of this activity, the wheeling and dealing was global in nature. Spain's

Endesa sought to construct a power-generating empire throughout Latin America, while Dutch grocery power Ahold expanded both in the United States and South America.

While firms from all around the world became more actively engaged across national frontiers, a new debate arose about the erosion of the nation-state. In some quarters there appeared to be a certainty that the nation-state was destined for the trash can of history as companies divided the world into more logical regional economic trading units. Along the same lines, concerns were raised about the "clear and present danger" of mega-mergers in their concentration of economic power. This had special ramifications in the international arena, as a foreign company buying a local firm raised the oftentimes-delicate issue of nationalism. At the same time, there was a fundamental questioning about the way companies went about globalization and the often-unintended consequences on local cultures.

▶ EVOLUTION OF THE FIRM AND GLOBALIZATION

Companies have been around for a long time.[1] From the loosely linked trading families of the ancient world to the joint stock trading firms that emerged in the seventeenth century, the company has evolved. It had to for the sake of survival. As John Micklethwait and Adrian Wooldridge observe: "Companies have proved enormously powerful not just because they improve productivity, but also because they possess most of the legal rights of a human being, without the attendant disadvantages of biology: they are not condemned to die of old age and they can create progeny pretty much at will."[2] What is significant in what Micklethwait and Wooldridge note is that companies are not condemned to die of old age. If a firm's leadership has vision, patience, drive, and a little bit of luck, it will live a long time and create plenty of progeny. If not, companies die. As market conditions change for a vast array of reasons, firms are forced to evolve. As Micklethwait and Wooldridge state: "Throughout its history, the company has shown an equally remarkable ability to evolve: indeed, that has been the secret of its success."[3] This was certainly the case during the 1990s as globalization became a force that could not be ignored.

This is not to argue that there is anything new to the idea of companies traversing borders in the pursuit of business opportunities. Clearly early companies, such as those of the northern Italians and Hansa in the Baltic, were actively engaged in international trade and commerce. In the sixteenth and seventeenth centuries there was the birth of joint stock companies, many of which had an international orientation—the Dutch East India Company, the Virginia Company, and the Muscovy Company. These were to be followed by other international firms, including the large global oil companies, Royal Dutch/Shell and ExxonMobil, and many others. Despite an expansive literature on the evils of MNCs during the 1970s and 1980s, the scope of penetration in world affairs was not complete.

For U.S. companies, the 1980s were a period of structural change, where an emphasis was placed on greater cost efficiencies and eliminating shop-worn ideas like lifetime employment with the same firm. Technology gradually began to make inroads, with the personal computer (PC) replacing teams of word processing workers, files made the transformation from paper to disc, and secretaries increasingly became obsolete. The pace of technological change accelerated during the 1990s, becoming a central part of the new mantra of doing more with less. Although it is debatable how much technology actually increased productivity, one thing is certain—the daily pace of the business world certainly felt accelerated. In addition, new technology came with its own set of unforeseen problems. Talk about the paperless office proved to be the opposite—it just became easier to print more copies. PCs opened up new ways to waste time in the office, from Solitaire to Minesweeper, while the Internet opened up universes of new distractions, including online auctions, shopping, and porn. As the new tech entered the workplace, "futzing around" with the computer ate up time. Indeed, Nielsen Media Research Inc. found that workers at IBM, Apple, and AT&T together logged onto Penthouse's site on the World Wide Web 12,823 times during one month in 1996, equaling 347 eight-hour days in lost work.[4]

Globalization and technology improved access to new markets that were previously closed because of cost, regulation, and indirect barriers, while allowing firms the ability to tap resources such as labor, capital, and knowledge on a worldwide basis.[5] McDonald's locations climbed to more than 120 countries, with more than 50 percent of revenues coming from outside the United States. Yum! Brands, owner of KFC, Pizza Hut, and Taco Bell, with its headquarters in Louisville, Kentucky, served up chicken, pizza, and burritos to hungry consumers in one hundred countries. Pepsi and Coca-Cola came to fight the "cola wars" in India and Argentina. Nike sportswear was made in Indonesia and China and clothed thousands in Africa. And the entertainment business, dominated by a handful of companies in the United States, Europe, and Japan, pumped out movies, videos, and CDs into every corner of the planet. Technology helped open the door, and firms stepped inside to reach new customers in the global market. As Richard J. Barnet and John Cavanagh noted in 1995: "Global corporations are the first secular institutions run by men (and a handful of women) who think and plan on a global scale. Things that managers of multinational companies dreamed of twenty years ago are becoming reality—Coca-Cola's ads that reach billions in the same instant, Citibank's credit cards for Asian yuppies, and Nike's network for producing millions of sport shoes in factories others paid for."[6] The bottom line was that technology helped push globalization as it facilitated the firm's ability to reach a larger market for its goods.

Consequently, evolution came in many forms.

- First and foremost, companies that had largely catered to domestic markets could no longer ignore the bigger world either because of foreign competitors muscling into their markets or because they operated in mature or saturated markets and needed to go international to generate profits.

- Second, foreign companies came into local markets and acquired local companies. For the remaining local companies, foreign competition suddenly was not a long distance concept but one that could be reached out and touched.

- Third, for more proactive managements, mergers and acquisitions were one means of growth and of achieving size and scope to fend off competitors in a globalized marketplace.[7]
- Fourth, globalization challenged firms to become more streamlined and efficient while simultaneously extending the geographic reach of their operations.
- Fifth, as MNCs expanded their presence in foreign markets, their production chains became global. For many companies, access to less expensive pools of expertise, as in India and China, represented cost savings and allowed them to offer cheaper prices.

One of the most successful companies during the 1990s to emerge as a global giant was the retailer Wal-Mart. Wal-Mart was initially established in the 1960s and gradually expanded in the United States. The 1990s, however, marked a massive surge in the company. By 1997, Wal-Mart was in all fifty states, expanding overseas, and the largest employer in the United States, with ninety million customers worldwide. One of the major cornerstones of the company's success was its ability to offer a growing range of consumer goods, some of it locally produced, but increasingly produced in low-cost labor countries, such as China. The combination of low wages for its sales force, low-cost production, often from overseas manufacturers, and a wide range of products offered at low prices proved to be difficult competition for many other retailers. In many regards, Wal-Mart came to represent many of the positives and negatives of globalization. On the positive side, Wal-Mart employed more than 962,000 workers in the United States and 252,000 workers internationally. It offered consumers worldwide reasonable prices. It also helped the economic development of many lower-income countries, such as China, from which it purchased goods. And Wal-Mart was the darling for the global investor, with most major mutual funds holding the stock.

Wal-Mart also represented some of the negatives of globalization. The relentless push for lower-cost products meant turning to overseas producers to the detriment of U.S. employment. Unemployed U.S. workers have more than once grumbled about the view that a large amount of goods sitting on Wal-Mart shelves are made in China, not the United States. In addition, there are concerns that the U.S. economy is becoming "Wal-Martized", i.e., converted from an economy with well-paid manufacturing jobs into an economy where the jobs are exported and cheap goods imported, with only low-paying jobs at Wal-Marts left to make up the difference.

All the same, Wal-Mart represented a major trend for firms in the 1990s, a fulsome embrace of globalization as a means of doing more with less. In an age of low-cost energy, easy transportation and relentless consumer spending, Wal-Mart emerged as a poster-child of U.S. corporate reconfiguration in a globalized economy, ready and able to adapt to changing market conditions. For investors, this was magic; for U.S. workers losing jobs in the manufacturing sector it was poison. Despite the global economic downturn in the aftermath of the carnival on Wall Street, Wal-Mart remained one of the world's more profitable companies.

Yet, the evolution of MNCs into more global institutions was not limited to the more industrialized economies. Globalization also had an echo in a number of developing economies. In the oil industry, Malaysia's Petronas, Venezuela's PDVSA, and Brazil's Petrobras spread their operations across national borders and into the larger world. In the telecommunications sector, Telekom Malaysia and SingTel moved out of their home markets and into Australia, Ghana, and Indonesia. Hong Kong's Hutchinson Whampoa, a diversified conglomerate, set up business operations throughout the world, including Asia, Latin America, and Europe. These companies were hardly alone and represent one of the changing dynamics of globalization and firm change that occurred during the 1990s and into the next decade.

Consider Petronas, Malaysia's largest company. It is owned by the Malaysian state and has long managed the country's hydrocarbon sector. Initially focused on Malaysia, Petronas in the 1990s increasingly turned to international operations to generate revenues. It was understood that Malaysia's oil reserves were dwindling and that by 2008 the Southeast Asian nation could become a net oil importer. The obvious path was to go international. The first major step in this direction came in 1995, when Petronas bought a 30 percent share in South Africa's biggest oil refiner and marketing company. This was followed by a successful exploration and production operation in Sudan, a country known for its political instability. Today, Petronas operates in thirty-two countries outside of Malaysia, overseas operations account for more than 75 percent of its revenues, and the company is highly regarded as a partner for many older and more established international oil companies. On average, Petronas earned $5 billion a year through the late 1990s and into the 2000s.

The 1990s, therefore, brought considerable change to the firm. Technology and globalization pushed many companies to think differently on how to approach old markets, reach new customers, and re-examine growth. One of the major areas that a number of companies considered was mergers and acquisitions. As cross-border solutions increasingly presented themselves to management teams looking for growth, cross-border mergers entered a new era.

▶ THE 1990s M&A GOLDMINE

One of the most dramatic reflections of the changes facing the firm in the 1990s was the spurt in mergers and acquisitions (M&A). Some of the world's largest corporations were the byproduct of mergers and acquisitions. This was certainly true in the U.S. experience (Table 7.1).

While the 1980s were once regarded as a Golden Age for M&A, the 1990s were even greater. The 1990s began with a slow shift out of recession, but a considerable pick up in M&A activity soon occurred, due to ongoing deregulation under the Clinton presidency (working with a Republican-dominated Congress). By the end of the 1990s, M&A activities were awash in a sea of money. According to data compiled by the U.S. Government in the *Statistical Abstract of the United States 2000*, the value of M&A in 1990 stood at $205.6 billion, with 4,239 mergers.[8] That number was destined to climb throughout the decade, reaching a substantial $3.4 trillion and 9,599

TABLE 7.1   Top Fifteen U.S. Companies, by Earnings (2002)

Company and Rank	Earnings, in Billions of $
1. General Electric (multiple mergers)	15.133
2. Citigroup (merger of Citibank and Travelers Insurance)	13.448
3. Altria Group (formerly Philip Morris, Kraft Foods, and Nabisco)	11.102
4. ExxonMobil (merger of Exxon and Mobil)	11.011
5. Microsoft	9.541
6. Bank of America (merger of Nations Bank and Bank of America)	9.249
7. Pfizer (includes Parke-Davis, Warner-Lambert, and Goedecke)	9.181
8. Wal-Mart Stores (Asda)	7.698
9. SBC Communications	7.473
10. Merck	7.150
11. Johnson & Johnson (multiple acquisitions)	6.651
12. Freddie Mac	5.764
13. Wells Fargo (multiple acquisitions)	5.710
14. IBM	5.334
15. Procter & Gamble (Clairol)	4.907

Source: BusinessWeek, February 24, 2003.

transactions in 1999. (That $3.4 trillion was a greater sum than the combined gross domestic products of Canada, Italy, and the Netherlands.) Among the big-name mergers in the last years of the decade were Viacom–CBS, Daimler Benz–Chrysler, BP–Amoco–ARCO, Travelers–Salomon–Citicorp, AOL–Netscape, SBC–UBS, Dean Witter–Morgan Stanley, NYNEX–Bell Atlantic, and Wall Mart–Asda. See Table 7.2 for the five biggest deals of the 1990s. These deals were all of hefty size and scope, which according to one of the major players in the M&A business, Bruce Wasserstein, suggested that the merger trend starting in the 1980s and accelerating during the 1990s was "a seismic shift in the structure of the world economy."[9] For Wasserstein and many others the urge to merge was driven by globalization, technological innovation, and falling regulatory barriers. To this he added: "Corporate managers view acquisitions and mergers as critical tools to position their companies for success in the face of their industry's competitive dynamics."[10]

The combination of the end of the Cold War, the opening up of Eastern and Central Europe, the European Union's creation of a single market (1992), and technological innovations opened the door to a brave new world of mega-deals. Indeed,

TABLE 7.2 Five Biggest Deals of the 1990s

Rank	Acquirer	Target	Deal Value ($U.S., in Billions)	Year Announced
1	Exxon	Mobil	86	1998
2	Travelers Group	Citigroup	73	1998
3	SBC Communications	Ameritech	72	1998
4	Bell Atlantic Corp.	GTE Corp.	71	1998
5	AT&T Corp.	Tele-Communications	70	1999

Source: Aladdin Capital Management Research.

the ten largest mergers and acquisitions in history were announced in 1998 and 1999. The announced top ten mergers alone in those years equaled $747 billion, including the ultimately failed acquisition by MCI WorldCom of rival Sprint. Telecommunications, oil and gas, and finance dominated the merger mania, but the movement was not limited to just those sectors. The strategic imperative to grow by acquisition was clearly a force in driving management to seek out new takeover candidates that would eventually contribute to the bottom line of profitability.

Despite the negative publicity about M&A since the market crash, the fact is that most of the world's successful companies have expanded by following this business strategy. General Electric (GE) is often regarded as one of the major M&A success stories. Under the leadership of its longstanding CEO Jack Walsh (who retired in 2001), GE reorganized during the mid-1990s and made a concerted effort to grow the company's business, in part through acquisitions, which were geared to rapidly accrue revenue for GE. The strategy emphasized that by growing the stable of companies under the GE banner, there would be greater diversity among operations, including short- and long-cycle businesses as well as geographies. All of this would provide a moderating effect on its core business cyclicality. At the same time, there was an awareness that size would provide a scale of operations and breadth of reach throughout its global markets which would provide greater staying power to weather industry and/or economic downturns. In addition, such an approach would allow GE the ability to invest opportunistically and strategically in anticipation of the eventual up-cycles. GE's total assets went from $131 billion in 1994 to a little over $381 billion in 2001, with the company producing everything from aircraft engines and kitchen appliances to nuclear reactors as well as providing a wide range of financial services.

Two critical aspects of the GE program were evident: globalization and an ability to quickly and almost seamlessly absorb new businesses and make them part of the GE family. As a Moody's Investors Service report noted: "Globalization is critical to enhance the modest growth prospects, to exploit less saturated and higher growth potential markets, to source lower cost labor as well as intellectual knowhow, and to provide its global customers with seamless products and services on a global scale."[11] Considering that GE now does business around the planet, it clearly has taken the idea of globalization very seriously and has made it a cornerstone in growing its sales from around $49 billion in 1997 to $68 billion in 2001.

The other aspect of GE's M&A strategy centers around what is called the Six Sigma Program, which seeks to re-engineer everything from design times to manufacturing, marketing, and billing. The general overarching objective is to reduce errors and defects, which cuts costs, stimulates incremental demand from more satisfied customers, and augments revenues and profitability. This process has often encompassed the reduction of staff and placing greater responsibilities into the hands of fewer workers. While this has delighted shareholders, it also earned Walsh the moniker "Neutron Jack," as his acquisitions often left the facilities and operations intact but devoid of people—much like a neutron bomb was supposed to function. Despite such criticisms, GE emerged during the 1990s to become one of the world's most admired and consistently profitable companies. Moreover, it was able to weather the economic downturn that followed the bursting of the stock market bubble in 2001.

GE is hardly alone in its successful use of M&A to grow business and maintain it as a profitable venture. Other companies in this bracket would include the United Kingdom's Vodafone and Spain's Telefonica in telecommunications as well as Hong Kong Shanghai Bank (HSBC) and Citigroup. The commonality in each case has been a very focused approach to what is being acquired, dominated by concerns over how quickly and easily the acquired can be brought into the family while maintaining a high degree of profitability. While a number of companies get it right, more than a few get it wrong.

▶ THE DRIVEN: DAIMLERCHRYSLER

If any sector of the global economy was wrapped up in the merger mania, it was autos. The forces behind consolidation were similar to those of many other industries—overcapacity, technology, and an international environment more open and welcoming to cross-border acquisitions. Of the forty or so world automakers, only a handful were profitable. In the United States, three giants held sway—Ford, General Motors, and Chrysler. In Europe, Daimler-Benz dominated, sharing lesser shares of the market with Fiat, Volkswagen, Volvo, Audi, Renault, Saab, and Peugeot. In Asia, Toyota and Honda were the key players, though other Japanese automakers Nissan and Mitsubishi and Korean companies such as Kia and Daewoo slugged it out for whatever parts of the global auto market were left.

By the end of the 1990s, consolidation had worked its way through the auto industry's ranks. Daimler–Benz bought Chrysler, Renault captured a dominant share of Nissan, and Ford took Volvo. Indeed, consolidation became the buzzword of the decade. As Toyota's President Hiroshi Okuda stated in January 1999: "In the next century, there will be only five or six auto makers."[12]

Taking a step back from the emotions evoked by the Daimler–Chrysler merger and looking at the deal from the standpoint of building a bigger, more global company, capable of contending with the tempest of globalization, what was proposed in May 1998 was nothing less than the world's largest industrial merger. The combined company was to be the fifth largest carmaker in the world, with combined revenues of around $130 billion, a combined operating profit of $7 billion, and a workforce of more than 420,000 employees. Significantly, both companies were expected to complement each other, with the German company serving the high and luxury range car market, while Chrysler would have a medium-range car, van, and sports-utility product line. In a sense, the new company was to bring together a rigorous and disciplined German focus on luxury vehicles, with brash American inventiveness in its sports-utility vehicles.

Chrysler had long been a part of the lexicon of U.S. business legends, as celebrity chairman and CEO Lee Iacocca cleverly wrapped the company in the U.S. flag, positioning the revival of his company from its late 1970s doldrums as a critical part of the struggle of American business to regain its past glory and effectively deal with tough (especially Japanese) foreign competition.[13] The new Chrysler that emerged from this low point soon became known for innovative and brash new products, such as its minivan line. By the mid-1980s, Chrysler was firmly affixed in the public mind as part and parcel of Americana. The Chrysler brand had become as American as apple pie.

Daimler–Benz's move toward the acquisition of Chrysler came from its own set of compelling reasons. Following the 1979–1980 oil hikes, management decided to take the automobile maker in a different direction. Beginning in the mid-1980s, the company moved beyond its traditional automobile manufacturing role and embraced aerospace, electrical engineering, and software services. It was believed that by moving into these sectors the company could augment profitability, which could then be funneled back into better innovation in the auto lines. Daimler soon gobbled up MTU Motoren and Turbinen Union, a manufacturer of aircraft engines, Dorneir GmbH, Germany's second largest airplane maker, and Messerschmitt-Boelkow-Blohn GmbH (MBB), the country's most significant aerospace company. Other major acquisitions included electrical engineering group AEG, which produced everything from refrigerators to computer chips. The AEG purchase in 1985 also made Daimler-Benz Germany's largest industrial group, ahead of Siemens. But Daimler-Benz was not done. In 1991, it bought Cap Gemini Sogeti, Europe's largest software developer, and in 1992, the Dutch commuter aircraft maker, Fokker.

Although Daimler–Benz had created a large, broadly diversified conglomerate, stretching across several European borders, it found the massive challenge of integrating them into an effective whole. The situation was complicated by then-rigid European labor laws that made downsizing difficult; by the survival of quarrelsome minority shareholders who complicated the implementation of rational business plans; and by the end of the Cold War, which reduced the significance of the defense industry. Instead of the creation of a diversified company that fed back and supported the automotive part of the company, it was the automotive part of the company that kept the other parts afloat. By 1994, when Schrempp became CEO of Daimler–Benz, the company was struggling. Billions of dollars had been spent and lost in businesses that were not capable of giving back adequate returns.

The new CEO soon was busy restructuring and streamlining the Daimler–Benz empire. Within a period of two years, some sixty thousand jobs were eliminated,

Fokker was allowed to go into bankruptcy (to the considerable irritation of the Dutch government), AEG was dismantled and parts of it were sold off, and the number of corporate divisions was reduced from thirty-five to twenty-three.

Schrempp's other long-term objective was to strengthen Daimler–Benz's position as a global auto company. Although the German firm was international, it lacked the same global reach as Ford, GM, and Toyota. To reach those heights, Daimler–Benz needed additional assets outside the country, preferably something in the United States. At the same time, there were similar thoughts in Chrysler about the need for a stronger global business presence. By 1998, Schrempp and Daimler–Benz had cast their eye on Chrysler, then fighting off a takeover from Kirk Kerkorian, one of the company's largest shareholders. The nasty fight between Kerkorian and his ally, former Chrysler CEO Iacocca, against the current management of Chrysler, led by Bob Eaton, left the latter open to discussions with Daimler–Benz that ultimately turned into a German takeover bid.

With a price tag of $36 billion, Daimler–Benz was buying a piece of history. As journalists Bill Vlasic and Bradley A. Stertz commented: "… every oil deal, bank marriage, and phone merger paled in comparison to the shocker of the year, Daimler–Benz AG's $36 billion buyout of Chrysler Corporation. Daimler, the biggest company in Germany, reached across the Atlantic and grabbed an American industrial icon, setting off an unprecedented frenzy of consolidation in the global automotive industry."[14]

These words were echoed by Nick Smee, then an automotive analyst for J. P. Morgan: "The formation of DaimlerChrysler changes the landscape of the automotive industry. Daimler–Benz has captured one of the industry's most attractive prizes and staked out its claim on the global market … perhaps doing permanent damage to the global ambitions of its rivals."[15]

Despite these high hopes, the difference in business cultures was not easy to bridge. As *The Economist* noted at the time of the merger: "Chrysler likes to pride itself on its buccaneering approach, where speed and ingenuity are prized. It builds cars around common platforms, with teams of engineers, designers, and marketing people working on each model. Daimler–Benz was a more traditional 'chimney' structure, in which designers and market people mattered less—and engineers are in charge."[16] Pay scales were also different, with the Americans usually paid considerably more than their German counterparts.

For all the hype and high hopes, the Daimler–Chrysler merger was not a raging success in its early years, and the verdict of its long-term success is also still questioned. Once the new company set to the task of integrating two very different business cultures, complicated by different nationalities, things did not go according to plan. The U.S. part of the business saw many of its most talented managers leave, some enriched by the merger and others rubbed the wrong way by their new CEO Schrempp.

At the same time, Chrysler was hit by growing operational inefficiencies, in part due to management's focus on the merger instead of the car business. While Chrysler tinkered, making small modifications instead of bold new designs, Toyota and Honda, aided by a weaker yen, marched into the market, offering more car for the same money. Consequently, Chrysler ran into problems in late 2000, post-ing a massive $1.3 billion loss in the fourth quarter. The stock fell considerably. Schrempp was forced to fire much of the U.S. management and placed Dieter Zetsche in charge of turning the American operation around. In 2001, Chrysler lost another $2 billion, and recovery was slow in coming in the following years.

DaimlerChrysler remains important as one of the largest cross-border merg-ers in history. If cross-border consolidation in a number of sectors is to succeed, firms like DaimlerChrysler must show the way. Thus far, DaimlerChrysler has not been a raging success. Sadly, the merger occurred shortly before the U.S. econ-omy headed into a difficult economic downturn, complicating the task of integra-tion. The task that lies ahead will continue to be difficult but hardly impossible.[17]

▶ FINANCIAL MERGERS

Financial services played a key role in the 1990s wave of M&A activity. Throughout the 1980s and early 1990s, the Glass–Steagall Act in the United States was gradu-ally dismantled, blurring the lines between the activities of commercial and invest-ment banks. The coup de grace in the liberalization of the U.S. financial sector was the Financial Services Modernization Act of 1999, which officially repealed the Glass–Steagall Act. The old barriers between commercial and investment banking were finally lifted. With this, many financial service companies saw the opportunity to diversify their product lines and offer one-stop shopping for their clients.

At the same time that these changes occurred in the United States, financial markets around the world were liberalized, facilitating an unprecedented wave of cross-border acquisitions. In Europe, the creation of a single European market in 1992 was a big step forward in the financial services industry, while Japan embarked upon its own Big Bang in financial services liberalization later in the decade. The opening up of Central and Eastern Europe also brought countries such as Poland, Hungary, and Czech Republic into the new wave of M&A activities. Not to be left out of the cross-border financial consolidation, many Latin American countries opened their borders. Large European banks, mainly in Spain and, to a lesser extent, Italy and the Netherlands, moved into key Latin American markets. By the late 1990s, a considerable part of the banking sector in Argentina, Brazil, Mexico, and Venezuela was in foreign hands. Cross-border acquisitions occurred even in Asia, with Newbridge–GE Capital buying Korea First Bank and other financial interests buying into the battered Japanese banking sector.

The largest and most significant mergers were Travelers–Citigroup, Deutsche Bank–Bankers Trust, Nations Bank–Bank of America, J. P. Morgan–Chase Manhattan, and CSFB–Donaldson, Lukfin & Jenrette (DLJ). The Travelers–Citigroup merger in 1998, for instance, combined one of the world's premier insurance companies with one of the world's most globally oriented banks. Also under the wing of Citigroup was the firepower of earlier mergers with Salomon Brothers and Smith Barney. Indeed, the new Citigroup was a true financial supermarket, capable of offering insurance, banking, and investment bank services all under one global brand name. An added plus was broad diversification of products and markets, a factor that was regarded as important in reducing risk. Travelers cost Citigroup $73 billion, making it one of the largest deals of the decade. (Only two years later Citigroup would make yet another acquisition: Associates First Capital, for $31 billion.) Despite the slowdown in the U.S. economy and the bursting of the stock market bubble in the 2001–2002 period, Citigroup's appetite for new acquisitions was hardly sated.

Among the companies to take advantage of the changing regulatory environment were Chase Manhattan Bank and J. P. Morgan. Both institutions were well-established, with traditions of success in the banking industry. J. P. Morgan was founded in 1854 and was long regarded as one of the blue bloods of the banking world. Chase's foundations date back to 1799, when the Manhattan Company was formed with the support of Alexander Hamilton and Aaron Burr to improve New York City's water supply, with the provision that extra capital could be used for buying stock. Through various transformations, Chase eventually emerged as the largest bank in the United States in 1927.

The competitive pressures facing J. P. Morgan and Chase Manhattan were increasingly difficult. Long rivals, both banks were increasingly aware of the growing costs of technology, product innovation, and keen and growing competition from both banking and nonbanking financial institutions. Forced to compete in international markets against universal European banks and fighting for market space with nonbanking financial institutions for savings and other financial services, not to mention waging an uphill battle to gain access to investment banking activities, each institution tried different strategies. J. P. Morgan started its own investment banking division. In 1999 alone, the bank hired one hundred investment-banking professionals and concentrated on six major business segments, including bank credit markets, asset management, equities and equity investments, and interest rate and currency markets. Although J. P. Morgan managed to make it into the top ten in many business segments by year-end 1999, it still lagged the other, larger, and ultimately better capitalized, firms.

Chase's road to the merger was different. It clearly felt the same competitive pressures through the late 1980s and early 1990s, and pressure was particularly intense to break into the lucrative investment banking market, in particular, equity underwriting. While the 1996 Chemical merger gave Chase greater size, this did not convert it into an investment bank. In 1999, Chase acquired Hambrecht and Quist, a well-respected San Francisco–based technology underwriting boutique, for $1.4 billion. Soon to follow were the acquisitions of Robert Flemmings Holdings (a U.K. investment bank) and The Beacon Group (a New York M&A firm). While these acquisitions gave Chase some degree of clout in investment banking, success continued to elude the bank. In particular, Chase failed to break into the top ten in equity underwriting and in M&A. Consequently, Chase hoped that a merger with J. P. Morgan would help it climb into the upper tier of investment banking. From J. P. Morgan's perspective, merging with Chase would remedy its own costly and disappointing move from commercial banking to investment banking. After a few months of courting, Chase acquired J. P. Morgan in January 2001. The cost was $36 billion.

Many initially regarded the merger with considerable skepticism. One J. P. Morgan employee stated: "J. P. Morgan must be turning in his grave." Yet, Chase quickly emerged as one of the major forces in investment banking, and despite the difficult market conditions that followed the market crash in 2001, the new institution is poised to eventually do well. In 2001, close to ten thousand employees lost their jobs, departments were merged throughout the bank, and management sought to create a new business culture that captured the best of both institutions. At the same time, the merged entity was able to generate considerably greater revenue than before. Its profitability, however, remains to be seen, especially in light of the difficult market conditions facing the investment banking industry in the early 2000s.

Credit Suisse's acquisition of DLJ did not have an easy start. Credit Suisse was founded in 1856 and had became a major investment bank force in the United States by 1988, when it gained a controlling stake in First Boston. Like its national rival, Union Bank of Switzerland, Credit Suisse's management recognized that if it were to survive in the highly competitive world of international banking, it needed to grow both within Switzerland, its home market, and globally. During the 1990s, Credit Suisse acquired Bank Leu (Switzerland) in 1990 and Swiss Volksbank (1993) and developed strategic alliances with Swiss Re (a major insurance company) in 1994 and the Winterthur Group (1995). In 1997, Credit Suisse bought Winterthur for around $9 billion. By 1998, the Credit Suisse Group was a large international player, involved in almost every major financial business segment. Despite a somewhat fractious business culture, its investment bank, CSFB, was profitable.

DLJ was founded in 1960 on the idea that research should lead the investment process. The company managed to expand rapidly through the following decades, gaining a strong reputation for its expertise in high yield bonds, an area in which CSFB had lagged. Under the leadership of CEO John Chalsty, DLJ sought to become a more international firm in the 1990s, establishing offices in London, Hong Kong, and Moscow. Management understood that for DLJ to make the next step into the upper level of investment banks it needed to become more global as a firm. Despite the company's expansion into foreign markets, it remained very American in its orientation.

Although DLJ had not put itself up for sale, it was being closely watched by CSFB. CSFB's pressing need to develop a high-yield franchise had driven CEO Allen Wheat to decide that he needed DLJ to secure CSFB's place in high-yield markets. While the high-yield department was a logical fit between the two firms, it was not clear that the rest of the two companies matched. Indeed, there was considerable overlap in both debt and equity areas as well as other services. Yet, CSFB decided in the end to buy DLJ for $11.5 billion.

The DLJ acquisition was not a failure for CSFB. The firm did achieve a more substantial presence in high-yield bond capital markets in terms of investment banking, trading, and research. At the same time, considerable money was spent in merging the two companies. The usual downsizing occurred, and new teams were brought together from both institutions. Money was put aside to keep key people, many of whom later walked away. As one disgruntled ex-DLJer stated: "For all the money thrown into the deal, CSFB basically bought a high-yield department with a company attached to it. The real trick will be to make it work." Unfortunately, the high-yield market hit a difficult period as the U.S. economy slowed in 2001 and 2002. The wisdom of the merger has yet to be fully seen—tough market conditions have reduced profitability and made it hard to fairly judge whether the merger will pay off in the end. In addition, Credit Suisse has faced problems related to its earlier acquisition of Winterthur. In the massive securities sell-off of May–July 2002, Winterthur, like many insurance companies, was hard hit by a decline in value in its stock and bond portfolios. It was reported that Credit Suisse would have to inject more capital (possibly up to $2 billion) into its insurance unit to make certain that it was adequately capitalized according to Swiss regulatory standards.[18]

Banks were not alone in the process of financial consolidation during the 1990s. Large insurance companies such as France's AXA, the Netherlands' ING, and Germany's Allianz moved to acquire strategic assets around the planet. Under the leadership of chief executive Henning Schulte-Noelle, Allianz went on a major acquisitions spree in the late 1990s and early 2000s. The reasons for this strategy were simple—for Allianz to grow it had to become global and broaden the range of products. Beginning in 1998, the German insurance giant bought Assurances Generales de France, which was followed in 2000 with the purchase of 70 percent of Pimco Advisers Holdings LP, the largest bond fund manager in the United States, for $3.3 billion. Also in 2000, Allianz took over another U.S. asset manager, Nicholas-Applegate Capital Management LP, for $2.2 billion. The crowning glory of Schulte-Noelle's tenure at the helm of Germany's insurance powerhouse was the $17.4 billion acquisition of Dresdner Bank, one of the top three banks in the country.

It is often said that timing is everything. Allianz bid to create a global insurance/financial services empire occurred at a time when the spurt of global growth was slowing. The company was also hard hit by the September 11, 2001, terrorist attacks in the United States, paying out $1.3 billion on insurance claims. Net profit was down in 2001, and results were worse in 2002. The Dresdner Bank merger brought some unexpected challenges. While the bank failed to make adequate profits, top investment bankers left. In November 2001, Bruce Wasserstein, whose firm Wasserstein, Perella & Co. had been acquired by Dresdner in 2000, quit to become CEO of Lazard LLC.

Equally problematic for Allianz's management was integrating the insurance company and bank. Business cultures and practices were very different. Moreover, there was resistance to the idea of selling insurance products from banks. As Helmut Ahrens, a labor coordinator at Verdi, Europe's largest union, which represents six thousand Allianz employees, stated: "We've had cases where the Dresdner branch manager refuses to recognize the new Allianz employee. In some cases, the Allianz agent walks in and says, 'Our company bought your bank, so I'm in charge now.'"[19]

Allianz's management insists that the merger will work—over time. In the short-term, the company made some big reaches. However, in the highly competitive global market for financial services, Allianz must enhance its earnings power for the future and achieve greater earnings diversification. All of this requires tough actions, including the unwinding of industrial holdings, assuming full ownership of formerly partially owned subsidiaries, expanding its life assurance business, and creating third-party asset management capabilities, most notably through the acquisition of PIMCO, Nicholas Applegate, and now Dresdner Bank. The message is clear: Allianz feels compelled to globalize, the alternative being a slow death within the parameters of the German insurance market. Globalization has given it few choices.

The Impact of Global Capital Markets

Mergers and acquisitions during the 1990s had a substantial impact on global capital markets. The M&A trend was not limited to the United States. It appeared almost everywhere, with Spanish banks buying and merging Argentine and Brazilian banks, France Telecom buying Poland's TPSA, and Malaysia's Petronas buying a major South African refinery. As the global economy liberalized, it appeared that everything was up for sale. Germans, French, and Japanese vied for cheap, yet strategically placed assets in Central and Eastern Europe or in Central Asia. Although it sometimes seemed that U.S. companies were always stalking other companies, in fact the U.S. market too was highly attractive for Europeans, Japanese, and others throughout the decade.

In September 1999, in the midst of the global M&A boom, Alcatel's chief operating officer summarized the prevailing view of European senior managers toward the United States: "So much of company strategy is driven out of the United States today that no serious player can afford not to have a presence here."[20] As Morgan Stanley economists Joe Quinlan and Rebecca McCaughlin stated: "Over the late 1990s, European corporations plowed $600 billion into U.S. acquisitions out of fear of missing out on the most dynamic, innovative market in the world, marking one of the most aggressive and intense periods of European integration with the U.S."[21]

Consider the Dutch. The Netherlands has had a long relationship with the United States as a place of investment. After all, Manhattan was founded by the Dutch, and they long remained one of the major investors in North America. During the 1990s Dutch companies found the United States an appealing location for business. In 1999, the Netherlands' stock of investment in the United States passed the $100 billion mark, putting the Dutch a little ahead of the Japanese and behind only the British. Table 7.3 provides some idea of what Dutch companies bought in the United States.

Explaining the attraction of investing in the United States, Alexander Rinnooy Kan, a director of the large insurance financial services company ING, stated "… it is the largest market, and we cannot afford not to be there if we want to present ourselves as a global player."[22] Another Dutch executive active in buying U.S. companies was Cees van der Hoevan, president of Ahold, a major grocery chain. He explained: "It is more important to have strong local or regional positions than a thinly spread total position in Europe."[23] Ahold was to put into the United States with around $10 billion to buy an empire of grocery stores with a strong presence in the eastern part of the country. (Unfortunately, Ahold's expansion was too rapid and consolidation was sloppy, and in early 2003 the company announced that it had overstated profits by $500 million. Shortly thereafter the CEO and CFO were fired, and Ahold found itself under investigation by the Securities & Exchange Commission.)

TABLE 7.3   Acquisitions by Dutch Companies in the United
                States in 1999

Acquirer	Target	($U.S., in Billions)
Aegon (insurance)	TransAmerica	$10.81
Fortis	American Bankers Insurance Group	2.80
Numico	General Nutrition	2.51
Buhrmann	Corporate Express	1.75
Ahold	Pathmark Stores	1.75
Getronics	Wang Laboratories	1.49
Philips Electronics	VISI Technology	1.16

Source: Financial Times, July 31, 1999, p. 12.

For the United States, the huge inflow of mainly European and, to a lesser extent, Japanese capital for M&A was highly useful in offsetting the current account balance of payments deficit as well as making up for the decline in national savings and helping to prop up the U.S. dollar. In 2000, the peak of M&A activity in the United States, some $175 billion in M&A money flowed in from abroad. The flow slowed to $68 billion in 2001. In the first half of 2002, net flows actually reversed, totaling a net outflow of $14 billion, reflecting the flight of foreign investors from what appeared to be a scandal-plagued corporate world.

In July 2002, the Organization for Economic Cooperation and Development (OECD) released data on global foreign direct investment flows. Global foreign direct investment (FDI) had tumbled 56 percent to $565 billion in 2001, from an all-time high of $1.27 billion in 2000.[24] Leading the way was the United States, which observed FDI fall more than 57 percent to $131 billion in 2001, down $177 billion from $308 billion in 2000. This was the lowest level since 1997. Germany, Japan, Ireland, Sweden, and the United Kingdom also saw large declines in FDI flows. As the OECD stated: "The decline in international investment flows could represent a 'return to normal' following the extremely high transactions of the late 1990s and in 2000, and so the end of a recent mini-boom in FDI."

The implications of the retreat from M&A and the decline of international capital flows into the United States clearly had an impact on the value of the U.S. dollar. The loss of confidence in Wall Street helped weaken the U.S. dollar. Scandals at Enron, Arthur Andersen, Tyco International, and WorldCom did much to instill many investors (at least in the short term) with a fear that management and accountants lie, investment-bank research analysts misrepresent, and chief executive officers operate in a fog. Investors, both foreign and domestic, had become leery of the U.S. corporate sector and apprehensive of when the next Enron or WorldCom would blow up. They needed to be persuaded that corporate governance standards in the vast majority of U.S. companies are still solid—

that Enron et al. are the outliers, not the mainstream. Although the vast majority of U.S. companies did not have any corporate governance issues, the perception of a tainted few outweighed the reality of the many.

Equally important, WorldCom and other recent scandals bolster a negative perception about the U.S. corporate world at a time when the economy is struggling to recover and needs ongoing foreign investment. As one of the authors observed in an earlier publication: "The loss of confidence on Wall Street could lead foreign investors to demand a premium for holding U.S. corporate assets to offset higher credit risks. European corporations, most of which have not benefited from as extensive deregulation, could look more attractive. As funds leave the U.S., those foreign investors who remain could also ask for a premium to offset currency risk."[25]

Who Benefited?

There will no doubt be considerable debate as to who benefited from the 1990s merger boom. Was it the investment bankers, lawyers, or public relations firms? Was it the shareholders? Was it the employees of the merged companies? What was the public good? The danger of writing so close after the decade under study has dangers—it certainly is difficult to adequately judge the ultimate success or failure of mergers that are less than two years old in some cases. The 1990s merger mania, however, does provide some initial views that are worth noting.

Clearly, the large investment banks were a dominant force in M&A activities, as reflected by Table 7.4. Goldman Sachs was the leader in the 1990–1999 period, closely followed by Salomon Smith Barney, Merrill Lynch, Morgan Stanley Dean Witter, and CSFB.

The large number of deals meant strong cash flows for Wall Street firms. In 1999, disclosed fees for M&A were led by Goldman Sachs at $523 million, Morgan Stanley Dean Witter at $368.5 million, and CSFB at $323 million. Even for the smaller players, such as Wasserstein Perella ($64.8 million) and Blackstone ($28.7 million), M&A activity brought in substantial profits. Yet, the investment bankers were hardly alone. Legal advisors also took their fair share of the money flow. Long hours of sometimes around-the-clock work on documents and creative interpretations of the law translated into big payoffs. Among the most active law firms in the M&A world during the 1990s were Skadden, Arps, Slate, Meagher & Flam; Sullivan & Cromwell; and Shearman & Sterling (Table 7.5).

As these data suggest, investment banks and law firms were big winners in the merger mania of the 1990s. But what about the stockholders? In November 1999, the accounting and consulting firm KPMG caused a moment of panic in the market when it released and then withdrew a merger study that concluded that 83 percent of cross-border mergers did not deliver shareholder value.[26] The firm, which was itself involved in M&A activity, later stated: "We didn't want people to read into a negative spin."

The KPMG study was commissioned by the company, but was carried out by confidential interviews conducted by a third-party consultant. It examined a sample taken from the top seven hundred cross-border deals by value between 1996 and 1998. In sum, 107 companies worldwide participated. The study found that of

TABLE 7.4 Top Advisors for Announced and Completed Deals, 1990–1999

Adviser	Number of Deals	Value of Announced and Completed Deals ($U.S., Millions)
Goldman Sachs	1,730	2,141.3
Salomon Smith Barney	1,653	1,389.3
Merrill Lynch	1,463	1,675.1
Morgan Stanley Dean Witter	1,441	1,698.7
Credit Suisse First Boston	1,215	1,023.9
Donaldson, Lufkin & Jenrette	1,111	604.8
Deutsche Bank AG	1,096	402.3
Lehman Brothers	1,004	734.8
Chase Manhattan	700	512.1
Warburg DillonReed	670	473.1
J. P. Morgan	658	622.8
Lazard Freres	645	645.2
Bear Sterns	516	524.0
Banc of America Securities	490	194.8
Broadview	477	NA

Source: Mergers & Acquisitions, Security Data Publishing, Inc., February 2000.

the 107 companies involved in a merger, 53 percent saw shareholder value rescued. Another 30 percent of mergers produced no discernible difference. The conclusions came after an analysis of share price movements in relation to those of similar competitors in the first year following the merger.

While KPMG quickly sought to bury what appeared to be an embarrassingly negative assessment of a business line in which it was very active, other observers also questioned the value of mergers. *The Economist* magazine, hardly a bastion of anticapitalist left-wingers, noted: "But just as certain as the flow of deals is that most will be failures. Study after study of past merger waves have shown that two of every three deals have not worked; the only winners are the shareholders of the acquired firm, who sell their company for more than it is really worth."[27]

Along the same lines, mergers also represented a tough challenge to the companies involved. Too much growth at too rapid a pace raises concerns about the ability of companies to integrate newly acquired units. Integration risk is real. As the *2001 Goldman Sachs Annual Report* stated: "It is no easy task in the face of great growth and change. To meet this challenge, in 1999 we initiated a multiyear process to adapt our culture to a large and growing global organization without becoming too bureaucratic." This came from a successful company of twenty-two thousand employees spread around the globe and having recently acquired a smaller specialist firm, Spear, Leeds & Kellogg.

TABLE 7.5   Top Ten Most Active Law Firms, by Number of
Announced and Completed Deals, 1990–1999

Legal Advisers	Number of Deals	Value of Deals ($U.S., Millions)
Skadden, Arps, Slate, Meagher & Flam	1,068	1,672.0
Sullivan & Cromwell	786	1,294.6
Dorsey & Whitney	741	62.9
Simpson, Thacher & Bartlett	661	1,720.4
Shearman & Sterling	620	1,233.4
Gibson, Dunn & Crutcher	602	183.1
Latham & Watkins	478	229.6
Davis, Polk & Wardwell	451	757.6
Wachtell, Lipton, Rosen & Katz	451	1,242.5
Wilson, Sonsini, Goodrich & Rosati	412	109.0

Source: Mergers & Acquisitions, Security Data Publishing, Inc.,
February 2000.

The Relationship between the Corporation and the Nation-State

The great surge in mergers and acquisitions and the movement of many companies
into operations and activities across national borders all had an impact on the nation-
state.[28] Indeed, there developed a debate about the withering away of the nation-state.
Simply stated, large multinational corporations and even smaller firms aided by technology were able to leap over single countries in a single bound. With the Internet
and other forms of e-commerce, national borders came to mean very little. The nation-
state, the dominant political actor in global politics and economy since the Treaty of
Westphalia in 1648, was being bypassed by new economic actors that carried considerable economic clout. As Richard Barnet and John Cavanagh noted: "The most disturbing aspect of this system is that the formidable power and mobility of global
corporations are undermining the effectiveness of national governments to carry out
essential policies on behalf of their people."[29] Indeed, Barnet and Cavanagh warned
that the nation-state "looks more and more like an institution of a bygone age."

Yet, the nation-state did not wither away. Rather, it changed much like the firm.
Globalization and technological changes left governments in both the industrialized
and developing world grappling with regulatory deficiencies, corporate governance
issues, questions over the adequacy of legal regimes, and doubts about the transparency
of political systems. For the transnational firm, the main drive was to take advantage
of the movement toward a single global market. After all, a single global market would
create a situation in which the consumers would be able to buy the best products at

the lowest prices, which would be supplied by those companies that were the most innovative, the most able to adapt. Weak governments made poor referees for MNCs seeking to penetrate and gain control of local markets. In addition, weak governments opened the door for transnational crime, some of it disguised as legitimate business.

The problem in all of this was the labor issue. The advent of new technology required companies to "brain up," i.e., hire people who were better educated with cognitive and interactive skills. This was evident as a number of major international tech firms were willing to set up shop in India, tapping that country's pool of Ph.D.'s, at much less cost than in the United States, Canada, or Europe. What this meant was that job growth was to come from the high end of creativity and skill sets and from the low end in retail, healthcare, domestic service, gardening, and janitorial work, which are likely to expand due to demographics.[30] Many other jobs, in particular, those that have been regarded as blue collar jobs in manufacturing, increasingly feel the pinch of hard times. Some of these jobs went to developing economies (as in the case of India with high-tech positions). Others simply disappeared. Cross-border mergers and acquisitions only increased the size and scope of this process of labor downsizing. In addition, there was a tendency for consolidation of companies in a number of sectors, with a group of very dominant MNC giants buying out smaller regional and local players (as in mining and pulp and paper industries).

Consequently, globalization and new technology became a source of inequality in the system. While the firm struggled to evolve in this environment, the state was left struggling with its traditional role of providing for its citizens, including accommodating in some fashion the losers in the new economy. In a sense, the losers in the labor pool disappeared from the firm's roster, but they could not fade away from the nation-state, especially as the unskilled and underskilled workers still had a vote. The evolution of the firm in a globalized world demanded change, which unfortunately often meant personnel downsizing.

The transformations that occurred in the global economy, including how globalization impacted the firm, did not result in the state withering away. Voters remained voters even if they were unemployed. Indeed, globalization was to stir up discontent related to the labor issue. In the United States, antiglobalization voices with a particular view to MNCs included Pat Buchanan on the right (who railed against "amoral behemoths") and Ralph Nader (who attacked "unaccountable transnational corporations") on the left. Although the United States remained one of the major forces in globalization and its firms demonstrated a substantial capacity for morphing, both the national and state governments became more sensitive to the negative impact of globalization on the firm and the worker. In addition, the ups and downs in the global economy, especially the crashes in capital markets that occurred with Mexico in 1994–1995 and Asia in 1997–1998, brought the same issues to bear on emerging markets.

If anything, the volatility in the global economy and the gut-wrenching slowdown experienced in the early 2000s reinforced the role of the nation-state from the standpoint of the necessity of the rule of law, standard sets of rules and regulations, and level playing fields for all actors. In a sense, the nation-state functions as an anchor in a globalized world, dominated by MNCs. Horst Kohler, head of the IMF, stated in May 2003 that it was necessary to create a "better globalization," on the condition that "… international cooperation and solidarity should not weaken or even replace national self-responsibility. At the end of day, what matters is also, and, above all, good governance, sound institutions, and respect for the rule of law."[31] In essence, the IMF chief recognized the need for the nation-state in a globalized market system to improve the process of globalization.

▶ CONCLUSION

The years that marked the Carnival on Wall Street clearly made an imprint on the firm. Companies were forced to contend with sweeping technological changes, a more global entrepreneurial economy, nation-states struggling to adapt to a new world disorder, a changing environment concerning transparency and corporate governance, and easy access to capital markets. With deregulation and liberalization in local markets from the United States and Argentina to China and India, MNCs and FDI became the drivers of integration as they spread their production chains around the world. Transnational firms were powerful actors on the global economic stage and clearly had developed considerable political influence. Countries, regions, and even towns willingly competed for FDI and a chance to become part of the production chain. The rewards of such arrangements were jobs, capital inflows, and growth. The risks were an erosion of the authority of the state by the increasing power of the multinational corporation; an institution by its nature usually did not place a tremendous emphasis on national loyalties. However, the argument that MNCs were the instrument of doom for the nation-state was overstated. At the end of the decade, when the stock market bubble burst, economic growth cooled, and geopolitical risks mounted, it was the nation-state that stepped up to enforce the rule of law, protect citizens' rights, and generally provide an environment that was still conducive to multinationals and cross-border trade and commerce. In the aftermath of 9/11, the so-called imperial firms demonstrated that they still preferred to work under the protective shade of a national flag.

▶ NOTES

1. For a history of the company see Alfred Chandler, *Strategy and Structure: Chapters in the History of the American Industrial Enterprise* (Cambridge, Mass.: MIT Press, 1962) and Jonathan Barron Baskin and Paul Miranti, *A History of Corporate Finance* (Cambridge, UK: Cambridge University Press, 1997).

2. John Micklethwait and Adrian Wooldridge, *The Company: A Short History of a Revolutionary Idea* (New York: Modern Library, Inc., 2003), p. xv.

3. Ibid, p. 181.

4. Bob Davis and David Wessel, *Prosperity: The Coming 20-Year Boom and What It Means to You* (New York: Times Books, 1997), p. 101.

5. Kenneth L. Kraemer, Jennifer Gibbs, and Jason Dedrick, "Impacts of Globalization on E-Commerce Adaptation and Firm Performance: A Cross-Border Investigation," Center for Research on Information Technology and Organizations, University of California, Irvine, December 20, 2002, p. 2.

6. Richard J. Barnet and John Cavanagh, *Global Dreams: Imperial Corporations and the New World Order* (New York: Touchstone, 1995), p. 15.

7. Theories about mergers and acquisitions typically consider questions concerning motivations for mergers, the empirical evidence related to those motivations, and valuation issues (i.e., valuation

of merger candidates, how purchase prices are determined, and the effects mergers can have on stock prices). Also taken into consideration are the different kinds of mergers. Three broad categories of merger are identifiable: horizontal mergers between firms that are direct competitors in the same market; vertical mergers between firms that stand in a supplier-customer relationship; and conglomerate mergers between companies operating in unrelated markets that are endeavoring to diversify their activities and revenue streams.

All three categories are driven to some degree by the potential for added value offered by economies of scale, better management, and coordination of cost savings. Horizontal mergers usually are motivated as well by hopes of enhanced market power, industry consolidation, and geographic expansion. Another driver in the 1990s was the quest for technology or intellectual property—a key issue in the tech boom in the later half of the decade. One last key factor pushing mergers and acquisitions in the 1990s was globalization. As the world became a smaller place, cross-border rivalries were more discernible and the need to expand into new markets more pressing. Scale suddenly no longer pertained to a national economy but to a global economy. The table of top fifteen U.S. companies by earnings is instructive, as the overwhelming majority have grown via mergers and acquisitions.

It should be added that not all mergers are welcome but that some are advanced in the form of hostile takeovers, providing us with the vision of fur-clad and sword-swinging barbarian raiders seeking entry into the corporate castle. The 1990s were full of hostile takeover bids. This of course led many companies to strengthen their defenses via such mechanisms as "poison pills." This tactic, popular among firms concerned about an unwanted takeover bid, ensures that a successful takeover bid would trigger some event that drastically reduces the value of the acquired firm. According to one source: "Examples of such tactics include the sale of some prized asset to a friendly company or bank or the issue of securities with a conversion option enabling the bidder's shares to be bought at a reduced price if the bid is successful." Quoted from Brian Butler, David Butler, and Alan Isaacs, editors, *Oxford Dictionary of Finance and Banking: From International to Personal Finance* (New York: Oxford University Press, 1997), p. 272.

8. U.S. Government, *Statistical Abstract of the United States 2000* (Washington, D.C.: U.S. Statistical Office, 2001), p. 551.
9. Bruce Wasserstein, *Big Deal: 2000 and Beyond* (New York: Warner Books, 1998, 2000), p. 1.
10. Ibid.
11. Richard J. Lane, John D. Moore, and Robert Konefal, *General Electric Company Report*, Moody's Investor Service, July 2002, p. 2.
12. Quoted from "The Global Six," *BusinessWeek*, January 25, 1999, p. 70.
13. A quick history of Chrysler is as follows. Walter P. Chrysler founded Chrysler in the 1920s. Indeed, the first Chrysler car was launched in January 1924 at the New York Auto Show. The company's early years were marked by expansion, partially through acquisitions, as was the case of the Dodge Brothers in 1928. Under Walter's guidance and vision, Chrysler not only survived the Great Depression but also expanded market share and came to be regarded as cutting edge in terms of design and innovation. By the 1940s, when Walter died, Chrysler was well-established as one of the Big Three auto companies, alongside General Motors and Ford, holding a quarter of the U.S. market. Although the company was to see several ups and downs, following the business cycle, it remained at the helm alongside the two major U.S. firms.

The 1970s proved to be a particularly difficult period for Chrysler. Management was lackluster, the company became heavily indebted, and questions were raised over its liquidity. The oil embargo by the Organization of Petroleum Exporting Countries (OPEC) in 1973–1974 only made matters worse, as Washington put the automakers under pressure to shift from large, gas-guzzling cars to smaller, more energy-efficient autos. While these pressures hit Ford and General Motors, the impact was mitigated in part by lucrative international operations. In contrast, Chrysler's international operations were smaller and poorly managed and actually in some cases required government help. By 1978, when Lee Iacocca joined the company, it was a deeply troubled institution. By 1979, when Iacocca became Chrysler's chairman and CEO, the situation was becoming terminal. As journalist David Waller noted: "Chrysler was in far worse shape than Iacocca had imagined when he took the job. Morale was appalling, the balance sheet was shot to pieces, the plants were dirty and dangerous." Ultimately, Iacocca was forced to turn to the

U.S. government for help. This came in the form of $1.5 billion in loan guarantees from Washington, which helped clear the way for a restructuring of Chrysler's $4.5 billion debt.

14. Bill Vlasic and Bradley A. Stertz, *Taken for a Ride: How Daimler-Benz Drove Off With Chrysler* (New York: Harper Business, 2001), p. 1.
15. Quoted from Waller, *Wheels on Fire*, p. xiv.
16. "How to Merge," *The Economist*, January 9, 1999, p. 23.
17. Another example of a nonfinancial company involved in mergers was Tyco. Throughout the 1990s, Tyco International was a company on the move. Imbued with an acquisition-oriented growth strategy and led by Dennis Kozlowski, Tyco was often regarded as an up-and-coming GE. Founded in Waltham, Massachusetts, in 1960, the company started with semiconductors and research and became a multifaceted conglomerate. By 2000, Tyco International boasted companies that were involved in electronics, making electrical connectors, conduits, and printed circuit boards; fire and security services for security and fire-protection systems; healthcare products such as bandages, crutches, and respiratory care equipment; and undersea fiber-optic cable. It also owned CIT, a large finance company. While the list of companies coming under the banner of the Tyco empire is impressive, it was also a point of weakness that eventually came close to destroying the firm in 2002.

While the years prior to the 1990s were built around numerous acquisitions, the last decade of the twentieth century was almost frantic. According to the company, acquisitions were based on the following criteria: an acquisition candidate must be in a business related to one of Tyco's four business segments; it must be able to expand the product line and/or improve product distribution; it must have excellent long-term growth prospects; and it must be using a manufacturing and/or processing technology already familiar to one of the four business lines.

Under the guidance of CEO Kozlowski and Mark Swartz, first director of mergers and acquisitions from 1993 to 1996 and then CFO from 1996 to 2002, the company emphasized that it was using "synergistic/strategic guidelines and stringent financial requirements" to guide the acquisition process. With this in mind, Tyco moved at a rapid pace with major acquisitions. Beginning in 1991, with the purchase of Worwald International Limited, a fire protection company, Tyco was off to the races. With the $9.6 billion acquisition of finance company CIT in 2001, it was estimated that Tyco had spent around $60 billion on acquisitions and mergers during the previous ten years.

Throughout the 1990s, Tyco managed to grow its income. Sales rose from $8.1 billion in 1996 to over $20 billion in 1999. Profitability also rose, with the company shifting from a net loss of $835 million in 1997 to a profit of $985 million in 1999. In 2000, sales rose to $34 billion. Although Tyco had its critics, the company was regarded as an up-and-coming firm. Even Moody's Investor Service was positive about the company, providing it with a positive outlook in a review conducted in December 2001. As the rating agency stated at the time: "The positive outlook is based on Tyco's demonstrated track record of integrating acquisitions, as well as the expectation of further improvements in earnings and free cash flow generation of Tyco's diversified business line."

Yet, by late 2001 Tyco International found itself under pressure. The Enron scandal sapped investor confidence and cast analysts looking for companies that could have similar off-balance sheet liabilities. Tyco, with its conglomerate structure, numerous acquisitions, and official domicile in Bermuda, fit the profile for nervous investors. Doubts had arisen as early as 1999 over the integrity of the company's numbers, especially in the area of acquisitions. Although the U.S. Securities and Exchange Commission undertook an informal investigation in December 1999 and ended the probe in July 2000 with no action other than to recommend some accounting changes, doubts had lingered. The Enron debacle brought those doubts to the surface again with a vengeance. The company responded with considerable indignation, claiming that its accounting and disclosure were second to none, and in January 2001 it announced a plan to break up the conglomerate into four companies.

Things did not go according to plan. Kozlowski's strategy for splitting the company did not sway investors. In late April 2002, Tyco announced that the breakup plan was being shelved. Kozlowski said that the decision had been a mistake and that he misjudged the "extraordinarily fragile market psychology." The response to this decision was captured by an investor report on a fixed income investment fund: "Tyco has an uphill battle in regaining investor confidence. The lack of consistency in direction cost its investors billions of dollars and put the company back in terms of focusing on its core businesses … we do not see the company failing, but the name will clearly have a stink attached to it in both bond and equity markets for a long time to come …"

By July 2002, Tyco Finance was sold off and returned to being The CIT Group. Kozlowski was under criminal investigation, CFO Swartz was in the process of departing, and the Manhattan District Attorney and SEC were investigating whether Tyco corporate funds were improperly used to enrich executives with artwork and homes. In addition, Tyco's general counsel Mark Belnick resigned his position in June 2002 after being accused of making secret pay plans with Kozlowski without the board's knowledge. Allegations of corporate wrongdoing were also leveled against Frank Walsh, a board member. Tyco filed lawsuits against Belnick and Walsh, alleging that Kozlowski agreed to pay Walsh $20 million for his help in the acquisition of CIT but did not tell the board until seven months later. While these allegations left questions about Tyco's top management, they also made the company's board of directors appear, at best, out of touch and unaware of questionable practices and, at worst, willfully blind.

What caught the public's attention was the downfall of Kozlowski. In the January 2001 edition of *BusinessWeek*, he was named as one of the magazine's top twenty-five managers and lauded as "one of Corporate America's most aggressive dealmakers." Well-known in high society as a generous benefactor (with Tyco's money) to an array of institutions from the New York Botanical Garden and the Whitney Museum of Modern Art to the University of New Hampshire and the United Way, Kozlowski, the son of a police detective, enjoyed a lavish lifestyle, complete with a yacht and expensive homes. He gave his wife a $2.1 million birthday party. Since 1997, Tyco and its subsidiaries also gave more than $600,000 to national political organizations, the bulk going to the Republican Party. It was his taste for fine art, however, that got him into trouble. According to the Manhattan district attorney's charges, Kozlowski had embarked upon a $13 million fine art shopping spree, during which he sought to evade more than $1 million in sales tax.

Following the departure of Kozlowski, Tyco International entered an exceedingly difficult period, with questions raised over its ability to survive. Swartz, the CFO, soon departed under a cloud. Public disgust with Tyco's problems mounted with the disclosure that the former CFO was ranked as the highest paid CFO in the United States in 2001, collecting nearly $47 million in compensation. One of the most challenging aspects facing the new management was whether it could recapture investor confidence. After all, the buildup of a major international conglomerate had been done in the name of the shareholders. In 2002, when stock prices were trading at a seven-year low, many shareholders were wondering what exactly had been done in their name. However, the new management moved to provide greater transparency and disclosure in the company's operations, a new board was elected, and assets were sold to guarantee that debts were repaid. Tyco International will probably survive, but it is a smaller and far lesser M&A player than it was before.

18. Daniel Huegli, "Credit Suisse May Need to Put SF3 bln in Winterthur, Study Says", *Bloomberg*, July 16, 2002.
19. Quoted from Kevin O'Brien, "Allianz Bets on the Bank," *Bloomberg Magazine*, June 2002, p. 43.
20. Quoted from Joe Quinlan and Rebecca McCaughlin, "Global: Cross-Border M&A Update," *Morgan Stanley Global Economic Forum*, July 8, 2002.
21. Ibid.
22. Quoted in Gordon Gramb, "Off to New Amsterdam: Dutch Companies Are Taking America By Storm," *Financial Times*, July 31, 1999, p. 12.
23. Ibid.
24. "OECD Reports a 56% Decline in Foreign Direct Investment," *Wall Street Journal*, July 5, 2002, p. A2.
25. Scott B. MacDonald, "The Impact of Wall Street's Scandals on Japan," *Asia Times*, July 16, 2002.
26. Norma Cohen, "KPMG Withdraws Merger Study," *Financial Times*, November 29, 1999.
27. "How to Merger: After the Deal," *The Economist*, January 1999, p. 21.
28. As Sylvia Ostry, University of Toronto, stated: "There is a growing view, approaching conventional wisdom, that the power of the nation state is eroding from above, by globalization, and from below, by devolution." *Globalization and the Nation State: Erosion from Above*, Timlin Lecture, University of Saskatchewan, February 1998, p. 1.
29. Barnet and Cavanagh, *Global Dreams*, p. 19.
30. Ostry, *Globalization and the Nation State*, p. 16.
31. Horst Kohler, "The Challenges of Globalization and the Role of the IMF," Speech given at the Annual Meeting of the Society for Economics and Management, Humbolt University, Berlin, May 15, 2003.

CHAPTER 8

A DECADE OF FINANCIAL WRONGDOING

"Al-Qaeda: Complex finances defy global policing" … "Banks in London handled $1.3 bn linked to Abacha" … "Case still open on 'terror's quartermasters'" … "Citibank admits to lapses in dealings with offshore shell banks" … "How to avoid the dirty money" … "Deal at Enron gave insiders fast fortunes" … "FBI in Global Crossing probe" … "How Enron's money won friends and influenced people" … "Mexico drug lords exploit NAFTA" … " Wall Street faces rules on money laundering" …

Our decade begins in the early 1990s, when the Bank of England and the Federal Reserve finally shut down the greatest rogue financial institution in modern history, Bank of Credit and Commerce International, or BCCI (better known in banking circles as the Bank of Crooks and Criminals International). BCCI had raised financial wrongdoing to a fine art. It provided banking services for everyone from petty con artists and drug dealers to multimillionaire dictators and terrorists (not to mention the CIA). When the Bank of England finally closed it down, the list of charges against BCCI provided a veritable laundry list of financial wrongdoing: tax evasion, money laundering, and gross negligence were only the tip of the iceberg. The bank also left a list of damaged parties across the globe, ranging from the Central Bank of Jamaica to hapless depositors in the United Kingdom.[1]

And our decade ends in the early 2000s, marked by the frantic search for terrorist funds in the global financial system in the aftermath of 9/11 and by the stories of Enron and WorldCom, the biggest bankruptcies in U.S. corporate history—a saga of corporate governance gone sadly astray that becomes more complicated and more worrisome with every passing day.

So a decade that began with a serious effort to clean up financial wrongdoing ended in another welter of financial scandal. This is not new, of course; the 1980s, for instance, elevated insider trading to a fine art. The history of corruption and financial wrongdoing is long and multifaceted, from the Teapot Dome scandal back to the earliest days of banking and finance. Indeed, scandal has historically been a shipmate to boom-bust cycles and bubbles in the financial world.

The 1990s, however, did witness some important trends in the nature and perception of financial misdeeds. For the purposes of this discussion, our definition of wrongdoing is somewhat impressionistic: it refers to an illegal and/or immoral act that serves the individual or group at the expense of those who the wrongdoers are supposed to be protecting or serving, such as taxpayers, investors, or shareholders. Note that an act that is wrong in this sense may not necessarily be illegal! The world of corporate governance and regulation includes many areas that are considered "gray"—not illegal, but of questionable moral nature. In fact, one of the most dismaying aspects of Wall Street scandals in the 1990s may be how much of the executives' self-serving, self-dealing activity was perfectly legal. Thus our definition of wrongdoing encompasses crime, corruption, *and* acts that may be technically legal but seem just plain wrong to most onlookers—acts that fail to pass the so-called sniff test. In other words, actions that will look bad if they are exposed on the front page of *The New York Times* will be considered here. (Or, as a Supreme Court justice famously explained with regard to pornography: I know it when I see it.)

The 1990s were supposed to be a time in which good triumphed over bad, at least in the financial world. BCCI was closed, the great insider trading excesses of the previous decade had passed into history, and the United States launched a determined battle to spread American rules against bribery and corruption to other countries. A renewed focus on the importance of good governance at both the corporate and country levels emerged in the wake of financial crises in Asia and company crises in the United States. (Governance is defined as the method of control over an organization or country; the United Nations Development Program explains that "good governance is, among other things, participatory, transparent, and accountable. It is also effective and equitable. And it promotes the rule of law. Good governance ensures that political, social and economic priorities are based on broad consensus in society. ...")[2] In 1995, for instance, the International Corporate Governance Network (ICGN) was founded at the behest of major institutional investors to represent investors, companies, financial intermediaries, academics, and others interested in the development of global corporate governance practices. Then, in May 1999, ministers representing the twenty-nine OECD countries voted unanimously to endorse the OECD Principles of Corporate Governance, acknowledging the great importance of corporate governance in the twenty-first century global economy.[3]

However, in the end the decade saw some of the worst-smelling excesses in the history of financial markets. Globalization, free markets, and technology should make the financial world cleaner—thanks to better transparency and disclosure—thus enabling good governance practices. And they do. But it appears that these developments are also great enablers of less noble trends as well. Blind faith in markets, models, globalization, and technology during the past ten years laid the foundation for some of the most blatant deviations from good governance practices of the decade.

This chapter examines some of those episodes, keeping a close eye on the relationships between blind faith, globalization, and financial wrongdoing. In particular, the increasing complexity of financial markets and transactions, which are impossible to regulate or sometimes even to comprehend on a global level, has facilitated all sorts of unintended problems: rogue traders, high-tech money launderers, and even a rogue company named Enron (or, in insiders' parlance, the crooked E).

► CORRUPTION AND BRIBERY

The decade of the 1990s was marked by a growing wave of revulsion, worldwide, against bribery and corruption (generally defined as the abuse of public office for private gain). The president of the World Bank identified bribery as one of the greatest threats to global economic development, Web sites sprang up to rank countries on their perceived level of corruption (Table 8.1), and U.S. officials tramped through Asian, European, and Latin American capitals to lobby for worldwide adoption of U.S.-style laws against bribery of foreign officials.

Underlying much of this activity was a growing awareness on two fronts:

■ Recognition of the high and growing *level* of corruption in many parts of the world, including, but hardly limited to, emerging and transition economies, and

■ A growing recognition of the *costs* of corruption, especially for the more vulnerable countries of the world.

A Corruption Eruption

Bribery and corruption certainly are not new. But the opportunities for financial misdeeds afforded by unstable, chaotic emerging and transition economies are breathtaking. As a result, the world has experienced what Moises Naim, editor of *Foreign Report*, calls a "corruption eruption." According to a 1999 survey by Transparency International, the well-respected group that tracks corruption levels worldwide, in two-thirds of the countries surveyed (66 of 99), companies are likely to encounter a bribe request.[4] Another survey found that bribery and corruption are widespread in the formerly communist countries of eastern Europe, to the point that companies operating in this region generally pay bribes equivalent to between 2 percent and 8 percent of their annual revenue. The survey authors conclude: "When added to what is already considered by firms to be an extremely high level of official taxation, the bribe tax imposes a severe burden on enterprises in the region."[5]

Greasing the Wheels?

Not surprisingly, this growing recognition of the high level of bribery and corruption has led to a reexamination of its effects on business, growth, and development. At one point, it was popular to believe that a reasonable level of corruption may actually "grease the wheels" of what would otherwise be a chaotic and inefficient economy. It has been argued that payoffs and bribes may actually *increase* efficiency by introducing at least a primitive market mechanism into a poorly functioning economy—thus putting capital into the hands of those who value it most highly.[6]

This sentiment was enshrined in a revisionist view of corruption that emerged in the 1970s and 1980s. Basically, some economists looked at the world and

TABLE 8.1 2001 Corruption Perceptions Index (1 = Least Corrupt)

Rank	Country	Rank	Country
1	Finland	35	Uruguay
2	Denmark	36	Malaysia
3	New Zealand	37	Jordan
4	Iceland, Singapore	38	Lithuania, South Africa
6	Sweden	40	Costa Rica, Mauritius
7	Canada	42	Greece, South Korea
8	Netherlands	44	Peru, Poland
9	Luxembourg	46	Brazil
10	Norway	47	Bulgaria, Croatia, Czech Republic
11	Australia	50	Colombia
12	Switzerland	51	Mexico, Panama, Slovak Republic
13	United Kingdom	54	Egypt, El Salvador, Turkey
14	Hong Kong	57	Argentina, China
15	Austria	59	Ghana, Latvia
16	Israel, United States	61	Malaysia, Thailand
18	Chile, Ireland	63	Dominican Republic, Moldova
20	Germany	65	Guatemala, Philippines, Senegal, Zimbabwe
21	Japan	69	Romania, Venezuela
22	Spain	71	Honduras, India, Kazakhstan
23	France	75	Vietnam, Zambia
24	Belgium	77	Cote d'Ivoire, Nicaragua
25	Portugal	79	Ecuador, Pakistan, Russia
26	Botswana	82	Tanzania
27	Taiwan	83	Azerbaijan, Bolivia, Cameroon
28	Estonia	84	Kenya
29	Italy	88	Indonesia, Uganda
30	Namibia	90	Nigeria
31	Hungary, Trinidad & Tobago, Tunisia	91	Bangladesh
34	Slovenia		

Source: Transparency International 2001 Corruption Perceptions Index, available at www.transparency.org/cpi/2001.

observed that many reputedly corrupt governments were in fact effective economic managers for quite long periods of time. In Latin America, for example, the highest growth countries—Venezuela and Colombia—were among the most corrupt. In fact, according to one school of thought, there may be an optimal level of corruption—which is greater than zero—at which the economy functions most efficiently. Esteemed political scientist Samuel Huntington observed: "In terms of economic growth the only thing worse than a society with a rigid, overcentralized, *dishonest* bureaucracy is one with a rigid, overcentralized, *honest* bureaucracy."[7] (Italics were added.)

Thus, development experts wondered if corruption might grease the wheels for development in some circumstances. Columbia University's Nathaniel Leff, for example, argued that "corruption may introduce an element of competition into what is otherwise a comfortably monopolistic industry ... payment of bribes [becomes] one of the principal criteria for allocation. ... Hence, a tendency toward efficiency is introduced into the system." This "grease the wheels" argument suggests that bribery, for example, may be a relatively efficient means of getting around burdensome regulations and an ineffective legal system in some countries.[8]

Indeed, it does seem plausible to believe that corruption may actually play a useful role in developing or transition economies. By introducing a market mechanism of sorts, corruption may put resources into the hands of people who value them and thus can use them most effectively. If the economy is badly distorted to begin with, corruption may make it work better—or indeed may be needed to make it work at all.

The Moralists Win

Does corruption improve economic or organizational efficiency? Fortunately for the moralists, a body of empirical evidence gathered over the past decade indicates that the harmful effects of corruption greatly outweigh its occasional benefits. First of all, corruption conveys important losses in efficiency due to the waste and/or misallocation of resources. Because of corrupt government procurement policies, for example, governments in developing countries typically pay between 20 percent and 100 percent more than they would pay in a noncorrupt situation; this effect has been well-documented by a series of studies.[9] Economist Daniel Kaufmann tells the following story:

> In Ukraine, a construction firm submitted a bid of U.S. $10 per square meter for tiling a major public building; the official disqualified it immediately, because the contractor had 'dared' to submit a bid for less than the 'minimum' bidding cost of US $30 per square meter. The winner of the bid was hardly the most cost-effective firm![10]

Second, corruption plays a mischievous role in redistributing resources within a country. Most studies indicate that the rich and privileged benefit from corruption at the expense of the poor, the rural, and the disenfranchised. Corruption tends to drive large swathes of economic activity underground, depriving the government of badly needed resources and contributing to the dilapidated state of infrastructure and public services. Finally, corruption distorts the energies of officials and citizens toward socially and economically unproductive activities. And corruption tends to be self-perpetuating, so once a country has entered a cycle of corruption, the habit is hard to break.

As noted, numerous empirical studies during the 1990s supported the economists' contention that corruption should be harmful to the economic performance of a developing or transition country. The World Bank found in a sample of thirty-nine countries that high levels of corruption tended to reduce the rate of investment in gross domestic product (GDP) from 28.5 percent to 12.3 percent. The bank suggested that investment levels are especially vulnerable to corruption because of the accompanying unpredictability of the political environment.[11] A few blocks away at the IMF, economist Paulo Mauro demonstrated convincingly that high levels of corruption are associated with lower levels of investment. Furthermore, he showed that corrupt countries are likely to lose about one-half percentage point of GDP growth per year, compared to relatively clean countries. Another study, by economist Shang-Jen Wei, demonstrates that corruption essentially adds a "tax" of around 20 percent to investments.[12]

The example of Angola is both instructive and painful. As *The New York Times* recently reported, Angola is "sub-Saharan Africa's second-largest oil producer and the seventh-largest supplier of crude oil to the United States. Yet 70 percent of the people live in poverty and the hardships have only worsened as oil exports have surged. ..." How can this be? Obviously, poor government and years of civil war are part of the explanation. But so is corruption. In 2000, for example, as the advocacy group Global Witness reports, the government was supposedly paid $3.8 billion in oil taxes—but the Finance Ministry says that only $3 billion was received.[13] The missing $800 million is emblematic of the obstacles to development, even in a country with rich natural resources.

Mexico is another example; by the early 2000s, according to A.T. Kearney management consultants, Mexico had slipped from fifth to ninth place in attractiveness to foreign investors worldwide, largely because of crime and corruption. Extra security costs cut into export competitiveness, while frequent kidnappings (often with police complicity) scare off executives. The IPADE business school reports that corruption costs Mexico $650 million, or 5 percent of foreign direct investment receipts, every year. And according to Transparency International, the average Mexican household spends 8 percent of its income on bribes.[14]

While the bottom line is difficult to quantify with any precision, it is increasingly clear that bribery tends to corrupt markets; in a system where decisions are made on the basis of bribes rather than quality and pricing, economic actors are rewarded for diverting resources from quality actors to bribe-payers. But the human costs are increasingly evident as well. Buildings that collapsed in Turkey's 1999 earthquake, for example, had not been built to code because it was more cost-effective to erect substandard buildings and bribe the building inspectors than to build stronger buildings that could withstand an earthquake.[15]

So as the 1990s progressed, decision-makers around the world became increasingly convinced of the high costs of this corruption eruption: dead bodies in an earthquake, higher levels of poverty, and lower levels of investment in an immature market economy. As economists made a convincing case, their efforts were complemented by a spate of corruption scandals in the 1990s that proved the straw to break the proverbial camel's back. And all at once, a consensus formed: corruption was a serious problem, and it had to go. Accordingly, the 1990s saw a variety of efforts to combat corruption in its many forms.

The Reformers Strike Back

The most obvious of these efforts was the U.S. drive to extend its Foreign Corrupt Practices Act (FCPA), which was enacted in 1977, to the rest of the world. The

FCPA had long been a thorn in the side of U.S. multinationals, since it forbade them from bribing foreign officials. Predictably, U.S. companies lamented that they were at a severe disadvantage relative to their rivals in other, more tolerant countries; until recently, France, Germany, and other nations not only countenanced their companies' paying off of foreign officials but even allowed them to treat the bribery payments as tax-deductible expenses.

By the late 1990s, revulsion against the size and costs of the world corruption eruption had turned the tide in the Americans' favor. In 1997, the twenty-nine OECD nations signed an antibribery treaty to bring laws into line with the U.S. position—scoring a huge success for American diplomacy. Bribery of foreign officials, not to mention tax deductions for bribery expenses, was to become a thing of the past. The Organization of American States (OAS) soon followed suit with a treaty requiring its members to also criminalize transnational bribery.

Predictably, though, the drive against international corruption has had mixed results at best. U.S. officials are visibly disappointed at the lack of progress in some countries, such as France, toward implementing enabling legislation and suitable penalties. Americans are especially critical of Japan's new antibribery law, which imposes a maximum fine of just $2 million for corporations found guilty of violating the law. France and Germany too have been reportedly cited in an internal U.S. government report as countries whose companies pay most bribes and where legislation to implement the OECD accord has lagged.[16]

Indeed, surveys indicate that businesspeople report no change in behavior despite the industrial world's commitment to criminalizing bribery of foreign officials. Low-level bribes ("dash" in Nigeria) are still widely accepted as the only way to get a job done in many parts of the world. *The Financial Times* reports: "Today, in India, corruption is the rule, not the exception." In the Indian state of Uttar Pradesh, for example, about one-half of the state's 403 legislators have criminal backgrounds, and experts estimate that less than one-third of development aid actually gets to its intended beneficiaries in the state.[17] According to a study by Control Risks Group in 2002, fully 40 percent of companies in the United States, United Kingdom, Germany, Netherlands, Hong Kong, and Singapore believed that they had lost business in the past year because a competitor paid a bribe. The 1997 OECD antibribery convention was still an enigma; Control Risks found that only 56 percent of U.K. companies and fewer than 40 percent of Dutch and German companies were even aware of the convention. (This is perhaps not surprising, since the new laws had not resulted in any criminal convictions, which probably would have caught people's attention.)[18]

A 2002 study by Transparency International (TI) is similarly downbeat, finding that bribery of foreign public officials by multinationals from rich countries is still commonplace despite the efforts to stamp it out. TI finds that U.S. companies are, in fact, among the worst offenders more than twenty years after passage of the FCPA (Table 8.2) and that the OECD's convention against bribery has failed to make much of an impact.

Further, TI's *Corruption Perceptions Index 2002* indicates that corruption is actually on the rise in many industrialized and developing countries. Around

TABLE 8.2 Transparency International (TI) Bribe Payers Index, 2002

Rank	Country	Score
1	Australia	8.5°
2	Sweden, Switzerland	8.4
4	Austria	8.2
5	Canada	8.1
6	Netherlands, Belgium	7.8
8	UK	6.9
9	Singapore, Germany	6.3
11	Spain	5.8
12	France	5.5
13	US, Japan	5.3
15	Malaysia, Hong Kong	4.3
17	Italy	4.1
18	South Korea	3.9
19	Taiwan	3.8
20	China	3.5
21	Russia	3.2

°Higher score indicates that the multinational companies from that country are perceived as less corrupt, on the basis of a survey carried out in the fifteen emerging market countries that trade most with multinationals.

Source: Transparency International Bribe Payers Index 2002, available at www.transparency.org.

seventy of 102 countries scored less than five out of ten possible points for "highly clean" countries; the previous year, fifty-five of ninety-one countries scored below five.

TI concludes: "There is no end in sight to the misuse of power by those in public office—and corruption levels are perceived to be as high as ever in both the developed and developing worlds." Its chairman adds: "There is a worldwide corruption crisis." The most corrupt countries in the world include Azerbaijan, Bolivia, Cameroon, Kenya, Indonesia, Uganda, Nigeria, and Bangladesh[19]—countries where the lost growth and investment due to corruption are a national tragedy.

► FINANCIAL WRONGDOING ON WALL STREET

While conversations on bribery and corruption tend to focus on poor, emerging market countries, some of the highlights (or low-lights) of the decade actually center around the most sophisticated and developed financial markets in the world.

Crony Capitalism, American-Style?

When the Asian financial crisis erupted in 1997–1998, commentators bemoaned the omnipresence of crony capitalism, which had laid the foundations for the crisis and endangered future prospects for the ailing economies. Crony capitalism meant, among other things, that bankers allocated resources to the best connected rather than the most efficient, with predictably disastrous results. However, a closer look at the decade suggests that crony capitalism is deeply rooted in the New York–London axis of financial power—with, perhaps, even more alarming implications.

Long-Term Capital Management

The story of Long-Term Capital Management (LTCM) is not one about crooks and criminals. It may be a morality play, but there are no rogue traders, no market manipulators, no inside traders, no smoking guns. No one went to jail. In fact, the tale starts with a group of Nobel Laureates and financial whiz kids—with math degrees from the finest universities–who formed a hedge fund (an investment pool for well-heeled, sophisticated investors that generally operates beyond the realm of national regulators). The whiz kids created a financial model that enabled them to take huge, highly leveraged risks in global financial markets. Unfortunately, the markets in 1997–1998 took an unexpected and unprecedented turn, upsetting LTCM's models which were, of course, based on historical trading patterns. A lot of things went wrong at once, the models crashed and burned, and LTCM stood on the verge of collapse. In many regards, LTCM was hit by the perfect financial storm; all of its bets went wrong at the same time.

Thus in September 1998, the Federal Reserve Bank of New York (the Fed) summoned the top executives of the city's leading commercial and investment banks to an extraordinary gathering. Senior officers of Merrill Lynch, Goldman Sachs, J. P. Morgan, and other Wall Street leaders met at the New York Fed's headquarters in Manhattan to coordinate an emergency rescue for LTCM. The Fed put no taxpayer money on the table, but it used its considerable jawboning power (cooperate or else) to pressure the banking executives into crafting a rescue package. In the end, fourteen leading Wall Street institutions put up $3.625 billion to bail out the sinking hedge fund.

The markets breathed a sigh of relief, but there was dismay as well. Critics charged that the rescue was a glaring example of moral hazard—the economic equivalent of rewarding a toddler for sticking his wet finger in an electrical socket. In effect, the Fed was signaling to big investors that it would provide a safety net if they were in danger of incurring big losses on their bets, a dangerous extension of the "too big to fail" doctrine. The financial moral hazard involved seemed quite clear: if hedge funds, and the banks that lend them money, are not punished for poor behavior—then their incentive is to take ever-bigger risks in the comfortable certainty that someone will bail them out should they falter.

Even more worrisome to critics was the suggestion that so-called crony capitalism, a term generally reserved for cozy relationships in emerging markets between lenders and borrowers, was alive and well on Wall Street. Merrill Lynch, a leading member of the rescue group, confirmed that its executives had invested $22 million of their own money with LTCM, including $800,000 of the chairman's money. And why exactly was the Fed stepping in to broker a rescue that would benefit wealthy, savvy investors—not a widow or orphan among them? Speaking in Boston, former Fed chairman Paul Volcker wondered aloud: "Why should the weight of the Federal Government be brought to bear to help out a private investor?"[20]

On the other hand, government officials explained that they were not bailing out LTCM's rich investors. In fact, the government was worried that a forced sale of LTCM's financial holdings would disrupt New York's financial markets, perhaps catastrophically so. Fed chief Alan Greenspan defended his organization's role in brokering the rescue, explaining that it had acted out of concern for financial market stability rather than a desire to assist the hedge fund's wealthy owners.

Given the still-simmering financial crises in Asia, Russia, and Brazil—as well as the near-implosion of major financial institutions that followed the 1980s debt crisis—this was a plausible argument. Global financial markets were exceedingly fragile following the Asian crisis, and it was believed that if LTCM went down, it could pull a good chunk of Wall Street down with it. Still, the episode did not play well on the front page of *The New York Times*. Detractors believed that if it had happened in Indonesia, it would be pilloried as yet another example of Asian crony capitalism. Given the robust and vast nature of U.S. capital markets, skeptics had trouble imagining that the collapse of one high-flying but relatively obscure hedge fund could really undermine the stability of world financial markets.

Bubbles and Conflicted Analysts

Accusations of crony capitalism emerged again amidst the debris left when the Internet and telecom bubbles burst. In particular, increasing attention has been focused on the Wall Street analysts who touted these stocks when even the most rudimentary financial analysis might have suggested otherwise. The example of Jack Grubman, the "resident guru on telecoms at Salomon Smith Barney and one of Wall Street's highest-paid analysts," is instructive.

During the height of the boom in telecom stocks, 1999–2000, Grubman maintained buy recommendations on thirty companies in the sector (much more than other analysts). Certainly, stock-pickers can be the victims of exogenous events or of their own poor judgment, but an examination of the role of Grubman and others like him raises disturbing questions about the ability of Wall Street analysts to produce objective and timely recommendations for their clients. (Of the thirty-six stocks that Grubman covered in 1998–2002, sixteen eventually went bankrupt.) An independent research firm, Gimme Credit, by contrast,[21] did manage to foresee crashes in key stocks, including WorldCom, Tyco, and Qwest. Said Gimme Credit's research director: "We look at the same numbers everybody else looks at. It's just surprising how having no conflict of interest improves your batting average. ..."

According to one securities lawyer, in 1997–2001 Grubman's firm, Salomon Smith Barney (SSB), earned more investment banking fees from telecom companies than any other Wall Street firm. (In 1997–2001 SSB earned $809 million from underwriting telecom stocks and bonds and $178 million more for giving merger advice to the telecom companies.) This lawyer, not surprisingly, calls Grubman "the king of conflicted analysts." *The New York Times* observed:

> Anyone can make mistakes, but Mr. Grubman's cheerleading epitomizes the conflict of interest questions that have dogged Wall Street for two years. Even as he rallied clients of Salomon Smith Barney, a unit of Citigroup, to buy shares of untested telecommunications companies and to hold on to the shares as they lost almost all their value, he was aggressively helping his firm win lucrative stock and bond deals from these same companies.[22]

Grubman, of course, was not alone in his conflict. Another star analyst, Henry Blodget, earned fame as Merrill Lynch's Internet guru who encouraged clients to buy into the Internet bubble at the same time that his firm was earning huge sums advising and underwriting deals for those very companies. Grubman himself, though, is scornful toward those who question the propriety of having one analyst— whose job is to provide investors with objective investment advice—work closely with the investment bankers doing deals for the subjects of his investment advice. He explained, "What used to be a conflict is now a synergy. Objective? The other word for it is uninformed."

When the bubble burst, however, the reputations of Grubman, Blodget, and others like them were badly tarnished. Predictably, the lawyers and government investigators found rich material to investigate, mindful of an angry public in the background. By mid-2002, both the Securities and Exchange Commission (SEC) and New York attorney general Eliot Spitzer had struck pay dirt in their investigations into conflicts of interest among big Wall Street analysts like Grubman and Blodget. While looking into the question of whether SSB, Merrill Lynch, and other firms used their research analyses as an incentive to attract investment banking clients, Spitzer "learned from thirty thousand internal e-mails obtained from Merrill [that] at the height of the dot-com mania only the clients were deluded, not the analysts."

These internal e-mails, in fact, revealed that while research analysts were publicly telling their investor clients to buy shares, at the same time the analysts were privately highly critical of those very same shares. Star Internet stock analyst Blodget was writing and speaking favorably about the prospects of hot dot-coms like GoTo.com, InfoSpace, Pets.com, and others, but in private Merrill Lynch analysts were singing quite a different tune. Internal communications among analysts called the stock of Excite@home, for example, "such a piece of crap" and InfoSpace "a piece of junk."[23]

In fact, the Internet/telecom bubble of the late 1990s is dotted with instances of questionable behavior. In early 2002, the Wall Street giant CSFB (Credit Suisse First Boston) agreed to pay $100 million to settle charges brought by the SEC and National Association of Securities Dealers (NASD) relating to hot Internet IPOs (initial public offerings) during the bubble years. The regulators examined how CSFB rationed shares of sought-after high-tech IPOs at the height of the bull market and concluded that the firm received kickbacks from the lucky buyers of these hot stock offerings. In fact, there was apparently an elaborate scheme in which CSFB earned millions of dollars in inflated commissions from its clients, in return for allotments of the hottest IPOs. The charges indicate that between April 1999 and June 2000 CSFB arranged for more than one hundred clients to funnel 33 percent to 65 percent of their IPO profits to CSFB in exchange for the IPO allotments.

Worse was yet to come. During 2001–2002, a series of investigations into IPO allotments to key executives raised troubling questions about how level the Wall Street playing field really is. The issue revolves around allotments of stock in hot IPOs. Since the shares in these deals were routinely underpriced (to make room for a big jump in early trading, lending some fizzle and excitement to the new stock), the fortunate first owners of the shares were virtually guaranteed huge gains in early trading. Shares routinely surged on the first day of trading, doubling or even tripling in value. Not surprisingly, the allotment of these sought-after shares left much room for shenanigans.

In 1999, the SEC looked into the practice of allocating shares in these IPOs and concluded that there was no legal case to bring against investment banks that favored certain clients over others. Some SEC staffers found the practice unethical, but there was no apparent violation of securities laws. But then the issue exploded in 2001–2002, when it became clear that executives involved in some of Wall Street's biggest implosions were also among the greatest beneficiaries of the practice. Bernie Ebbers, for example—former CEO of WorldCom, which filed the largest bankruptcy in U.S. history in 2002—was one beneficiary. An internal SSB memo from 1999 detailed requests for shares in a hot new IPO issue from twenty-six wealthy and generally well-known clients. Twenty of these twenty-six clients were affiliated with companies that had recently generated hefty investment banking fees for SSB, raising the question of whether SSB was dispensing free money in the form of IPO shares to Ebbers and other executives to ensure a strong bond with their firms.

New York attorney general Eliot Spitzer describes this as a form of "commercial bribery." There was no obvious quid pro quo—no smoking gun memos promising investment banking business in return for IPO shares—so bribery will be hard to prove. But the practice leaves outsiders with a queasy feeling. "Wall Street is a scam," declared analysts in *The Financial Times*, citing a new congressional report that finds the system "rigged" against ordinary investors.[24] The most efficient, transparent, and best-regulated capital market that the world has ever seen—Wall Street—was not, it appears, as transparent and fair as we would like to believe.

Rogues and Other Traders

Halfway around the world, another kind of trouble brought down an even more venerable financial institution. In mid-1992, an ambitious young man named Nick Leeson arrived at Barings Bank Singapore. His job was to arbitrage (make risk-free trades) to take advantage of the tiny differences between prices quoted for the same contracts on the Singapore and Japanese exchanges. Typically, traders accomplish this by entering into hedged (matched, or offsetting) purchase and sales contracts on the two exchanges almost simultaneously in order to capture favorable price differences. The trader is usually allowed to maintain an unhedged, intraday position up to specified risk limits and no unhedged overnight positions.

This should have been a low-risk, low-profit operation. Since price differences between the two exchanges should generally be quite small, the trader does a high volume of low-margin deals; it's the Costco of the trading business. Leeson, however, took quite a different approach.

Making unauthorized trades on options and futures through a secret account, number 88888, Leeson developed huge positions—one-way directional bets, not hedged by any matching or offsetting positions. Unfortunately for Barings, Leeson was no George Soros. His positions were losers almost from the very beginning. (To some extent, of course, Leeson was the victim of exogenous events as markets moved against him.) Moreover, Leeson was, almost from the very beginning, trading far in excess of his authority at Barings—and losing money on those positions. Then, like many unlucky gamblers, Leeson took bigger and bigger bets to try and reverse his losses. To bring in cash needed to finance his losing positions, he sold whopping big options contracts giving purchasers the right to cash in should the markets move in their favor (and, by definition, against Leeson). In the end, he left behind liabilities of $1.3 billion, and Barings—banker to the British royal family—was suddenly insolvent. Leeson fled, leaving a handwritten note that said, simply, "I'm sorry." The Bank of England chose not to intervene, and eventually the Dutch bank ING agreed to assume most of Barings' liabilities for the princely sum of one pound. The venerated Barings name, sadly, disappeared from the world of banking.

The shocking piece of the Barings story, of course, is not Leeson's perfidy—unexpected market shifts put traders into losing positions with unfortunate frequency—but the fact that one undistinguished trader could, single-handedly, bring down a 232-year-old British financial institution. Where were the checks and balances? Leeson was hardly a star trader to begin with; he was originally hired to manage the back office, where trades are processed and recorded. When he moved up to the trading floor, he was essentially unsupervised. Worse, from an internal controls perspective, he was allowed to control both the trading operation and the back office. This violates, of course, the basic principle of internal control; the same person should never be writing the checks and reconciling the checkbook. Combining those operations is practically an invitation to malfeasance.

This lack of supervision reflected institutional neglect and a power vacuum in Barings' Asian operations to some extent. But there are structural issues too. With the Big Bang, London's "sedate financial sector was deregulated in the 1980s—and suddenly the aggressive American and Japanese came crashing in with giant salaries. … Traders were made overnight," says Valerie Thompson, who traded for Salomon Brothers in London for fifteen years and watched the change. "Managers did not have time to train them properly." Thompson points, in particular, to "the inexperience and hubris of youth" among the hard-driving traders of the post-Big Bang era. Moreover, the increasing complexity of those new-fangled financial derivatives was profoundly perplexing to staid British bankers. One former Barings manager later admitted, "There was no one in Barings top management who understood derivatives"—the very instruments that Leeson was trading.[25]

They did understand profits, though. In fact, Leeson was viewed as a wonder boy in London, who single-handedly contributed one-half of Barings

Singapore's 1993 profits and one-half of the entire firm's 1994 profits. Violating yet another axiom of internal control, managers were admiring, not skeptical, of these reported profits (which, of course, excluded the growing river of red ink on account number 88888). When Leeson needed funds to finance his losses and margin deposits for the Singapore exchange, he easily obtained funding from other Barings companies.

And in a precursor of the Enron affair, the auditors too asked no hard questions. Five years after Barings collapsed, a British tribunal found PricewaterhouseCoopers guilty of professional failings by the Coopers part of the now-merged auditing firm. Like Enron, many Barings shareholders lost their life savings in the mess. Criticism has been heaped on both management and auditors for failing to detect Leeson's unauthorized trading activity. The Bank of England found: "It was this complete lack of effective controls, which provided the opportunity for Leeson to undertake his unauthorized trading activities and reduced the likelihood of their detection." In particular, Bank officials criticize Barings management for:

- *lack of segregation* of Leeson's duties (his management of both back- and front-office operations);

- *improper supervision* of Leeson (the back-office operations were never really monitored, and Barings managers seemed uncertain as to who was really responsible for supervising Leeson's trading activities); and

- perhaps most critical, *failing to question* his reported profits. As the Bank of England points out, Barings management did understand that Leeson was supposed to profit from his trades by "switching" between the Singapore and Japanese exchanges with fully matched trades, at no real risk. How on earth could Leeson have generated such large profits from this low-risk arbitrage operation? And how on earth could no one at Barings have asked this question?[26]

Leeson is not the only rogue trader of the decade, of course. In early 2002, a foreign exchange trader at Allfirst Bank in Baltimore, Maryland, a U.S. subsidiary of Allied Irish Banks, quite remarkably managed to lose $750 million of his bank's money in unauthorized trading (like so many before him, he bet the wrong way on the yen). The trader, John Rusnak, was reportedly responsible for quintupling the bank's foreign exchange revenues in 1995–2000. The persistence of these episodes seems to reflect some common elements:

- *The discomfort of both management and auditors* with highly complex financial markets, especially in derivatives. Once again, this highlights the gap between the financial innovations being introduced—and the ability of institutions to properly accommodate them in a prudent regulatory fashion. Certainly, the proliferation of complicated and sophisticated financial transactions enables rogue traders, who rely on the fact that their bosses or regulators do not understand their trading. Says one expert, "It is a standard feature of these situations that the people these traders are reporting to either don't want to ask what appears to be a silly question and look ignorant, or simply don't understand."[27]

■ *A disinclination to question extraordinary profits,* even from wildly improbable sources (a currency trader in a Baltimore bank, for example, or arbitrage trading in the Far East); and

■ *Serious misalignment of incentives,* to the point that individual traders may come to believe that their best interest lies in deceiving management. Undoubtedly, these traders think that if their unauthorized trading were to result in profits rather than losses, they would be rewarded.

Enron India: The Story Begins

If BCCI represents the ultimate in rogue financial institutions and Barings the ultimate in rogue traders, Enron may be the standard-bearer for unprincipled corporations. The Enron story is still unfolding, of course—and will probably continue to unfold in courtrooms around the country for many years to come. It is already clear, though, that the Enron tale contains a veritable litany of financial wrongdoing. It is a failure of corporate governance in every sense of the phrase. *The Financial Times* editorialized: "The damning report delivered by a special committee of the Enron board describes an unholy convergence of greed, incompetence, and deceit."[28]

Indeed, the most striking feature of the Enron debacle is the extent to which it is truly a systemic failure. While Barings, Allfirst, and others may be dismissed as examples of individual perfidy enabled by a flawed system, the Enron story highlights the perfidy of the very system itself. Not one piece of the system—company executives, directors, auditors, lawyers, market analysts, bankers, or regulators—functioned as it should. Economist Paul Krugman laments, "The Enron debacle is not just the story of a company that failed; it is the story of a system that failed. And the system didn't fail through carelessness or laziness; it was corrupted."[29]

To fully understand Enron's corporate environment, it is instructive to step back and examine the company's history in India. Enron entered the Indian market in the early 1990s with the $2.9 billion Dabhol power plant project in Maharashtra state. The deal quickly became problematic. In April 1992 Enron was invited to bid for the project as part of India's liberalization drive. The deal was struck remarkably swiftly, so fast that the process was criticized almost immediately for its haste, lack of transparency, and absence of competitive bidding. As a result, a "widespread belief" developed that "corruption played a role in the project's implementation."

In 1995, the Maharashtra state government issued a detailed report criticizing the deal, finding: "Thus, in a matter of less than three days, an MoU [Memorandum of Understanding] was signed ... in a matter involving a project of the value of over 10,000 crore rupees [almost $3 billion] at the time, with entirely imported fuel and largely imported equipment, in which, admittedly, no one in the government had expertise or experience."

The World Bank also reviewed the deal, concluding that it was "one-sided" in favor of Enron, and refused to finance the project because it was "not economically viable." Perhaps most damning, the bank found that the project did not satisfy the test of least-cost power and was too large for the power demands of Maharashtra. In particular, the Bank underlined the following concerns:

- The agreement guaranteed Enron a steady income in dollars, regardless of demand or of the rupee/dollar exchange rate.

- The Maharashtra state government waived its right to sovereign immunity, so that if it was unable to make a payment, the company had the right to seize state assets.

- The central government also guaranteed payment in the event of a state default, and the central government of India also waived its sovereign immunity.

These provisions seemed to justify complaints by World Bank officials and Indian opposition leaders over the lack of competitive bidding for the project; the project costs (the cost of electricity from Dabhol would be significantly higher than in other areas); and the state government's promise that it would purchase all the high-priced electricity generated by the project, whether warranted by demand or not.[30] One Indian columnist summed it up this way: "If Enron remains the most controversial multinational in India for the last eight years, it is because there is substantial basis for the charges made against it."[31] (And, of course, there were considerable questions pertaining to the corruptibility of Indian officials and the amazingly complicated bureaucratic red tape imposed by local governments.)

The pessimists had it right. By 2001, the cash-strapped state government was locked in a nasty dispute with the Enron-controlled Dabhol Power Corporation. Following in the steps of the Clinton administration, which had also stepped in to support Enron in India during the mid-1990s, Bush aides lobbied vigorously in 2001 to avert a shutdown of the Dabhol plant. White House aides acknowledged that Vice President Cheney and other U.S. officials had pressed Indian officials to pay Enron the money owed to it for past power purchases.

A testimony to Enron's skill in gaining influence with both Democrats and Republicans in Washington, the lobbying on Enron's behalf seems, with the benefit of hindsight, to be remarkably tone-deaf. From the beginning, critics of the project had warned that the power plant was economically unsound, suggesting that corruption was involved in the awarding of the contract. The project's troubles by 2001 underlined the concerns of its critics: Its woes stemmed directly from the structure of the deal, which pegged payments in dollars at a price that proved too high for the government to pay. Little wonder, then, that "the struggle against Enron has become symbolic of the struggle against globalization in India."[32]

Enron: A Cancer on Capitalism

Given what is now known about the company, it is particularly unfortunate that Enron may represent the face of globalization in India. One financial pundit writes, "Argentina's financial collapse looks at first like a blow to the 'Washington consensus' brand of market-based economics. ... But another record bankruptcy—Enron—could be a bigger and more insidious threat to the Washington consensus." Enron's demise, she adds, "strikes at the heart of American capitalism."[33]

How did Enron come to be the poster child for capitalists behaving badly (or, as Paul Krugman put it, "a cancer on capitalism"[34])? The company did so many things so wrong that it is difficult to sum up quickly. Simply, Enron established a network of affiliated companies to hold assets that were thus removed from the corporate balance sheet. Not surprisingly, these assets performed very poorly, so removing them from the balance sheet helped preserve the image of Enron as a strong company. (Actually, setting up an incredibly complex web of special-purpose vehicles like this was a common practice among U.S. corporations.) In this case, though, the result of this asset-migration was that the company's reported earnings were about $1 billion higher than they should have been, greasing the way for a soaring stock price. Adding insult to injury, top executives enriched themselves by various self-dealing schemes and generally managed to sell off their own shares before the bottom fell out; shareholders and employees lost everything.

As in the Barings case, the remarkable and disturbing fact of the Enron story is how thoroughly the checks and balances failed to operate. Indeed, some of the most prominent names in world finance figure in this story. Merrill Lynch, Citigroup, J. P. Morgan Chase, and Deutsche Bank all helped finance the company; Arthur Andersen audited its books. Company management worked closely with government officials and regulators, to the point that CEO Kenneth Lay advised Vice President Cheney in formulating U.S. energy policy. Board directors included some of the best-respected and best-connected names in the business.

So the implosion of Enron hits squarely at the reputation of U.S. capital markets. Clearly, in this case, the system failed. Some of the most obvious culprits include the following.

■ *Wall Street's lack of objectivity and conflicts of interest.* Investment banks earn far more from underwriting and advising big deals than from broker fees. Thus analysts have conflicting loyalties, as noted in the Grubman example: Do we offend the management of a major client company, or do we inform investors that the company may be heading for trouble? In early December 2001, with Enron stock flailing at less than $1 per share, twelve of seventeen analysts who covered the company still rated it a buy or hold. It was an open secret on Wall Street that firms with negative ratings on Enron's stock would not win its business.

While details remain hazy, as more information emerges about Wall Street's ties to Enron, the picture grows progressively more disturbing. An investigation by *The Financial Times* found that Enron depended heavily on a team of bankers at CSFB in setting up the controversial web of partnerships that helped hide poorly performing assets. Moreover, the reporters calculated that Enron paid more than $250 million in fees to bankers during 2000 alone. "Wall Street's links with Enron were complex, intimate, often antagonistic, but above all, lucrative," the report concludes. (One banker who worked with Enron said, "They were the golden goose.")[35]

In some ways, the bankers' failings are reminiscent of those experienced in Latin America, Asia, and Russia and at LTCM. And they were duly punished: Citibank recorded a $228 million pretax loss in fourth quarter 2001 due to Enron; Bank of America dismissed three veteran bankers who were responsible for its Enron loans and took a $231 million write-off. J. P. Morgan Chase, which provided a wide array of financial services to Enron (from commodities trading to commercial loans), wrote down a whopping $451 million in the fourth quarter, with around $2 billion more in potential losses still on its books.

And yet the bankers were hardly alone. Another set of Wall Street players, the credit rating agencies, also appear to have been blindsided by the Enron debacle. These agencies are supposed to be independent securities analysts who judge a company's financial health and issue unbiased, objective reports periodically. The credit rating agencies, however, did remarkably little to warn investors of Enron's troubles until long after evidence of substantial problems had become public. Many investors were left wondering why the rating agencies were so slow in acting, even after much of the bad news was public.

■ *The auditor's inherent conflict of interest.* Observers have heaped opprobrium on Arthur Andersen, for good reason. The auditing firm was aware of the partnerships used to manipulate earnings at Enron and in fact had earned big fees for advising Enron on those partnerships. Arthur Andersen signed off on a variety of earnings manipulation and self-dealing schemes, no doubt to placate a big and profitable client. The auditor's conflict between pleasing a rich customer and preserving a reputation is age-old, of course, but brought into new relief by the Enron debacle.

■ *Crony capitalism.* All of the above, and more, enabled Enron's executives in their activities. Enron had plenty of help—its lawyers, accountants, lobbyists, consultants, board members, and government allies all helped the company look respectable long after it began to implode. An embittered-sounding Krugman observes:

> Four years ago, as Asia struggled with an economic crisis, many observers blamed 'crony capitalism.' Wealthy businessmen in Asia didn't bother to tell investors the truth about their assets, their liabilities, and their profits; the aura of invincibility that came from their political connections was enough. Only when a financial crisis came along did people take a hard look at their businesses, which promptly collapsed.[36]

Substitute 'Enron' for 'Asia' in the second sentence, and many see classic crony capitalism, American-style.

As the details continue to emerge, there is much speculation about what should be done to prevent another Enron. Reams of legislation are in the pipeline; auditors and board directors are struggling with proposals for reform; and Wall Street analysts are vowing, once again, to eliminate conflicts of interest. Investors, some of them badly burned by Enron, have become much more cynical and more focused on examining company financial statements—taking note of who the auditors are and, in some cases, shunning companies with substantial off-balance-sheet liabilities.

It is far from clear, though, that Enron is an isolated case. Because of an unlucky set of circumstances, the Enron scheme unraveled quickly and dramatically. But does anyone seriously believe that the system that produced Enron has not spawned many other mini-Enrons? Indeed, much of the utilities and energy sector has come under intense regulatory and investor scrutiny. Companies such as Williams and Calpine have been severely punished by investors and the rating agencies for questionable accounting practices. Many other energy companies, such as El Paso, were forced to take drastic measures, including putting off-balance-sheet liabilities on the books, incurring substantial losses as a consequence. Even relatively clean utility companies were punished as investors fled for the exits.

Moreover, Enron quickly lost its title of biggest bankruptcy in U.S. history to WorldCom—an even grimmer tale. The former CFO and controller of WorldCom were arrested in mid-2002, charged with falsifying balance sheets to hide more than $3.8 billion in expenses, thus causing a huge overstatement of earnings.

Former SEC chairman Arthur Levitt, in fact, believes that Enron is just a symptom of a much larger problem. "What has failed," he told the Senate in recent testimony, "is nothing less than the system for overseeing our capital markets."[37] The gatekeepers who are supposed to keep our markets efficient and fair all failed simultaneously. Thus, a columnist concludes: "… the system of corporate governance and market scrutiny that is supposed to allow free markets to flourish to the benefit of all, not just the privileged few, failed."[38]

As Krugman explains, capitalism depends on a set of rules and institutions that limit the potential for insider abuse. These institutions include accounting rules, independent auditors, securities and financial market regulators, and laws against insider trading. The Enron and WorldCom affairs, however, illustrate the flaws at the heart of these institutions. "It's a matter of what it takes to make capitalism work," he explains.[39] Faced with an absence or weakness of these institutions, free markets will inevitably invite and enable financial wrongdoing. In other words, good governance practices rest on a set of shared institutions and values—so good governance is vulnerable to any weaknesses in these institutions and values. At the same time, as institutions catch up in their ability to deal with financial innovations, many of these financial misdeeds are more easily and quickly identified and rooted out.

▶ CASH, CRIMINALS, AND TERRORISTS

Perhaps the most alarming face of financial wrongdoing in recent years is the intersection of terrorists, cash, and crime in the increasingly globalized, high-tech world economy. Terrorists, often financed by drug trafficking and other criminal activities, move their funds through the international financial system with remarkable ease and sophistication. A former U.S. government official writes, "Victims of wrongdoing have found that global evil-doers are better at taking advantage of the financial infrastructure of globalization than the world's police and regulators are at catching them."[40] Enabled by unwitting (or witting) bankers and by astonishingly efficient banking technology, criminals and terrorists have reaped great benefits from the international financial system. *The Financial Times* notes: "The terrorist attack on America of September 11 exposed the dark side of globalization that allowed al-Qaeda to operate freely around the world. In particular, Osama bin Laden was able to send funds to his followers through the international banking system, exploiting weaknesses already used by criminals and corrupt politicians to launder dirty money."[41] Today, bin Laden no doubt is earning healthy returns from money residing in the very financial world that he attacked so viciously on September 11, 2001.

The Globalization of Crime

Many industries have globalized successfully—think McDonald's, Coca–Cola, and Microsoft—but perhaps none have embraced globalization as enthusiastically as crooks and criminals. Crime is thriving in the new international economy, thanks to the proliferation of free expression, global communications, and technology. A Clinton administration report found that "Russian, Chinese, Nigerian, Middle Eastern, and Italian gangs have enthusiastically embraced globalization and technology." Organized crime, it observed, has become diversified internationally and is so deeply intertwined with political elites in some countries that it is increasingly difficult to combat.[42] Remarking on a rumored summit meeting in 1998 of Russian, Colombian, Italian, Chinese, and Japanese crime bosses, a senior British policeman notes, "There has been an astonishing growth in transnational crime. ... The legal economy has gone global and the crime economy has gone global as well."[43]

In Japan, for example, the *yakuza* gangs have reacted to the prolonged contraction of their domestic economy in the best business school tradition: by going global. Yakuza gangsters have increased their cooperation with criminal counterparts in China and Russia, forging stronger links with Chinese "snakehead" smugglers of illegal immigrants and joining with the Russian mafia to import prostitutes for Japan's hostess bars.[44] In addition, global criminals have learned to harness technology for their peculiar needs. In spring 2002, *The New York Times* reported that "tens of thousands of stolen credit-card numbers are being offered for sale each week on the Internet in a handful of thriving, membership-only cyberbazaars, operated largely by residents of the former Soviet Union, who have become central players in credit-card and identity theft." Buyers come from all over the world—a true measure of globalization!—especially the former Soviet Union, Eastern Europe, and Asia.[45]

Law enforcement strategies, however inadvertently, may have contributed to the globalization of crime. More than 3,500 criminals are repatriated from the United States to the Caribbean every year, and these deportees are blamed for an upsurge in violent crime across the region in recent years. Deportees have been involved in murder, armed robbery, kidnapping, and gunfights between rival drug gangs, overwhelming the small and unsophisticated police forces of the tiny Caribbean countries. In effect, the deportees are graduates of a veritable finishing school for violent criminals—the U.S. prison system—and they bring those well-honed skills and connections back home with them when they are kicked out of the United States.[46]

Crooks, criminals, and terrorists are engaging in technology transfer as well. A congressional investigation in early 2002 found that "the Irish Republican Army has formed part of a global terror network based in Colombia, training Marxist guerrillas alongside Iranian and Cuban officials as well as Basque terrorists." Training by the Irish, Basque, and other terrorist groups has improved the skills of the Colombian guerrillas, especially with regard to urban terrorism. For these services, the IRA was reportedly paid around $2 million—the equivalent of a single day's proceeds for the Colombian group from its drug trade.[47]

Russia: "The World's Leading Kleptocracy"

Russia has struggled with economic and political reform since the breakup of the Soviet Union, with mixed results at best, but it has scored extraordinary success in the art of crime and corruption. In Russia during much of the 1990s, "crime is not at the margin of society; it is at its center," making the country "the world's leading kleptocracy."[48]

From the dying days of the USSR onward, billions of dollars flowed out of the crippled giant to be reinvested in London flats, nightclubs in Budapest, and U.S. Treasury bonds. While much of Russia's economy struggled to survive in the new environment, its money laundering network adapted remarkably well to the change in political and economic climate—facilitating capital flight first by aging Soviet apparatchiks and then by youthful Russian entrepreneurs. According to Fitch IBCA, an estimated $136 billion in capital fled Russia between 1993 and 1998. One expert explains, "By the time all the CPSU [Communist Party of the Soviet Union] money had been laundered and legitimized, the mechanisms that had been set up started accepting other clients. It was a business arrangement available to a fairly large group of people with the right connections."[49]

Indeed, Russia quickly became a role model for crooks and criminals worldwide, with special expertise in financial fraud. In 1996, the Russian central bank spirited $1 billion out of the country to a company that it controlled in the Channel Islands without telling the IMF—under whose auspices the government was supposedly implementing an economic reform program in return for massive loans. An auditor's report concluded in 1999 that the Russians had lied to the IMF about the level of foreign exchange reserves in order to encourage the Fund to continue lending. This action, of course, would normally put the country out of contention for funding well into the foreseeable future. But Russia was a special case. Just after the report was released, the IMF agreed to lend Russia another $4.5 billion despite the Channel Islands caper.

Financial crime and corruption were not invented after the fall of the Soviet Union, but the evolution from communism to some "Wild West" form of market economy has certainly democratized the crookedness. Throughout much of the 1990s, the country's interior minister estimated, organized crime controlled around

40 percent of the economy (other figures are even higher). One-half of Russia's banks were thought to be run by crime syndicates. Thus, the endorsement of Russia's biggest banks, companies, and state organizations meant little, since many were suspected of close ties to criminal groups. Crime was so deeply entrenched in the economy that it was virtually impossible for an onlooker to figure out if money was earned legitimately or not (this made it impossible to apply normal anti–money laundering tactics to Russian businesses, for example).[50]

From a safe distance, the world could observe the criminalization of Russia with fascinated horror, much as observers clucked over the descent of Colombia into narco-terrorist hell in the 1980s. Unfortunately, though, globalization means that the risk of contagion outside Russia's borders is real and alarming. If the Russian economy enters another period of stagnation—not an outlandish prospect, given the still-warped nature of basic market institutions—then growth opportunities for ambitious crooks and criminals within Russia's borders are poor. This leaves several avenues for the growth-oriented crook to pursue:

- *Export Russian organized crime abroad.* The Russian mafia is already well established in smuggling and prostitution, for example, in countries with large Russian immigrant populations, like Germany and the United States.

- *Cooperate with foreign criminals in areas where the Russians enjoy a competitive advantage.* The Russian mafia has developed expertise in some basic criminal skills and enjoys a reputation for ruthlessness. Thus, Russian professional assassins are in demand worldwide, and Russian money launderers have lent their professional expertise to Israeli practitioners.

- *Fusion of the corrupt state with powerful gangsters.* The most alarming scenario, this in effect projects the worst-case scenario onto a worldwide stage. Russia could become a major staging point for smuggling weapons and drugs, for instance, or for counterfeiting—which would be well-nigh impossible without the close cooperation of state institutions. The potential for Russian criminals to essentially coopt the state and turn it into a global gangsters' headquarters is terrifying, especially in the context of increased European integration. One security expert says, "Organized crime interests are global, not isolated. They would love it if Russia was in the EU."[51]

Since the Wild West days of the 1990s, though, Russia has made a serious effort to deal with the pernicious impact of criminalization. Money laundering laws have been enacted, greater transparency and disclosure are now expected in the corporate world, and Russian legal authorities are more inclined to cooperate with their foreign counterparts. The situation is still challenging, but Russia's political elite came to recognize that unless measures were taken, their country would continue its slide into a developmental cul-de-sac. One reward of the effort to deal with widespread corruption and criminality: foreign investment is finally flowing in at a higher and more sustainable level. However, Russia is likely to be plagued by crime for the foreseeable future.

A Guerrilla's Best Friend: Crooks, Guerrillas, and Terrorists

Russia's mafia is generally apolitical—the crooks want money, not political goals. Political power is a means to this end, rather than an end in itself.

In other cases, though, the unholy fusion of criminals, guerrilla fighters, and terrorists has opened up new and equally alarming vistas. Proceeds from criminal activity are used to fund terrorist and guerrilla operations; in return, the fighters often provide protection and other services for the criminals. In many parts of the world, the line between terrorism and banditry is increasingly blurred.

So-called conflict diamonds, for example, originate in the deeply troubled countries of Sierra Leone, Angola, and the Democratic Republic of the Congo. The diamonds are mined and sold by rebel forces, who then use the proceeds to finance a brutal military campaign against the (often equally brutal) government. The UNITA rebel group in Angola sold $3.7 billion of uncut diamonds in Antwerp between 1992 and 1998, enabling rebels to continue a costly and bloody battle against the government.

In fact, research suggests that some of the bloodiest wars of the past half-century have been waged over control of diamonds and other commodities, rather than ideology. In 2000, a World Bank study found that "Rebels fighting civil conflicts around the world are more often motivated by greedy pursuit of lucrative commodities, like diamonds and drugs, than by political, ethnic, or religious goals." After examining forty-seven civil wars from 1960 to 1999, researchers concluded that the single biggest risk factor for outbreak of civil war was a nation's economic dependence on commodities. "Diamonds are the guerrilla's best friend," commented the study's author.[52]

Conflict diamonds have been an important source of funding for al-Qaeda and other global terrorist organizations as well. Al-Qaeda has reportedly earned millions of dollars in recent years from illicit sales of diamonds mined by rebels in Sierra Leone, according to U.S. and European intelligence officials. Diamond dealers working directly with al-Qaeda operatives bought gems from rebels at below-market prices and then resold the stones for large profits in Europe.[53]

Conflict diamonds are a sideshow, of course, compared to the center-ring attraction: drug trafficking. Close financial ties between drug traffickers, terrorists, and guerrillas in Latin America have been well documented, but the connection between drug sales and Islamist terrorists is perhaps less well understood.

Colombia alone has three armed groups that the U.S. government identifies as terrorists, who control vast chunks of the country's territory and are all deeply involved in the drug trade. Colombia is the source of 90 percent of the cocaine consumed in the United States, an incredibly lucrative business. The link between these two groups—terrorists and drug traffickers—is quite straightforward and businesslike: guerrillas (both left-wing and right-wing) take a tax on every shipment of cocaine out of the country. In return, the fighters provide protection for the drug traffickers from government forces. The World Bank likens Colombia's left-wing FARC (Revolutionary Armed Forces of Colombia) guerrilla group to a giant narcotics corporation, with twelve thousand paid fighters and annual revenues of $700 million from drug sales.

Publicly acknowledging this alliance, the U.S. government in early 2002 launched a series of anti-drug advertisements warning American teens, for example, that by buying a joint or snorting cocaine, they may be helping terrorists buy AK-47s. The tag line: "Drug money supports terror. If you buy drugs, you might, too." While the ads proved intensely controversial, the facts support the basic concept. (The idea was born when State Department officials identified twenty-eight terrorist organizations after 9/11, nearly half of which were closely linked to drug trafficking.) A Web site developed to educate the public, especially U.S. teens, states: "There is an undeniable link between drugs and terror. ... The bottom line is simple: terror and drug groups are linked in a mutually-beneficial relationship by money, tactics, geography, and politics."[54]

Colombian terrorists have, for the most part, confined their violent depredations to their own country. Not so, of course, for the Islamist terrorists. They do share, though, a reliance on drug trafficking (and other forms of criminal activity) for financing. By the late 1990s, Afghanistan was easily the largest source of opium and heroin in the world. Before 9/11, the CIA estimated that Afghanistan's Taliban government earned much of its income from the country's $6.5 to $10 billion a year drug trade.

In 2000, the Taliban banned opium production, a move generally hailed by Western governments. However, with the benefit of hindsight this move was more cynical than moralistic. *The Financial Times* reports, "After the last record harvest, 1999–2000, the then-Taliban government announced that it was freezing further production. However, Western officials now believe that the Taliban was simply stockpiling in order to stabilize the price of raw opium." (During the one-year freeze on production, opium crops continued to flourish in lands controlled by the Northern Alliance, a key U.S. ally.) Following the ouster of the Taliban, Afghanistan reportedly reaped a record harvest of opium in 2002. The profits, presumably, will flow to various tribal leaders whose support remains essential to the United States.[55]

At any rate, Osama bin Laden's legitimate business ventures generally flopped, but Afghanistan's rich and beautiful poppy fields were one of his most powerful sources of funding. A study by a U.K. journalist suggests that bin Laden may have been taking a cut of up to 10 percent from Afghanistan's drug trade by early 1999, providing his organization with an income stream of perhaps $1 billion per annum.[56] Perhaps not surprising, there are persistent rumors of ties between al-Qaeda and organized crime figures; at the very least, they probably share resources.

The combination of failed nations, rich drug fields, and terrorists with global ambitions is particularly combustible. One observer writes:

> ... as anti-drug campaigns have advanced in relatively coherent states like Pakistan, Iran, Thailand, and Bolivia, more of the world's drug supply has begun to come from so-called rogue states, or from regions that government authority simply doesn't reach. After Afghanistan, the world's biggest opium producer these days is

Burma. Most of the world's supply of coca, the raw material for cocaine, comes from regions of Colombia dominated by leftist rebels and right-wing paramilitary forces.[57]

This means that the intersection of crooks and terrorists is likely to become even more dangerous as their activities become increasingly concentrated in rogue nations. Should Russia go down the worst path described, the possibilities become limitless.

Enter the Bankers

To this combustible mix of crooks and terrorists, now add a third element: bankers. Criminals, terrorists, and bankers all come together against the murky landscape of money laundering, the act of transforming illegal gains into legitimate-looking money safely ensconced in the global banking system. Knowingly or not, bankers enable financial sleaze and worse, through their willingness and ability to provide increasingly sophisticated financial services for the bad guys. A former U.S. government official says flatly, "Globalization has rapidly democratized money laundering."[58]

The Scope of Money Laundering

"Dirty money makes the criminal underworld go 'round," says one expert. According to the IMF, somewhere between $500 billion and $1.5 trillion, or up to 5 percent of gross world product, is laundered through global financial institutions every year.[59] Hugely aided by new computer networks and technologies, money laundering is now the fastest growing sector of crime.

Conventional wisdom has it that money laundering is primarily the province of secluded tropical islands, small Alpine countries noted for their neutrality and discretion, and pariah states. No doubt, offshore financial centers offering banking secrecy, lax regulations, and a lovely climate attract a great deal of criminal attention. But in fact, vast sums of money are laundered through the best-regulated financial markets of the world—London and New York. U.K. intelligence experts guess that 200 *billion* pounds per year is laundered through the City of London; of that, police locate around 55 *million* pounds per year.[60] One U.K. official explains it this way: "If you are in the business of trying to hide needles, you look for large haystacks."[61] So the largest haystacks of all—London and New York—have hosted some of the most egregious money laundering spectacles of the decade.

Perhaps most embarrassing was the Abacha episode. U.K. authorities have determined that twenty-three London banks, including some of the city's finest and best-respected institutions, handled $1.3 billion on behalf of former Nigerian ruler General Sani Abacha and his associates. The money was allegedly looted from Nigeria by a host of Abacha's friends and family and was eagerly accepted by London's best bankers. Under the U.K. government's new "name and shame" powers, authorities released the names of the banks to the public in 2001.

The Bank of New York/Russian mafia case, though, probably wins the prize for most brazen money laundering scandal of the decade; it also demonstrates quite palpably the power of global banking technology to support networks of crooks and criminals worldwide. In an effort to build its lucrative business in Eastern Europe,

Bank of New York (BONY) aggressively pursued relationships with Russia's biggest banks (which, as mentioned, often have close ties to Russia's seamy underworld). BONY specialized in setting up cash and securities accounts for Russian banks in New York, an operation tailor-made for the needs of money launderers anxious to convert their ill-gotten gains into legitimate accounts in safer corners of the world. The accounts allowed Russian banks to quickly and easily transfer money out of Russia, using a sophisticated software system provided by BONY.

And so they did! Between October 1998 and March 1999 alone, some $4.2 billion (in more than ten thousand transactions) passed through BONY from its Russian clients, making this one of BONY's most profitable customer relationships. In total, $7 billion was transferred through the BONY accounts from Russia in 1995–1999. According to lawsuits that are still pending, senior managers of the Russian banks—which were controlled by organized crime—used the BONY accounts to embezzle bank customers' deposits and illegally transfer assets out of Russia.

Perhaps what is most striking about this scheme is its ease. BONY insiders used three standard-issue computers to perform 160,000 transactions on behalf of their Russian clients, underlining the enabling role of technology in financial wrongdoing. For moving the $7 billion out of Russia, the BONY managers earned millions in fees. The scheme was seamless and smooth, and it was only discovered by a fluke—a $300,000 ransom fee intended for the kidnappers of a Russian businessman went through the BONY pipeline, setting off an FBI investigation.

BONY, of course, is not alone. Citibank has admitted to handling billions of dollars for all manner of allegedly corrupt leaders and their kin, including Omar Bongo, president of Gabon; Jaime Lusinchi, former president of Venezuela; and, most famously, Raul Salinas, brother of Mexico's former president. The Salinas case came to light through an extraordinarily bizarre set of circumstances that eventually included witches, buried bodies, and drug snitches. Citibank's involvement, no doubt, ranks as one of the bank's most distressing episodes.

Salinas opened a private banking account in Citibank New York's offices in the early 1990s, during his brother's presidency. (Private banking, the provision of financial services for high-net-worth individuals, can be an important conduit for money laundering.) As a midlevel government employee, Salinas earned less than $200,000 per year—but as a Citibank client in 1992–1994, he transferred around $100 million out of Mexico to accounts in the U.K. and Switzerland. Citibank officials were told that the money came from the sale of a construction company and that Salinas needed to effect the funds transfers with the utmost discretion so that his brother's political enemies would not discover that a Salinas was moving money out of Mexico.

On the face of it, this is not an implausible tale. But Citibank violated its own "know your customer" guidelines by failing to ask even the most basic of questions (such as the name of the construction company). Citi never requested any information on Salinas's financial background and made no effort to verify the source of his income. Only after Salinas was arrested on murder charges in 1995 did Citibank perform a routine background check; eventually it turned out that his millions were earned by providing protection to drug traffickers, not by selling lumber and nails.

Anti–Money Laundering Reforms

Cynics and skeptics suggest that Citibank, BONY, and others earn enough from money laundering operations to compensate them for the occasional Salinas-style embarrassment. But all other things being equal, most bankers would probably prefer *not* to provide banking services for criminals and terrorists, regardless of the fat fees involved. Moral considerations aside, the downside of criminal investigations, fines, and public opprobrium is fairly significant for institutions whose greatest asset is their name.

So bankers and government officials have worked together over the past decade to fashion anti–money laundering rules that might make it more difficult for crooks and terrorists to enlist the banking services of legitimate financial institutions. The war against money laundering dates from 1989, when the Group of Seven industrial countries set up the Financial Action Task Force (FATF). The FATF has established forty principles covering financial regulations, law enforcement, and international cooperation to bolster anti–money laundering efforts. The FATF also publishes a blacklist of financial centers that fall short of these international standards, which has included Russia, Ukraine, and Israel.

In addition, the discovery of funds linked to former rulers, from Ferdinand Marcos to Sani Abacha, has prompted banks to strengthen "know your customer" rules that require bankers to know the identity of their customer, the source of his/her funds, and the nature of his/her business. (Of course, as the Salinas case illustrates, even the best banks can fall afoul of their own guidelines.) Most countries also require banks to report suspicious transactions to the authorities. In the United States, all cash transactions over $10,000 must be reported, as well as any other transactions that may appear "suspicious" (whatever that means!).

Nonetheless, as the Salinas and BONY cases illustrate, it remains remarkably easy for bad guys to use the international financial system for their own purposes. In late 2001, a French parliamentary committee condemned the City of London and the United Kingdom's offshore financial centers for its "feeble" attempts to combat money laundering. "Great Britain ... offers a totally unacceptable haven for criminal funds," opines the report's author.[62]

Even allowing for French anglophobia, there is too much truth in this statement for comfort. The anti–money laundering system is riddled with holes, as the post-9/11 hunt for terrorist funds has revealed. One of the biggest holes of all is the system of correspondent banking, in which large international banks offer services and provide accounts for other financial institutions. Correspondent banking is a lucrative line of business, especially for the leading U.S. banks, but it has allowed high-risk foreign banks to enjoy virtually unlimited access to U.S. financial markets. Some big established banks (BONY, Chase Manhattan, Citibank, and American Express in New York) even had correspondent relationships with the Afghan central bank during the late 1990s, for example![63] The trouble with this is that these relationships can lure well-respected banks into accepting payments from less reputable correspondents. A U.S. Senate investigation found that weak control over correspondent banking had created a gateway for rogue foreign banks to launder cash from illegal activities, including Internet gambling, investment scams, and, of course, drug trafficking.

Ironically, the proliferation of anti–money laundering regulations may also have a perverse effect on law enforcement. Regulations requiring the reporting of suspicious transactions are cumbersome at best, and at worst they lead to defensive overreporting by banks anxious to absolve themselves of any possible blame. (Most of the transactions reported by banks are, of course, perfectly legitimate payments involving homebuyers or business deals.) The sheer volume and complexity of global financial transactions overwhelm the reporting system; the United States currently handles hundreds of thousands of suspicious-transaction reports and twelve million currency-transaction reports (of cash deals over $10,000) per year. As a result, the authorities receive way too much undifferentiated information, which goes largely unread and unanalyzed.

Lack of communication between banks is another big hole, as the example of Barakat Boston illustrates. Barakat, part of a Somali-owned money transfer group, was asked to close its account at Bank Boston in 1999 because alert officers there noticed that it tended to make lots of payments just below the $10,000 threshold that would trigger a currency transaction report to the feds. But the company was easily able to reopen accounts as Barakat North America at Citizens Bank and Key Bank, since the bankers do not communicate with each other about potential clients. (In the wake of 9/11, Barakat's accounts were frozen when the U.S. government accused it of close ties to the al-Qaeda organization.)

Before 9/11, in fact, the Bush administration itself was openly dubious about the efficacy of anti–money laundering regulations. Prodded by banking lobbyists, the government was weighing the idea of raising the $10,000 reporting requirement threshold. Treasury Secretary Paul O'Neill commented that the current regulation "imposes a significant cost on society" and questioned whether that amount of information was really necessary. He went so far as to say that the $700 million spent annually in efforts to crack down on money launderers may not be money wisely spent.[64] In the post-9/11 world, of course, the U.S. government is leading efforts to use anti–money laundering regulations to track down terrorist funds.

Terrorist Funds

If the worldwide drive against money launderers and drug traffickers has produced spotty results at best, the hunt for terrorist funds may be even less promising. In the horrified aftermath of 9/11, President Bush launched a drive to combat the terrorists by locating and freezing their funds, which presumably repose somewhere in the world financial system. Abruptly reversing its previous position, the administration imposed more record-keeping and reporting requirements on U.S. financial institutions. Among other things, a new law limits U.S. banks' business with "shell banks"—banks without a physical presence, which are frequently used for money laundering. New regulations also extend to many industries that handle large amounts of cash (mutual funds, brokerage houses, check-cashing and foreign currency services, commodity dealers) the same anti–money laundering rules long imposed on banks. Eventually, the regulations will cover still more sectors, such as jewelers, travel agents, and automobile dealerships.

In addition, the Bush administration has leaned on U.S. allies around the world to join in the hunt for terrorist funds. Under the auspices of the FATF, new measures now require financial institutions to report not only suspicious transactions but also any transactions in which the bankers have "reasonable grounds" for believing that the funds will be used for terrorism.

Not surprisingly, Bush aides claimed early victory on this front. In early 2002, the administration announced that the campaign to crack down on funding for terrorist organizations had significantly disrupted the activities of those groups. By midyear, officials estimated that just over $100 million of terrorist funds had been seized worldwide so far.

Even so, all but the staunchest Bush supporters admit that this is only the tip of the iceberg. U.S. and U.K. officials say that they have tracked down "only a fraction" of the funds used to finance terror. By the end of 2002, a more realistic and more depressing assessment of the hunt for terrorist assets had emerged. A draft of a United Nations report stated that al-Qaeda's financial network was "fit and well," and that United States–led efforts to freeze the assets had slowed to a crawl. Furthermore, the report notes that these efforts are largely stymied by:

- Al-Qaeda's increasing reliance on gold and gems, partially facilitated by a penetration into Muslim areas of West Africa;

- informal money-changing networks known as *hawalahs,* which operate largely outside the formal financial system; and

- the ability of al-Qaeda's financial people to resume operations under new names and in new locations, which makes it very difficult to trace and identify them.

As a result, the report concludes, al-Qaeda's financial operatives are still managing anywhere between $30 and $300 million for the organization.[65]

These findings were underlined by a subsequent study from the Council of Foreign Relations, which points out that the intransigence of key countries (think Saudi Arabia) has further stymied the hunt for terrorist assets. The Council states: "For years, individuals and charities based in Saudi Arabia have been the most important source of funds for al-Qaeda, and for years Saudi officials have turned a blind eye to this problem." As a result, the study finds "little disruption to the web of charities, businesses, and other fund-raising activities that provide al-Qaeda with huge sums of money." Other reports have stated similar findings. Canadian intelligence sources, for example, estimate that Saudi-based charities alone funnel $1 to $2 million per month to al-Qaeda.[66]

As these reports suggest, it is difficult to see financial sleuthing as a serious antidote to terrorism. First of all, the most likely impact of the new spate of regulations is an even more massive flood of defensive "suspicious transaction" reports from nervous bankers—overwhelming a system that is already drowning in paper-work (as Bush officials noted, pre-9/11). Indeed, investigators have discovered that Mohamed Atta, one of the 9/11 hijackers, opened a bank account in southern Florida in mid-2000. A wire transfer from the Gulf some months later made SunTrust bankers wary enough to file a report with the government, but, like most of the 125,000 similar reports filed every year, it went unnoticed until the post-9/11 investigation unearthed it.

Second, terrorism is a bargain basement business. Drug trafficking, in the end, is all about money—and it produces massive sums of money that cannot help being noticeable, even in the huge global financial system. By contrast, security experts figure that it cost no more than $500,000 to organize and implement the horrors of 9/11. With $1.2 trillion sloshing through global foreign exchange markets *every day*, the odds of finding such relatively minute amounts seem long indeed.

And third, terrorist funding is really the reverse of money laundering—and those differences really matter. Money laundering is the process of placing illegally sourced funds in the banking system and then whipping them through enough accounts (and countries) that in the end the money looks clean and its origins are entirely obscured. By painstakingly tracing the money back to its original depositor, investigators can *sometimes* (note the emphasis!) locate the drug barons themselves. In terrorist financing, though, the opposite is true. This involves depositing money that may even have been earned legally into the banking system, to be withdrawn by terrorists for the purpose of illegal acts. Changing the emphasis from the deposit to the withdrawal is an important change indeed. The only way for banks to monitor those who with-draw funds from perfectly legal accounts is to practice some form of profiling, an uneasy and possibly illegal practice in most Western countries.

Last but not least, any serious effort to block terrorist funds will require inter-national cooperation of an unprecedented nature. Horrified by the acts of 9/11, some previously reluctant U.S. allies were willing to join hands, but this is fading fast. As of April 2002, the IMF reported that only forty of its 180 member coun-tries had responded to its request to report steps that they are taking to deny sus-pected terrorists access to funds. Without the total cooperation of countries like Bahrain and Saudi Arabia—which, frankly, appears unlikely—it is simply not pos-sible for U.S. authorities to trace and seize funds deposited halfway around the world. The situation is exacerbated by the terrorists' use of Islamic charities and other organizations to help fund and move funds, as well as the widespread use of hawala money-transfer networks.[67] A thorough investigation by *The Financial Times* demonstrates how easy it has been for al-Qaeda to move money through the global banking system, making extensive use of correspondent bank accounts and the hawala system.

No doubt, terrorists and criminals have coopted the international financial sys-tem. In one particularly egregious example, European Union authorities are investi-gating persistent rumors that terrorists engaged in insider trading on European stock markets in advance of 9/11, apparently guessing that insurance and airline stocks, for example, might take a tumble. Even if these charges prove to be unfounded, the pos-sibility still illustrates the extent to which bad guys take full advantage of the financial world. All in all, the investigation into al-Qaeda's finances has revealed how easy it is for terrorists to exploit the international financial system. They can look for the weak link—one of the nineteen financial centers cited by the FATF, for example, or correspondent banking accounts—and gain access to the most sophisticated and globalized capital markets of the world. One expert concludes: "Terrorism has highlighted the shortcomings of the global financial system in a brutal way. The use of it to fund global terrorism is, of course, an aspect of globalization that was not emphasized by those who sang its praises a short while ago."[68]

▶ THE GREAT ENABLERS

Thus developments that should pave the way for better governance practices at both the corporate and country levels—technology, globalization, and the spread of free markets—seem to, at times, facilitate the spread of financial wrongdoing instead. Bribery, corruption, financial crime, and unethical business practices have all flourished in the past decade, side by side with unprecedented advances in global free markets and technology. As we noted in the introduction, this is not a coincidence. Good governance practices rely on a foundation of solid institutions such as government regulators, arms-length bankers, and well-informed market participants. The absence, or weakness, of these facilitators undermines good governance at all levels.

Globalization, free markets, and advancing technology should be the great enablers of transparency, disclosure, and therefore good governance in financial markets. And they are. But a byproduct of high-tech global markets, clearly, is unprecedented opportunity for financial wrongdoing—originating both with insiders, such as a small group of Wall Street executives, and with outsiders, such as criminals and terrorists. One expert predicts: "Transnational organized crime will proliferate in the next century because the crime groups are among the major beneficiaries of globalization. Benefiting from increased travel, trade, telecommunications networks and computer links, they are well positioned for growth."[69] Technology promises to make money launderers' and drug traffickers' lives much easier; in a few years, drug dealers could arrange to have digital dollars zapped into their Palm Pilots—and then tap a few keys to have the funds transferred to Liechtenstein within seconds. Globalization, it appears, is the great enabler of financial wrongdoing—at least in the short term.

At the same time, financial wrongdoing poses a huge threat to continued progress toward free global markets. Growing evidence of—and outrage toward—financial misdeeds emboldens antiglobalization activists, giving them new fuel for their arguments. Even more fundamental, wrongdoing corrupts markets, thus damaging prospects for growth, investment, and eventual prosperity. So it is a two-way street: free markets, globalization, and technology enable crooks, terrorists, and unethical operators; the wrongdoers, in turn, threaten progress toward free and efficient global markets, growth, and prosperity for all.

Yet, before we totally despair of globalization, it must be understood that the gap in the institutional development needed to maintain a system of checks and balances for the vast majority of prudent businesses is beginning to close. It will take time, but the weight of the world's legitimate economic life still far outweighs the illegitimate and undesirable economic activity. In this, there is great hope.

▶ NOTES

1. For one of the better accounts of BCCI, see Peter Truell and Larry Gurwin, *False Profits: The Inside Story of BCCI, the World's Most Corrupt Financial Empire* (Boston and New York: Houghton Mifflin, 1992).
2. "Governance for sustainable human development: A UNDP policy document," available at magnet.undp.org/policy/chapter1.htm.
3. The ICGN Web site at www.icgn.org contains a wealth of information on corporate governance and the OECD Principles.
4. Philip M. Nichols, "Dealing with an eruption of corruption," *The Financial Times*, May 30, 2000.
5. John Reed and Erik Portanger, "Bribery, Corruption Are Rampant in Eastern Europe, Survey Finds," *Wall Street Journal*, November 9, 1999.
6. There is a wide body of literature on this topic. See, for example, "Bribonomics," in *The Economist*, March 19, 1994, and Daniel Kaufmann, "Corruption: The Facts," *Foreign Policy*, No. 107.
7. Samuel Huntington, *Political Order in Changing Societies* (New Haven, Conn.: Yale University Press, 1968).
8. Kaufmann, Daniel, "Corruption: the Facts," *Foreign Policy*, No. 107, p. 114.
9. Andrei Shleifer and Robert W. Vishny, "Corruption," *The Quarterly Journal of Economics*, August 1993. Also see Robert Klitgaard, *Controlling Corruption* (Berkeley, Calif.: University of California Press, 1988).
10. Daniel Kaufmann, op. cit.
11. Martin Wolf, "Corruption in the Spotlight," *The Financial Times*, September 16, 1997.
12. There is a wealth of material available on this, including these articles (all available on Nouriel Roubini's Web site): Cheryl W. Gray and Daniel Kaufmann, "Corruption and Development," Paul Mauro, "Why Worry About Corruption?" (*IMF Economic Issues*, No. 6), and Vito Tanzi and Hamid Davoodi, "Road to Nowhere: How Corruption in Public Investment Hurts Growth" (*IMF Economic Issues*, No. 12). Also see Paulo Mauro, "Corruption and Growth," *The Quarterly Journal of Economics* 110, No. 3, August 1995.
13. Rachel L. Swarns, "Angola Urged to Trace Its Oil Dollars," *The New York Times*, May 14, 2002.
14. Alexander Hanrath, "Mexico gets tough as crime hits economy," *The Financial Times*, October 11, 2002.
15. Philip M. Nichols, "Dealing with an eruption of corruption," *The Financial Times*, May 30, 2000.
16. Alison Maitland, "Costs of trouble ahead," *The Financial Times*, March 11, 1999.
17. Edward Luce, "Hands-on politics," *The Financial Times*, October 12–13, 2002.
18. Jimmy Burns, "Laws fail to halt international business bribery," *The Financial Times*, October 15, 2002.
19. Information available at the Transparency International Web site, www.ticpli.com.
20. Richard W. Stevenson, "Officials Assess Impact of a Fed-Brokered Deal," *The New York Times*, September 23, 1998.
21. Gretchen Morgenson, "Don't Count on Corporate Bonds for Safety," *The New York Times*, March 2, 2002.
22. Gretchen Morgenson, "Telecom's Pied Piper: Whose Side Was He On?" *The New York Times*, November 18, 2001.
23. "Disinformation on Wall Street," Editorial, *The New York Times*, April 11, 2002.
24. Charles Pretzlik and Gary Silverman, "Wall Street under fire: daily complaints grow of unfair treatment and unethical deals," *The Financial Times*, October 4, 2002.
25. Howard G. Chua-Evan, "Going for Broke," *Time*, March 13, 1995.
26. Report of the Board of Banking Supervision, "Inquiry into the Circumstances of the Collapse of Barings 18 July 1995," Bank of England, 1998.

27. Vincent Boland and Charles Pretzlik, "A suburban rogue trader," *The Financial Times*, February 9, 2002.
28. "Editorial Comment: Holding Enron to Account," *The Financial Times*, February 3, 2002.
29. Paul Krugman, "A system corrupted," *The New York Times*, January 18, 2002.
30. Canute James, "Deportees blamed for crime surge in the Caribbean," *The Financial Times*, January 6, 2000.
31. Suchata Dalal, *The Indian Express*, August 12, 2001.
32. Canute James, op. cit.
33. Caroline Atkinson, "America's crony capitalism," *The Financial Times*, February 6, 2002.
34. Jonathan Alter, "Which boot will drop next?" *Newsweek*, February 4, 2002.
35. Joshua Chaffin and Stephen Fidler, "Enron's alchemy turns to lead for bankers," *The Financial Times*, March 1, 2002.
36. Paul Krugman, "Crony Capitalism, USA" *The New York Times*, January 15, 2002.
37. Jonathan Alter, op. cit.
38. Caroline Atkinson, op. cit.
39. Paul Krugman, "A system corrupted,"
40. Jonathan M. Winer, "How to clean up dirty money," *The Financial Times*, March 23–24, 2002.
41. "Banking Diligence," Editorial, *The Financial Times*, July 4, 2002.
42. Joseph Kahn and Judith Miller, "Getting Tough on Gangsters, High Tech and Global," *The New York Times*, December 15, 2000.
43. John Lloyd, "Freedom to corrupt," *The Financial Times*, December 19–20, 1998.
44. David Ibison, "Gangsters steal march on legitimate business," *The Financial Times*, January 26, 2002.
45. Matt Richtel, "Credit Card Theft Is Thriving Online as Global Market," *The New York Times*, May 13, 2002.
46. Canute James, op. cit.
47. Richard Wolffe and John Murray Brown, "IRA linked to global terror base in Colombia," *The Financial Times*, April 24, 2002.
48. "Russian Organized Crime: Crime Without Punishment," *The Economist*, August 28, 1999.
49. John Thornkill and Charles Clover, "The robbery of nations," *The Financial Times*, August 21–22, 1999.
50. Ibid.
51. "Russian Organized Crime: Crime Without Punishment".
52. Joseph Kahn, "World Bank Blames Diamonds and Drugs for Many Wars," *The New York Times*, June 16, 2000.
53. Douglas Farah, "Qaeda linked to diamond trade," *Washington Post*, November 2, 2001.
54. www.theantidrug.com.
55. Jimmy Burns and Carola Hoyos, "U.S. and UN ignoring 'menace' of drugs cultivation," *The Financial Times*, February 18, 2002.
56. Mark Hubbard, "Bankrolling bin Laden," *The Financial Times*, November 29, 2001.
57. Tim Golden, "A War on Terror Meets a War on Drugs," *The New York Times*, October 25, 2001.
58. Jonathan M. Winer, "How to clean up dirty money," *The Financial Times*, March 23-24, 2002.
59. "Russian Organized Crime: Crime Without Punishment."
60. John Lloyd, op. cit.
61. John Willman, "Cleaning up," *The Financial Times*, September 21, 2001.
62. Victor Mallet and John Willman, "City 'feeble' in battle against dirty money," *The Financial Times*, October 10, 2001.
63. Richard Wolffe and Jimmy Burns, "Huge obstacles in global search for terrorist paper trail," *The Financial Times*, September 24, 2001.
64. "Bush reviews money laundering rules," Associated Press, June 7, 2001 (available at www.russianlaw.org/ap).
65. Edmund L. Andrews, "The White House Denies Report Qaeda Funds Are Flowing," *The New York Times*, August 30, 2002.
66. Edward Alden, "The money trail: how a crackdown on suspect charities is failing to stem the flow of funds to al-Qaeda," *The Financial Times*, October 18, 2002.

67. Hawala is a trust-based, time-tested method of money transfer that is widely used in Asia, Africa, and the Middle East. It works worldwide through networks of money-changers, who generate no records of their transactions. See "Elusive terror money slips through government traps," by Jane Hughes, *USA Today*, November 28, 2001.
68. Leif Pagrorsky and Joseph Stiglitz, "Blocking the terrorists' funds," *The Financial Times*, December 7, 2001.
69. Louise Shelley, Testimony before the House Committee on International Relations, October 1, 1997.

CHAPTER 9

JAPAN AND CHINA: POTENTIAL ASIAN EARTHQUAKES

"Asia's Tiger Economies Roar" … "Institutions Plan to Boost Asia Equities Holdings, Survey Shows" … "Vietnam—The Next Tiger Economy" … "Singapore's Growth Jumps" … "Softbank Soars" … "Korea's Industrial Might Flexes Its Muscles in International Markets" … "South Korea—Is This Recovery for Real?" … "Beijing Acts to Support Waning Export Growth" … "IMF Admits Errors in Asia but Defends Basic Policies" … "Bank Reforms in Japan—Hampered" … "China and Japan—Wary Dragons"

Asia's two largest economies were not untouched by changes in international capital markets during the 1991–2001 period. New financial innovations, globalization and the volatility in capital markets, had multiple impacts on Japan, Asia's long-standing economic trendsetter, and China, newly emergent from several decades of chaotic Maoist rule. Japan entered the 1990s marked by a bursting of its own "bubble economy" and spent the rest of the decade seeking to regain some degree of growth. Sadly, the country's leading institutions—the long-dominant Liberal Democratic Party (LDP), the bureaucracy, and much of the business sector—had great difficulty in adjusting to a new global economic landscape. Instead, Japan entered the twenty-first century without economic recovery, with record bankruptcies, and with serious questions about its future. The once high-flying Nikkei Stock Exchange staggered through the 1990s, entering the new century a pale reflection of its former wealth.

While Japan struggled, China motored ahead. The 1990s were a period of ongoing economic reforms, strong growth, and a massing of foreign exchange reserves in excess of $100 billion. China underwent a transformation from being an inward-looking and agriculturally top-heavy economy into one of the world's major manufacturing nations, producing a vast range of manufactured goods, geared for export to the world's major markets. In many regards, China embraced globalization and liberalization of its economy, but at its own pace. Membership

220

into the World Trade Organization (WTO) in 2001 was a crowning moment of achievement in China's push into the global economy. Yet, the Asian country had considerable unfinished business in terms of large problematic state economic organizations (SEOs), a bad loan–laden banking sector, and economic inequalities between the coastal and inner regions of the country. While China was a siren song for many global investors throughout the 1990s and into the next decade, there were others who were deeply concerned that the Asian country was becoming an investment bubble—largely with foreigner's money. Japan had experienced a bubble, which had burst; would China follow the same path?

What is compelling in the case of Asia's two economic giants is that both countries found themselves in a position where they were forced to deal with a plethora of external pressures, some hostile, while grappling with the need to make difficult structural changes, which would clearly have domestic societal ramifications. Ironically, it was "communist" China that was to adopt a more entrepreneurial-oriented economy (sometimes with very free-wheeling results). Japan, Asia's long-standing capitalist giant and former model of development for much of the region, however, was straddled by the contrary pulls of a highly competitive export sector and a highly protected and inefficient domestic sector. Despite the different paths to development over the second half of the twentieth century, in particular during the 1990s, there are similarities between the two Asian countries. In particular, Japan and China had to deal with the gap between robust, usually export-oriented parts of their economies, and sheltered domestic/state-owned parts of their economies. That gap had a political extension: local institutions have been forced to deal with the impact of economic changes and the new demands leveled on them by their populations. It can be argued that the globalization of capital markets was a major force in pushing that gap wider. One result was Japan's decline and China's rise during the 1990s. The question is how each country will respond in dealing with the gaps between their populations' aspirations and what institutions can accommodate.

▶ CHINA AND JAPAN IN ASIA'S GREAT CAPITALIST LEAP FORWARD

Following the Second World War, most of Asia was an economic backwater. The regional economic dynamo, Japan, had lost the war and was occupied by the United States. Its once-powerful industrial infrastructure had been bombed into useless rubble. Korea was divided between a Communist North and a Western-leaning South. Although some of Japan's colonial industrial infrastructure survived in Korea, the looming threat of war eclipsed hope of sustainable economic growth. China was also finishing one conflict—the Second World War—and gearing up for a bloody civil war between the Nationalists and Communists. In Southeast Asia, Europe's colonial embrace was loosening and new nationalistic forces were competing for control. In Malaysia and Singapore, this would result in relatively peaceful transfers of power (after the defeat of a Communist insurgency), while in Indonesia and Vietnam, the Dutch and French, respectively, proved reluctant to depart. India was also restive, and the days of the British Raja were clearly numbered. A central theme running through almost every country in the region, with the exception of Japan, was a political awakening in which nationalism was rising, sometimes leading to conflict with and other times to be commandeered by communist forces, as in China, North Korea, Vietnam, Laos, and Cambodia. Political concerns overrode economic concerns.

While much of Asia was rocked by political problems during the 1950s through the 1970s—the Korean War, the Vietnam War, the Cultural Revolution and political succession in China, and the rise and fall of Sukarno in Indonesia—Japan began the gradual process of economic reconstruction. No longer burdened by heavy military expenditures and protected by the U.S. nuclear umbrella and troops, the Japanese were able to turn their attention to rebuilding the economy. As historian R. L. Sims noted, the emphasis placed on the economy "provided a nationally and internationally acceptable outlet for Japanese nationalism."[1] The Korean War (1950–1953) also helped the Japanese economy, as the Asian nation functioned as a backup base for U.S. and United Nations forces.

During the 1950s and 1960s, a combination of factors helped elevate the Japanese economy: close coordination between the government, the ruling LDP, and the business sector; a talented and skilled population with a strong work ethic; initial U.S. assistance in economic reconstruction, which led to all-new industrial plants; a strategy based on export growth; and a willingness on the part of the population to make personal sacrifices for the national good. The government's role was to provide stability and guide the public and private sectors into a coordinated effort, much as a country would be mobilized for war. The Ministry of International Trade and Industry (MITI) acted as the coordinating agency for government, industry, commerce, and banking. Bank lending was guided to key industries. This system was soon to be called "Japan, Inc.," and was known for its picking winners and losers in catching up with the West.

From being a defeated imperial power, Japan steadily rose to become Asia's leading economic heavyweight. Real GDP growth rates of close to 10 percent were achieved in the 1956 to 1973 period. By 1970, Japan had achieved a production level twice that of China, three times that of Africa, and twice that of Latin America. In 1972, gross national product stood at an impressive $290 billion—a substantial up-tick from $1.5 billion in 1945.

By the late 1970s, the "Made in Japan" label was no longer looked down upon. Japan was now a major economic player in international markets. It was also increasingly looked upon as a model for other Asian countries, many struggling to move beyond political issues and focus on economic development. For various reasons, Singapore, Taiwan, South Korea, and Hong Kong emerged as the first group of Asian "dragons" or "tigers" to follow Japan into a higher level of economic development. Although smaller than Japan, the four economies were similar in that they lacked natural resources but had comparatively well-educated populations capable and willing to learn new skills. Taiwan and Korea had both been Japanese colonies, a factor that perhaps helped them adopt the system of close government-business cooperation. In addition, Korea and Taiwan benefited from a close political and military relationship with the United States. In the cases of Singapore and Hong Kong, both were virtual city-states, surrounded by potential enemies, which augmented a sense of urgency to make economic success a maximum objective relative to elevating their populations' per capita income and making their commercial enterprises more competitive. As Korea, Taiwan, Singapore, and Hong Kong developed, they also became more attractive to foreign investors. This came in two forms: direct investment by large multinational corporations and portfolio investment via institutional investors and small investors [through mutual funds and ADRs (American Depository Receipt)]. The multinational corporations increasingly found that setting up shop in this handful of Asian countries made strategic sense. These countries offered cheap, yet relatively well-educated and motivated work forces, geographic proximity to potential growth markets (such as China), adequate infrastructure, and usually a high degree of political stability. Hong Kong and Singapore also offered two of the best harbors in the world.

A second wave of tiger economies emerged in the 1980s, encompassing Malaysia, Thailand, and Indonesia. Each country had adopted export-oriented economic policies, had benefited from the U.S. economic boom, and had a strong government that was able to focus largely on policy matters. Real GDP rates were to pick up considerably (Table 9.1). A third wave of tiger development came with China, which began the economic reform process in 1978 but slowly moved to a faster pace, especially in the early 1990s. A fourth wave appeared to be forming in the mid-1990s, consisting of the Philippines, India, Vietnam, Pakistan, and Burma.[2]

Of the last two waves, China was by far the most significant newcomer, in light of its large, billion-plus population and geostrategic position. China went from being an inward-looking and heavily agriculturally oriented economy in the 1970s to the

TABLE 9.1 Asian Real Gross Domestic Product (GDP) Growth (%)

Country	1980–1990	1990–1998
China	10.2	11.1
Hong Kong	6.9	4.4
India	5.8	6.1
Indonesia	6.1	5.8
Korea	9.4	6.2
Malaysia	5.3	7.7
Myanmar (Burma)	0.6	6.3
Philippines	1.0	3.3
Singapore	6.6	8.0
Thailand	7.6	7.4
Vietnam	4.6	8.6

Source: World Bank, *World Development Report 1999/2000: Entering the 21st Century* (New York: Oxford University Press, 2000), pp. 250–251.

manufacturing workshop of the world by the early 1990s, with its share of world trade quadrupling from the pre-reform period. As Nicholas D. Kristof and Sheryl WuDunn stated in 1994: "If China can hold its course, it will produce the greatest economic miracle in recorded history. Never before has such a large proportion of humanity risen from poverty so rapidly. Studies that measure the size of an economy in terms of purchasing power indicate that China's economy is already the third largest in the world, after those of the United States and Japan. At present rates, the Chinese economy will surpass America's within a few decades to become the biggest in the world."[3]

As globalization made inroads into Asia and capital markets were relaxed, foreign investment rushed in. While China was one of the major beneficiaries, the rest of the region was very much on the investment map. Indeed, the amount of capital flowing into non-Japan Asia was considerably larger than that flowing into Latin America, the Middle East, and Africa (Table 9.2).

While countries such as Malaysia, Thailand, and Indonesia attracted foreign investment, it was China that increasingly stole the show as the 1990s progressed (Table 9.3). Three key reasons dominated foreign investment decisions about China: the sheer seize of the potential China market dwarfed the rest of Asia (and Latin America and other emerging markets); the Chinese government was actively seeking to attract foreign investors with a wide range of incentives; and China was moving to further open its economy as part of joining the WTO. Another factor was China's relative political stability. Gone were the days of the chaotic Cultural Revolution in the 1960s and the democratic fervor of the late 1980s. China was clearly focused on its economic development.

The combination of foreign investment and implementing market economics resulted in a substantial transformation of China. China's export sector enjoyed a substantial takeoff. Between 1978 and 1996, the Asian country's total exports expanded from $9.5 billion to $151 billion, a fifteen-fold increase. At the same time, Chinese disposable incomes rose and Chinese consumers gradually began to develop more sophisticated tastes, including for imported goods. For most major multinational companies, the changes occurring in China could not be ignored. Despite concerns over the lack of transparency, official corruption, the creaky state of the banking system, and the problematic nature of the state-owned companies, the threat of being left out of China was a key force in the country's investment boom during the 1990s and its continuation into the 2000s.

TABLE 9.2 Emerging Markets: Net Private Capital Flows ($U.S., Billions)

Region	1983–1988	1989–1995	1996	1997
Africa	3.5	7.2	12.3	16.8
Asia	11.9	43.6	114.0	13.4
Western Hemisphere	–2.0	33.0	62.8	68.1

Sources: IMF, *World Economic Outlook*, May 1997, and *World Economic Outlook*, May 2001.

TABLE 9.3 Foreign Direct Investment in China and Selected Economies (in $U.S., Billions)

Country	1991	1992	1993	1994	1995	1996	1997
China	4.4	11.2	27.5	33.8	35.8	40.2	44.2
Mexico	4.7	4.4	4.4	11.0	9.5	9.2	12.5
Brazil	1.1	2.0	1.3	3.1	4.9	11.2	19.7
Korea	1.2	0.7	0.6	0.9	1.8	2.3	2.8
Thailand	2.0	2.1	1.8	1.4	2.1	2.3	3.0
Malaysia	4.0	5.2	5.0	4.3	4.2	5.1	5.1
Philippines	0.5	0.3	1.2	1.6	1.5	1.5	1.3
Indonesia	1.5	1.8	2.0	2.1	4.4	6.2	4.7
Singapore	4.9	2.2	4.7	8.4	7.4	7.4	8.6

Sources: International Monetary Fund, *International Financial Statistics,* and UNCTAD, *World Investment Report, 1998.*

▶ THE END OF ASIA'S GREAT CAPITALIST LEAP FORWARD AND JAPAN'S SICKLY ECONOMY

In 1997–1998 Asia's great capitalist leap forward came to an abrupt and bruising end. The combination of a massive inflow of foreign investment, a fulsome (though varying) embrace in globalization, liberalization of capital markets, weak local regulatory institutions, and real estate bubbles, compounded by overvalued currencies, eventually lead to a region-wide implosion, ignited by the Thai government's ill-fated decision to devalue their currency after months of depleting foreign exchange reserves in an effort to defend the baht in international foreign currency markets. The great rush of capital had flowed in, and now it flowed out with a vengeance. Thailand, Indonesia, and Korea were ultimately forced to seek aid from the IMF, while the better-managed economies of Malaysia, Hong Kong, Singapore, and Taiwan came under severe pressure. China, however, was able to weather the storm. Moreover, it did not devalue its currency, something that it could have done to improve its competitive export advantage. While China emerged as a concerned Asian power and partner, Japan was a point of deep concern for policymakers throughout the rest of Asia and in Washington.

Although Japan's economy was in the doldrums throughout the 1990s, it was not until the Asian crisis rocked the global financial system that the dire nature of Tokyo's financial problems came sharply into focus. While the Asian Tigers had moved along at rapid paces of growth, at least until 1997, Japan spent the 1990s in an awkward twilight zone of slow to no growth. Deflation, the decrease in the general level of prices, became the primary concern for Tokyo. With very weak growth, the once inflationary nature of the Japanese economy gave way to an era of declining prices and asset valuations. This was to become a problem for the financial sector and certainly was watched with concern in the rest of Asia. The roots of Japan's problematic economy dated back to the 1970s and 1980s, especially during the bubble economy.

Japan's bubble economy was caused by a number of factors. At the 1985 Plaza Accords between the G-7 leading industrial economies, it was agreed to let the U.S. dollar decline and let the yen appreciate, in order to help address U.S. external economic imbalances. The result was that the yen soared in value, reducing the long-standing trade surplus, hence curtailing that route to growth. The Japanese economy began to cool. This left the government at a policy crossroads. The traditional path to economic growth—export expansion—was now hindered by a strong currency. The situation was further complicated by earlier decisions taken in 1973 and 1979 during the oil crises, to intensify the protection of domestic basic industries. Consequently, the Japanese government moved in the easiest and least confrontational direction, making a policy shift from promoting winners to protecting losers. The result was the development of an inefficient dual economy. As Japan watcher Richard Katz noted: "... Japan turned into a deformed dual economy—a dysfunctional hybrid of superstrong exporting industries and superweak domestic sectors," which meant "over the course of the 1970s and 1980s, the country's economic arteries became increasingly clogged and rigid."[4]

Currency appreciation in the mid-1980s, therefore, only masked the problems that faced Japan and narrowed policy options. For the LDP, with its many connections to the protected domestic sectors of the economy, painful though necessary structural adjustment and liberalization were not attractive options. Instead, Japan responded to currency appreciation by artificially pumping up real estate, stock, and capital investment with monetary steroids.[5] Referred to as "zaitach" or financial engineering, Japanese corporations turned to speculation as an integral part of corporate earnings statements. At the same time, Japanese investors went on a buying spree of international assets. The appreciation of the yen, partially behind Japan's surge to global economic colossus, made the land upon which the Imperial Palace sat allegedly worth the entire state of California. In 1989, Japan looked set to rule the world. By 1997, Japan was a major concern for international policy-makers.

One of the major reasons for Japan's economic mess was the inability of its institutions to deal with change. In light of the country's amazing turnaround starting in the 1860s, which transformed Japan from an inward-looking and agricultural-based economy into Asia's leading industrial and military power by the 1910s, and its ability to reconstruct its economy in the aftermath of World War II, it is difficult to understand why its leading institutions proved so inept in pulling Japan out of the problematic tract it found itself in following the bursting of the bubble economy in 1989–1990. Part of the answer is found in the LDP.

The LDP's long period of rule from the 1950s to the present, with only a few brief interruptions, has stemmed from its ability to provide stability founded upon policy coordination between public and private sectors. This has appealed to many Japanese, especially those in parts of the economy that sought and received protection from foreign competition: retail companies, construction firms, and agriculture. Construction, in particular, was the heart of the traditional political economy. As Gaven McCormack explained of the central role of construction: "... during the long period of one-party rule in postwar Japan, a collusive system of exploiting the public by massive corruption evolved, sometimes called the *dokken kokka* or construction state, in which construction is incidental to the reproduction of power and the distribution of profit. It became a massive welfare system, with beneficiaries numbered in the millions, an incubus on the state and society comparable to the mafia in other countries."[6] In all fairness, the system initially worked well, providing strong economic growth from which everyone benefited. It was difficult to argue that the 9.3 percent average annual growth rate in the 1956–1973 period and the 4.1 percent average growth rate in the 1975–1991 period were bad. It should also be clarified that not all of Japan's corporate world was caught up in a web of corruption and that many Japanese companies played by the rules.

However, economic development was lopsided in a way that became painfully apparent in the 1990s. Those economic sectors that were forced to compete in the rough-and-tumble of international markets weathered the 1990s comparatively better than the protected areas, which were allowed to plod along, never developing competitive instincts. As Japan became a world leader in automobiles and electronics and maintained those positions during the 1990s, the retail sector remained inefficient, agriculture ran at a high cost and was decidedly not consumer-friendly, and the construction sector remained bloated and highly dependent on the public sector for ongoing largesse. In addition, there was a marked aversion to allowing companies to go into bankruptcy. In this system the banks were an important factor, providing loans and keeping many weaker companies afloat by loose accounting standards. Banks were willing to keep the "zombie" companies from bankruptcy by providing even more loans or not categorizing the companies as troubled. What this meant was that the Japanese banking system, already hurt by the massive depreciation of securities valuations and real estate with the bursting of the bubble economy, spent the 1990s dealing with an increasingly uglier loan portfolio.

Considering Japan's position as the second largest global economy and its major role in Asia, the state of Japan's banks emerged as a major worry by the late 1990s. Indeed, Declan Hayes, a Professor of International Business at Tokyo's Sophia University, stated: "Because the Japanese banking system is currently the biggest threat there is to world stability, the rest of the world is concerned."[7] Yet cleaning up the banking system would also mean forcing many zombie companies into admitting that they were indeed bankrupt, incapable of living without exceedingly lenient bank terms. Although corporate bankruptcies did rise in the late 1990s and into 2000–2001, many more were postponed, in large part because of political considerations.

The LDP's ability to raise considerable cash from its key supporters was another element in the coordination and stability system. As political historian Richard L. Sims noted, the "LDP, either as a party or through its various factions and Diet members, acquired enormous funds—far beyond the amounts which rival parties could raise—notably from big business, the construction industry, and numerous small businesses which owed gratitude to LDP politicians or sought their aid."[8] In the 1990s, members of the LDP were happy to help their constituents in postponing painful reforms, some of which would have led to more short-term pain in terms of bankruptcies and fewer donations.

The postponing of reform was not accepted by all sectors of the Japanese population. The country's largely urban population came to resent the constant bailing out of rural agricultural concerns and the higher prices passed on to the consumer. Moreover, in the late 1990s and early 2000s, the government willingly used taxpayers' money to bail out the banks. Following the inept Mori administration, Koizumi, riding a wave of considerable public support, became prime minister in April 2001, promising to change Japan. Despite Koizumi's efforts to implement reforms of the postal system, the banks, and the public sector, Japan continues to have massive problems. These include too much public sector debt (it stood at 133 percent of GDP at the end of 2001, equal to $5.6 trillion and rising); high unemployment (around 5 percent); strong deflationary pressures; a weak banking system, burdened with a heavy load of nonperforming loans (estimated at yen 52.4 trillion or 10 percent of GDP in March 2002); an ineffective and inequitable taxation system; ongoing issues with corporate transparency and disclosure (despite new legislation and some improvements); a strong yen that threatens to undermine export competitiveness (and the major support for economic recovery); and an aging population, which will put large long-term spending pressure on the country's finance.[9]

▶ JAPAN: HEADING INTO EMERGING MARKET STATUS?

The acute nature of Japan's economic crisis raised the issue in the media that the Asian country was becoming like Argentina—top heavy with debt and unable to make the right policy decisions because of political paralysis. Complicating matters was a higher degree of political turnover at the top, with one commentator stating: "... prime ministers came and went from the national stage faster than actors at a music hall variety show."[10] In a deeper sense, the problem for Japan was that its system of coordination and stability, which long served it well, proved unable to effectively deal with changes in the global economy: in part, the greater liberalization of capital flows as well as the rise of new economic competitors such as Korea and China. This issue came into sharper focus when the two major international rating agencies, Moody's and Standard & Poor's, downgraded Japan from its pristine AAA status to much lower levels.

In May 2002, Moody's downgraded Japan's domestic yen rating from Aa3 to A2, which put the ratings on the same level as the African country of Botswana. Moody's stated that the ratings action reflected "the conclusion that the Japanese government's current and anticipated policies will be insufficient to prevent continued deterioration in Japan's domestic debt position." Moody's said that Japan's general government indebtedness, however measured, will approach levels unprecedented in the postwar era in the developed world and that, as such, Japan will be entering "uncharted territory."[11] (See Table 9.4.)

Later in 2002, Standard & Poor's put Japan's AA-domestic rating on watch for a possible downgrade. The rating agency was critical of the limited scope of deregulation of the postal system (touted as a pillar of the reform agenda), the announcement

TABLE 9.4 General Government Gross Financial Liabilities
(as a Percent of GDP) for G-7 Countries

G-7 Country	1998	1999	2000	2001	2002F	2003F
Japan	103.0	115.8	123.5	132.8	143.3	152.0
United States	68.3	65.3	59.4	59.5	58.9	57.6
Germany	63.2	60.9	60.8	60.3	61.3	60.9
France	65.0	64.6	64.1	64.8	65.6	65.7
Italy	117.5	115.9	111.4	108.7	106.3	103.1
United Kingdom	61.4	56.4	54.0	52.5	51.8	51.6
Canada	115.2	113.2	103.0	101.6	99.7	96.2

Source: Organization for Economic Cooperation & Development, *Economic Outlook June 2002* (Paris: OECD, 2002), p. 238.

Note: "F" stands for forecast.

of a mere 3 percent cut in public works spending in the fiscal 2003 budget (especially in view of the fact that one of Koizumi's promises was fiscal consolidation); and the government's shift to maintaining full deposit insurance on certain bank accounts past the April 2003 termination deadline set under the government's bank reform measures (regarded as backsliding on making the bank's adhere to tougher guidelines). As Standard & Poor's noted: "Whatever the case, in our view any further dilution of the reform agenda will undermine the prospects for an economic recovery, further reduce the government's future fiscal flexibility, and lead to an increase in Japan's already massive public sector debt."[12]

Yet for all the public criticism of the slow approach taken in dealing with Japan's economic problems and deep-seated worries about deflation eroding the retirement savings of the country's aging population, conservative elements in the LDP and other parties have consistently sought to block reforms. Consequently, the ongoing problem of the zombie companies followed Japan into the 2000s. Despite opposition to bailing out companies that were not central to national security, the government was still willing to pump a little life into dying companies. This sits in sharp contrast to the United States, which allowed the failure of large companies such as Enron, WorldCom, and Kmart. In contrast, Japan was willing to keep alive Snow Brands, a meat and dairy distributor involved in food poisoning cases and fraud, and Daie Inc., a grocery store chain.[13] One could question the importance of such companies to the national security of Japan. Indeed, in the case of Daie, the company was allowed a three-year restructuring program and provided massive debt forgiveness by its main lenders as part of a bailout scheme formulated with the strong support from the Ministry of Economy, Trade and Industry, as well as financial assistance from the Development Bank of Japan.[14] It would appear that moral hazard was not an issue.

The danger represented by Japan is that having survived the 1990s without dealing with the many challenges facing the economy and its governing institutions, the first decade of the twenty-first century takes the world's second largest economy into uncharted territory of massive public sector debt, a lopsided economy increasingly dragged down by the unproductive and protected domestic side, and a seemingly gridlocked political system. Although Japan's debt burden is largely domestic and held by local investors, the interrelated nature of the global financial system means that Tokyo's problems are the rest of the world's, especially if the banking system were to fail. The wobbly nature of Japan's public finances and banks creates uncertainty, which is something that never helps markets. Moreover, Japan's problems hurt other countries in terms of capital flows. Indeed, global direct investment by Japan declined 26.3 percent in 2001, plunging 40.6 percent in the United States.[15] While the decline in capital flows to the United States could be attributed in part to the deflation of that country's tech bubble, outflows to other Asian nations, with the exception of China, also fell.

The worrisome thing about Japan is its failure to find a new equilibrium. Despite the efforts of Prime Minister Koizumi in the first part of the 2000s, the Japanese economy remains sickly. Antireform elements of the LDP fought an ongoing battle against reforms and continue to sidetrack Koizumi's programs. The result of the political warping of reform policy was that the Nikkei stock average, which reached an all-time high of 38,915.87 on December 29, 1989, stood at 8,002.69 on March 14, 2003. The banking sector remains a major policy concern, unemployment was at a postwar high, and the central bank was actively buying stocks from the banks to shore up their capitalization. Corporate bankruptcies hit their worst record in postwar history with 19,458 cases (the record number of bankruptcies was set in 1984 at 20,841 cases).

While it can be argued that Japan has embraced globalization and is a world leader in a number of areas, the ongoing problem of a two-tiered economy has left Japan as an ongoing worry. As one Japanese editorial opined: "But the old system, which has been sustained largely by the Liberal Democratic Party, has clearly arrived at a terminal stage, at which it is now writhing."[16] What must replace the "writhing old system" is yet to be formulated, though there is hope that the country will eventually move more fulsomely to reform. Looking back over the decade of 1991–2001, however, it appears that Japan missed the carnival on Wall Street because of its earlier binge but is still suffering from a hangover.

▶ CHINA: WILL THE BOOM GO BUST?

Unlike Japan, China was not a worry during the Asian financial crisis. In fact, China continued to move ahead with economic reforms, opening up its economy (in selected areas) and maintaining strong economic growth. In November 2001, China joined the WTO, a landmark event and something that the government of President Jiang Zemin had doggedly sought. In 2002, China reported that it had received more than $50 billion in foreign investment, while real GDP growth was 8 percent, one of the fastest in the world. This made a sharp contrast to the slowdown in the rest of the global economy. It also made the usually pessimistic Morgan Stanley economist Stephen Roach comment in March 2003:

China always stands out. But in this growth-starved world, the Chinese dynamic is all the more visible. It is certainly the topic du jour in investment circles, even in these times of geopolitical angst. Everyone now wants to come to China and see the story first-hand. My phone is ringing off the hook these days with requests to be invited on my proverbial "next China trip."

The excitement about China was hardly limited to investors in the United States, Europe, and Japan. Even other developing countries such as India found China attractive. Several Indian software companies entered China, including Tata, Asia's largest software company. They are hardly alone.

Yet, for all the hype, China's reform process is far from complete and there are considerable risks. The same economy that has become a major exporter of manufactured goods, ranging from toys to weapons, also has a deeply troubled banking system and a highly problematic state-owned enterprises (SOE) sector and public finances, which are under pressure. The Chinese Communist Party remains bent on maintaining control but is confronted by widespread corruption that undermines its position and social unrest in different parts of the country, related to varying degrees of economic opportunity. In addition, the WTO membership entails opening up further the Chinese economy to outside competition, a process that will take the country through the decade. For the Communist Party, this means that the process of change will have to be accelerated. For a party geared to control, this raises substantial challenges.

China came into the 1990s with considerable economic momentum, despite the political hiccup related to Tiananmen Square in 1989. Politics remained under the control of the government, which was dominated by President Jiang Zemin and his allies, such as Zhu Rongji and the People's Liberation Army (PLA). The focus remained on economic development, albeit in a gradualist fashion. China had earlier rejected the rapid, shock treatments that a number of the Central and Eastern European countries had embraced in the early 1990s. There would be no big moves on privatization, overnight price reforms, or the immediate dismantling of trade barriers. However, the government decided to advance reforms to deal with the three core areas of concern (banking, SOEs, and public sector finance). In 1993 reform was enacted to commercialize the banking system and to change the structure of governance of SEOs by converting them into modern share-holding institutions. The banks were loaded with bad loans, many of them the result of politically guided loans to SOEs. By commercializing the banks, a new, tougher credit culture was to be introduced, while the state banking sector would be consolidated into the "Big Four" state banks. What kept the state banks from being insolvent were regulatory leniency and the fact that households continued to add large amounts of funds to their savings accounts.[17]

While the country's large deposit base kept the banks liquid and prevented a crisis, the situation was not sustainable in the long term. Greatly complicating matters, the SOEs represented a major problem. Badly in need of reform and a drag on the banks, they were a politically difficult issue. Initially created to help industrialize China, they were also to provide lifetime employment and a number of social services. They were not created with the idea of profit-making. As China modernized, the emphasis of reform fell on an emerging private sector. Although there were a few SOEs that did manage to make the adjustment to a market-oriented economy, most did not. However, in 1993 the SOEs accounted for 109 million workers, equal to 68 percent of the urban workforce.[18] Throwing large numbers of workers out of work in urban areas was not politically appealing to the Communist Party. For an organization dedicated to control, unemployed workers in the cities had the potential for opening the door to social unrest.

The 1993 reforms were followed by additional measures, including a major tax reform designed to reverse the long-term trend of declining tax revenue relative to output and to reduce the size of a bloated bureaucracy that was regarded as stifling business. Although the pace of economic growth slowed in the mid-1990s to the 7 percent to 8 percent range, China was able to steer its way through the 1997–1998 Asian financial crisis. Some credit can be given to the government, as it used fiscal stimulus to pour money into the economy, largely through infrastructure programs (mostly needed). At the same time, China's gradualistic approach to economic modernization helped. China was able to sidestep the worst of the crisis, as it was less well integrated into the international economy as were countries such as Korea and Thailand. Simply stated, hot money could not move in and out of China as quickly as it could elsewhere in Asia where financial liberalization had taken place.

By the end of the 1990s, the policy of gradualism was under question. The Big Four banks had an estimated 25 percent to 50 percent of their loans considered nonperforming, with some 80 percent of all lending going to the SOEs.[19] As for the SOEs, in 1999 they still produced around 28 percent of China's output, with about 53 percent of its industrialized fixed assets and 41 percent of its urban work force, hardly efficient ratios.[20] With the WTO membership in 2001, there is a more pressing demand for a quick conclusion to the SOE problem. WTO membership offers China a more stable access to foreign markets, as it intends to reduce disruptions in foreign trade that are caused by unpredictable policy shifts. Along these lines, China will be in a better position to attract foreign investors who use China as their export platform. It also is expected to attract foreign investors who feel more secure about developing China's domestic market. Beyond this, foreign direct investment helps bring in management, technology, market information, and global production and distribution networks that link China more tightly to the rest of the global economy. Yet, the ongoing existence of a large and unprofitable state sector represents a hurdle to gaining the benefits from WTO membership.

The SOE challenge clearly has an international element. The highly successful part of China's reform program has been with exports. Tellingly, the state-owned sector has played a limited role in China's economic success. While it is readily acknowledged that the sector represents a problem in terms of government support, it also carries another, more subtle danger. Economist Nicholas R. Lardy noted: "Not only do state-owned firms exhibit lagging export performance, but in some sectors high tariff and nontariff barriers have insulated them from competition from foreign firms, even on their own home turf."[21] In many regards, the strategy of keeping SOEs alive even though they are in difficult economic straits looks very much like Japan's strategy with zombie companies. It could provide the foundation for a major financial crisis early in the twenty-first century.

Ironically, China's retail sector has had considerable problems since the Asian country joined the WTO. Foreign competition, such as Wal-Mart and Carrefour, have aggressively moved into the Chinese retail market, pushing many of their local and more inefficient rivals out of business. The survivors throughout China, like their counterparts in Japan, have sought help from their local political establishments. As the elements of the LDP gave an ear and help to Japanese zombie retailers, members of the Chinese Communist Party have sought to do the same for their countrymen. China is caught in a dilemma between continuing the marketization of the economy and controlling competition—which runs contrary to WTO membership. As one Japanese observer noted: "It remains to be seen how Beijing will go about reconciling its market opening commitment as a WTO member with ensuring survival of domestic retailers."[22] Lurking somewhere in this issue is the related question of whether China will develop into a more pronounced two-tiered economy, with all the negatives that trend implies.

▶ POLITICAL CHALLENGES FOR CHINA

All of the previous discussion reflects the danger that as China accelerates the restructuring of its economy, it will suffer from an institutional/political lag—much like the rest of Asia did in 1997–1998. Having more open borders means greater vulnerability to capital flight. Consequently, any future disruptions in global capital markets could have a much greater impact on China. Conversely, any crisis in China could result in the rapid flight of capital.

There is also a political dimension to China and its linkages to global capital markets coming out of the 1990s. As China took major steps forward in modernizing its economy, political development lagged behind. The leadership around Jiang Zemin had little desire to slip back into the turmoil that erupted around political liberalization in the late 1980s. Yet, the same push on the economic side helped maintain pressure to change on the political side. As Nicholas Lardy stated: "Historical experience elsewhere in East Asia, particularly in Taiwan, suggests that an economy that is market oriented and open to the outside world will eventually stimulate a demand for choice in governance and political leadership."[23]

While there are many worries related to the issue of China being a bubble economy, there are other factors to argue that it is not. China's leadership is deeply concerned about economic policy direction and any other problems that could jeopardize sustainable growth. This includes political succession, always a difficult issue in nondemocratic political systems, and the future form of government. In late 2002 and early 2003, the "fourth generation" of leadership assumed power from the "third generation" led by outgoing President Jiang Zemin. The new leadership, centered around President Hu Jintao, took power in a planned and bloodless transfer of power. This was a departure from the past changes at the helm of China in which intense and bitter political intrigues between competing cliques often boiled over into purges and violence.

The Chinese leadership strongly desired that political change at the top was a peaceful, though competitive, affair. The new leadership is younger than the last, more technocratic in training, and more pragmatic in thinking.[24] The transfer to power also reflects that the political and economic model pursued by China is that of Singapore's neo-authoritarian system of tightly controlled elections and government-inclined courts, which serve to control potential social disorder and guide the population along clearly defined developmental paths.

The political challenge to China is not limited to political succession. Other issues include what type of institutions should govern, how much authority should be given to local governments, and how China should deal with the issue of globalization. The last is probably one of the most complicated issues and easily touches upon the themes in this book. While entrepreneurial states such as the United States, the United Kingdom, and The Netherlands embraced much of the challenge of globalization and had the institutional capacity to deal with many of the ramifications, the issue in China is much more starkly driven between economic strength and economic security.

Deng Xiao-ping saw economic success via implementing market reforms as the path to economic security. From Deng through Jiang, this was the guiding light of Chinese economic policy. However, as China enters the twenty-first century, globalization in all its aspects is fogging the straight line between economic success and security. WTO membership highlighted this. As veteran China journalist Bruce Gilley noted: "… the faster opening has sparked a debate about how China can defend its economic security—safeguarding its ability to generate wealth in the face of external threats—as it becomes more intertwined with the rest of the world."[25] Although the majority of dominant policymakers favor continued integration into the global economy and regard WTO membership as a major milestone in China's development, there are those that look back to the Maoist era and favor the creation of a "new Great Wall" to protect their country against (in Gilley's words) "rapacious foreign investors to dependence on world petroleum and grain markets." They also would seek to limit the "bad influences" associated with globalization, such as the freedom of the Internet to express ideas and political views. In this light the spread of Fulan Gong represented a threat related to globalization—a group seeking to have freedom of expression and right of assembly challenged the power of the CCP as the sole power and institution to provide such guidance of thought. Fulan Gong benefited from globalization: the Internet helped it organize.

The political dimension is also observable in how China governs. The CCP still regards itself as the leading light of Chinese civilization. However, the party faces widespread corruption, an erosion of popular support among large elements of society, and a pressing need to provide a more defined and understood rule of law. The last represents a major challenge for a one-party state. Without a system of balances and checks, keeping the party clean of corruption is difficult. Yet, as China becomes more integrated in the global economy, it is being forced to re-examine the role of the CCP and the state and their interrelationship. This situation has forced the central government leadership to take a stronger stance on corruption, seeking on occasion to make an example of corrupt party members.

In some cases, corruption has become so blatant that the government has been forced to strike. This was the case in 2000, with the south China port city of Xiamen, where a major $3 billion smuggling ring was broken. As one report noted: "A shady local businessman methodically bought off representatives of almost every arm of the state, including the local Communist Party committee, the customs administration, the police and even, if popular reports are to be believed, the local bureau of the Ministry of State Security and the People's Armed Police. The businessman transformed the black economy into the city's mainstream economy, and bred in Xiamen's bureaucrats a set of interests directly in opposition to the interests of the central government."[26] The government's slow response was a full-scale purge of local institutions and crime groups, with a number of executions. Despite the government's clamp-down, the events surrounding Xiamen reflected the depth to which corruption challenges chains of authority and institutional loyalties in China. Ultimately, official corruption could sink the CCP as it will continue to erode its legitimacy vis-à-vis the population. As an increasingly larger part of the country's population has access to alternative forms of information and, more critically, opinion, the ruling party's claims to be the leading light of Chinese civilization will look less than truthful.

Directly related to the issue of how to deal with corruption is the need for greater transparency in government. Considering the roots of the CCP and the long tradition of factional infighting that have marked the party's history, the idea of transparency is not an easy issue. However, the SARS pandemic which hit China in 2003 clearly underscored the major problem faced by the government. Although the disease was initially discovered as early as November 2002 in southern China, local officials sought to cover up the problem. By the time the disease spread into Hong Kong and from there the rest of the world, China had a very serious health problem. It was also acutely embarrassing for the new government of President Hu, which had signaled that it was bringing a newer, more modern China. Criticized from abroad, much of the Chinese population was not thrilled to learn that their country had given birth to a dangerous new disease, which local officials had sought to conceal. Although the Health Minister was forced to resign, the Hu administration had been forced to start under a cloud that pointed to one of the major flaws in ruling China—the lack of transparency in day-to-day government.

▶ CHINA'S PARADOXICAL POSITION

China entered the twenty-first century in a paradoxical position. On one side of the ledger, it has managed to maintain relatively strong economic growth, has accumulated massive foreign exchange reserves (in excess of $250 billion), and has a low level of foreign external debt. It has one of the world's highest levels of domestic savings: 40 percent of the GDP. With steady economic development it has gained in influence throughout Asia, gaining more clout in terms of its military strength and political influence in Southeast Asia. The other side of the equation is that China still faces many problems. It remains an economy still very much in transition, a situation complicated by the ruling Communist Party's battle to remain in control. This explains the harsh reaction to Falun Gong, a quasi-religious group that was able to mobilize more than ten thousand people in Beijing in 1999. After a protest against the government for tolerance, authorities moved later in the year to outlaw the group and arrested a number of its members. Falun Gong, however, is only one problem of many, the most pressing of which remain the SOEs and banks.

The government plan is now to use the country's stock markets to float issues of SOEs as they are privatized. The capital for the buying of such shares will come from the country's savings. As equity money flows into the more bottom-line-driven former SOEs, loans will be repaid to the banks and everyone will be happy. A virtuous circle of investment will be made. There is a major danger that this will not work. As a Standard & Poor's study report noted: "However, the stock market could easily follow the banking system and also misallocate China's savings unless it is modernized and better regulated. The listing of over one thousand state-owned enterprises on China's stock exchanges has done little thus far to change their governance or improve their performance."[27] The sad truth is that China is a long way from having a legal and court system that functions independently of the Party and the State or is supportive of a stock market operating with the same level of disclosure as in the West.

China sits in a position of dealing with a number of contradictions, all of which make it the source of potential new Asian earthquakes. As Gordon Chang noted: "Party cadres say they want the benefits of the Internet, but they also want to be able to censor it. They say they want to be a technological leader of this century, but they restrict innovation. They say they want a modern society, but they cannot relinquish their hold."[28] While a country remains largely buffered from the outside world, these contradictions are problematic but limited in their scope to do damage beyond national frontiers. However, with globalization of markets—in particular, global capital markets—the danger has a distinct possibility of spreading throughout the entirety of the system. This is the growing danger that China represents in the early twenty-first century. Simply stated, many of the reforms that should have been accomplished during the 1990s have now been left to a much shorter time frame in the 2000s, increasing the difficulty of an already very difficult task.

Deflation as Slow Contagion?

China and Japan are afflicted by deflation. It is more acute in Japan, but China is helping to spread the problem in a slow-motion contagion to the rest of Asia. Because of the Chinese government's policy of strong economic growth based on exports, the rest of Asia is suffering from deflation. Does this make any sense? In a strange way it does. China exports large amounts of cheaply produced goods, which undercuts other regional exporters, forcing them to cut costs to keep up. At the same time, manufacturing firms are increasingly moving to China, also reducing regional wages and real estate prices throughout Asia.

In 2002, consumer prices declined in major East Asian countries and regions, with Hong Kong observing a sharp 3 percent slide. This was the fourth consecutive year that witnessed a drop in prices for Hong Kong. The problem is that the growing integration between the city and the rest of China is pushing prices down in a number of areas. This is evident in the fact that Hong Kong citizens are buy-ing homes in neighboring and less expensive Shenzen (opting to commute to work) and shopping in China (where prices are lower) and the fact that there is an inflow of cheaper Chinese goods. Adding insult to injury, many foreign companies are leav-ing Hong Kong for Shanghai, a city seeking to regain its lost luster as East Asia's financial center, which it was before the Chinese Revolution. Making matters worse, Hong Kong was hard hit by SARS, which further cooled economic activity, in par-ticular tourism for which the city is well known. Unemployment shot above 8 per-cent by mid-2003, a very high level for Hong Kong.

Hong Kong is not alone in dealing with the deflationary threat. While Japan already suffered from deflation, the movement of growing numbers of Japanese industrial firms to China is only making the situation worse. At the same time, Taiwan is being hit by Chinese-related deflationary pressures. Taiwan is suffering from a "hollowing-out" of domestic industry as its technology companies move manufac-turing bases to China.[29] Singapore is also watching international companies depart for China, leaving its economy in a much lower level of growth than in prior decades.

While the deflationary impact of the Chinese economy should not be over-stated, it also should not be ignored. China is one of the key economic heavyweights in Asia. If deflation were to emerge into a more severe problem (through over-supply), the ripples of such a trend would only reinforce that tendency in Japan and harm Singapore, Taiwan, Korea, and Hong Kong. This would be a slow yet highly damaging development, especially in a global economy recovering from the investment binge of the 1990s.

▶ CONCLUSION

While Wall Street went through a period of development characterized by rising pro-duction, technical innovations, and the application of those innovations to finance, Japan entered a period marked by deflation and an inability to come to terms with the problems that burst the bubble economy of the 1980s. The 1990s, therefore, were a lost decade for Japan. Innovation and globalization seeped into the economy, but a fulsome embrace was deferred by a conservative political elite that largely pre-ferred a state-guided economy over the hurly-burly of a more entrepreneurial-driven economy. The ensuing decade of economic stagnation postponed dealing with dif-ficult issues, though Japan clearly suffered the consequences. As long as the rest of Asia moved along at a brisk pace of economic growth, Japan was not a problem. However, following the 1997–1998 Asian financial crisis, the situation changed, and Japan became a point of concern for policymakers throughout the world. Japan's eco-nomic problems since then have only grown in significance: globalization has made the risk of slow-motion reform and the accompanying deflation a wider worry of eco-nomic implosion on a slow fuse.

Despite its strong economic growth, China potentially represents many of the same risks as Japan. Although the central government leadership has done an amaz-ing job of modernizing the Chinese economy, it also has numerous problems that could be highly disruptive. The SOEs remain a major problem, threatening to develop into an even more explosive issue. Too rapid a closure of state-owned companies would mean more unemployed, which could equal social unrest. This would be a clear threat to China's leading institutions, from the CCP to various branches of government. Related to the SOEs is the issue of domestic Chinese companies seeking protection from foreign competition: everything from retailers to banks. The risk is the creation of a two-tier economy, much like in Japan, with all the related political dilemmas. A collapse of the Chinese banking system would have major ramifications for the country's economy as well as the regional economy. Last, but hardly least, China's deflation represents a challenge to regional economies and the leadership in Beijing, requiring tough decisions about maintaining employment, creating oversupply of goods, and undermining regional economies.

Ironically, the two largest economies in Asia, China and Japan, having managed to exit the 1990s without a crash, remain two potential sources of new shocks to the global capital markets. The carnival on Wall Street may be over, but risks of new bursting bubbles are hardly gone. And China's long run of strong economic growth and inflow of foreign capital sounds and feels like a possible bubble. Though substantial differences exist between China and Japan, they are both troubled by banking systems hobbled by high levels of nonperforming loans, heavily indebted and protected sectors of the economy (largely on the domestic side), and weak regulatory institutions. The need for reform is understood, but the politicization of the reform process leaves the door open for new meltdowns. Globalization has both enhanced and complicated the economies of Japan and China. As in most countries, the Chinese and Japanese leadership elite cannot avoid globalization, and efforts thus far to control it have left legacies of problems that loom on the horizon of the international economy.

▶ NOTES

1.   R.L. Sims, *Japanese Political History Since the Meiji Renovation 1868–2000* (London: Hurst & Company, 2001), p. 288.
2.   The Philippines was by far the most advanced of this group but had gone through the trauma of the fall of the Marcos dictatorship and a period of democratic consolidation before the authorities could fully concentrate on economic reform.
3.   Nicholas D. Kristof and Sheryl WuDunn, *China Awakes: The Struggle for the Soul of a Rising Power* (New York: Vintage Books, 1994), pp. 14–15.
4.   Richard Katz, *Japanese Phoenix: The Long Road to Japanese Revival* (Armonk, New York: M.E. Sharpe, 2003), p. 17.
5.   Richard Katz, *Japan—The System That Soared* (Armonk, New York: M.E. Sharpe, 1997), p. 13.
6.   Gaven McCormack, *The Emptiness of Japanese Affluence* (Armonk, New York: M.E. Sharpe, 1996), p. 33.
7.   Declan Hayes, *Japan's Big Bang: The Deregulation and Revitalization of the Japanese Economy* (Boston: Tuttle Publishing, 2000), p. 9.
8.   Sims, *Japanese Political History since the Meiji Renovation,* p. 337.
9.   See Scott B. MacDonald and Jonathan Lemco, "Japan's Slow-Moving Economic Avalanche", *Current History,* April 2002, pp. 172–173.
10. David F. DeRosa, *In Defense of Free Capital Markets: The Case Against a New International Financial Architecture* (Princeton: Bloomberg Press, 2001), p. 2.

11. Moody's Investors Service press release, "Moody's Lowers Government of Japan's Local Currency Bond Rating to A2; Maintains Foreign Currency Rating at Aa1," Moody's Investors Service, May 30, 2002.

12. Takahira Ogawa, "One Step Forward, Two Steps Back: Koizumi's Reform Setbacks," Standard & Poor's Press Release, August 18, 2002.

13. Snow brands was Japan's sixth largest meat packer. In 2002, it was made public that the company mislabeled foreign beef as domestic beef to take advantage of a government program that spent billions of yen buying and disposing of older domestic beef potentially contaminated with mad cow disease.

14. "Daei's Restructuring Lacks Sense of Crisis," *The Nikkei Weekly*, March 10, 2003, p. 7.

15. "Japan's Total Investment Overseas Falls Sharply," *The Business Times* Online Edition, June 14, 2002, business-times.asia1.com.sg/latest/story/0,2276,48289,00.html.

16. Masahiko Ishizuka, "Voters Fed Up With Politics as Usual," *The Nikkei Weekly*, March 3, 2003, p. 7.

17. Nicholas R. Lardy, *China's Unfinished Economic Revolution* (Washington, D.C.: Brookings Institute, 1998), p. 5.

18. Ibid, p. 27.

19. David Logue, "A Finger in the Dyke," *Far Eastern Economic Review*, December 20, 2001, pp. 30–32.

20. Gordon G. Chang, *The Coming Collapse of China* (New York: Random House, 2001), p. 66.

21. Lardy, *China's Unfinished Economic Revolution*, p. 211.

22. Toru Shimoharaguchi, "Foreigners Muscling Into China Retail," *The Nikkei Weekly*, March 17, 2003, p. 18.

23. Lardy, *China's Unfinished Economic Revolution*, p. 216.

24. Andrew J. Nathan and Bruce Gilley, *China's New Rulers: The Secret Files* (New York: NYREV, Inc., 2002), p. 21.

25. Bruce Gilley, "Building a Wall Or a Bridge?" *Far Eastern Economic Review*, February 7, 2002, p. 30.

26. Susan V. Lawrence, A City Ruled by Crime:, *Far Eastern Economic Review*, November 30, 2000, p. 15.

27. Joydeep Mukherji and Terry Chan, "Privatization in China: To Sell or Not to Sell," *Standard & Poor's CreditWeek*, August 14, 2002, p. 18.

28. Chang, *The Coming Collapse of China*, p. 13.

29. "Deflation Affects Rest of Asia," *The Nikkei Weekly*, March 10, 2003, p. 19. Also see Tsyyoshi Kurokawa, "Singapore, Hong Kong Face Decline," *The Nikkei Weekly*, March 10, 2003, p. 20.

CHAPTER 10

9/11 AND BEYOND: IT'S THE SYMBOL, STUPID

The September 11, 2001, attack on the World Trade Center marked the symbolic end of a remarkable decade: a ten-year period of dynamic economic growth, amazing yet largely ephemeral wealth creation and a great leap forward in terms of technological innovation, punctuated by episodes of greed, greatness, and crisis on the world financial markets. Doubts about that carnival had already arisen: the decade-long global expansion had ground to a halt, antiglobalization protesters were taking to the streets, and former top officials of the IMF and World Bank were publicly questioning the roles of those august institutions in the world's most vulnerable countries. By mid-2002, the twin implosions of Enron and Argentina left no doubt in any minds that the carnival was over. Indeed, from March 2000 to July 2002, the value of the U.S. stock market fell by $3.7 trillion.

The decade of 1991–2001 magnified both the strengths and the weaknesses of today's global financial system. This "system" is founded on an unshakeable faith in the power of markets, technology, models, and globalization, a faith that was tested as never before in the past decade. At the close of this historic era, it is clear that financial markets are the worst possible method of allocating resources—except for all available alternative methods. Like it or not, we are stuck with a global financial system dominated by the market. And, like it or not, the alternatives of closed markets, excessive state controls of capital flows and economic self-sufficiency don't work and will not work. Nor does anyone really want to adopt the models of Enver Hoxha (Albania's long-time Stalinist dictator) or Kim Jung-il of self-imposed isolation and poverty. Yet, there is a desire for something that works better. Consequently, the trends that marked the carnival decade are worth summarizing one last time.

▶ BLIND FAITH REVISITED

The Mantra of Globalization

The siren song of globalization drove much activity in financial markets over the past decade. Energized by the belief that integration into the global economy is the key to prosperity, developing countries have moved aggressively to liberalize their trading and investment regimes, lure foreign capital, and adopt Anglo-American-style business models.

The results, however, did not match the hype. Some countries have, indeed, discovered that their ability to compete effectively in global markets has sent them galloping along the path to higher living standards (for instance, Ireland, Malaysia, Korea, Taiwan, Singapore, and China). But many more countries have been buffeted mercilessly by the vagaries of international capital flows, commodity prices, and economic conditions. Empirical work by globalization proponents finds that, for the most part, poverty and inequality have fallen during the past two decades of fast-paced globalization; empirical work by the antiglobalists finds exactly the opposite result.

Data and academic research aside, it is clear that billions of people around the world have been disappointed by the globalization process, either because they live in a region that is thoroughly marginalized by the process, like sub-Saharan Africa, or because they live in a country that has been undone by the risks while seeing few of the benefits, like Argentina. The developing countries that have globalized most successfully (China and India) have done so via their own idiosyncratic and oftentimes non-IMF-guided policies, heightening the doubts about the efficacy of those policies. If "do no harm" is the physician's primary rule, has the IMF fallen afoul of even this most basic of guidelines?

It is also clear that just as the markets vote with their money, people vote with their feet. Worry about the problem of brain drain in developing countries is usually eclipsed by worries about capital flight. However, labor mobility is just as much a factor as capital mobility. Lawrence Summers (treasury secretary in the Clinton administration and now president of Harvard University) has observed that the benefits of globalization could be undone if labor and educated people continue to flee their homes in developing countries. Medical students, for example, leave the Philippines to work in the United States, and Russians invest in Western Europe. There have to be incentives for people and capital to remain in their home markets, and that involves everything from rule of law and personal safety to encouragement of small and medium-sized businesses and clean government.

These doubts have created an antiglobalization movement that is more vibrant and more intelligent than is commonly believed. Steve Hilton writes, "Global capitalism has a problem—a problem that the brutal efficiency for which capitalism is routinely lambasted can reduce to just three words: Seattle, dot-com, Enron."

Indeed, by the early 2000s the well-publicized failures of global capitalism had come to dominate the headlines. The anticapitalist orthodoxy holds that global brands exploit people by creating a desire for "junk with a logo, sold at extortionate prices to feed the insatiable demands of shareholders for even higher profits." Then there's the dot-com fiasco: "From cutting edge to laughing stock in just a couple of years, dot-com mania saw corporations falling over themselves to pour shareholders' money into fatuous ventures." And finally, Enron, which "stands for old-fashioned villainy."

But while the antiglobalists have plenty of ammunition, they founder, ultimately, on their inability to produce a viable alternative paradigm. Like financial markets, capitalism is the worst possible system—except for its alternatives. Hilton continues by noting that thanks to capitalism, life expectancy is up, infant mortality is down, education is richer, and environmental awareness is greater. Capitalism, he believes, is "the most powerful force for good the world has seen."[1] Related to this is that globalism works only when all parties agree to it. As already noted, people often vote with their feet. The reason is often that there are better opportunities elsewhere—places that have the proper institutional frameworks for globalization, i.e., to handle free capital flows. Too many countries around the world lack adequate institutions to safeguard contracts, property rights, and other laws necessary to make global capitalism work.

In all of this, there is an ideological component that has helped make the United States (New York City, in particular) the core of global capital markets. This is not by any means to argue that the belief in the market to deliver a greater social good is special only to the United States, and because of this there has been a greater tolerance of the massive swings of sentiment in the market. Rather, the United States, because of its core position in the global economy, has a special place in global finance. As Richard Leone, president of the Century Fund, observed: "Still, it seems true that Americans tolerate a greater degree of market risk than do many other wealthy societies. They do not because they are exceptionally reckless, but rather because they place a high value on the positive results of a relatively unfettered free market."[2] Compared with any other alternative views, the belief in the market, though sullied by the tech crash of 2000–2002, remained far more attractive than anything else.

Markets, Models, and Technology

The most well-known episodes of the past decade in financial markets make for depressing reading:

- The dot-com and telecoms bubble of the late 1990s, which will no doubt go down in history as one of the greatest financial follies;

- The endless quest for mergers and acquisitions on Wall Street and worldwide, fueled in part by the avarice of investment bankers and lawyers (often the only parties to actually profit from these deals);

- The Age of Currency Crises in emerging market countries, which decimated the nascent middle classes and threw millions back into poverty;

- Enron, the poster child for rogue companies;

- Long-Term Capital Management (LTCM), the poster child for crony capitalism, American-style; and

- Argentina, the poster child for globalization's failure, especially the inability of local authorities to construct adequate institutions to handle capital flows.

At the same time, every one of these episodes reflects, to some extent, the vast increase in market activity and importance over the past decade. Enron and LTCM made (and eventually lost) their money as traders; Argentina and other emerging market countries were attacked and decimated by traders; dot-coms were celebrated and cursed by traders.

Peter Martin writes in the *Financial Times*, "We are collectively indulging in far more trading activity than the world needs—and more than is in the interests of the participants and shareholders." Every day, he points out, $1.2 trillion in foreign exchange is bought and sold, and $580 billion is traded in over-the-counter currency and interest rate derivatives. This activity vastly oversets the productive economic activity that it supposedly represents; it is, as Shakespeare would have said, full of sound and fury and signifying nothing.

This oversupply of trading activity, Martin continues, confers liquidity on the markets, which is good, but super-liquid markets do not convey extra benefits. In fact, they bring extra dangers, by increasing volatility and by adding to the mistaken belief that you can always trade your way out of difficulties (a contributory factor in LTCM's troubles). Moreover, the danger of frenzied trading for its own sake is that it raises the risks of bad traders, such as:

- Toshihide Iguchi, who lost $1.1 billion for Daiwa,
- Robert Citron, who lost $1.6 billion for Orange County, and
- John Rusnak, who lost $750 million for Allfirst.

The late, great economist James Tobin commented with remarkable prescience in 1984:

> I confess to an uneasy physiocratic suspicion, perhaps unbecoming in an academic, that we are throwing more and more of our resources, including the cream of our youth, into financial activities remote from the production of goods and services. ... I suspect that the immense power of the computer is being harnessed to this "paper economy," not to do the same transactions more economically but to balloon the quantity and variety of financial exchanges.[3]

Fooled by Randomness

As these financial exchanges ballooned, so too did the ambitions of traders associated with the exchanges. The markets rose ever-upward for prolonged periods of time, making the acquisition of riches look easy. But, as Nassim Nicholas Taleb writes in *Fooled by Randomness: The Hidden Role of Chance on the Markets and in Life*, few people truly understand the rules of probability. Traders attribute their good results to skill, when it is often just luck. Many traders who made money in the 1990s, for instance, were "dip buyers"—traders who poured more money into the markets on price dips. This was successful in 1992–1998 but has been disastrous ever since. These traders, in Taleb's parlance, were fooled by randomness.[4]

The Role of Complexity

Many were fooled, too, by the complexity of the markets and financial instruments in which they operated. Outside observers such as regulators, shareholders, and analysts were sometimes flummoxed, sometimes deceived by the sheer complexity of financial life. Rogue traders and rogue companies, like those at Enron, Barings, and Allfirst, used this complexity to their advantage. A *New York Times* commentator notes,

> The trading in these devilishly complex financial tools known as derivatives did not contribute much to Enron's collapse, [but] the contracts did allow the company to conceal the aims of its financial dealings. The veil of complexity, whose weave is tightening as sophisticated derivatives evolve and proliferate, poses subtle risks to the financial system—risks that are impossible to quantify, sometimes even to identify.

One professor adds, "Complexity allowed Enron to hide the true picture from the financial markets."[5] Substitute Barings, Allfirst, LTCM, or many others for Enron in that sentence, and the power of complex financial transactions to obscure the truth becomes apparent.

But outsiders are not the only players to fall afoul of complexity. Sometimes insiders too fail to understand the financial intricacies of their own companies, with predictably disastrous consequences. The company's own CEO, Board of Directors, and even CFO may not understand its derivatives portfolio. Remarkably, the CEO of American Express, Kenneth Chenault, admitted that the company "did not fully comprehend the risk it was taking" on its derivatives activities, which eventually resulted in an $826 million write-down. The CEO of Wells Fargo adds, "There are all kinds of transactions going on out there where one party doesn't understand it."[6]

And if the companies themselves are befuddled, imagine the plight of regulators and supervisors struggling to make sense of their finances! The bottom line was forgotten by many investors: If you don't understand it, don't buy it. The more opaque the investment process, the greater the probability that something is not as it should be. Sadly, in cases of outright fraud, there is little to safeguard investors who believed in what corporate management and its accountants and lawyers told them. Consequently, the confidence lost on account of rogue management teams such as at Enron, Global Crossing, and WorldCom will be difficult to regain.

Models and Technology

Complex financial instruments, of course, are facilitated by the proliferation of ever more complicated models and technology that purport to value these derivatives based on fantastically complex financial models. Another commentator notes, "Finance is now a high-technology business, the province of technocrats with advanced degrees in statistics."[7]

In fact, complex, model-based technology is implicated in virtually every financial market debacle over the past decade. LTCM, for example, relied heavily on some of the most sophisticated financial models that the world has ever seen, created by some of the best financial minds in the business. But the weakness in their view of the world, according to Roger Lowenstein, author of *When Genius Failed: The Rise and Fall of Long-Term Capital Management*, was their belief that the world worked as smoothly as their models. In effect, they placed a giant bet on market liquidity.

But in doing so, they ignored the human factor. LTCM assumed that the markets were continuous, that you could trade your way out of a bad position even when the markets went sour. In practice, though, people panic when the markets go sour, and liquidity evaporates. This pitfall is summarized by writer G. K. Chesterton, whom Lowenstein quotes: "Life," he writes, "looks just a little more mathematical and regular than it is; its exactitude is obvious, but its inexactitude is hidden; its wildness lies in wait."[8]

Reexamining the Human Factor

These spectacular miscalculations should lead, in turn, to a reexamination of the role of risks in financial markets—and of methods to evaluate these risks, including human judgment.

Subjective analysis, or human judgment, has become passé in financial markets over the past decade. It is supplanted by computer models, the more complex the better. In the foreign exchange markets, for instance, trading is increasingly dominated by models that use historical patterns to predict the future; "macro" specialists like George Soros who see the currency as the bottom line of the country are out. Students in business school classrooms around the globe disdain classes that and instructors who emphasize judgment and experience; they want spreadsheets and econometric models.

Over-reliance on these models, though, coupled with a misunderstanding of the role of randomness as Taleb describes, has created an environment in which train wrecks are inevitable. Our tendency to underestimate the role of chance in creating great successes is dangerous—it leads us to overestimate our abilities and thus to take ever-greater risks. Similarly, our tendency to overestimate the ability of models and technology to control risks and confer rewards is just as dangerous. Peter Martin, in discussing his concern about the oversupply of trading activities, remarks, "Why is there so much trading? The basic reason is that the participants underestimate the risks they run and overestimate the long-run rewards."[9]

But in the end, business and trading are still risky. Technology does not eliminate these risks; on the contrary, it magnifies them by increasing complexity and by enabling those who wish to obscure their activities. Martin, again, says:

> At its heart, business is a gamble. … This fundamental uncertainty at the center of business is so unsettling that most of the time we choose to ignore it. We have developed techniques to analyze and manage the risks it implies and we tell ourselves that we have made the gambles go away. They have not.

As Martin notes, many of the financial techniques that are now routinely used in business decisions are, at their heart, attempts to gloss over or control the risks of doing business–which are essentially uncontrollable. Discounted cash flow valuation, for example, is a basic and universally used method of assessing the value of a business activity by calculating the current value of all the future cash flows it will produce. This valuation is then used for everything from buying and selling companies to valuing stock.

However, financial market participants almost never acknowledge that all such methods, in the end, rely on the analyst's ability to predict future cash flows. Absent a crystal ball, there is little magic to this process. In fact, it can founder on our inability to guess the future, as well as our temptation to invent the future that we want. The much-revered discounted cash flow valuation of a company thus rests largely on wishful thinking about future income streams!

In the end, there is no way to eliminate uncertainty from business and financial markets. In fact, our attempts to manage these risks may instead magnify them, by distorting and concealing risks and by giving us a false sense of confidence about our abilities.

Martin concludes:

> Just vowing not to misuse the techniques we use to measure and manage risk is not enough. Even scrupulous caution will not save us if we place too much faith in techniques that are inherently limited. The solution is not to invent ever more sophisticated measures of risk or ever more elaborate means of parceling it out to others. It is to face up to the inherent riskiness of business activity and to understand where the vulnerabilities lie. ... The underlying challenge, though, is to accept the inherent uncertainty of business activity, rather than covering it up with a layer of apparently rigorous calculation.[10]

This brings us back to people again. The classic movie *WarGames* begins with the decision to "take the people out" of the nuclear launch sequence, because computer judgment is not subject to the vagaries of human emotion and thought. As the movie proceeds, though, the disastrous consequences of this decision unfold. In the end, the military brass puts the people back into the nuclear silos, viewing human judgment as the only way to prevent nuclear catastrophe.

Blind faith in computer models and technology during 1991–2001 brought some of the most egregious episodes of the decade. Perhaps one lasting lesson is the need for the human factor in financial markets. Computer models cannot calculate away risk; only people can really understand and manage the uncertainties that lie at the heart of global financial markets. Human judgment is the worst possible technique for understanding financial markets—except for all available alternatives.

▶ CONCLUSION

There is a place and time for everything. The 1990s were a time of many hard and fast truths—at least until they were proven to be lacking. All the same, it is important to emphasize that while new ground in terms of technology and its uses was broken, human behavior remained as it has always been: attracted to new ideas that promise brave new worlds. As has often happened, part of that brave new world was delivered and part of it was deferred. The part that was delivered has made the PC and the Internet firmly entwined in daily life. Even in remote parts of the planet, people are able to communicate via the Internet, helped along by satellites and other means of wireless communications. A traveler from Stamford, Connecticut, can go to an automatic teller machine in Edinburgh, Scotland, or Hong Kong and withdraw money from a bank account. The medical field also made improvements, with plenty of pills available to deal with hair loss and to maintain sexual vitality, as well as technological advances enabling surgeons to look into the human heart without surgery. Furthermore, the new wave of technology has improved productivity, helping in myriad ways such as better inventory control, quicker routing of goods to markets, and cutting time on changing fashions. All of this costs money—much of it raised during the 1990s in global capital markets.

The part of the promise of a brave new world that was not delivered was freedom from corruption and scandals. The weakness of institutions to either regulate or channel capital flows (without a heavy hand) created its own set of problems around the world. The lagging ability of institutions even within the most developed countries to adequately deal with new financial instruments led to abuses and criminal acts. Sadly, the acts of a few corporate leaders, traders, accountants, and lawyers left a certain taint on the 1990s. Not every corporate leader, trader, and accountant was corrupt during the 1990s, not every use of quantitative modeling led to a disaster, and not every derivative blew up unsuspected investors. Yet, one of the legacies of the 1991–2001 period is that in the short term it will appear that was indeed the case.

The first decade of the twenty-first century will be one in which institutions and people play catch up with the advances made during the last decade. No doubt new threats to the stability of global capital markets will arise. In addition, efforts to liberalize capital flows are likely to be slower and more measured. In some cases, there is also likely to be slippage back to capital controls. However, if history is any measure, mankind will eventually go back to globalization and capital market liberalization, much as it did to varying degrees following the First World War, after the Great Depression and the Second World War, and at the end of the Cold War. The same belief in interdependence bound by commerce and finance, as articulated by Angell in London prior to the Great War, will no doubt resurface in a stronger fashion. Maybe then the other half of the brave new world offered in the 1990s will be delivered.

▶ NOTES

1. Steve Hilton, "The Corporatist Manifesto," *Financial Times,* April 20–21, 2002.
2. Quoted in Charles R. Morris, *Money, Greed, and Risk: Why Financial Crises and Crashes Happen* (New York: A Century Foundation Book, Random House, 1999), p. xvi.
3. Peter Martin, "Trading on Dangerous Ground," *Financial Times,* February 12, 2002.
4. Nassim Nicholas Taleb, *Fooled by Randomness: The Hidden Role of Chance on the Markets and in Life* (London: Texere, 2001).
5. Daniel Altman, "Contracts So Complex They Imperil the System," *The New York Times,* February 17, 2002.
6. Floyd Norris, "They Sold the Derivatives, But They Didn't Understand It," *The New York Times,* July 20, 2001.
7. Gary Silverman, "Banks break the old boundaries," *Financial Times,* February 18, 2002.

8. Roger Lowenstein, *When Genius Failed: The Rise and Fall of Long-Term Capital Management* (New York: Random House, 2001).

9. Peter Martin, "Trading on Dangerous Ground."

10. Peter Martin, "Always expect the unexpected," *Financial Times,* January 29, 2002.

Selected Bibliography

Abelson, Alan. "Eruption of Corruption." *Barron's*, 1 July 2002, 7–8.

Alletzhauser, Albert J. *The House of Nomura: The Inside Story of the Legendary Japanese Financial Dynasty.* New York: Harper Perennial, 1990.

Banerjee, Neela and Shaila K. Dewan. "For Executives of Enron Unit, The Skill Was in Leaving." *New York Times*, 15 February 2002, C1, C6.

Berman, Arnold. "Tactics: Now's Not the Time for the Next Big Thing." *Red Herring*, 18 December 2000, 238.

Blanton, Kimberly. "Nightmare on Wall Street as Market Soars Closer to Once-Unthinkable Height of 10,000, Analysts Detail Their Worst Fears." *Boston Globe*, 10 January 1999, J1.

Blustein, Paul. *The Chastening: Inside the Crisis that Rocked the Global Financial System and Humbled the IMF.* New York: Public Affairs, 2001.

Brooks, John. *Once in Golconda: A True Drama on Wall Street, 1920–1938.* New York: John Wiley & Sons, 1969, 1999.

Caragata, Warren. "Union of Giants: Exxon and Mobil Create a Colossus." *Maclean's*, 14 December 1998, 44–46.

Chancellor, Edward. *Devil Take the Hindmost: A History of Financial Speculation.* New York: Farrar, Straus & Giroux, 1999.

Cheng, Ien and Caroline Daniel. "The Dice Are Loaded, The Losers Take All." *Financial Times: A Special Anniversary Magazine*, November 2002, 44–45.

Chernow, Ron. *The House of Morgan: An American Banking Dynasty and the Rise of Modern Finance.* New York: Simon and Schuster, 1990.

Clow, Robert. "Investors Pile Into Alternative Fund Strategies." *Financial Times Survey—Hedge Funds*, 30 April 2002, 1.

Colbert, David, ed. *Eyewitness to Wall Street: Four Hundred Years of Dreamers, Schemers, Busts and Booms.* New York: Broadway Books, 2001.

Cringley, Robert X. *Accidental Empires.* New York: Penguin Books, 1996.

Davis, Bob and David Wessel. *Prosperity: The Coming 20-Year Boom and What It Means to You.* New York: Times Business, 1998.

Dent, Harry S. *The Roaring 2000s: Building the Wealth and Lifestyle You Desire in the Greatest Boom in History.* New York: Simon & Schuster, 1998.

DeRosa, David F. *In Defense of Free Capital Markets: The Case Against a New International Financial Architecture.* Princeton: Bloomberg Press, 2001.

Dhume, Sadanand and Susan V. Lawrence. "China Investment and Trade: Buying Spree Into Southeast Asia." *Far Eastern Economic Review*, 28 March 2002, 30–33.

Donlon, Thomas G. "Good Omen?" *Barron's*, 28 October 2002, 46.

Dungey, Mardi, Renee Fry, Brenda Gonzalez-Hermosillo, and Vance Martin. *International Contagion Effects from the Russian Crisis and the LTCM Near-Collapse.* IMF Working Paper no. 02/74, 1 April 2002.

The Economist. "Nasdaq and Its Rivals: Uncertain Future." *The Economist*, 25 May 2002, 71–72.

————. "How to Merge: After the Deal." *The Economist*, 9 January 1999, 21–23.

Fox, Justin. "Show Us the Money." *Fortune*, 3 February 2003, 76–78.

Galbraith, John Kenneth. *The Great Crash 1929.* London: Penguin Books, 1954.

Gapper, John. "The Secret Formula That Saved Salomon North." *Financial Times Special Anniversary Issue*, November 2002: 52–54. Originally published 25 September 1998.

Garten, Jeffrey E. "Corporate Standards: Raise the Bar Around the World." *Business Week*, 13 May 2002: 30.

————. "Megamergers Are a Clear and Present Danger." *Business Week*, 25 January 1999: 28.

Gao, Bai. *Japan's Economic Dilemma: The Institutional Origins of Prosperity and Stagnation.* New York: Cambridge University Press, 2001.

Geisst, Charles R. *Wall Street: A History.* New York: Oxford University Press, 1997.

Gordon, John Steele. *The Great Game: The Emergence of Wall Street as a World Power 1653–2000.* New York: Charles Scribner's Sons, 1999.

Grant, Jenny, "Suharto Cash Linked to 12 Parties," *South China Morning Post,* 2 February 1999: 14.

Greenberg, Herb, "Expecting Tech's Comeback?" *Fortune,* 3 February 2003: 116.

Haacker, Markus and James Morsink. *You Say You Want a Revolution: Information Technology and Growth,* IMF Working Paper, April 2002.

Hayes, Declan. *Japan's Big Bang: The Deregulation and Revitalization of the Japanese Economy.* Boston: Tuttle Publishing, 2000.

Hitt, Greg. "Enron's 'Sham' Trading Fueled West's Power Crisis, Officials Say," *Wall Street Journal,* 12 April 2002, A4.

Hughes, Jane. "Elusive Terror Money Slips Through Government Traps," *USA Today,* 28 November 2001.

Huntington, Samuel P. *Political Order in Changing Societies.* New Haven, Conn.: Yale University Press, 1968.

Ingram, Mathew. "Enron Was a 'Black Box', But Few Cared," *The Globe & Mail,* 16 January 2002.

International Monetary Fund. *World Economic Outlook April 2002.* Washington, D.C.: International Monetary Fund, 2002.

———. *World Economic Outlook May 1997.* Washington, D.C.: International Monetary Fund, 1997.

———. *World Economic Outlook May 2001.* Washington, D.C.: International Monetary Fund, 2001.

———. *World Economic Outlook October 1998.* Washington, D.C.: International Monetary Fund, 1998.

Jackson, Karl D., ed. *Asian Contagion: The Causes and Consequences of a Financial Crisis.* Boulder, Colo.: Westview Press, 1999.

Johnston, David Cay and Reed Abelson. "G.E.'s ex-Chief to Pay for Perks, But the Question Is How Much?" *The New York Times,* 17 September 2002, C1–C2.

Kaplan, David. *The Silicon Boys and Their Valley of Dreams.* New York: Perennial, 2000.

Katz, Richard. *Japan The System That Soured: The Rise and Fall of the Japanese Economic Miracle.* Armonk, N.Y.: M.E. Sharpe, 1998.

Keegan, John. *The First World War.* New York: Vintage Books, 1998.

Klitgaard, Robert. *Controlling Corruption.* Berkeley, Calif.: University of California Press, 1988.

Kristof, Nicholas D. and Sheryl WuDunn. *China Wakes: The Struggle for the Soul of a Rising Power.* New York: Vintage Books, 1994.

Kuttner, Robert. *Everything for Sale: The Virtues and Limits of Markets.* Chicago: University of Chicago Press, 1996.

Laing, Jonathan. "After the Bubble," *Barron's,* 1 July 2002: 19–21.

Lamfalussy, Alexandre. *Financial Crises in Emerging Markets: An Essay on Financial Globalization and Fragility.* New Haven, Conn.: Yale University Press, 2000.

Landler, Mark, "Crisis Recedes In Hong Kong, With Economy Back in the Black," *The New York Times,* 28 August 1999: C1–C2.

Larsen, Peter Thal, "War of Words After Tyco Sacks Legal Executive," *Financial Times,* 11 June 2002: 17.

Loomis, Jay. "Brokers Battered, Bearish," *The Journal News* (White Plains, N.Y.), 2 September 2002: D1–D2.

Lowenstein, Roger. *When Genius Failed: The Rise and Fall of Long-Term Capital Management.* New York: Random House, 2000.

MacDonald, Scott B. "Japan's Regional Banks: Neglected Troubles," *Asia Times Online,* 19 November 2002. www.atimes.com/Japan/DK19Dh03.html.

———. "The Impact of Wall Street's Scandals on Japan," *Asia Times Online,* 16 July 2002. www.atimes.com/atimes/Japan/DG16Dh01.html.

———. "Japan: Standing at the Crossroads," *Asia Times Online,* 11 January 2002. www.atimes.com/japan-econ/DA11Dh01.html.

MacDonald, Scott B., Jane Hughes, and David L. Crum. *New Tigers and Old Elephants: The Development Game in the 20th Century.* Rutgers, N.J.: Transaction Press, 1998.

MacDonald, Scott B., and Albert L. Gastmann. *A History of Credit and Power in the Western Hemisphere.* Rutgers, N.J.: Transaction Press, 2001.

MacDonald, Scott B. and Johathan Lemco. "Japan's Slow-Moving Avalanche," *Current History,* April 2002: 172–176.

MacDonald, Scott B. and Jonathan Lemco. "Indonesia: Living Dangerously," *Current History,* April 2001: 176–182.

Malik, Om. "Qwest's Napoleonic Ambitions," *Red Herring,* 15 October 2001: 47–52.

Mayer, Martin. *Wall Street: Men and Money.* New York: Harper and Row, 1959.

Meesook, Kanitta, Il Houng Lee, Olin Liu, Yousesh Khatri, Natalia Tamirisa, Michael Moore, and Mark H. Krysl. *Malaysia: From Crisis to Recovery.* Washington, D.C.: International Monetary Fund Occasional Paper 207, 2001.

Morris, Charles R. *Money, Greed, and Risk: Why Financial Crises and Crashes Happen.* New York: A Century Foundation Book, 1999.

Murray, James B. Jr. *Wireless Nation: The Frenzied Launch of the Cellular Revolution in America.* Cambridge, Mass.: Perseus Publishing, 2001.

Nelson, Emily and Laurie P. Cohen. "Why Jack Grubman Was So Keen to Get His Twins Into the Y," *Wall Street Journal,* 15 November 2002: A1.

Norris, Floyd, "Can Investors Believe Cash Flow Numbers?" *The New York Times,* 15 February 2002: C1.

Organisation for Economic Co-operation & Development. *OECD Economic Outlook, June 2002.* Paris: Organisation for Economic Co-operation & Development, 2002.

———. *OECD Economic Outlook June 1999.* Paris: Organisation for Economic Co-operation & Development, 1999.

———. *OECD Economic Outlook June 1998.* Paris: Organisation for Economic Co-operation & Development, 1998.

Rabin, Keith and Scott B. MacDonald. "The U.S. Economy: A Few Bad Apples or Tip of the Iceberg?" *KWR International Advisor,* September/October 2002.

Robison, Richard and David S.G. Goodman, eds. *The New Rich in Asia: Mobile Phones, McDonald's and Middle-Class Evolution.* London: Routledge, 1996.

Romero, Simon. "Panel Turns Focus to Founder In Global Crossing Investigation," *The New York Times,* 30 August 2002: C1–C2.

Root, Hilton. "Asia's Bad Old Ways," *Foreign Affairs,* March/April 2001: 9–14.

Sandberg, Jared. "Bernie Ebbers Bet the Ranch—Really—on WorldCom Stock," *Wall Street Journal,* 12 April 2002: A13.

Schroaeder, Michael, Jerry Guidera, and Mark Maremont. "Accounting Crackdown Focuses Increasingly on Top Executives," *Wall Street Journal,* 12 April 2002: A1, A2.

Sims, R.L. *Japanese Political History Since the Meiji Renovation 1868–2000.* London: Hurst & Company, 2001.

Skidelsky, Robert. *The Road to Serfdom: The Economic and Political Consequences of the End of Communism.* New York: Penguin Books, 1995.

Smith, B. Mark. *Toward Rational Exuberance: The Evolution of the Modern Stock Market.* New York: Farrar, Straus & Giroux, 2001.

Smith, Randall and Susan Pulliam. "How a Star Banker Pressed for IPOs," *Wall Street Journal,* 5 September 2002: C1, C14.

Smith, Rebecca. "Energy Traders To Issue Rules On Disclosure," *Wall Street Journal,* 19 November 2002: C1, C14.

Spiegal, Peter. "The Architect of Enron's Downfall," *Financial Times,* 21 May 2002: 22.

Vlasic, Bill and Bradley A. Stertz. *Taken for a Ride: How Daimler-Benz Drove Off with Chrysler.* New York: Harper Business, 2001.

Waller, David. *Wheels on Fire: The Amazing Inside Story of the DaimlerChrysler Merger.* London: Hodder & Stoughton, 2001.

Waters, Richard. "Global Crossing and XO Edge Nearer Precipice," *Financial Times,* 18 June 2002: 19.

Weiss, Gary. "A Sorry Legacy The Street Can't Shake," *Business Week,* 13 May 2002: 43.

Wicker, Elmus. *Banking Panics of the Gilded Age.* New York: Cambridge University Press, 2000.

Yeager, Holly. "Tyco's Open Cheque Book Opened the Doors for Kozlowski," *Financial Times,* 18 June 2002: 19.

Index